HOW WE FLOURISH

The Surprising Path to a Just Prosperity

Earl L. Grinols[1]

[1]Distinguished Professor of Economics Emeritus, Baylor University; Professor of Economics Emeritus, University of Illinois.

Truth will ultimately prevail where pains are taken to bring it to light.

George Washington, 1794

Do good in every possible kind, and in every possible degree to all men.

John Wesley, 1799

Contents

List of Tables

List of Figures

Why Read This?

This book is about human flourishing and the science of how society should be organized to enable the most good for the most people. Of course, human flourishing requires flourishing in multiple realms such as Literature, Engineering, Astronomy, Arts, and Philosophy, but let's be honest: If we don't have Morality and do have Poverty, success in the other fields doesn't count for much. We need to get serious. In Lewis Carroll's words,

> "The time has come," the Walrus said,
> "To talk of many things:
> Of shoes—and ships—and sealing-wax—
> Of cabbages—and kings"[1]

of goods, of services, of businesses and trade;
Morality and Prosperity from which flourishing is made!

Humans **want** to flourish. Science is supposed to help us. *Essential economics* is the term we use in this book to mean the special instructions that economic science tells us must apply to buying and selling, to markets, to the working world, and so on if human flourishing is to be present. Stated equivalently in reverse terms: Without *essential economics*, human flourishing is not possible. The second message of this book is that *essential economics* is not enough. Morality must be present. *Morality* requires the Golden Rule to be honored and thus the Golden Rule becomes our working principle.

So why read this book? Because with each generation knowledge increases, and each generation must re-confirm what it believes. No one wants to be the "useful idiot" that a selfish group manipulates.

---

[1] Lewis Carroll (1832-1898), "The Walrus and the Carpenter."

1

This book is written for those who want to know what economics and morality jointly have to say about what promotes human flourishing and what does not.

The science is incomplete if it leaves unaddressed any of the tasks that an economy must perform. For example, economists have long known that the mathematics of general equilibrium require that the individuals inhabiting the models they study have sufficient wherewithal that they will be viable in market equilibrium.

The question of rightful ownership of assets, therefore, also enters the discussion. Because you may be innately more capable than I am and find it effortlessly easy to acquire more than you need, does that entitle me to take the work product of your effort and consume it for myself? What if a majority votes to take from you and give to me? Most would say the morality or immorality of the taking does not change, but there are those who might disagree. It is a cliché to say that if you rob Peter to pay Paul, you can always count on the support of Paul.

Economics must coordinate with justice and morality. In this book we make explicit the assumptions from which we work, deducing from as few axioms as possible what society must look like to be both successful and moral. Choosing between capitalism and socialism, between rightful government and wrongful government, can be grounded in light of 70 years of additional economic progress.

Today we have the means to present a coherent picture of what morality and economics jointly say about social organization. My hope is to explain the implications that derive from three assumptions: First, human flourishing requires economic efficiency. This has implications. Second, human flourishing requires morality, which requires the Golden Rule. This, too, has implications. Third, humans are entitled to own themselves. If we agree that slavery or its equivalent violates the Golden Rule, then the third axiom follows from the second, and we can work from two. Deriving the implications of these axioms is the methodology and the purpose of this book.

What follows from human flourishing, morality, and ownership of oneself distinguishes capitalism and market competition from socialism and state control. Being able to say analytically *why* one system works and is moral, and the other does not work and is immoral, is our discovery.

My most treasured compliment received as a teacher was unintended. At the end of a semester covering health care and some of the material that has found its way into this book, one of my best students was excited to remark at the end of a class, *"Now I understand how the American economy works."* It is my fervent hope that the reader also understand how the economy works and maybe feel excitement about it, too.

Note on organization: **Part 1** describes the essential economics implied by human flourishing and morality. **Part 2** provides added material for selected chapters of Part 1 whose numbers match those in Part 2.

Acknowledgements

The following individuals provided comments on early versions of this book. Each brought perspectives based on their own professions and experience for which I am grateful. Law, research meteorology and computer modeling, business, computer programming, chemical engineering and entrepreneurship, voluntary private organization leadership, applied economics, and business communication are represented. In the order help was received, I thank the Hon. Peter C. Bradstreet, Gary A. Achtemeier PhD, Gregory E. Mapes, Patricia J. Mapes, Gregory W. Leman PhD, John Pisciotta PhD, and James W. Henderson PhD. My wife Anne B. Grinols PhD provided invaluable help and encouragement throughout.

PART 1

Chapter 1

Essential Economics

But to care about the economy is to care about human life, since the economy is how life is sustained. It is a source of meaning, as well as sustenance, binding humans to each other in a web of voluntary exchange.

Heather McDonald.

You are walking through the forest as lovely as any in a Grimm's fairy tale. Gentle sunlight dapples through the lush ferns, grass, and the leafy canopy overhead. The log from a fallen tree forms a perfect resting place. Examining the tree nearby, you learn you are not alone as you had thought: to your side an active honey bee colony is busy in its hollow.

Some might start to move away, but others begin to think: Say, isn't the colony in many ways just like a human economy? After all, it has citizens, it has resources, it has production. The little bees are born and die. They raise their young. It probably doesn't make sense to ask if they are happy, they certainly don't engage in trade, but might it still make sense to wonder if their colony, their little "economy," is doing as well as it can? This is starting to get interesting. What does it mean for an economy to be doing as well as it can, i.e. to be "optimal?" How would you know if it were not?

1.1   The Meaning of Optimality

When economists began to parse carefully what they meant by the word "optimal," they quickly realized that it was not good enough to say that "being optimal means to operate at peak efficiency." Peak efficiency sounds good, but what is peak efficiency for an economy? Saying that the economy "cannot do any better" sounds good, too, but numerous definitions for "do better" are possible.

So the early thinkers started with something noncontroversial. It makes sense to believe that human flourishing should respect *all* people of the economy. Were we to find that re-arranging the economy in some way hurt no one but made one, some, or all people better off, it would mean that the original economy was not optimal.

It turns out that this simple observation is good enough to provide a definition of optimality. Why? Because we use it to eliminate arrangements of the economy that are not optimal. Anything left is defined to be "optimal." We will, in fact, formalize the definition just given as our meaning for optimality in the section labeled "Pareto Optimality." We add here a small clarification. Some economists prefer to speak of "efficiency." Efficiency and optimality are synonyms. In this book we will use the two interchangeably and make no distinction between *economic* efficiency, or just "efficiency," and optimality.

1.1.1   What is an Economy?

Humans are multi-dimensional and complex, which is why we need farmers, plumbers, mechanics, bankers, electricians, artists, poets, insurance agents, social workers, musicians, philosophers, psychologists, and scientists. These are participants in the economy. A lawyer might talk about the need for rule of law, a musician about uplifting music, while an economist focuses on arrangements regarding production and trade in goods and services. For human flourishing, an economy certainly requires economic efficiency.

But what, exactly, is an economy? Is it the same thing as society?

A "society" is a group of individuals living together as members of a community. An "economy" is slightly different. An economy is a group of participants, assets ("endowments"), and the production technology that allows the economy to function. The first component of the economy is its persons. These might be called individuals or sometimes households or sometimes "consumers" to reflect the fact that the participants are separate decision-making units involved in making decisions about consumption of goods and services, supply of labor and so on. When members of the economy are called households it reflects the fact that families tend to be the primary units for decision making. Households can also consist of other groupings of individuals. For our purposes, the terms "individual" and "consumer" are satisfactory. As stated, the primary requirement is that the member of the economy be a decision-making unit that decides about its consumption of goods and services and its supply of goods and services to the rest of the economy.

> **Economy: An economy is people as individuals for decision making, assets available to be used, and production technology or know-how.**

The second element of an economy is the list of assets it has. Economists use the term "endowments" to mean those assets available to the economy that are provided by nature or past production. Buildings from the past are resources that do not come from current activity. So are stocks of minerals and ores, which may be stockpiled from previous mining or even be still in the ground. Land is an endowment. Whatever tangible good or goods inherited from nature or the past, owned by the members of the economy and available for use are endowments.

The third ingredient of an economy is its production technology ("techniques" or know-how). Technology can be thought of as the techniques, recipes or blueprints for production methods that are known to the households, individuals, and consumers that make up the economy. Technological progress is merely the adding of new and improved production methods to the list of known techniques. At any point in time, individuals, endowments, and currently known techniques constitute the economy and define it.

Note that an economy is *not* necessarily synonymous with a geographic area on the globe defined by boundaries, government, and so on, though it could be. Usually, the persons that make up the economy live together as members of a community. In that case "society" is the people of the economy.

1.2   Allocations

Moving on, presume you have the participants, assets, and production know-how that define an economy. How do you describe how the economy is functioning? Listing the consumption and production of every good and service by every producer, consumer, and decision making unit leaves nothing out. Call such a list an *allocation*. For example, for an accountant the section of the allocation related to him might include 2000 hours of accounting work supplied per year plus whatever quantities of goods or services the accountant consumed. For a business firm the allocation would list the quantity of every input used—electricity, steel, accounting hours, whatever— and the amounts of each good or service supplied. Voluntary private organizations and government are also decision-making units. We list all of their inputs and outputs as well. The lists might be extremely large, but by listing everything, the *allocation* identifies everything the economy is doing.[1]

> **Allocation: An allocation lists the consumption and production of every good and service by every producer, consumer, and decision making unit.**

Let's return to our original question about optimality.

1.3   Pareto Optimality

The concept of optimality or efficiency for an economy is associated with Italian economist Vilfredo Pareto (1848-1923). Talking about optimality makes sense only with respect to *feasible* allocations, meaning allocations that are physically possible for the economy to achieve given its technology and endowments. A feasible allocation

---

[1]The endowments of the economy, available at the start of the production period, are stocks. Production is a flow where the production period is usually taken to be a year. When labor hours supplied by a worker are discussed, they might be measured in hours per week, and so on. Fortunately, it is not too hard to keep stocks and flows straight.

is defined to be *Pareto Optimal* if it is impossible to replace it with a different allocation in which one or more consumers are better off and no one worse off. After all, if Mr. Green, Mrs. Blue, and Mr. Red are the members of the economy, who would be willing to describe it as optimal if Mr. Green and Mrs. Blue can both be made better off without harming Red? The same goes for Blue being helped without harming the other two. In an optimal economy, it must be impossible to help any one or more people, unharmfully to the rest.

> **Pareto Optimality: To be optimal, it must be impossible to help any one or more people, unharmfully to the rest. Eliminating non-optimal allocations leaves Pareto Optimal allocations.**

Similarly, an allocation is Pareto Optimal if replacing it by any other feasible allocation harms one, some, or all individuals, or at best leaves all of them unaffected.[2]

Adjustments and Optimality

The plumber in a large city repaired pipes for the leading high-powered lawyer who was surprised by the bill.

"I don't even earn that much in my own billable hours."

"I know, I didn't get that much when I was a lawyer either."

We may smile that a lawyer made himself better off by becoming a plumber (the story sometimes pairs a plumber and a brain surgeon), but if citywide plumbing rates are unchanged and the rest of the economy unaffected, one person was helped and no one harmed when there was one more plumber and one fewer lawyer. The ability to improve shows that the original allocation could not have been Pareto Optimal.

A small detail needs to be added. The decision about whether a participant is better off or worse off must be decided by the individual himself or herself. Mr. Green does not get to say when Mrs. Blue is better off or worse off; that is left solely to Mrs. Blue. The same is true for every other consumer. Notice that this individualistic

---

[2]That is, indifferent between their original bundle and the post-change bundle.

approach rules out authoritarian approaches to economic efficiency or measuring economic success in terms of some private idea of national pre-eminence, glory of the leader, and so on. Honoring everyone's *own* assessment of whether they are better off or worse off implies that individuals do not live to sacrifice themselves for some externally imposed betterment of the state.

1.3.1   Production

Recall the honey bees and what you know about them: Bees need to produce food just like humans do, and they have two types. If the colony is efficient, it must be impossible to make any change that results in more honey without diminishing the quantity of Royal Jelly. This rules out certain ways of doing things.

This all seems pretty simple, and it is. Pareto Optimality requires efficiency in production, and later we will see that it also requires efficiency in distribution and the right choices of goods produced. Production involves using up a list of inputs and getting a list of outputs in return. If identical output could be achieved using less of one or more *inputs,* while using no more of any input, then the original production cannot have been optimal. The point is that we are led to know certain things that have to be true of input use. We need only to investigate.

International trade is a type of production. Goods are sent abroad and "used up" in return for getting a list of different goods back. Whatever Pareto Optimality requires of production, it requires of international trade, and so on.

1.3.2   Other Requirements

Economists have discovered a number of things that must be true in order for the economy to be Pareto Optimal. This book talks about six in Part 2. Three requirements have to do with production. One has to do with distributing goods once they are in existence, and two have to do with choosing the right mix of goods to produce. These are called necessary conditions because the presence of Pareto Optimality implies that they must hold. Without them, we cannot have Pareto Optimality. We will return to these briefly in Chapter

4 after providing the two main results about Pareto Optimality in Chapter 2.[3]

1.4 How Much Do Social Arrangements Matter?

The reasoning just described found that efficiency places restrictions on production. Total production is generally measured by the size of Gross Domestic Product[4] (GDP) which we want to be as large as possible. We have not yet introduced prices to value different types of output, so for now we can either think of output as a single substance or accept it on faith that valuation is possible until prices are described later.

In either event, GDP can be measured and reasonably compared across countries. Comparisons provide us a window into the question of how much social arrangements might matter to efficiency and well being. For example, if country A produces $80,000 worth of goods and services per capita in a year, while country B produces just $500 per capita in the same time frame, which country would you rather live in?

Thankfully, from time to time history offers natural experiments from which to learn. Strictly speaking, an experiment holds constant all relevant factors except the one under consideration that is allowed to differ. While natural experiments do not rise to this standard, they are nevertheless worth knowing.

1.4.1 East and West Germany

Perhaps one of the best natural experiments is the differential progress experienced by East and West Germany after World War II. East and

---

[3]Chapters 1 and 2 in Part 2 show that "social bookkeeping" can be set up to simplify thinking about the requirements of Pareto Optimality. Conventions like listing production inputs as negative numbers and outputs as positive numbers enormously reduce the needed notation. While these arrangements are accessible to any reader, they are provided in Part 2 to augment what is in Part 1 with proofs, documentation, and greater details. Chapters in Part 2 correspond to the same-numbered chapters in Part 1.

[4]GDP is the total value of all goods and services produced within the economy during the production period.

West Germany, of course, were part of Germany, a single nation, before the end of World War II in 1945. Their citizens had the same
language, the same culture, a common history, and a common legal
structure. After 1945, East Germany was placed under control of
the Soviet Union, a socialist country, whereas the sectors controlled
by the United States, England, and France became West Germany
and adopted capitalism and free markets. By 1970, twenty five years
later, GDP per capita in West Germany exceeded that in East Germany by 41 percent. Ten years later, it exceeded it by 55 percent.[5]
The part of the country that become capitalist noticeably outper-
formed the part of the country that became socialist.

Germany was re-unified on October 3, 1990, leading to years
of transition and disruption in the difficult economic merger that,
understandably, included significant out-migration of much of the
eastern population once it was possible to them. Effects of the
separation continued for years. Nevertheless, differential GDP per
capita in the east noticeably began to improve. By 2018 the east
trailed the western part of the country by only 27 percent.[6] We
might expect that the gap will narrow further.

Government and social arrangements matter.

1.4.2   North and South Korea

North and South Korea were parts of a single nation and a single people prior to the events leading up to World War II and the subsequent
Korean War that lasted from June 25, 1950 to July 27, 1953. Ko-
reans spoke the same language, had a common history, and derived
from the same culture. Aided by the socialist Soviet Union, North
Korea became a communist country "one of the world's most centrally directed and least open economies"[7] and South Korea adopted
western capitalism. The Korean War began when socialist North Korea invaded South Korea in 1950. War is destructive and both sides
suffered until the armistice in 1953. The North became communist,
the South remained capitalist. Sixty-three years later in 2015, the

---

[5]Ehrlich and Boros-Kazai (1991), p. 90.

[6]"East Germany," *DW*, https://www.dw.com/en/east-germany-its-not-just-
the-economy-stupid/a-45454241, online.

[7]*CIA Factbook,* "North Korea," https://www.cia.gov/library/publications/the-
world-factbook/geos/kn.html, online.

GDP per capita in North Korea was estimated to be an astonishingly low 4.5 percent of that in the South, $1,700 compared to $37,600.[8]

Government and social arrangements matter.

1.4.3 Haiti and Dominican Republic

The Republic of Haiti and the Dominican Republic were once a single nation, together occupying the west and east halves of the same island of Hispaniola in the Caribbean. Haiti was established on January 1, 1804 after winning its independence from France in the Haitian Revolution of 1791-1804. Haiti is the first independent nation of Latin America and the Caribbean, and it is the second independent nation in North America after the United States, also once colonies, obtained their independence.

The Dominican Republic, on the east side of the island, in turn declared its independence from Haiti on February 27, 1844. The Dominican Republic had to defend itself from raids and military engagements that lasted as late as 1855. Ultimately, however, the two nations with common origin, occupying a common island, with the same climate, in the same region of the globe, operated as separate nations with separate leaderships, separate governments, and separate legal structures. Many things that go beyond natural resources, location, climate, and people, account for a country's progress including the competence and corruption exhibited by its government.

In 2018 the Dominican Republic (July 2017 estimated population of 10.7 million) had GDP per capita of $16,900. This was 9.4 times the $1,800 GDP per capita of its older sister Haiti (July 2017 estimated population of 10.6 million).

Government and social arrangements matter.

1.4.4 A Cautionary Note: Venezuela 1999-2018

Examples of absolute decline are rare, but exist among the case studies, and should be considered in the larger context.

Apologists for countries with poor performance have suggested many factors to explain differential progress. Perhaps being a former colony presents challenges. Perhaps having valuable natural

---

[8]op cit., "North Korea," and "South Korea."

resources provides opportunities. Perhaps there is a difference between English common law and Spanish legal traditions.

The problem with many of these explanations is the prominent outliers. The United States is a former colony, as is Canada, as is Mexico. The citizens of the United States have made their nation one of the wealthier nations of the world. Canada and Mexico, also former colonies, produce output that places them in the top 6 percent and 8 percent of world countries, respectively.

Mexico and Canada have oil deposits, but so does Venezuela. Venezuela's GDP growth rate in three years (2015, 2016, 2017) was -6.2, -16.5, and -14 percent, respectively![9] What could account for the destruction of one-third of GDP?

Governmental philosophy provides one possible answer. Venezuela was governed by a series of democratically elected governments after 1959. In 1999 Hugo Chavez, a socialist, became president, a position he held until his death in 2013. Thereafter handpicked successors followed. Chavez gradually concentrated power and changed governmental and legal structures to implement his "socialism of the 21st Century" agenda. While the people of Venezuela suffered under his leadership, his daughter Gabriela did quite well.

Government and social arrangements matter.

State Control

Power is gathered into the hands of a governing few who reward themselves and take steps never to lose it. The face of the oligarchy typically rests on a single individual such as Hugo Chavez in Venezuela, or Fidel Castro who earlier took power in Cuba.

Two years after Chavez's death, news reports began appearing in Latin American, United Kingdom, US and other sources with rumors that his favorite daughter, Maria Gabriela Chavez, had somehow become the richest woman in Venezuela. According to stories, her bank accounts in the U.S. and Andorra had assets totaling nearly $4.2 billion.[10]

---

[10]Nick Fagge, "The Rich Kids of Venezuela" (2009).

---

[9]Op cit., *CIA World Factbook*, "Venezuela."

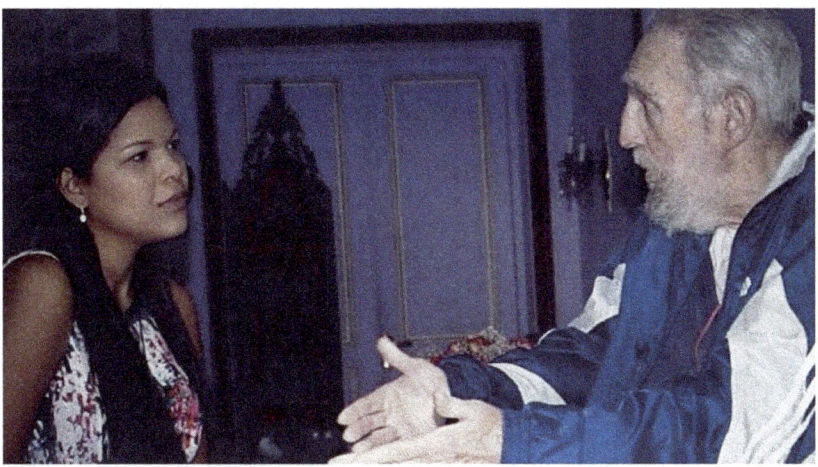

Figure 1.1: **Maria Chavez meets Fidel Castro in Havana, April 2014.**

1.4.5 Ehrlich's Pairings

The twentieth century itself can be seen as a grand social experiment. It provides many possible pairings of countries that, for a time, could be argued to have sufficient similarities and comparable economic prospects that they could be used to make comparisons.

Argentina, whose name means "silver" or "land of silver," in the beginning years of the twentieth century could have been paired with Australia. Both countries have large endowments of land and other natural resources. Both were associated with European colonizers. Argentina could sensibly have been said to have had the advantage. The phrase "rich as an Argentine" in common use at the end of the 19th century derived from Argentina's obvious wealth and early twentieth century prospects. In the hundred years after World War I, however, Argentina's history included the Peron era, the establishment of a socialist regime and much political instability. Argentine GDP per capita (population 44.3 million) in 2017 was $20,900 compared to Australia's GDP per capita (population 23.2 million) of $50,300, more than twice Argentina's level.[11]

The differential progress of country pairings where at the begin-

---

[11]GDP per capita in purchasing power parity, op cit., CIA World Factbook

Table 1.1: **Comparing the Effectiveness of Socialist Economies and Market Economies Using Relative Per Capita GDP Over Time**

.

Country Pairings (Capitalist/Socialist)	1937	1970	1980
Austria/Czechoslovakia	1.12*	1.29	1.43
Austria/Hungary	1.58	1.96	1.91
Austria/Poland	1.90	2.14	2.21
Austria/Yugoslavia	2.38	3.00	2.76
Greece/Czechoslovakia	0.54	0.51	.64
Greece/Hungary	0.76	0.76	.86
Greece/Poland	0.92	0.86	1.00
Greece/Yugoslavia	1.15	1.20	1.24
Italy/Czechoslovakia	0.80	0.94	1.02
Italy/Hungary	1.12	1.43	1.36
Italy/Poland	1.35	1.57	1.58
Italy/Yugoslavia	1.69	2.20	1.97
Spain/Czechoslovakia	0.56	0.69	0.98
Spain/Hungary	0.79	1.04	1.12
Spain/Poland	0.95	1.14	1.30
Spain/Yugoslavia	1.19	1.60	1.62
Average	**1.18**	**1.40**	**1.44**

*I.e. In 1937, Austrian GDP per Capita was higher than Czech GDP per Capita by 12 percent ($\frac{\text{Austria GDP per Capita}}{\text{Czechoslovakia GDP per Capita}} = 1.12$). By 1980 capitalist Austria was 43 percent better off than socialist Czechoslovakia.

Source: Ehrlich and Boros-Kazai (1991), Table 9, pp. 94-95.

ning of the comparison period a socialist government was chosen by the people (or imposed on them) in one of the pair but not the other country gives insight into how much social structure—socialist versus capitalist—might matter. Table 1.1 displays just a few of these capitalist versus socialist pairings studied by economist Eva Ehrlich. Each of the countries shown—half that would remain capitalist (Austria, Greece, Italy, Spain), half that would become socialist (Czechoslovakia, Hungary, Poland, and Yugoslovia) is intentionally made part of four pairings so that the displayed pairings in the table being shown are balanced across the two groups.

In 1937, all countries were capitalist. World War II occurred. Thereafter the denominator country became socialist. What is the result? Whereas the numerator countries exhibit average GDP per capita 18 percent above their partner in 1937, by 1980 they are 44 percent ahead. The 18% starting point in 1937 is an inessential artifact of the pairings being selected and shown. Some numerator countries are worse off than their denominator country initially, some the reverse. *All numerator countries make gains against their soon-to-be socialist partner. In no case does a socialist country make gains over time against its capitalist partner.*[12]

Government and social arrangements matter.

1.5 Conclusion

Human flourishing requires economic flourishing, which we have determined requires Pareto Optimality. We use the term *essential economics* to mean the economics that support, and are required by (implied by), human flourishing and hence are required by Pareto Optimality.

Any sensible reading of the data suggests that social structure matters greatly to economic performance, efficiency, and human flourishing. Capitalist countries studied in the twentieth century seem to outperform their socialist counterparts by a good bit.

---

[12]Between 1970 and 1980, Italy gives back some of its 120% gains against Yugoslavia and its 43% gains against Hungary, which reminds us that no form of government is perfect all the time. The same observation applies between 1970 and 1980 to Austria giving back some of its 96% gains against Hungary or its 200% gains against Yugoslavia.

Starting from Pareto Optimality, production, distribution, and choice of goods produced will establish what the economy must look like. These are discussed in the next chapters.

References

CIA World Factbook (2020). "North Korea," "South Korea," "Venezuela."

DW.com (2018). "East Germany," https://www.dw.com/en/east-germany-its-not-just-the-economy-stupid/a-45454241, online, accessed 2 October.

Ehrlich, Eva and Andreas Boros-Kazai (1991). "The Competition among Countries, 1937-1986," *Eastern European Economics,* 29, 2 (Winter, 1990-1991), p. 90.

Fagge, Nick (2019). "The Rich Kids of Venezuela—Including Socialist Revolution Leader Hugo Chavez' Daughter—Flaunt their Wealth with Fist-fulls of Cash and Lavish Holidays while the Nation Starves," *Daily Mail*, UK, 4 February 2019, https://www.dailymail.co.uk/news/article-6667889/Rich-Kids-Venezuela-including-Socialist-leader-Hugo-Chavezs-daughter-flaunt-wealth.html.; *Fox News,* "Hugo Chavez daughter is the richest individual in Venezuela, report claims," 10 August 2015, https://www.foxnews.com/world/hugo-chavez-daughter-is-the-richest-individual-in-venezuela-report-claims.; "Maria Gabriela Chavez podria ser la mujer mas rica de Venezuela" (Maria Gabriela Chavez Could Be the Richest Woman in Venezuela). *Diario Las Americas* (in Spanish). Caracas. 7 August 2015.

McDonald, Heather (2020). "Four Months of Unprecedented Government Malfeasance," *Imprimis*, 49, 5/6, May/June.

Chapter 2

The Fundamental Theorems of Welfare Economics

How can we love our country and not love our countrymen? And loving them, reach out a hand when they fall, heal them when they're sick, and provide opportunities to make them self-sufficient so they will be equal in fact and not just theory.

Ronald Reagan, Inaugural Address

In the years following the 1930s, the word "welfare" has come to be associated with government-operated tax-supported entitlement programs. Such entitlement or "welfare programs" might provide to a special sub-group in-kind goods such as food, clothing, housing, transportation, medical care, dental care, vision care, and more. Sometimes the entitlement program takes the form of a government-granted pension.

However, to the economist "welfare economics" refers to its more originalist meaning: the study of community well being, the study of human flourishing in the economic realm, the study of arrangements for the production and consumption of goods and services that lead to the highest possible well being of the members of the economy. The focus of welfare economics is to have the economy provide the best possible outcomes for all its citizens, the reason for which, as explained in Chapter 1, is the selection of Pareto Optimal allocations so that no improvement in those allocations can be achieved. In this book it is in this sense that we use the term "welfare economics," and this is the reason we study its theorems.

2.1   From Individuals to the Nation

Few propositions are given the label "Fundamental Theorem of..." yet this is precisely the label applied to *The First and Second Fundamental Theorems of Welfare Economics*. This chapter is devoted to interpreting both theorems. We have already explained that more detail is provided in Chapters 1 and 2 of Part 2 for those who wish it.

Since everyone matters, the economy needs to account for everyone. There is a way to do all this that works out nicely for every quantity that is part of the economy's allocation.   Each column in

EVERYONE MATTERS

Figure 2.1: **Assessing the Economy Disregards None**

a rectangular array can be designed to list the numbers that apply to an economic decision maker (household, firm, voluntary private organization, government) and each row to list the numbers that apply to a given good or service. Using a positive number for outputs and a negative number for inputs makes thinking about the economy's effect on wealth easy. We *want* the economy to create wealth. But how exactly is that done?

Wealth is created when objects of lower value are converted by production into objects of higher value. Sticks and stones, for example, are just sticks and stones until they are worked into a spear. Presuming that you prefer the spear to sticks and stones, making the spear creates wealth. This leads us to consider the value of sticks and stones relative to spears and to the positive and negative numbers just mentioned.

2.1.1 Prices and Values

We haven't said much about prices yet, but as soon as people are able to trade a certain number of their apples for someone else's oranges—and they naturally will trade in apples, oranges, and all other kinds of goods—we will have a list of positive numbers that give relative importance. Two apples trading for one orange implies an "orange price" and an "apple price." If we pick apples to be the measure, then the apple-price of an apple is 1 (1 apple always trades for 1 apple), and the apple-price of an orange is 2 (2 apples trade for 1 orange). But if we pick oranges to be the measure, then the orange-price of an apple is $1/2$ ($1/2$ orange trades for 1 apple) and the orange-price of an orange is 1 (1 orange always trades for 1 orange).[1] Other prices are worked out from the other trades. How prices work is fairly basic, so little needs to be explained about them.

Now, take any production process such as making a spear and add the values (price times quantity) of all the inputs and outputs, where outputs are listed as positive numbers and inputs are listed as negative numbers. The result, called profit, tells us how much wealth has been created.

Profit and Making Wealth

---

[1]Selecting the "numeraire" determines the standard by which values are displayed.

It might seem that everyone should understand what profit is and that we should view it favorably. In 1987-88 I served as the Senior Economist for international trade for the President's Council of Economic Advisors. The Uruguay Round of Trade negotiations was in full swing, the Canada-U.S. Free Trade Agreement (later expanded to the North American Free Trade Agreement) was being negotiated, the Omnibus Trade and Competitiveness Act of 1988 (at the time of writing still the last large scale U.S. trade bill passed) was being debated in Congress, and many Section 201 and 301 trade disputes were prominent in the news during that time. In the U.S. Trade Representative's building one morning to participate in welcoming a delegation of young trade experts from Communist China, I was impressed by the collection of obviously intelligent, well spoken, tall and physically attractive men with whom I interacted among our Chinese counterparts. After a short discussion, the contents of which I have forgotten, one asked me a question that I have not forgotten, "What is profit?"

Tending to think at first the question was in jest, I hesitated and then answered the question straightforwardly. My questioner thanked me for my answer and the moment passed. I now think the question was sincere, given the false aversion to profit that can be found in socialist countries based on lack of understanding of what profit actually is.

Listing inputs as negative numbers and outputs as positive numbers aids in wealth and profit calculations. For example, an artist uses a particular recipe to make a sculpture. He takes a chunk of marble (p_{Chunk} = \$100 per chunk), uses 85 hours of labor on it (p_{Labor} = \$35 per hour) and 1500 kilowatt hours of electricity (p_{Kwh} = \$.15 per Kwh) to produce a finished sculpture ($p_{Sculpture}$ = \$4100).

The quantities and prices just stated are (-1, -85, -1500, 1) and (100, 35, .15, 4100). Valuing each quantity by its price and summing gives $-1 \times 100 - 85 \times 35 - 1500 \times .15 + 1 \times 3500 = -100 - 2975 - 225 + 4100 = \$800$. We conclude that marble in form of the sculpture is worth \$800 more than the inputs. \$800 is the sculptor's profit. Since it is positive, wealth was created.

2.2 Rationality and Revealed Preferences

As already stated, each consumer gets to determine for himself or herself whether one collection of goods is better or worse than another. No one else gets to decide for them. Let us use the word "bundle" to mean a collection or "basket" of goods. A basket of 3 apples, 2 oranges, and 1 pear would be a bundle. A basket of 3 apples, 3 oranges, and 2 pears would be another bundle. For the consumer to be rational there are a few basics.

1. We expect that consumers choose the best available bundle as judged by themselves (preferences are individualistic).
2. The consumer can rank any two bundles (preferences are complete).
3. If bundle A is better than bundle B, and B is better than C, then A is better than C and so on for any chain (preferences are transitive),
4. and any bundle is equivalent to itself in preference (preferences are reflexive).

Assuming rational consumers does not mean that we actually believe that all of the consumers, all of the time, satisfy all of the requirements. Rather it is a statement that studying *irrational* consumers would be essentially pointless, even if possible.[2] Various studies indicate that as children mature, their preferences become more stable. In cases where people have pointed out to them that they provided rankings that created a cycle (A is preferred to B, B is preferred to C, and C is preferred to A), without being told to do so they will often correct their answers to eliminate the cycle. Finally, we all recognize that there may be cases where we find it hard to choose between two options, but eventually manage to decide. All things considered, assuming rationality makes more sense that not assuming it.

An implication of rationality is that we can learn from what the consumer's choices reveal. If the consumer chooses bundle B when some other bundle A could have been chosen, then we know that bundle B must be strictly preferred to bundle A or at worst

---

[2]There is little that can be said about someone who cannot tell us which of two bundles is better for him or her, whose rankings lead to inconsistencies, and whose preferences can change from moment to moment so that a given bundle cannot even be said to be as good as itself.

is indifferent to A. Observing all such choices would identify the preferences of the consumer.

The main application of these obvious kinds of conclusions is to bundles whose cost we know. If bundle B, costing $85, were chosen, then by revealed preference we know it is preferred or indifferent to any alternative bundle A that costs less than or equal to $85 because A was a feasible choice when B was selected.

If a bundle B is known to be strictly preferred to a chosen bundle A, then B must have been too costly when A was chosen. Returning to our example, if I bought bundle A for $80, but did not choose bundle B, though I preferred it, it must be that it cost more than the $80 available to me to spend. Again, these are pretty much common sense, yet do not despise small things. "Revealed Preference" is the term that economists use to describe the conclusions we can make about consumers' likes and dislikes by observing what they actually do.[3] It figures prominently in deriving the first of the important two theorems discussed after the next section.

> **Revealed Preference:** "Revealed preference" refers to the conclusions we can make about consumers' likes and dislikes by observing what they do.

2.3   Competitive Equilibrium

To summarize,
1. people naturally engage in trade, which creates prices, and
2. assuming rational choices, we can infer things about the value to the consumer of chosen bundles relative to non-chosen bundles.

This inches us suspiciously close to familiar ground where markets exist, prices govern trades, and people sell some items in their bundle (say labor) to use the money to buy other items. Because we are assuming they are rational, certain things must be true.

Consider this logic: If a given trade harms one of the consumers making it, he or she can refuse the trade. Therefore, if consumers are rational, trade will be engaged in only if it is mutually beneficial. An economy with mutually beneficial trade *un-engaged in* cannot

---

[3]Chapter 2 of Part 2 provides more information on page 279.

be Pareto Optimal. Thus Pareto Optimality implies that trade will be engaged in and prices determined, until there is no further room for mutually beneficial trade. This is not quite a proof, but it comes close to explaining the close connection between markets, prices, and human flourishing. The First and Second Fundamental Theorems of Welfare Economics are that connection.

It is sensible that human flourishing naturally comes embedded with the requirement for certain kinds of allocations that relate to freely-engaged-in markets and not others. An allocation with these features is called a *competitive equilibrium*. We define this, and then move to the main event in the next two sections.

Presume that a list of prices is given and a firm's profit at these prices is calculated as we have already described. Then an allocation that satisfies the following three conditions is said to be a *competitive equilibrium*.

1. First, firms maximize profits. That is, from the available activities (given by current technology) known to the firm, the firm selects the one with highest profit.
2. Second, given their spendable income at these prices consumers choose the bundle that maximizes their satisfaction. For example, consumers may own some endowment of a natural resource that they can sell in addition to selling their own labor. The value of what they can sell and the cost of goods they can buy produces a budget, from which they buy the best bundle.
3. Third, demand by members of the economy for each good or service equals the available supply from current production and endowments.

That is pretty much all there is to competitive equilibrium: *Firms maximize profits, consumers maximize utility, and demand equals supply in all markets.*

Competitive Equilibrium: Firms maximize profits, consumers maximize utility, and demand equals supply in all markets.

2.4   The First and Second Fundamental Theorems of Welfare Economics

At this point we have no reason to expect that any particular allocation will be a competitive equilibrium. But supposing that one is, then that allocation is Pareto Optimal. You've just seen stated the First Fundamental Theorem of Welfare Economics![4] Likewise, there is no advance reason to expect that any particular allocation will be a Pareto Optimum. But supposing that one is, then the second fundamental theorem says that it is a competitive equilibrium![5]

In logic, a set is just a collection of objects. These objects could be the arrays representing different allocations for some economy. Call one such collection CE and another such collection PO. If set of objects CE is a subset of set of objects PO, and the set of objects PO is a subset of CE, we know that PO and CE are the same set of objects

We are left with no option except CE = PO! Now, let CE be competitive equilibria (you knew where we were headed), and PO be Pareto Optimal allocations. If we say that competitive equilibria *are* the set of Pareto Optimums,[6] you have just absorbed the message of the First and Second Fundamental Theorems of Welfare Economics.

There is a lot wrapped into this equivalency. The First Fundamental Theorem of Welfare Economics, and its companion the Second, have every right to be considered fundamental properties of the universe just like $E = mc^2$ or the First and Second Laws of Thermodynamics (energy is conserved, and entropy increases in natural processes). Like them, the simply and succinctly stated First and Second Fundamental Theorems contain a host of meaning. Since the 1950s, when they were mathematically proven using the arrays

---

[4]A competitive equilibrium is Pareto Optimal, or more precisely, any allocation (recalling Chapter 1, think of an allocation as the array of numbers for all quantities for all participants in the economy) that satisfies the conditions of a competitive equilibrium is Pareto Optimal.

[5]Let a^0 denote a particular allocation (a^1 might be a different allocation, and so on). If a^0 is Pareto Optimal, then a^0 could be made to be the outcome of a competitive equilibrium for the economy with appropriate assignment of asset ownerships.

[6]Optima and optimums are each grammatically correct as the plural of optimum.

of numbers describing the economy that we have already discussed, economists have expended much thought and ink to laying out all of the ramifications.

So what are some of these ramifications?

The most obvious is to recognize that if we want humans to flourish, then we want economic efficiency, and if we want economic efficiency then we want a competitive equilibrium. Pareto Optimality is not just *related* to competitive markets, it *is* competitive markets. If you want human flourishing, you want competitive markets. Getting close to one is getting close to the other. To oppose competitive markets, which are the essential element of a competitive

> **Pareto Optimality is not just RELATED to competitive markets, it IS competitive markets. If you want human flourishing, you want competitive markets.**

equilibrium, is to oppose human flourishing. To observe that conditions in the economy might not mimic the conditions for competitive equilibrium does not say that the First and Second Fundamental Theorems are wrong, or that they fail to apply, or that they are unimportant. It says only that there are ways the economy can do better.

A second ramification has to do with an implication of competitive free markets ("free" meaning no agent is compelled to produce or to trade if he or she does not want to) that immediately speaks to certain fallacies often heard in political discussions. Here is one:

> If you are part of the economy, the story goes, then you benefit from being part of it (this much is true). For example, you are better off than if you had been forced to live in isolation (again true). Further, the economy you are part of may have inherited endowments of buildings, machines, and capital that your forebears left in the land (true) that you didn't make (true again). Therefore, you "*owe*" something more back to "society" (false).

Exactly what the "something more" is that you "owe" to society is usually left to the speaker to tell you. Never mind. Whatever "it" is, the last statement is false. How do you know it is false?

Since Pareto Optimality is the same thing as competitive equilibrium, we can check to see what collection of activities agents are allowed-to-do/supposed-to-do in a competitive equilibrium. In a competitive equilibrium each consumer voluntarily sells goods and services at market prices and voluntarily buys goods and services at market prices. Restated, the consumer in a competitive equilibrium "serves" his or her fellow man by voluntarily providing goods and services to society and willingly receiving goods and services from society. Each consumer makes and receives payments at the market price for what he or she gives and takes. Payment at market prices is what Pareto Optimality specifies for any transfers. There are no "side payments."[7] Full stop. Period. They are not present. If side payments were present, the equilibrium would not be a competitive equilibrium and the allocation would not be a Pareto Optimum.

So where do kindness, loving your brothers and sisters in society, volunteering help, generosity, and charity enter? Don't those who make the "owe-to-society-claim" align themselves on the side of morality? The answer is no. Debts are legal obligations. Payments that are not debts *cannot* be forced on people in a competitive equilibrium. Charity is gifts voluntarily given from one's own assets to help another. Paying your debt is not voluntary; giving someone else's money is not a gift. You have a moral duty to be charitable but it is not a debt you owe society. Others can urge you to be charitable, but they are wrong to force on you side payments.

> **We continue to recommend charity, praise it, and discuss it as we go forward because we assign equal dignity and freedom to everyone.**

We continue to recommend charity, praise it, and discuss it as we go forward because we assign equal dignity and freedom to everyone. Helping others matters, as we will see in due course. Regarding side payments, however, the theorems are plain: All you "owe" to society

---

[7] "Side payments" are any transfers in the system that are imposed outside the rules of normal buying and selling at market prices. Involuntary payments for anything beyond buying and selling at market prices are side payments. For example, were a system of bribes present where a person had to pay a bribe to some official or other individual before being allowed to engage in trade at market prices, the bribe would be considered a side payment.

is to pay fully for what you take from it, and all society "owes" you is to pay you for what you provide to it.

Pay fully for what you take from society, be fully paid for what you provide. Human flourishing means everyone has the same freedom to trade or not trade as others.

2.5 Conclusion

The First and Second Fundamental Theorems of Economics show that the set of allocations in an economy that are Pareto Optimal is the same set of allocations in that economy that are a competitive equilibrium. In a competitive equilibrium consumers pay the competitive market price for what they receive from the economy and get paid the market price for what they provide.

The identification of efficiency with markets has been described in this chapter as a fundamental fact of the universe on par with natural laws. It suggests norms for economic interaction that fortunately conform to our rules of justice. Those who want to consume double what another does, must pay double, and those who are willing to contribute double what another does, get paid double. The same applies to those who want to contribute half or consume half.

For the equivalence between competitive equilibria and Pareto Optimality to hold, certain features must be present that the mathematics of a competitive equilibrium take as given. Following through on these is important, and will be taken up in due course in later chapters. Two important ones are these.

1. In a competitive equilibrium consumers must own some asset or assets of value that they can exchange for the goods and services they consume. In other words, a competitive equilibrium assumes that each consumer is directly viable or can trade to viability. Where does ownership come from? Who enforces the right to property? Does everyone have the right to property in themselves? Can someone else own the right to my labor, for example?

2. The mathematics of competitive equilibrium automatically presume that honesty and safety prevail. Consumers are safe from criminals, liars, and exploiters within the economy and from aggression from the outside. Who provides this safety?

There are several paths that need to be followed. Chapter 3 starts on the first item on the list above—the all important issue of where the property comes from that markets and efficiency require. After this path is briefly pursued, Chapter 4 talks about some of the implications of Pareto Optimality that provide fascinating and important conclusions about markets and how they function. A greater appreciation for prices and the free interaction between buyers and sellers is the benefit.

Chapter 3

Your Work, Your Rights, Your Property

> *"You raised the grain, and you will eat it, ... you your-selves will drink the wine you have pressed."*
>
> Isaiah 62: 9

Human flourishing requires economic optimality, and, as we have seen in the previous chapters, economic optimality is synonymous with competitive markets. However, buying and selling, even in barter, presumes the right of one person to exchange something in the form of a tangible good or a service with another. This chapter discusses human rights related to property, and why they exist.

3.1 A Grocery Story

Taking a cart as you arrive, you enter the grocery store with your list. After some time of filling the cart with your items you step away from it at the end of an aisle for just a moment to retrieve your last listed item, which is shelved a few steps away. As you turn toward your cart again your glance sees that it is gone, taken by another shopper who apparently wants the items you just gathered!

You are indignant, a little angry, and upset. But why? You have not yet paid for anything. Why do you feel rights to the property in the cart?

You are not alone in your reaction. Further, you would not be the first to believe that by virtue of having done the work to collect the items you mixed your labor with the items in the cart and created a claim to them that whoever just took your cart does not have. What you created is not quite your property yet, but it is close. The "rules" would say that you have the right of first refusal, meaning the claim to take them to the cashier and buy them. If you decide not to buy an item at that point, it is re-shelved and the right of others to purchase it restored.

3.2   Property, State of Nature, John Locke

Before there were towns, before there was farming, before there was recorded history, there were savannas and forests and wild areas in which collections of humans roamed, gathered food, lived and hunted. Fossil animal bones display cut marks and evidence of pro-cessing. We know that knives and spearheads were developed by ancient *homo sapiens.* Even in a primitive state of nature humans fashioned tools and capital, the means of production. They formed other implements to enhance their existence for clothing, shelter, and comfort.

Figure 3.1: **The 5,300 Year Old Finishing Tool Found with Oetzi the Iceman was his Property.**

Oetzi's Property

Made like a pencil and constructed from the wood of a linden tree, the tool was used in sharpening and re-knapping flint tools and arrowheads. It had hammered into its central core a fire-hardened deer antler whose point was sharpened. The Iceman, found thousands of years later in the Tyrolean Alps, is now believed to have spent his last days repairing his tools, including making arrows for himself and a new bow. These items were Oetzi's property.

The meaning of property in a primitive state has been well thought through. Probably the most famous and well regarded work was done by John Locke, writing in the 1600s. He adopted the term "state of nature," saying that "Men living according to reason, without a common superior on earth, to judge between them, is properly the state of nature." The lack "of a common judge, with authority puts all persons in a state of nature." The presence of appropriate or legitimately constituted government implies the existence of a political authority to judge between parties in a dispute and enforce decisions. Its absence defines a state of nature.

In addition to the state of nature where men "lived according to reason," there are conditions where appropriate government operates, and "a state of war" where men fail to abide by the law of reason. It is possible to move between states. For example, failure of government to adhere to its legitimate function could place men back into a state of nature. Acts of aggression create a state of war, and so on.

The main ideas relating to property are that people are born with status as free and equal persons. If this is not true, it is because of man's oppression. In the state of nature, the whole earth upon which they reside is commonly owned. Property is created when one mixes his own labor with an object from the state of nature, such as picking a fruit from a tree or a berry from a bush.

Naturally, scores of pages could be filled investigating details of what "mixing one's labor with it" means. If I pick a fruit from a tree, does that make the entire tree mine, the entire grove in which the tree sits, or just the fruit that I picked? If I take lemon juice squeezed from a lemon that I picked and do the work of stirring it into the ocean, have I "mixed my labor with the ocean" and therefore made it my private property? Or presume that I do nothing to change or improve the land, but merely travel across it as I hunt an animal from the forest it supports, does that make the whole forest mine, or just the deer that I killed?

At a minimum, "mixing his labor with it" would have to mean transforming one tangible good of value into another of greater value through converting it into something different, or transporting an item of value to a more valuable location, or using something as an input into the creation of a new product of value, and so on. Even this qualification might not rule out all difficulties. Locke himself recognized that while no permission in the state of nature is needed to pick a fruit or a nut, one should be restricted to take only what can be used. We will see later that part of government's legitimate function once it is appropriately contracted into existence is to enforce property rights and decide various of these details and issues.

According to Locke, acquiring property through the act of making or creating it confers rights. For example, all men are free to "dispose of their possessions and persons, as they think fit, within the bounds of the law of nature [rules of reason that govern human actions]."[1]

3.2.1   Right to Own Yourself

The key passage regarding property in Locke's Second Treatise reads,

> "every man has a property in his own person. This no-
> body has any right to but himself. The labor of his body,
> and the work of his hands, we may say, are properly his."

One particular conclusion from Locke is inescapable: Should anyone own the product of *another's* labor, then the property created from such accrues by definition to the owner, not to the one doing the labor, which is a direct violation of the statement that mixing one's labor with an object produces property of the laborer. It therefore follows that if "every man has property in his own person" slavery must be prohibited, since the labor rendered by the slave should belong solely to the one who labored and not to another.

---

[1] John Locke, *Second Treatise on Government*, 1689.

3.2.2   Right to One's Own Giftedness

Another implication flowing from the right to own yourself is that the labor that flows from your own giftedness also belongs solely to you who rendered the associated labor. If Pablo Picasso and you are more gifted than I am as an artist and painter, then you are rightfully the owner of what results from your painting, and I own what emits from my less stellar efforts. I cannot claim property in your painting. Maybe you paint effortlessly and I struggle. Your painting is still yours.

Arguing that not knowing before any of us is born which will be gifted and which will be mediocre in no way entitles the poor painter to product of the good painter. "Equal work for equal pay," if it is naively interpreted to mean that any painter who fills equal square footage of canvas with his artwork must receive what Pablo Picasso receives for his painting on same-sized canvas, is invalid.

3.2.3   Right Not to Be Stolen From

Ownership implies the right of the owner to use the owned property as he chooses, to prevent others from using it, and to dispose of it as he chooses. Included in the right to dispose of property is the right to trade it to another for something of value, sell it to another, or exchange it with another. Recognizing exchange, in turn, immediately adds another valid way to acquire property. Philosopher Robert Nozick's rules of justice in exchange are discussed briefly in the next section.

Taking another's property *without* voluntary exchange—in other words taking without consent—is stealing. Stealing has been universally condemned, denounced, and excoriated throughout history. A major function of government is to prevent stealing and punish those who engage in it to act as deterrent against future stealing. Many argue that it is possible for government to steal as well, and inappropriate forms of taxation are stealing. We will return to this topic later when we discuss morality in Chapter 7 and government and government failure in Chapters 10 and 11.

3.3   Voluntary Exchange and Nozick's Rules of Justice

One of the most influential thinkers of the twentieth century on this topic was Robert Nozick of Harvard University, and one of the several dozen or so most influential books was his *Anarchy, State, Utopia* published in 1974. In it Nozick works from first principles, such as of the type just discussed regarding property and others, to deduce what functions minimal government would engage in and whether ideal government should go beyond this.

> Nozick's rules of justice in property are so simple and useful that we quote his statement in full.

Nozick's rules of justice in property are so simple and useful that we quote his statement in full. He said that,

> the following inductive definition would exhaustively cover the subject of justice in holdings:
>
> 1. A person who acquires a holding in accordance with the principle of justice in acquisition is entitled to that holding.
> 2. A person who acquires a holding in accordance with the principle of justice in transfer, from someone else entitled to the holding, is entitled to the holding.
> 3. No one is entitled to a holding except by (repeated) applications of 1 and 2.
> (Nozick 1974. p. 151)

In other words, original property can be created by the mechanism described by Locke and later writers, but it also can be acquired by "just transfer" from someone else entitled to the property that is being justly transferred. In modern society, just transfer probably accounts for most of the property one acquires. I work for wages (justly acquired because my employer voluntarily hires me and I voluntarily work for the agreed pay) which are then used to buy goods that become my property (again, justly acquired because the sales are voluntarily agreed to by buyer and seller).

3.4 Pareto Optimal Slavery Shows Need for Morality.

In the long history of the world, slavery has been an ugly presence. Ancient Israelites were slaves in Eygpt. African tribes enslaved other African tribes. American Indian tribes did the same. North African Muslims enslaved American seafarers in the age of Barbary Pirates. Slavery is still present in certain places in the world. Mexican gangs that traffic women and young girls illegally into the United States across its southern border engage in a modern form of slavery. We consider slavery for what we can learn about economics.

Ted Bergstrom has been one of the more original and creative of economic thinkers. He wondered about the economics of slavery practiced in the American South prior to the Civil War. Stealing another's labor is wicked. Could a person be treated as nothing more than a productive asset? Would the outcome remain Pareto Optimal? What would competitive markets look like?

On one hand, we know that cattle are the property and assets of their owners. Even though the utilities of members of a cattle herd are not of direct concern, good animal husbandry generally means the cattle get fed, they are housed and sheltered, they are given good health care and so on, all for the sake of the ranch or farm's overall production effectiveness.

Why couldn't slave masters or government treat humans like cattle? One can certainly imagine particularly cruel and uncaring people who would treat another human no better than they would an animal they owned or beast of burden they controlled.

But Pareto Optimality differs from what is just described because it must take into account the well being of *all* members of the society as they themselves evaluate it. This includes the slave's estimation of his own well being. What if some humans or government *owned* other humans—controlled their use in the productive process, assigned them their consumption, and were able to assign them their tasks? Various details would have to be decided such as, Is the slave "obliged to surrender to his master a vector of commodities with" the "maximum possible present value"? (Ans.: yes.) Can a slave buy back his own freedom? "All that is required is that if he is to gain his freedom, he must pay his owner a price equal to his present value as a slave." In point of fact, manumission was often outlawed in antebellum American slave states.

The bottom line from such analysis is that Pareto Optimality is consistent with the ownership arrangements of some descriptions that are a slave economy. Stated in the negative, Pareto Optimality in and of itself does not rule out slavery as described by Bergstrom. In the slave economy's equivalent to competitive equilibrium, there is no way to increase the utility of anyone, slave or free, without harming someone else. If one applies a different description of slavery than covered in Bergstrom's analysis (for example does anyone anytime including the slave himself or herself have the legal right to borrow and buy the freedom of any slave?) then the conclusion that Pareto Optimality is consistent with slavery, as differently described, requires new analysis. If one starts from the premise that every human at birth owns himself or herself, then slavery is inconsistent with Pareto Optimality.

Bergstrom's paper makes the point that depending on the definition of slavery there may be nothing intrinsic to the goal of Pareto Optimality that rules out even slavery. Indeed, the need for morality from somewhere outside the rules of the economics of human flourishing is a major theme of the present book.

> **The need for morality from somewhere outside the rules of the economics of human flourishing is a major theme of the present book.**

The most simple code of morality to work from is morality's necessary condition, the Golden Rule. See how easily it dispenses with slavery. The Republican party was founded in 1854 to be an explicitly anti-slavery party.[2] It placed its first president in office in 1860. Abraham Lincoln[3]

---

[2]The anti-slavery reasons for the party's founding are well known. "The party was born of hostility to slavery (Cavendish, 2004)."

[3]Lincoln's anti-slavery plank reads, "Resolved, that we ... unite in the following declarations: 8. That the normal condition of all the territory of the United States is that of freedom: That, as our Republican fathers, when they had abolished slavery in all our national territory, ordained that 'no persons should be

applied the Golden Rule as follows:

> "As I would not be a slave, so I would not be a master. This expresses my idea of democracy. Whatever differs from this, to the extent of the difference, is not democracy." (Abraham Lincoln, 1 August 1858)[4]

3.5 Right to Defend

We have focussed on the most influential statements about property, but have been led inevitably to deductions that apply to related topics such as slavery, right to the product of one's own giftedness, rights against another's stealing your property, the right of voluntary exchange and purchase in the just acquisition of property, and, by

---

deprived of life, liberty or property without due process of law,' it becomes our duty, by legislation, whenever such legislation is necessary, to maintain this provision of the Constitution against all attempts to violate it; and we deny the authority of Congress, of a territorial legislature, or of any individuals, to give legal existence to slavery in any territory of the United States (Republican Party Platform, 17 May 1860)."

[4]Slavery is the extreme case of stealing the fruits of another's labor. The one stolen from does not agree to the taking of his or her labor and is not compensated for the taking.

   i. Locke rules out slavery, since each person owns himself.

   ii. The Golden Rule rules out slavery.

  iii. Robert Nozick's rules of ownership rule out slavery since they involve voluntary exchange from a preceding position and slavery provides no valid "chain of possession."

  iv. Finally, under various assumptions Pareto Optimality rules out slavery. For example, assume that the slave in freedom can produce surplus greater than or equal to the surplus that he produces in slavery and, taking into account his desire for freedom, understandably places a value on himself in the free state that equals or exceeds the value that the slave-owner places on his surplus in slavery. Since Pareto optimality is equivalent to competitive markets, which imply the possibility of borrowing and self-purchased manumission (BSPM), we have $Pareto\ Optimality \Rightarrow BSPM$. With few exceptions, slavery as practiced in the US South prior to the Civil War did *not* allow borrowing and self-purchased manumission, $US\text{-}practiced\ Slavery \Rightarrow \sim BSPM$. Thus, applying the contrapositive, $Pareto\ Optimality \Rightarrow BSPM \Rightarrow \sim US\text{-}practiced\ Slavery$. ($\sim$ means *absence* of the object following).

extension, the right to what justly emerges from one's own good luck and circumstances. We end with a final implication by quoting from "A Seasonable Plea for the Liberty of Conscience, and the Right of Private Judgment in Matters of Religion without any Control from Human Authority," published in Boston in 1744. Signed "Philalethes," the author is generally understood to be Elisha Williams, who clearly restates Lockean and Nozickean reasoning before turning to the right of defense.

> As reason tells us, all are born thus naturally equal, i.e. with an equal right to their persons; so also with an equal right to their preservation; and therefore to such things as nature affords for their subsistence....Thus every man having a natural right to (or being proprietor of) his own person and his own actions and labor, which we call property; it certainly follows, that no man can have a right to the person or property of another: And if every man has a right to his person and property; **he has also a right to defend them, and a right to all the necessary means of defense, and so has a right of punishing all insults upon his person and property.** (Emphasis added)

It will be the purpose of later chapters to work out the relationship between morality, essential economics (competitive markets), voluntary private organizations, individuals, and government in achieving the desired state of justice with human flourishing.

3.6   Conclusion

Property is created by the labor of an individual that removes something from the state of nature. The fruit of one's own labor is owned by the one that labored. The individual has the right to trade and dispose of property that is rightfully his. This includes gifting and exchange. Property, therefore, can also be justly acquired by purchase or by gift from its rightful owner.

One's own labor is one's own, including what emits from one's special talents, giftings, circumstances, and luck. Life may not be fair, but justice in transfer can be enforced. Slavery, stealing, and involuntary taking are all invalid. One has the right to defend one's property. This especially includes the right to defend one's person and family. Fair minded people would agree with this, should agree with this, and do agree with this.

References

Bergstrom, T. "On the Existence and Optimality of Competitive Equilibrium for a Slave Economy," *The Review of Economic Studies,* 38, 1, 1971, 23-36.

Cavendish, Richard, "The Republican Party Founded," *History Today*, 54, 7, 7 July 2004 (available online at https://www.history today.com/archive/republican-party-founded).

Locke, John. *Two Treatises on Government*, London: Printed for R. Butler, etc., 1821 (originally published 1689).

Nozick, Robert. *Anarchy, State, Utopia*, New York: Basic Books, 1974.

Chapter 4

Behind the Magic Curtain

*The economic problem of society is...the utilization of
knowledge not given to anyone in its totality.*

Friedrich Hayek, Nobel Economist.

In 1959 the Union of Soviet Socialist Republics Premier Nikita Khrushchev famously visited the United States. He came to the cornfields
of Iowa, a state that produced more corn, hogs, and finished cattle than any other state, on September 23 to learn how American
farmers were able to produce so much food for everybody.[1] While
acknowledging that Russia lagged in agriculture, he added that "it is
possible to overcome this lag within a short time." His idea was to
incorporate what he would learn into the socialist central planning
system of Soviet Russia.

An interesting story during his visit occurred when some of those
traveling with him talked to American farmers to ask how they knew
what to plant. Who told them how much of each thing to plan for?
The Americans replied that no one told them, they did whatever they
wanted. The Soviets did not believe them. How could something so
important as the food supply be left to people doing whatever they
wanted? It seems lunacy, but it raises a real question, How *does*
the economy know how to organize itself into an optimum without
a controller, overseer, government planner, or even a civil engineer
to design it? In fact, the absence of a single planner can be a *better*
policy than trying to plan from a central authority.

---

[1] Jack V. Fox (1959).

The analogy runs something like this: Imagine a deflated balloon that has flexible stretchable sides. It is potentially enormous, the size of a giant hot air balloon. Inside are weightless balloons, inflatable thin elastic membranes the size of marbles, peas, and BBs. Some are as small as grains of sand. The large balloon is the economy and the balloons inside it are consumers, households, firms, and voluntary private organizations. To make the economy as large as possible the strategy is to inflate each interior balloon. As each tiny balloon is fully inflated, their sum, the entire economy, begins to grow. If each interior balloon is as large as possible, the economy becomes as large as possible. This notion, really, is what Adam Smith was talking about in *An Inquiry into the Nature and Causes of the Wealth of Nations*. Capital was his word for the "stuff" that could be used to inflate each component.

> But the annual revenue of every society is always precisely equal to the exchangeable value of the whole annual produce of its industry, or rather is precisely the same thing with that exchangeable value. As every individual, therefore, endeavors as much as he can, both to employ his capital in the support of domestic industry, and so to direct that industry that its produce may be of the greatest value; every individual necessarily labors to render the annual revenue of the society as great as he can. He generally, indeed, neither intends to promote the public interest, nor knows how much he is promoting it. By preferring the support of domestic to that of foreign industry, he intends only his own security; and by directing that industry in such a manner as its produce may be of the greatest value, he intends only his own gain; and he is in this, as in many other cases, **led by an invisible hand** to promote an end which was no part of his intention. [Book 1, chapter 2, emphasis added]

In other words, the economy should not be thought of as a monolithic entity, but as the aggregation of parts. An individual productive firm inflates the value of its output—its share of contribution to GDP—when it makes its individual company profits as large as possible. It does not need to know what other firms are doing to maximize their profits, it needs only to know what it is doing with the prices that it sees.

This discovery about prices is important because the balloon analogy suggests possible coordination issues between producers and producers, consumers and consumers, and between producers and consumers. For example, if expanding the balloon of one firm for some range of its size uses resources that could have been used in expanding the balloon of another agent, we would want to be sure to act so as to expand the total of the two. How do we know that *our* use of resources is the best compared to the other ways that the same resources could be used? Thankfully—and this is the magic of the First Fundamental Theorem—prices in competitive equilibrium give the information that is needed to get past these difficulties.

Prices provide information. The high price of an input tells firms that others find the input extremely valuable and to conserve, in effect "use this input only if it is sufficiently productive." What about consumers? Their well being is the standard of usefulness for everything that is done. What firms do is ultimately for consumers. A high price for a good or service says that consumers find the item very valuable to their production of utility; the firm should strive to provide as much as it can and profits allow.

The consumer inflates his contribution to the ultimate produc- tion of utility when he chooses from his budget the least-cost means to generate his utility.[2] Notice that this is selfish activity because it isn't being done in consultation with what other consumers are doing with their budgets. Just as firms do not need to be told to maximize their profits (it is in their interest to do so) so households do not need to be told to generate their utility at least cost, it is in their interest to do so.

In this chapter we summarize some of the things that prices and competitive markets do for people.

4.1 Consumers

In your walk through the woods presume that you find a tiny Pareto Optimal economy tucked away somewhere. (Maybe this is the honey

---

[2]Utility is the term we use to denote a consumer's well being, happiness level, or satisfaction.

bee colony you found in Chapter 1.) Assume that you take a freeze-action-snapshot of it. Because the economy was Pareto Optimal what do you know about its parts?

One thing you know is that any two consumers from it can be selected, along with their bundles, and no further mutually beneficial re-arrangement of bundle contents is possible between them. Re-arranging bundles is equivalent to trade. Were any mutually beneficial trade remaining from the totals you just selected for review, it would indicate that it was possible to change things to increase the utility of one or both without harming either. Since the rest of the economy was not involved, someone has been helped without harming anyone, hence the original economy would not be Pareto Optimal. This contradicts the assumption that the economy *is* Pareto Optimal, hence you can conclude that such mutually beneficial trade must be absent.

4.2   Producers

The same argument applies to production.   Select any two productive firms along with their inputs. If by re-arranging any of the fixed total of inputs between them one or more firms could produce more of one good without lowering the output of any other, then it would imply that the original economy was *not* Pareto Optimal. In other words, no mutually beneficial trade of inputs between firms is possible if optimality is present.

Economists get excited about what this means for a number of reasons, but the main idea is that human flourishing implies that inputs end up in the hands of the firm that can best use them.

A second thing we know is that there must be full employment of inputs. Were there an input that was available for work[3] that was not at work, such input could have been put to work, more output produced, and one or more consumers made better off by giving them greater consumption. Since markets clear in a competitive equilibrium (quantity demanded of any input equals the quantity supplied), we know such unemployed resources are absent.

---

[3]If the input is labor, "wanting to work" means capable of the level of skill needed in the job description and willing to accept the associated wage.

Pareto Optimality requires a third property, which is proper coordination of production across sectors. What is a "sector"? In typical usage a sector is a collection of firms that produce a range of similar products, use similar inputs, or even are similar in location. For example, the chemical sector or the banking services sector are collections of firms grouped by similar types of outputs. A sector could be defined by firms that make use of similar inputs, as in the wood products sector. Or a sector could be defined geographically.

The best way to explain what human flourishing says about sectors is by example. Idaho is known for its potatoes and Texas for its cattle, though each state is certainly capable of producing the other good. In our simple-minded example presume that Idaho can produce the listed quantities $(Potatoes, Cattle) = (10, 0)^4$ if it specializes in potatoes, or $(0, 5)$ if it specializes in cattle, or it could produce something in between given by $((1 - i)10, i5)$ where the number i is chosen between 0 and 1. For Texas the numbers are $(Potatoes, Cattle) = (0, 20)$, $(5, 0)$, and $((1 - t)5, t20)$ where the number t is chosen between 0 and 1.[5] Human flourishing (Pareto Optimality and prices) mean that each state (sector) will be assigned what it does best to maximize GDP as Adam Smith explained, but imagine not. If Idaho has been assigned to produce exclusively cattle, and Texas has been assigned to produce exclusively potatoes, the two sectors combined produce 5 units of Potatoes and 5 units of Cattle. We could get 10 and 20 if the assignments were reversed. Somehow the prices in competitive markets guarantee that the right assignments across sectors will be made.[6]

---

[4]Units do not matter for the example. These can be millions of tons of potatoes and millions of cattle, or some other choice.

[5]We choose numbers 5, 10, and 20 for simplicity. Other numbers would work as well.

[6]We note in passing that efficiency across sectors has lessons for international trade. Two regions engaged in free trade will emphasize those products for which the regions have relative advantages. If Idaho were isolated, in autarky ("Autarky" is the state of having no economic dealings with the outside. A nation in autarky, for example, engages in no international trade.) it would have to produce all its own cattle and potatoes. Likewise Texas. But if the two regions can trade with one another, Idaho can go more heavily into potatoes— at which it greatly excels—and use them to trade for cattle, which Texas can supply cheaper. A reverse statement applies to Texas with the result that free trade leads to the right sectoral assignments.

4.3　Meeting Consumers' Needs and Wants

Imagine an economy going full tilt at producing, doing so in such a way that no good can be increased without lowering the output of any other. Further imagine that given the quantities of goods, there is no way to re-distribute them among consumers to make anyone happier without harming someone. Yet, people in the economy are miserable.

How is this possible? While the economy could be very good at producing stuff, and very good at getting such stuff into the hands of consumers so that no further trade between them is beneficial, it might be focused on an atrociously bad collection of stuff. In the days of the Soviet Union, the Russian people who might have been interested mostly in blue-jeans and consumer goods found the state's resources going instead to so much military equipment that blue-jeans and consumer goods were in short supply. If people's preferences are the highest priority, it must be impossible to alter the mix of what is being produced and re-distribute it so as to make any consumer better off without harming another.[7] Prices and competitive markets somehow get the job done.

Consumer sovereignty[8] says the consumer is king in deciding what gets done. Economists get excited about it because it can be explained using mathematics, graphs, and diagrams as we do in the companion chapter to this one in Part 2. The basic idea, though, can be explained by example. Assume quantities are measured in tons. If consumers value Blueberries as worth 10 and Blackberries as worth 1 (i.e. they are willing to forego 10 tons of Blackberries in return for 1 ton of Blueberries), and it is found that giving up production of 9 tons of Blackberries allows the freed resources to produce 1 ton of Blueberries, it means that consumers could be made better off by adjusting out of Blackberries and into Blueberries.

Competitive equilibrium means that prices and markets guarantee no such further improvements exist.

---

[7]When we talk about public goods in Chapter 6 we will address the question of how much goods like national defense should be supplied if the people's wishes are sovereign.

[8]This is the term that economists use to indicate that the consumer is sovereign in what the economy does.

4.4 The Magic of Prices

What we are saying is this: What began as a quest for human flourishing has ended by concluding that prices in competitive markets act as ideal valuators to the goods and services that firms, households, voluntary private organizations (VPOs) and government move around between themselves—i.e. "buy" and "sell." These prices cause "the right things" to be done. Even though from a theoretical standpoint an omniscient, omnipotent central planner could replicate all the assignments in the economy, we know in fact that there are just too many people, too many productive activities taking place, too many things going on, and too many things to know concerning what each person likes and dislikes, to maintain a serious belief that a human agency could work it all out as needed. It is insupportable, illogical, and absurd for government to think it can run the economy.

> **There are just too many people, too many productive activities taking place, too many things going on, and too many things to know concerning what each person likes and dislikes, to maintain a serious belief that a human agency could work it all out as needed.**

It is at this point that the best writers and minds of the 19th and 20th centuries have tried to explain the "magical" way that the economy is nevertheless maximized. In this chapter we used the hot air balloon analogy. Each internal balloon does not need to know what the others are doing, only what the cost is of the resources *it* is using and to make its balloon as large as possible. Vegetarians don't need to know what meat products cost or what others think of meat. Car drivers do not need to know what motorcycles cost or whether others like them.

Philosophers have also weighed in about economics and human flourishing in connection with the separate role of freedom. People like to be left alone to do what they want, to make their own choices and to learn from them, to be as much a person of goodwill as they can. People like liberty. People like freedom. This is what free markets deliver.

Economy planning inevitably means coercion, often a lot of it, and contradicts this kind of liberty and freedom. What we are beginning to see is that the economics of human flourishing and morality as they relate to personal liberty and freedom are moving in the same direction.

Those who want to see more about how prices work to *cause* the conditions to hold for Pareto Optimality that were sketched out in this chapter can read Chapter 4 in Part 2. Here we close with a verbal recapitulation.

Interest in human flourishing means interest in Pareto Optimality. Interest in Pareto Optimality means interest in competitive equilibrium. Interest in competitive equilibrium, means interest in firms choosing that activity that maximizes their profit at the prices they see as given to them. That, in turn, means that firms want to cost-minimize (produce whatever quantity of output they produce at least cost) and to prefer more efficient (think "newer," "better," "more technologically advanced") recipes for what they do over older, outdated, less efficient methods. No one has to tell the firm to do this, they *want* to do this on their own. Firms that don't will lose out and be replaced by those that do.[9]

There are at least four distinct ways that prices function to provide the means for firms and households to do what they want in their own interest, yet be coordinated with each other in the economy so that no one can be made better off without harming someone else in the process. Prices:

- **provide information**, making it possible for one part of the economy to know the value (to consumers) and cost (to producers) of what it is doing,
- **create incentives**, making each agent want to do what is right and in its own interest, but
- **coordinate between markets** so that one market's output can be the input into another as needed, and

---

[9]Examples abound. Readers may be surprised to learn that Eastman Kodak developed the first digital camera technology, but did not think it as promising as film, of which they were masters. Failing to move as they should have into digital technology, the giant firm eventually lost out and filed for bankruptcy in 2012.

- **equilibrate markets** so that everything is matched up and balanced in the end.

4.5 Conclusion

We have been following the implications of human flourishing that emerge from regarding each human being as the decider for himself or herself of what he or she likes. Do you want a ride-on mower or a push mower or a lawn service, grass-fed beef or vegetables only, organic food or cheaper non-organic?

What we found seems too good: People and firms working in voluntary competitive markets for their own good are coordinated in a way that leads to the best possible social good for all. Coordinated collective action is the "magic" work of prices and markets that we brought up in Section 4.4.

At the same time, discovering Pareto Optimality and the prices, markets, and competitive equilibria that emerge from it introduced certain features that needed to be thought through. Markets involve trade, buying and selling. You must own something to be able to trade it. We have already discussed in Chapter 3 what is ownership and what does a person rightfully "own."

Another issue that naturally arises is this: Who takes care of the needy? More broadly, how should society (a group of individuals living together as members of a community) and their economy (individuals, endowments, and their production technology) get done each of the things that need to get done? There is one means of individual action (the individual), but *three* means of collective action:[10] markets, voluntary private organizations, and government. Our method is to ask Pareto Optimality and the Golden Rule what means are ruled in and what means are ruled out.

Clearly all of this cannot be treated at once. Figure 4.1 explains the sequence that we follow in the next set of chapters. We start at the top and move down. Chapter 3, already covered, began with the question of where property and ownership come from. Chapter 4 (this chapter, not in diagram) dealt with prices. The next two chapters discuss the first of the means of collective action (markets

---

[10]By collective action we mean coordinated activity of individuals.

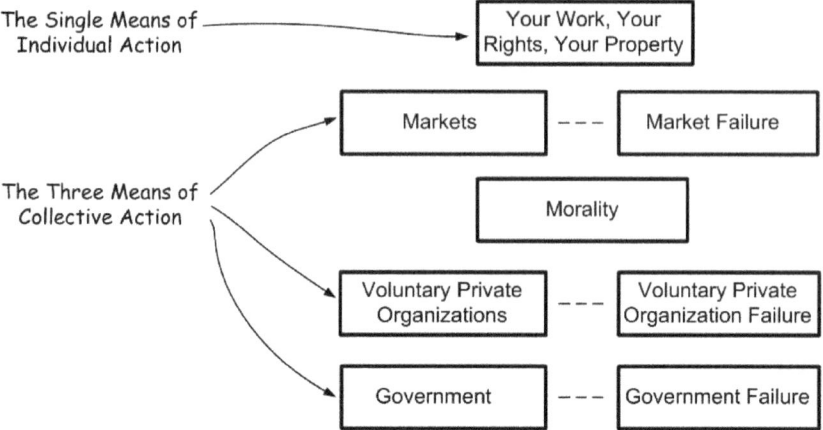

Figure 4.1: **Arrangement of Topics for the Economy: Deductive Flow**

and market failure). Market failure suggests the need for collective action from the other two means, one of which is government. In anticipation of the need for taxes Chapter 7 introduces morality and certain issues that have to do with who should pay. Chapters 8 and 9 on the other two means of collective action (voluntary private organizations and government) and their failure follow. By the time we reach the chapter on government, we will have done enough to consider the tasks that an economy must perform and the means by which they should be performed. Having finished with "the machinery" of the economy—the three means of collective action—charity figures prominently in Chapters 12 and 13 that come after those shown in Figure 4.1.

But those issues are reserved for later. At present, we need to look at the first means of collective action which is markets, how they work and when they don't.

References

Fox, Jack V. (1959). "Khrushchev Visits Iowa Cornfields," UPI, September 23, 1959. Online at https://www.upi.com/Archives/1959/09/23/Khrushchev-visits-Iowa-cornfields/1112442791026/

Chapter 5

Markets

In a true free market economy, you can't make yourself rich without enriching your community.

Robert F. Kennedy, Jr.

In this chapter we return to markets, which serve a coordinating function and are one of three means of collective action (the other two are voluntary private organizations and government). Prices and markets are mutually inclusive. Prices are the continuing wellspring for social harm or social good, and markets are the wellspring for prices. Prices need to be known and be the same across agents, and markets need to be consistent with competition for prices to be effective in promoting human flourishing. This chapter attempts to explain what equality and competition mean. Why do they personally matter? We begin with a story.

Fortune magazine reported that Jeffrey Bezos, the founder, chief executive officer, and president of the company Amazon had net worth of $138.5 billion.[1] Before his death, he will probably be richer still. Assuming his money earned the long-run average real return of 8 percent that one can get from investing in the U.S. stock market, and death at age 100, at the time of the article Mr. Bezos would have had to spend just under $11.5 billion annually to exhaust his fortune over 44 years. Presuming an average of 365.25 days per year, and an 8 hour day devoted to spending, this works out to $235.5

---

[1]Alexander, *et al.* (2020).

million spending per minute ($3.925 million per second). More likely, Mr. Bezos will die leaving a substantial fortune unspent.

Amazon began as a book retailer and expanded into other retail. Its activity, therefore, was not primarily inventing or manufacturing, but buying something at a price and re-selling it at a higher price. Jeff Bezos became wealthy, not by stealing from others, but by using prices to provide others what they wanted at a cost they were willing to pay. Mr. Bezos enriched himself, at the same time as he made others better off because of his ideas and activity. A true free market enriches the community.

While many fortunes have been made by producing a product, often one that is new or invented by the producer, and selling it— the Rockefeller oil fortune and the Carnegie steel fortune of the late 1800s and early 1900s or the Ford Motor Company fortune of the early 1900s are examples—it is surprising how much can be made merely by "buying low and selling high." Walmart, the source of another enormous fortune for its founder Sam Walton and family, was also engaged in retail.   Never underestimate the power of prices when they are working the way they should as signals and the value of joining a buyer to a seller. No wonder so much of world history revolves around trade. Christopher Columbus had personal, business, and religious reasons for believing he should "sail west to go east." Among them was to find a better trade route to join markets, buying low in one region and selling high in the other. "Arbitrage" is defined as making certain profit by purchasing an item (frequently a security or currency that can be quickly resold) at a low price and nearly immediately reselling it at a higher price. Price signals, and the differences in them, are a big deal.

5.1   Markets and Prices

No one who has never experienced enormous, constant, personal pain can fully understand its effect. I had a hip replacement in my 60s, ten years after an injury. My situation was mild compared to others, but I sought the surgery to relieve constant annoying pain. If your every move, or even your every absence of movement, causes you pain, how much would you be willing to pay to end the misery and restore your health? What good is money if you have no active life?

So, what keeps the hospital from charging whatever it pleases for a hip replacement?

The following is a real story from a book titled *The Price We Pay*.[2] Adam started feeling chest pains and went in to be checked. The hospital told him he had blockages that were life threatening. He did not require instant attention, but sometime in the coming year should arrange to have corrective surgery. He asked if they did that kind of surgery and what it would cost. They did. It would cost $250,000. Shocked and surprised, Adam said he would get back to them. Adam was from France originally. He did research, found that the identical surgery could be had in France, was just as safe and just as good. There it would cost him $15,000. Since he had not scheduled the surgery, at his next hospital visit the administrator asked if he wanted to schedule it. Adam said no, he could get it done for $15,000. Without a moment's hesitation the administrator revised his offer. Now the hospital would be willing to do the surgery for $50,000. Adam said no, rose to leave and just moments later was in the hallway nearing the hospital exit when the administrator hurried to him and reduced the price to $25,000. By this time, Adam was insulted and angered. He never went back to the hospital for surgery, which he eventually had done elsewhere for less.

From $25,000 to $250,000 is a factor of 10. Americans are used to prices that work and used to the good that competition causes. We do not want to pay 10% more than we need to and certainly feel cheated if we pay 90% more. The hospital wanted *900%* more than its final price and 1567% more than it could be done elsewhere!

Sadly, examples like Adam's are easy to find. You may even know more egregious ones. The point is this. It is fruitless to wish that all hospitals would be more honest and humane. It is fruitless to hope that all health providers would be more compassionate. Some might be, some not. But there will always be those who are not. A rule of thumb in life is you don't get what you expect, you get what you *inspect*. And competition is the inspector of the market place. Competition is what keeps market prices in line with the true cost of providing the good or service. The hospital did not lower its price to Adam because it had a sudden wave of honesty or compassion.

---

[2]Makary, 2019, pp. 15-17.

> **Competition is the only reliable way to keep prices as low as possible.**

The better world that we all long for comes from everyone paying the right price, meaning a price that everyone else is paying that reflects the true cost incurred by the provider in providing the additional unit of the good or service to us. Through other means we also know that this will leave them a reasonable profit. (If not, all would be out of business).

There is no other satisfactory mechanism yet found: Competition is the only reliable way to keep prices as low as possible.

5.2   Prices and Necessary Conditions for Optimality

In addition to being as low as possible to the buyer, prices must be equal to all buyers in at least six ways. These are *necessary* conditions, meaning each must be present if Pareto Optimality is present. By definition, any violation of efficiency is traceable to violation of one or more necessary conditions.

Because Chapter 4 in Part 2 covers these necessary conditions in more depth with relevant mathematics and diagrams, we add to what we have already said only by giving each condition a name and restating what it means in straight English.

Recall our methodology. Economies can function in miserable ways for decades and even lifetimes without collapsing but never reaching full capacity or human flourishing either. Here we are trying to learn what human flourishing looks like by learning what Pareto Optimality looks like. In other words, if we assume Pareto Optimality is present, then what?

Distributive Efficiency. If Pareto Optimality is present there is no mutually beneficial trade remaining, and competitive prices exist that allow us to talk value in terms of money. I know what being worth $12 means because I know how much spending $12 can do for me. Back to Distributive Efficiency: Everyone's money-value for a given good must be the same. Why? If the good is worth $12 to you and only $7 to me, there is a trade we can make at a price in between and both be better off.

Input Efficiency. If Pareto Optimality is present there is no mutually beneficial trade remaining between users of inputs, and competitive prices exist that allow firms to talk about value of inputs in terms of money. A firm knows what being worth $12 means because its knows how much spending $12 can do for it in terms of other inputs. Every firm's money-value for a given input must be the same. Why? If the input is worth $12 to your firm and only $7 to mine, there is a trade we can make at a price in between and both be better off. (Yes, Input Efficiency is a parallel concept and logically identical to Distributive Efficiency.)

Sector Allocation Efficiency. We have talked about sectors before. A "sector" is any grouping of producers, along with their inputs. We might talk of the oil sector, the agricultural sector, or even an entire economy as a "sector." If one sector reduces production of a good how much do the freed resources allow it to increase another good? The trade-off must match across sectors. Why? You can guess: If not, you could take the sector giving up little to get much, have it make such an adjustment, and instruct the other sector to do the reverse. More of one or both goods with less of any would result, violating the assumption that the original allocation was Pareto Optimal.

Full Employment. If Pareto Optimality is present, there can be no factors of production that would like to be employed, and could be employed, but are unemployed. Labor, of course, is the most important factor of production, but an input like energy should also be fully employed. If a hydroelectric plant is capable of producing more electricity with the water flow it has, but instead lets the water flow past its turbines unproductively, there is unemployed hydroelectricity. When all is said and done, an input that could have been available and used, but was not, represents wanton waste. More electricity could have been available to produce greater output, from which everyone could have been better supplied.

Full employment seems unrelated to prices and competitive markets, but is not. Its absence is a price inequality and competition issue. Let's focus on hydroelectricity for our example. Hydroplant BigGears has the capacity to produce more electricity at nearly zero cost (just let more water run through its turbines), but is not. Firms out there in the economy are paying a price for kilowatts of electricity higher than nearly zero. Have BigGears produce more electricity, sell it to firms above cost of production but below their current price. Everyone is happy, more electricity is used and no less of anything else, output is higher, meaning higher happiness is possible for some or all with no lower happiness for anyone. This sequence explains why unemployment is implicitly a price and competition issue. With competition, suppliers of electricity will cause any lower-cost supply to be put to use. No user willingly will pay a higher price for electricity when it can be had from BigGears for less. Purchases from BigGears in the end lead to full use of the water at BigGears, and equalized prices for electricity input.

Consumer Sovereignty. If Pareto Optimality is present, the prices this entails means consumers can value goods, producers can value goods and the inputs that it takes to make them, and sectors can value goods (or even baskets of goods) in terms of the value of the other good or goods that have to be given up to free the needed inputs for expanded production in a given direction. It should not be a surprise that the value a consumer places on a good or basket of goods needs to match the value placed on the same thing by producers or a sector. What this *means* is that the consumer is "king" (sovereign) over what selection of goods is produced. If you value a particular eye-shadow cosmetic at $12 and firms value it at $7, you and the firm can be made better off by having the firm increase its production of the eye-shadow at some price in between.

Consumer Sovereignty for Public Goods. Public goods have not yet been introduced (they appear in Chapter 6). We mention them here only for completeness as it relates to Consumer Sovereignty. If a good like a radio broadcast can be simultaneously consumed by multiple people without diminishing its ability to be consumed by others, Pareto Optimality requires that the value placed on the good, *summed over **all** the consumers of it* equal the value place on the same thing by producers or a sector. Consumer sovereignty relates to the single consumer's value relative to production, consumer sovereignty for a public good relates to all of its consumers' values.

Given the thousands of prices in a typical economy, equality for them as just described is massive, and massively important. Pareto Optimality means hospitals are not permitted to charge $250,000 to one buyer of surgery and decide $25,000 to charge another as we saw being done on page 59. Everyone having access to the same price is what equality means. Competitive markets provide this. Prices must be public, equally publicly known by all, and provide true information. Competition causes these equal, and equally publicly known, prices to reflect the true cost of provision so they are best for the buyer.

5.3 Capitalism and Personal Freedom, Socialism and Statism

Would you like to be rich? Here is how millions through history have done it: Buy low, sell high. Whenever prices that should be equal are unequal, there is a social improvement possible, and more importantly *personal* gain to you if you figure a way to serve others by getting to them what they want. Buy low, sell high, repeat. We are talking about honest commerce. It is said that God loves everyone, an honest rich person just as much as he loves an honest poor person. The choice of which you want to pursue is up to you.

> "Capitalism" is a generic term for the various buying, selling, producing, and trading activities involved in free markets, where there is personal freedom to enter, to leave, to buy, and to sell.

In a free market no one is forced to buy or to sell, to produce or not produce. Thus, no one "makes" such a market. That would involve telling others what to do. The market makes itself. "Capitalism" is a generic term for the various buying, selling, producing, and trading activities involved in free markets, where there is personal freedom to enter, to leave, to buy, and to sell. Sometimes government is needed to keep markets free (as when firms try to improperly abuse or eliminate their competitors, a topic we take up in Chapter 6), but freedom and capitalism are naturally linked. It was not for nothing that Economics Nobel Prizewinner Milton Friedman named his book *Capitalism and Freedom.*

Since capitalism involves complete personal freedom, subject to the limitations of honesty and competition as we have tried to make clear, it also follows that any system that deviates from this total freedom is *not* capitalism and must introduce coercion from some source. Nearly always the state is the source of coercion.

Socialism is not capitalism. Socialism is associated with Statism, the use of the state to control, limit, or in some way coerce the choices of citizens beyond what would be their freedom in a capitalist system. It is important to recall when the state offers to support its citizens or give something that it has nothing of its own to give. Newt Gingrich, Speaker of the House of Representatives during the presidency of Bill Clinton observes, "At the heart of all socialism is theft."[3] Because we adhere to the requirements of human flourishing in the economic realm and the implications of this for what we have called *essential economics*, we reject Statism. As previously promised, how a government might engage in theft will be taken up subsequent to introducing morality and the Golden Rule into the discussion in Chapter 7. We will discuss competition, keeping markets free, and other appropriate necessary functions of government in Chapter 10.

> **"At the heart of all socialism is theft."**

Business Honesty versus Dishonesty

Many criticisms of capitalism or socialism are really criticisms of personal dishonesty that could be practiced in either setting and are not failures of institutions so much as flaws of specific individuals. Dishonest practices often involve using time as a weapon to strip the other party of options. Once the other party has no alternatives, it is then cheated. Here are two examples.

Sam's Club has been accused of relying on the following practice. A vendor is tasked by purchase order with providing a batch of product to Sam's. The product may be perishable or an item tied to a specific sporting event after which demand will fall to zero. The manufacturing is undertaken, after which Sam's announces a pretext on which it must cancel the order. A short time passes. Sam's returns to the vendor and offers to "help them out" by taking

---

[3]Bartiromo, 2021.

the product off their hands at discount, sometimes for as little as 10 cents on the dollar relative to the originally agreed price.

Versions of the same form of dishonesty abound. Costco is a discount seller that regularly purchased Mango-Lime Salsa from its vendor.[4] "We would get purchase orders weekly and would ship weekly. It amounted to truckloads of product." In-store marketing involved providing free samples to the public, who would buy more if they liked what they sampled. A Costco in-house company would offer the samples. Naturally, the vendor received no payment for providing the "free" samples and had to pay Costco for services of the in-house company. "Sometimes Costco would want us to partner with a chip company (we would pay for our samples/sampling; they would pay for their samples/sampling)." This was the understood, accepted, and usual practice.

"During the course of several months, they chose for us to partner with a salmon vendor (we were to pay for our samples/sampling and the salmon vendor was to pay for its samples/sampling). The Salmon vendor backed out of the sampling early on..." At this point, Costco knew the original arrangements were at an end. Honest business therefore would have consulted with the salsa vendor and jointly chosen other arrangements. The salsa vendor would have been responsible for no more than it agreed to since the decisions that altered the original arrangements were made by the salmon vendor and Costco. Instead "Costco kept sampling Salmon with our salsa. At the end of that particular campaign, we got a bill for $25,000 for the salmon *they* used to sample/serve with our salsa."

By acting unilaterally as it did Costco seems to have followed the pattern described above. Its vendor's options were limited by lack of consultation, following which they presented the vendor with a surprise bill of $25,000.

"It's just how they worked....We finally walked away from that business."

---

[4] This account was provided to the author by the vendor involved.

References

Alexander, Sophie, Tom Maloney, Tom Metcalf, and Bloomberg. "The Global Economy is crumbling—and Jeff Bezos is $24 billion richer." *Fortune* , 14 April 2020. https://fortune.com/2020/04/14/jeff-bezos-net-worth-2020-billionaires-amzn-amazon-stock/

Bartiromo, Maria. "Interview of Speaker Newt Gingrich," Mornings with Maria Bartiromo, Fox News, 6 May 2021.

Kupfer, David. "Robert F. Kennedy Jr. interviewed by David Kupfer". *The Progressive Magazine*, November 2006.

Makary, Marty, MD. *The Price We Pay: What Broke American Health Care—And How to Fix It*. New York: Bloomsbury Publishing, 2019.

Chapter 6

Market Failure

We do not need to understand economics in order to experience the benefits of freedom of exchange and production. But we very well need to understand economics in order to sustain and maintain the institutional framework that enables us to realize the benefits that flow from freedom of exchange and production.

Peter Boettke

To fully understand markets, we must consider market failure as we do in this chapter. We will eventually apply the same logic to the two other primary means of collective action: Governments and Government Failure, Voluntary Private Organizations and Voluntary Private Organization Failure. In the case of markets, however, discussing their failure is a way to expand the range of discourse. We have said little about what economists call *public goods*. We have said nothing yet about pollution and externalities. This is our chance. By definition, markets have failed to deal with externalities if externalities are present. Markets are not expected to deal with public goods so it is not really a "failure" when they do not. We find a common connection among externalities, public goods, and goods intermediate to public goods and private goods called "club goods." In this chapter we consider what efficiency and morality mean when all are part of the discussion.

6.1   Externalities

Some things tend to be free. What we breathe, for example, tends to come to us without having to pay. In some places and from time to time (downtown Tokyo has oxygen bars, for example) even what we breathe can be for sale. Water is another essential. Sometimes it is taken from the ground by a homeowner's or farmer's well for "free," but when it needs to be purified before use, it can be bought from a municipal water supply or in grocery stores.

Consider then the following clipping from a news story. It seems almost certain that a less noxious way to do things exists. So why is the better way not being done?

> "The air is so bad in one Russian city, skies often turn black and people are regularly warned to stay inside. Some are even warned to get out of town if they have the chance. Krasnoyarsk is located 2,000 miles from Moscow in the Siberian forest. Toxic smog from coal-fired plants fills the sky in winter. And smoke from wildfires fills the sky in summer."

Later in the article we learn that although Krasnoyarsk suffers smoke from wildfires in summer, much of its year round air pollution is self-made.

Figure 6.1: **A Day in Krasnoyarsk**

> "Krasnoyarsk gets half its power from coal even though
> Russia has the largest gas reserves on earth. Some are
> calling for it to be connected to the national pipeline for
> the cleaner-burning fuel."[1]

It took a great deal of thinking by environmentalists, economists, and those simply worried about pollution to fully figure out what goes wrong in places like Krasnoyarsk and others. In the United States, the Cuyahoga River which runs through Cleveland is famous for having once been so polluted in 1969 that it caught fire.[2] Technically it was not the river, of course, that burned but enough flammable pollution in the river that flames burned on its surface. Even worse, while it was not a regular occurrence the river had caught fire on several earlier occasions!

What are the basics of pollution? In the case of river pollution, no one owns the river; those who dump their waste into the river personally benefit from the dumping or they would not do it; and dumping in the river harms the river and other users of it, otherwise there would be no problem. Economists call this an externality because the action of one decision maker, the dumper, has a direct effect on another economy participant—in this case a negative effect—that does not operate through markets or market prices. We will return to this distinction later, because it is important. If the direct effect is positive, we call it a positive externality. How have eminent economists dealth with these issues in the past?

A. C. Pigou. Let us continue with our river example. A.C. Pigou was a prominent economist working in the late 1800s and early 1900s. He noted that when a polluter decided to dump in the river, the cost imposed on everyone else was not included in the cost that the polluter personally experienced. Unlike a market situation where the cost imposed on society when a buyer takes a good or service out of the economy equals what the buyer experiences in having to pay the market price, the cost of disposing waste into the river to the one doing the disposing is below the total social cost. Pigou suggested that a solution might be to impose the extra cost onto the polluter with a tax, so the polluter would see an effective

---

[1]The Weather Channel, (2020).
[2]Rotman, (2020).

price (tax plus the polluter's original cost) that matched what taking the good or service from the system cost society. Facing a higher price generally means that less is chosen, just what you want if the externality is negative. If the tax is picked right, the stopping point balances the benefit and cost of doing the activity, just as the price does in a market.

Ronald Coase. Figuring out how to set the right tax if less of the activity is wanted (or the right subsidy if more is wanted), how the proceeds should be used, how money for the subsidy should be raised, plus similar issues attracted the bulk of attention through the 1950s. Then Ronald Coase, later to receive the Nobel Prize in economics, reminded everyone that the overarching goal was to adopt overall societal arrangements so that the best action was reached.[3] Sometime this involved applying a tax to the polluter/perpetrator, but sometimes not.

If the goal is that the overall right thing be done, then the party with the best ability to respond to the situation should have an incentive to take the right action. Sometimes this is not the perpetrator. Let's say that you have your two-year-old in the shopping cart and he knocks a glass jar of pickles off the shelf. The threat is that the broken jar will cause other shoppers to slip and hurt themselves. The socially best outcome is that the mess be cleaned immediately. You have no mop or bucket on site, but the store does. Wisely, our tort law places responsibility on the store to correct the hazard even though you (or your child) were the perpetrator. Placing some kind of tax or penalty on you if you break a jar in the aisle might move things in the direction of your being more careful, but the social arrangements can do better on an overall or holistic basis.

Coase adjusted a good bit of our thinking about externalities, social cost, and with them market failure. The following now seem almost obvious:

1. The presence of an externality indicates the absence of a market in the externality. Nobody was buying or selling the right to dump into the river.
2. The absence of a market indicates the absence of property rights. If someone owned the river, the polluter would not be allowed to pollute in it at all, or would have to pay for the

---

[3]Ronald Coase, (1960).

right.

3. The social arrangements should be set so the party with the best ability to deal with a situation has the incentives to take the correct action. Sometimes this involves imposing a tax or subsidy when the best solution is changing the quantity of a given activity, but sometimes not when another approach is better.

4. Property rights are government's domain to define and enforce.

Presence of an Externality ⇒ Absence of a Market ⇒ Absence of Needed Property Rights

⇒

Assign Property Rights So the Needed Market Can Exist and/or the Party with Best Ability to Take the Right Action Does So.

We said that externalities are direct effects, not operating through prices, of one economic decision maker on another. Externalities can be helpful or harmful, though negative externalities are generally the focus of attention. We end our discussion with another story and two lessons from it.

Green Grass Country Club (GGCC) has extensive golf course lawns for its golfers. These magnificent grounds are kept in perfect condition year round, which means extensively watering them, which means the club buys large amounts of water, which drives up the market price of water from the city water department. Higher priced water has a negative impact on everyone else in town who has to buy higher-priced water. Because the impact on others is not a direct effect, but operates *through market prices*, there is no negative externality present in this story. *Green Grass Country Country Club* is not a villain and is *not* obligated to pay anything beyond the same market price for its water that everyone else pays. Because there is a market in city water, the price properly reflects the cost to the system of a user using more of it. No externality, no side payment.

Now adjust the story a little. This time *Green Grass Country Club* has extensive lawns as before, keeps them in perfect condition as before, but because the natural rains are more than adequate GGCC does not need to buy water. However, it applies immense quantities of herbicides and fertilizer that run off in rains and pollute the local water table. It costs more for everyone else to clean their water before they can use it. This *is* a true negative externality. The Country Club does not experience the full social cost of the damage its fertilizers and herbicides cause. Externality is present. Pigou or Coase intervention is called for.

If the only way to mitigate water pollution is reduce the quantity of the damaging chemicals, then the Country Club "owes" the system a side payment to cause the club to experience the full true cost of the fertilizer and herbicides it uses. This is the Pigou-type tax we talked about earlier to induce the Country Club to choose the right amount to use. If other holistic solutions are present (maybe switching to natural chemicals that do not run off and harm water is possible), then arrangements that induce the Country Club to use them are called for. This is in line with Coase as well.

The first important conclusion is that effects on others have to be accurately understood. Direct effects on other economy participants that operate outside of market prices are externalities; effects operating through prices are not.

Without intending, we have also discovered a second important conclusion that needs to be framed in a different context to be understood: *If no externality is present, then you owe no additional side payments to society. You owe society only to pay the market price for what you take from the economy and to be paid the market price for what you provide to the economy.* This is the same conclusion, arrived at from a different starting point, that we reached in Chapter 2.[4] Those who say you "owe" something extra to society because you did not make the markets or the circumstances that allow you to thrive in the economy because of your own efforts, misunderstand when side payments are called for and when they are not. Voluntarily choosing to "give back" is a different matter. Understanding what you "owe" to society and what you do not owe to society is an important topic.

---

[4]See page 31.

6.2 Public Goods

An externality has to do with one firm or household's activity directly affecting another decision making participant in the economy. It was noticed for some types of goods, however, that just consuming them spontaneously implied externalities. Will we have the right amount of them?

Let's say you and I are traveling separately but settle near each other on the beach and happen to like the same kind of music. If you listen to your radio, I am automatically benefited by being able to listen to your music. Further, my listening in no way diminishes your ability to listen. In contrast, if we like the same kind of sandwich, your eating a sandwich on the beach does nothing for me. What is the difference between the two types of goods?

The sandwich is a *private* good. It is rival in consumption, meaning one person's consuming it prevents another from consuming the same good. Rivals are two individuals who want the same thing, which only one of them can have. A good is rival if only one person can consume it. In the beach example music was a *public* good. Its consumption was not rival.

You provided me music on the beach, a form of externality, because your personal benefits were high enough that you paid all the expense to bring your radio with you to the beach. But what about a public good like national defense? When the U.S. military makes your house safe from foreign aggression, my house next door is automatically safe, too. But there is no way you (or I) can fund the entire U.S. military.

Returning to the issue of provision, let us call a good *non-excludable* if there is no way to exclude individuals from consuming the good, whether or not they pay for it. Excludability speaks to provision and rivalness speaks to who benefits. *Private goods* are defined to be goods that are rival and excludable. *Public goods* are defined to be goods that are non-rival and non-excludable. Other types of goods can be imagined, but these are the main ones.[5] A fast-food-restaurant sandwich is a private good (only one person

---

[5]Logically there are four possible types of goods depending on rivalness and excludability. One could argue that rival + nonexludable goods do not exist unless they are self provided or received as charity, because it involves making a good at cost that another exclusively consumes for free.

can eat it and you can be prevented from eating it if you do not pay for it); national defense is a public good (if the country is defended, everyone is made safe at the same time and you are made safe whether you have paid for national defense or not). Goods which are less than perfectly non-rival, such as goods for which congestion effects matter, are added in the section on *club goods*.

Private Goods	ARE NOT	Public Goods
(Rival, Excludable)		**(Non-rival,**
		Non-excludable)

From the discussion so far and our expanded terminology the issues are now clearer. There is no problem about the provision of a private good if externalities are absent because the sole individual who benefits from it is the one who pays for it. By definition a pure public good involves externalities in consumption. (Recall music on the beach; there is a direct effect on you of a nearby beach-goer's music playing. This is a consumption to consumption externality.) If a public good is produced, every individual is benefited and no one can be excluded from consuming it even if he or she does not pay.

It is not rational to pay for something you can get for free. Thus the existence of public goods requires some form of payment different from the voluntary market.

6.3   Public Goods and Taxes

In the 1910s Swedish economist Erik Lindahl took up the question of how a public good could be financed so it could be produced and the taxes that support it be just.[6] What he discovered seems common sensical today, but represented a major step forward over one hundred years ago.

To explain what he found, remember first how a private good is "financed." The single individual who benefits from consuming the

---

[6]Erik Lindahl, "Die Gerechtigkeit der Besteurung" 1919 (translated from the German in 1958). Erik Lindahl, "Just Taxation—A Positive Solution," in: Musgrave, R.A. and Peacock, A.T. (eds.) *Classics in the Theory of Public Finance*. London: International Economic Association Series. Palgrave Macmillan, 1958.

good knows the price for the good and uses its price to decide the best amount to buy. Let's say this is 27 units at price p $/unit$. Were 26 units bought, we know by the assumption that 27 was chosen that adding one unit beyond 26 increases satisfaction to the buyer by an amount that matches p dollars. (More precisely, it matches the benefits that p dollars would produce if they were spent on other things.) After all, if adding the 27th unit generated *more* benefit than p, it would not be the last unit bought.

Now consider letting each consumer in like fashion independently decide how much of the public good they want to buy given the price per unit that is set for it. Presume Yellowstone National Park is a public good that everyone likes knowing is available and unspoiledly wild. What would it mean to "buy" a larger quantity of Yellowstone Parks? For our example purposes let's assume that we do this in acres. Doubling the acres of Yellowstone Park is "buying" two parks, tripling its acres is buying three parks and so on.[7] If I have to pay $50/year for one Yellowstone Park, I might decide to "buy" 10 of them. Lindahl reasoned that consumers would have to agree on the quantity of the public good, since by definition it is a public good and everyone consumes the same quantity. Jeff Bezos, worth $138 billion according to the last chapter, might decide to buy 20. Therefore we need to raise the price of national parks to Jeff relative to what I pay. The price I pay needs to be raised, too, because I want to buy too many. Calibrate the price for everyone so they voluntarily chose to buy one Yellowstone Park. (Maybe my example of Yellowstone is a bit fanciful since Yellowstone Park's features are unique, but stay with me.) Next, add the different payments made by everyone for one Yellowstone Park, and use that total to pay for Yellowstone Park. The amounts paid by each consumer, willingly given, are in fact taxes, and the prices are tax rates. Total taxes pay for the park, and government is the "producer" or contractor for the pure public good. Lindahl's pathbreaking achievement is named in his honor.

Lindahl Equilibrium has a number of nice properties, not least

---

[7]If you prefer, you can even imagine that the two Yellowstone National Parks occupy separate locations. If there is just one park, it is in Montana-Wyoming-Idaho, but if there are two, the second one is in, say, Alaska. The same idea applies for three and more parks.

of which is that it is Pareto Optimal, everyone agrees about the size of the activity, and just as in the case of a private good, everyone pays at a rate determined by the benefits they receive. A Lindahl Equilibrium is the counterpart to a Pareto Optimum, hence it is the counterpart to a competitive equilibrium for an economy with public goods present. Lindahl's discoveries explain how government should execute its assignment, since markets cannot be the source of a non-excludable public good. The following summary provides additional comments, which are explained in more detail in Chapter 6 of Part 2.[8]

Willing Participation. In a Lindahl equilibrium there is no disagreement about what government should be doing. This is because those who would want less done have had their tax rate adjusted down, just as those who would want more have had their tax rate adjusted up until they want the same. All of this is fair because the result is willingness to purchase the provided amount by everyone.

Unanimity. Objection to government often arises when it operates a program or policy to benefit one group at the expense of another. Lindahl equilibria show that it is possible in theory for government to operate in a way that benefits everyone. For discussion, let government activity consist of providing public goods. Then, in a Lindahl equilibrium it is not possible to find two identifiable-in-advance groups (young or old, urban or rural, coastal or interior, north or south, male or female, rich or poor, right or left, etc.) who would differ in their group's answer to the following question, "If government were to reduce all of its activity by 10%, at the same time reducing your taxes by 10%, would you favor such a change?" Failure of two groups to answer the same way implies failure to achieve Lindahl Equilibrium, hence failure of the economy to be Pareto Optimal. Any time two groups can be found that answer differently, it is possible to improve the wellbeing of one or more individuals in the economy without harming any other in the process. Such a poll or survey could actually be taken to test how different groups answer. Such a poll or survey could be applied to a single good or government activity as well. What do you suppose it would show? (In the example, 10% is meant to represent a small adjustment. A different small adjustment could be substituted.)

---

[8]See also Foley (1970).

In the Core. The "Core" is an idea we have not yet introduced, but is needed to fully appreciate Lindahl Equilibria. We explain it as follows. If you felt that a particular purchase would make you worse off, you have the freedom not to make that purchase. Thus voluntary exchange protects you as an individual. A firm that would be harmed by selling something likewise has the freedom not to sell. Just as voluntary exchange protects the individual, so the Core protects the group. The Core is a collection of allocations that have the property that no subgroup can withdraw from the economy (taking their property and assets with them) and do better for themselves using technology known to the economy.[9] In other words, if something government is doing makes you and others worse off, and there is a way you and your group could "take your marbles and go home," doing better for yourselves, then the original allocation is not in the Core.

Lindahl Equilibria are in the Core. They do not force harm on one group to benefit another. If government provides public goods and satisfies the requirements of Pareto Optimality, not to mention morality, it does not behave this way either.

Equilibrium Exists Starting from Existing Endowments. The fourth feature of a Lindahl Equilibrium that Lindahl himself was not able to prove, but which is known today is that a Lindahl Equilibrium always exists and can be supported (or reached, or attained) while respecting each individual's starting private property and rights under reasonable assumptions. For example, the economy must be productive enough that it is capable of producing some allocation for which everyone survives. A Lindahl Equilibrium will not exist for an empty desert isle with people but no food or water and no way to get them, so assumptions need to rule out these kinds of situations. The survivability assumptions also presume that each individual owns enough assets of some suitable form, whether actual physical assets (goods, capital, resources of some form), labor that is able to be supplied, or human capital (educated salable labor skills) to be able to provide for his or her needs. In reality, we acknowledge in the real world that individuals might exist who never will be able to take care of themselves and will always be dependent on someone else. We have agreed that for now we bypass discussion

---

[9]The role of allocations was introduced in Chapter 2.

of these and take them up later when we discuss charity.

Benefits-Principle Taxation. In some ways, the most important discovery is that if public goods are present and the economy is Pareto Optimal, it must find itself in the form of a Lindahl Equilibrium. As described, a Lindahl Equilibrium is a mock market in the public good where "the value of public goods received by each individual is equal to the total tax he pays."[10] The tax paid for an additional unit of the public good equals the marginal benefit received, playing the role of price. The problem is that we do not observe the price to tell us what the payment by the individual should be as we do in the case of a private good. Various fixes and ways to infer values exist, but are beyond our scope and interest here. There is at least one case, however, where there is not a problem setting the tax rate. When an individual receives no benefits whatever from a particular public good, the proper tax for that individual is zero.

> **When an individual receives no benefits whatever from a particular public good, the proper tax for that individual is zero.**

In Chapter 14 we will consider how federalism and regional jurisdiction tend to apply appropriate tax rates for those who do not benefit from a regional public good, by which we mean a public good whose benefits extend only to residents within a specific region. Residents outside the region, who benefit zero from the public good, should pay nothing for its provision. A simple contrived example suffices: If you live in a landlocked state you should pay nothing for harbors used by yachts in Chesapeake Bay, which you never visit. Likewise, the richest Manhattan banker should pay nothing for the city park in Indianapolis that he will never see. Notice the interesting conclusion reached by logical deduction that progressive taxation does not apply. What optimality and Lindahl Equilibria do imply is that government provision of public goods can be mentally broken down into a good-by-good basis where each taxpayer pays for each public good to the extent that he or she receives benefits from it. Total taxes become the total of all such payments for benefits received. Where zero benefits are received, the individual pays zero

---

[10]Foley, 1970, p. 70.

taxes toward support of that public good.

Publicly Provided Private Goods. From our definitions of private goods and public goods it should be clear that a private good does not magically become a public good just because government may be providing it. A loaf of bread is a private good, and remains a private good, even if government were to set up a bread distribution depot. In fact, many things that government provides are not public goods at all. Storing land deeds and titles at the county courthouse is an excludable service both to those who need to prove their title and to those who need to ascertain who has title. User fees should be charged for access and storage.

> **A private good does not magically become a public good just because government may be providing it.**

The principle in these cases is this: Whenever possible government should pay for the goods and services it supplies through the use of user fees, where the user fee plays the role of market price and is the same to every like user. On interstate highways, for example, windshield-mounted electronic payment systems like E-ZPass allow highway use to be recorded without forcing cars to slow or stop. This was not true in the past. Interstate highways no longer need to be supported by taxes, including taxes on those who never drive on them, but instead could today be supported by user fees in proportion to the amount of use. User fees can vary by vehicle type depending on damage done to the roads that require maintenance (i.e. trucks should be charged more than cars), and so on. When technology improves to make user fees possible, payment structures need to keep up.

As an application of our study of externalities we can also address a question that is sometimes raised. The little old grandmother who never drives herself does eat food that is transported to her store in trucks that use the highways. Is she therefore a beneficiary of the highway and should pay to maintain it?

The answer is that, yes, she is an indirect beneficiary of the highway, but, no, should not pay taxes or fees to maintain the highway. She pays for her food which has transportation costs built into the price the grocery store charges. That is sufficient. No externality is present, so the little old grandmother owes no payments beyond paying the market prices for what she takes from the economic system. She takes no highway services directly, so should pay nothing for highway services.[11]

6.4   Congestion, Club Goods, and Club Rules

One can imagine other ways that goods intermediate to private goods and pure public goods might exist. For example, a movie theater designed to hold 150 viewers is non-rival up to the seating capacity, after which more viewers diminish others' ability to enjoy the movie. The movie theater exhibits a form of congestion. An interstate highway experiences congestion when too many cars are present at one time. Goods for which congestion is present but which exhibit excludability, such as a golf course, are called "club goods" because in addition to deciding quantity or size of such a good, we must also decide how many should participate. Golf courses generally play rounds in foursomes because too many on the course at one time ruin the play.

Intermediate goods such as club goods are often provided by voluntary private organizations (VPOs), the topic of the next chapter. A golf club (VPO) admits members, each of whom pays toward the total costs, and the club decides what the right number of members is by balancing the benefits of an extra member against the extra costs. If extra benefits to everyone in society, which by definition in the case of a club good means benefits to those in the club, exceed the costs to society, which again in this case means the existing members of the club, then the extra member is admitted. Membership stops growing when extra benefits equal extra costs.

In this book we view a VPO the same way we do a market or the government. It is also a means (or mechanism) of collective action.

---

[11] How would we handle a public good like national defense where the military drives on the highways? In this case, highway user fees paid by the military would be considered part of the cost of the military and the little old grandmother would pay for the public good (military) in proportion to the marginal benefits she receives from the military. As before, no highway externalities apply and she should make no side payments for highway.

6.5 Induced Quantity Change: Government & the Theory of Best Possible Policy

Many times some quantity in the economy takes a value that we imagine should be different. When the Cuyahoga River caught fire near the Republic Steel Mill in 1969, many decided that it would be better if the quantity of industrial waste regularly dumped into the river was a smaller number. What is the best possible way to go from a big number to a small number? In other words how should we nudge the economy's allocation from one location in numerical goods space to another location nearby, doing least damage to the rest of the economy, meaning the rest of us citizens?

Presume that ABC, XYZ, and RST are the only companies known to dump waste. One solution would be to impose a tax on the company for every laborer hired by these companies. This raises the companies' hiring cost, thereby diminishing their use in production in favor of more expensive alternatives, thereby raising the cost of production, thereby raising the market price, thereby diminishing the quantity demanded, thereby diminishing the production, thereby diminishing the amount of waste by-product, thereby diminishing the amount that will be dumped into the Cuyahoga. Another solution might be to find every consumer of ABC, XYZ, and RST products and tax their consumption of the firms' goods directly. You probably can think of other ways and more direct ways to get the job done.

The point is that many "policies" might be imaginable that would achieve the target quantity change, but do different amounts of collateral damage. In addition, politicians are not always the best at thinking things through. At one time it was thought that the United States should reduce dependence on foreign oil. One proposal was to tax U.S. gasoline consumption at the pump. Another proposal was to subsidize U.S. production of oil. A third proposal was to place a tariff on imports of foreign oil! Which should we choose? Were the politicians even clear about which quantity they were trying to change?

The theory of policy intervention is inherently a question of cost-benefit analysis, measuring the current well-being against the well-being that would be obtained if a particular quantity or quantities were changed to another value. Measuring should be done in dollars and the well-being from different policies compared. Fortunately we can summarize in plain English what the mathematics boils down to.

The best way to accomplish a quantity change is to apply a tax or subsidy (depending on which direction the change needs to go), narrowly directed at the margin to be affected, and applied at a level just sufficient to accomplish the new target. This principle is called the intervention principle. For example, if you want hours of employment of loggers between age 30 and 40 who work in Oregon to rise to a particular level, you apply an hourly subsidy to the employment of 30-40 year old loggers who work in Oregon. Furthermore, you raise the hourly subsidy just high enough to hit the numerical target and no higher. You do *not* subsidize all loggers' hours, you do not subsidize loggers of all ages, you do not subsidize all loggers who work in every state, and you do not create a loggers employment entitlement program. The mathematics of economic efficiency says that *any* policy other than the hourly subsidy first set forth above will ultimately cost more because it has higher collateral damage in the economy.

We have come full circle. In essence, you just applied a Pigouvian tax (in this case it took the form of a subsidy narrowly directed to the margin of interest—logging employment of a specific type—and at a level just high enough to accomplish the purpose), since the issue is to change a particular quantity through some binding means. Coase's insight about holistic alternatives applies as before. That is, if the Oregon governor instead could have costlessly caused the target to be exceeded just by publicly praising the work of 30-40 year old Oregon loggers in his next speech, then doing so is obviously the holistic best.

6.6   Conclusion

Externalities and public goods are linked because both involve direct effects of one economy partipant's action on another participant. Effects that operate through the normal functioning of markets and prices are not externalities. Pigou and the theory of policy intervention say that a targeted intervention just sufficient to accomplish the goal is best, qualified by Coase's holistic observations.

Because public goods are non-excludable they will not be sold in markets. Configuring the economy with public goods present as a Pareto Optimum means it must be configured as a Lindahl Equlibrium, which is the counterpart to a competitive equilibrium. Interpreting the payments by each individual for a public good as taxes and government as the provider of public goods, reveals that taxes should be paid in proportion to the benefits received by the taxpayer. The right quantity of public good is achieved when the benefit to the taxpayer from an additional unit of public good determines the tax rate. Several strong implications result. One is that individuals agree about the size of government production. Another is that since the allocation is in the Core, no group of individuals is harmed in order to enrich or help another. Progressive taxation is ruled out. Individuals who receive no benefits from a particular public good, pay nothing for its provision.

Finally we learn that the amounts you "owe" to society because you did not make the markets and circumstances of the economy that allow you to work and thrive, are zero. What you do owe is to pay the appropriate prices for what you take from the economy, and to be paid for what you provide to the economy. What you choose to voluntarily give in charity is your choice, a moral issue that we consider in Chapter 13.

References

Coase, Ronald (1960). "The Problem of Social Cost," *Journal of Law and Economics*, 3, October, 1-44.

Foley, Duncan. (1970). "Lindahl's Solution and the Core of an Economy with Public Goods," *Econometrica*, 38, 1, January, 66-72.

Lindahl, Erik (1919). "Die Gerechtigkeit der Besteurung" (translated from the German in 1958). Erik Lindahl, "Just Taxation— A Positive Solution," in: Musgrave, R.A. and Peacock, A.T. (eds.) *Classics in the Theory of Public Finance.*

Rotman, Michael (2020). "Cuyahoga River Fire," *Cleveland Historical*, https://clevelandhistorical.org/items/show/63, accessed June 2020.

The Weather Channel (2020). "Russian City So Polluted Skies Turn
    Black, Residents Urged to Leave," 15 June 2020. https://weather.com/
    en-CA/international/videos/video/russian-city-so-polluted-skies-
    turn-black-residents-urged-to-leave.

Chapter 7

Morality

Martin Luther King, Jr.: *We cannot be truly Christian people so long as we flaunt the central teachings of Jesus: brotherly love and the Golden Rule.*

Arbitrary: *having or showing a tendency to force one's will on others without any regard to fairness or necessity.*

According to the Encyclopedia Britannica, the Golden Rule has existed for thousands of years in two equivalent forms.[1] The 1st century book of Matthew (7:12) reads, "In everything, do to others what you would have them do to you." The *Analects* of Confucius from the 6th and 5th centuries BC reads, "Do not do to others what you would not like done to yourselves (Analects 15:23)." The Golden Rule in this form is also found in 1st century BC Jewish sources and the Babylonian Talmud: "What is hateful to you, do not to your neighbor (Shabbat 31a)."

> In this book, the Golden Rule will be the working principle or axiom from which we derive conclusions about morality.

Hinduism, Buddhism, and Taoism have recognizable Golden Rules.[2]

---

[1]Encyclopedia Britannica "Golden Rule: Ethical Precept," https://www.britannica. com/topic/Golden-Rule.

[2]**Hinduism:** "Do nothing to others that would hurt you if it were done to you (Mahabharata 5:1517)." **Buddhism:** "Do not offend others as you would not want to be offended (Udanavarga 5:18)." **Taoism:** "Regard your neighbor's

Even Linus Pauling, two-time Nobel Prizewinner (Chemistry and Peace) explained his modification: "Do unto others twenty-five percent better than you expect them to do unto you. The twenty-five percent is for error." Morality means little if it omits honoring the Golden Rule.

In this book, the Golden Rule will be the working principle or axiom from which we derive conclusions about morality. We assume that anything that violates the Golden Rule violates morality and is rejected.

7.1 Morality and the Golden Rule

Children in play are quick to complain if something is "not fair." They believe that each child should get his turn on the swing and going out of turn is wrong. It is not fair if another child hits you unprovoked. You, in turn, should not provoke or hit another child. If you don't like something done to you, then you should not do that thing to another.

"The Rules" from childhood are so natural that children seem to accept them without being taught. What children need to be taught is to *follow* the rules.

In philosophy, *natural law* is the view that certain rules of right and wrong are universal and inherent in human nature. They are innately known to be right as well as can be deduced through reason. In this chapter, we derive *economic* direction from the most basic of moral rules, the Golden Rule.   We take the Golden Rule as axiomatically true and an implication of morality.[3]

We also pick up the trail again of the following discovery from Chapter 6. Recall that Pareto Optimality implies Lindahl Equilibrium when public goods and private goods are present, which in turn implies tax rates in proportion to the benefits received by the

---

gain as your own gain and your neighbor's loss as your own loss (T'ai-Shang Kan-Ying P'ien)."

[3] "Morality implies the Golden Rule" ($Morality \Rightarrow GoldenRule$) means: if the rules of Morality are being followed, then the Golden Rule must be followed. The contrapositive is logically equivalent, "Not Golden Rule implies Not Morality" ($\sim GoldenRule \Rightarrow \sim Morality$). Since we want Morality, we want the Golden Rule.

taxpayer. In the special case where the taxpayer receives *zero* benefits, the taxes paid for that purpose should also be zero. Working instead from revealed preference and the Golden Rule, this chapter shows that in addition to failing to be Pareto Optimal, collecting tax from individuals who receive nothing in return from the tax's use fails to be moral.

7.2 The Nathan and Black-Tie Patterns

The following incident is from a black-tie social event. Income numbers are adjusted to be meaningful at the time of writing.

At this university occasion I was assigned dinner seating to the left of a university vice president. Her husband, not near us at the table, was the respected dean of a college. Learning that I was an economist, she was excited to talk about the "feminization of poverty," a topic with which I was familiar, including knowing the results of a study I sometimes taught from finding that roughly half of the always-poor in the decade studied consisted of unmarried females with children. I was very interested in her account of national trends and the hardships experienced by women in the United States who suffered poverty.

When my turn came to speak, I said I agreed with all she had said, sympathized with the cause, and asked if she had thought to give charitably to organizations that specifically focused on combating feminine poverty. I learned that she was indeed giving, but was unwilling to do more, and wanted government to get involved because she wanted more to be done. Might I ask, I gingerly said, what percentage of her income was she giving? Her answer of 7 percent impressed me, and I said so, because I knew that typical charitable giving reported on US tax forms was more in the 2-3 percent of income range. Wanting to be encouraging I explained that in my own case I too had decided that personal charitable giving was important and had settled on the Biblical norm of ten percent of gross income annually as a minimum to devote to charitable causes.

I then said that for her to want more done through government, however, when she did not want to do anything more herself, had unforeseen implications. I said that I did not intend to pry, but from what she had already told me about herself and her husband, they were both comfortably paid, had no children at home, and probably had a combined income exceeding $530,000 annually,[4] a guess to which she assented. Thus, by her own account, I said, she and her husband gave $37,000 to charitable causes, probably paid taxes in the neighborhood of $70,000-90,000 annually, and thus lived on more than $410,000. They thereby demonstrated that it was more important to them to keep $410,000 for themselves each year than for those in poverty to have even one more dollar of it. This startled her, but I quickly explained that using their own money as they chose was certainly their right and I was doing nothing more than summarizing what she had already said.

If government became involved, though, it would mean taking money away from a young couple in their early twenties, just starting out in life, and earning less than $27,000.[5] Taking from them would give them nothing in return and reduce them to living on less than $27,000 when she and her husband were unwilling to live on less than $410,000.

Instead of acknowledging the obvious injustice of this, she hurriedly added that she had a sister not doing well financially whom she and her husband helped and no one else would know about that. I replied that *the young couple also has a sister they help, about which no one knows.* Rather than facing the question of how help could be given plus this kind of injustice avoided, she turned away and ended our conversation.[6]

A similar story from the Old Testament is recounted in II Samuel chapters 11 and 12. In the relevant portion Nathan the prophet is speaking the following parable to the reigning King David:

> There were two men in a certain city, the one rich and the other poor. The rich man had very many flocks and herds, but the poor man had nothing but one little ewe lamb, which he had bought. And he brought it up, and it grew up with him and with his children. It used to eat of his morsel and drink from his cup and lie in his arms,

---

[4]Their income placed them well into the top 1 percent of US households. $531,020.00 was the 1 percent lower threshhold for households in 2020.

[5]I chose the example of a couple whose income was 40 percent of median.

[6]This story appears in Grinols and Henderson (2009), pp. 84-85. The numbers are adjusted to the time of writing.

and it was like a daughter to him. Now there came a traveler to the rich man, and he was unwilling to take one of his own flock or herd to prepare for the guest who had come to him, but he took the poor man's lamb and prepared it for the man who had come to him. Then David's anger was greatly kindled against the man, and he said to Nathan, "As the Lord lives, the man who has done this deserves to die, and he shall restore the lamb fourfold, because he did this thing, and because he had no pity."

(II Samuel 1: 1-7, English Standard Version)

A great deal can be said about this story, but the gist of it is that the rich man acted immorally because he wanted the poor man's lamb to be used for the traveler instead of his own. He wanted done to the poor man what he did not want done to himself. Notice that the rich man did not take the lamb for himself. The lamb was taken to supply the needs of the "traveler." A similar observation applies to the pattern of helping implied by the Black-Tie story. The University Vice President wanted money to help "the traveler," in this case represented by those suffering from the feminization of poverty. She wanted done to the poor couple's standard of living what she did not want done to her own, thus violating the Golden Rule.

Prophet Nathan chose his story to portray an obvious injustice, and no explanation was needed. Taking more from the poor man than from the rich man is arbitrary and wrong. Indeed, King David was immediately incensed against the rich man.

7.3 Golden Rule and the Nathan Pattern

People reveal by their actions what their preferences are. We saw this already in Chapter 2 when we used revealed preference to make statements about the ranking of consumption bundles. A key deductive tool is: *People are always free to give charitably of their own money as much as they want until further giving is harmful to them.* Giving stops when the marginal net value of giving has been reduced to zero and enters the negative range. An identical statement applies to expenditures for the purchase of a private good. When further purchase lowers the buyer's well-being, purchases stop.

Tax for benevolence purposes is money forcibly taken from the taxpayer (it is tax after all) and used to benefit third parties. Taxes not providing goods or services to the tax payer are different from charity, which is money voluntarily given from one's own assets to benefit a third party. We saw in Chapter 6 that Pareto Optimality requires that taxes collected be used to pay for goods and services provided by government that benefit the taxpayer, where the size of the taxes paid reflects the benefits received. No individual should pay taxes to support an expenditure that provides the taxpayer zero benefits.

Tax for benevolence is also different from purchases for consumption. Payments for market transactions provide something back in return to benefit the payer. True charity reveals that the giver receives something of value in the satisfaction that another human being of one's choice has been helped. The Golden Rule is not violated by charity. Nor is it violated when a rich man leaves the grocery store having paid for a bag of groceries and the poor man leaves having identically reduced his wealth to buy an identical bag of groceries. (In fact, optimality *requires* that they are presented with the same prices.) Each was given something in return for his loss of wealth; each voluntarily engaged in the exchange.

Taxing the poor man and the rich man to provide benefits to a third party that their *actions reveal they would not choose* is different because (1) it is involuntary and (2) nothing is given to the poor man (or to the rich man) in return. Taxes for "charitable" purposes, therefore, are not technically charity, but theft. If theft violates the Golden Rule, it violates the most basic of codes.

> **The university vice president wanted government to create a system that revealed preference showed would force harm on another that she did not want for herself.**

The university vice president wanted government to create a system that revealed preference showed would force harm on another that she did not want for herself. Creating *a system* that forces harm on others that you are unwilling to accept for yourself does not reduce or eliminate the harm in it. Such a system does not become immune to the Golden Rule. In fact, a *system* of Golden Rule breaking is probably worse than non-systematic breaking of it because the system forces those in it to do things they would never have chosen as individuals. For example, it is scarcely possible to imagine the University Vice President intentionally extracting money from the struggling young couple once she was no longer willing to give more of her own.

Assume that money taken from A and B is given charitably to C or pays for a benefit that only C receives. By assumption A and B had the opportunity voluntarily to use their money charitably for this purpose but did not. By revealed preference, therefore, this taking is harmful to A and B. This is enough to show that the taxes imposed on A and B for C are immoral. The result is proven more formally in Chapter 7 of Part 2.

7.4 Conclusion

The Black-Tie story and the Nathan story should make us profoundly uncomfortable. Charity is using one's own money or resources to help another human being. Deciding to help is *always an available option* that can be freely chosen and expanded. Taking another person's money or resources when that person gets nothing from it and has not consented—even if it is for "the traveller"—violates the Golden Rule. This cannot be emphasized too much: Regardless of how the taking is done, the conclusion that it is immoral because it violates the Golden Rule remains.

In practical terms, taxes that are used in ways that return no benefit back to the taxpayer create a *system* that violates the Golden Rule. In Chapter 3 we learned that such taxes are inconsistent with the principle that you own yourself and the product of your own giftings and labor. In Chapter 6 we learned that such taxes are inconsistent with Pareto Optimality. The message of this chapter, therefore, is that taxes that are used in a way that provides no benefits to the payer are triply condemned.

One response is to ignore everything, employ such taxes anyway, and forge ahead regardless. Rather than pretending two wrongs make a right, however, in this book we choose to continue our patient, methodical, and logical investigation of how human flourishing, morality, and social structure can co-exist. Finding that *tax-supported charity* is immoral does not say there should be no charity or endorse selfishness. It says to use proper means. Markets are not designed for charity nor very efficient at it. If markets and taxes (government) are ruled out as the means of charity then by elimination charity needs to be rationally, calmly, and carefully assigned to the remaining possibilities, which are voluntary private organizations and individuals. Even after government is removed as the source, we will see that government-private initiatives can properly play a supporting role if they are truly efficiency-enhancing.

> **Finding that tax-supported charity is immoral does not say there should be no charity or endorse selfishness. It says to use proper means.**

References

Encyclopedia Britannica (2018). "Golden Rule: Ethical Precept," https://www.britannica.com/topic/Golden-Rule. Online, Accessed 13 November 2018.

Grinols, Earl L. and James W. Henderson (2009). *Health Care for Us All: Getting More for Our Investment*, New York: Cambridge University Press.

Chapter 8

Voluntary Private Organizations

> *I think the tendency when anyone thinks of a policy is that either individuals should do it for themselves or the state should do it. I'm struck by the fact that there are a number of situations where the policy expert doesn't understand that there are other institutions. There are many cases where these other institutions are probably superior, because the state has constraints on its actions, even the ideal state, leaving aside corruption and things like that.*
>
> *Kenneth J. Arrow, Nobel Economist*

Individuals doing what is in their best interest, as determined and evaluated by themselves and displayed by revealed preference, determine Pareto Optimality, which the First and Second Fundamental Theorems of Welfare Economics show to be equivalent to competitive markets (Lindahl Equilibria in the presence of public goods). We learned that markets coordinate, equilibrate, provide information, and create incentives through prices (p. 54). We covered markets and market failure in more detail in Chapters 5 and 6. In this chapter we continue our treatment of how the mechanisms, what we call "the means of collective action," get done what needs to get done. Kenneth Arrow's "other institutions" are taken up in this chapter. Government is considered in Chapter 10.

8.1   Voluntary Private Organizations

Among the constraints that the state faces is that it can never know all of the information that it would need to be competent to act on the many circumstances that myriads of households and firms face in multitudes of locations. Government is not omniscient or knowledgeable enough. But, individuals themselves, who know their circumstances that government does not know, are able to take action much more effectively. Society welcomes the most efficient way to accomplish needed tasks. Often that is the Voluntary Private Organization (VPO), whose name essentially defines it.

Any group of individuals willingly choosing in their private capacity to collaborate to achieve a common goal satisfies the status of being "voluntary," "private," and an "organization." A business firm, for example, is a VPO, as is a country club formed to operate and maintain a golf course for the group's benefit, as is a charity that collects donations to provide benevolent help to the needy. Recognizing the special status that we have already discovered for profit maximization, competitive markets, and Pareto Optimality, we focus in this chapter on the other forms of VPOs. In other words, we catalog for-profit business firms as a market feature.

Ironically, this will be a short chapter, not because VPOs are trivial and unimportant, but because the opposite is true. The following example of VPOs seen in the United States lists forty categories from the US Code by purpose and type. The list arguably could be longer.

1. religious
2. charitable
3. scientific
4. testing for public safety
5. literary
6. educational
7. foster national or international amateur sports competition
8. prevention of cruelty to children or animals
9. civic leagues for promotion of social welfare
10. local associations of employees
12. labor organizations
13. local associations of employees
14. agricultural organizations
15. horticultural organizations

16. business leagues
17. chambers of commerce
18. real-estate boards
19. boards of trade
20. professional football leagues not organized for profit
21. clubs for pleasure, recreation, and nonprofitable purposes
22. fraternal societies, orders, or associations, operating under the lodge system
23. fraternal beneficiary societies, orders, or associations
24. voluntary employees' beneficiary associations
25. teachers' retirement fund associations of a purely local character
26. benevolent life insurance associations of a purely local character
27. mutual ditch or irrigation companies
28. mutual or cooperative telephone companies, or like organizations
29. mutual or cooperative electric companies
30. cemetery companies not operated for profit
31. credit unions for mutual purposes without profit
32. domestic building and loan associations
33. cooperative banks for mutual purposes and without profit
34. mutual savings banks
35. certain insurance companies
36. organizations to finance ordinary crop operations
37. posts or organizations of past or present members of the U.S. Armed Forces
38. entities for relief, recovery, or preparation for a disaster or emergency
39. organization by a State for medical care and not organized for profit
40. co-op health insurance issuers

VPOs are as widespread and as different as the circumstances that lead like-minded individuals to band together for a common cause. Anything this large defies description. We can explain, however, something of the incentives and motivations behind them. In most countries not-for-profit organizations (NFPs) are governed by law, a few details of which we will also provide.

8.2   The VPO's Internal Arrangements

Hypothetically, one could ask why every person is not an independent agent, every task is not an independent event, and every transaction is not a market transaction. Firms often have an accounting department, for example. Why are such a firm's accounting services not bought in the marketplace from an independent accountant? Why does the firm have employees?

The same kind of question applies to VPOs, which consist of a bundling of activities and "nexus of contracts" linking stakeholders and patrons in the VPO.[1] Patrons are supporters or sponsors of the enterprise. Stakeholders are any agent that has an interest in some aspect of the VPO's operation. Stakeholders can be buyers of the VPO's product, vendors of inputs to the VPO, owners of the capital used by the VPO, financial lenders to the VPO, and so on. "Contracts" are the operating arrangements governing employment terms and conditions, loan agreements, rules for who controls the enterprise, rules for the purposes to which the VPO can be put, and how the stakeholders interact with one another.

Since the mid-twentieth century the concept of transactions costs and market imperfections or frictions has been used to explain how an enterprise is configured. This approach is found in the work of Ronald Coase whom we have already referenced with respect to externalities, for example.[2] The explanation seems straightforward: A VPO chooses its objectives, decides its controlling stakeholder and working arrangements to circumvent the kinds of market frictions, inadequacies, and transactions costs it faces in accomplishing its goals. If there were *no* transactions costs and frictionless perfection in all markets then the enterprise could farm out all functions to market transactions. Dishonesty can be a friction. If everyone were always fully honest it would not matter which stakeholder was the controlling agent. A firm may hire its own in-house accountant, but farm out the planning for its advertising campaign because each choice is best for the firm to get done what it wants to get done.

In what follows we remind ourselves what a for-profit business

---

[1] See for example, Hansmann (1996).

[2] Coase (1937) suggested the concept of transaction costs to explain the origins and structure of firms, a topic to which he returned many times. E.g. Coase (1988), (1990) and others.

firm does and then look at three examples. A business firm gathers together capital (financial and physical means of production), mixes it with other inputs to produce a product, and sells the product to make a profit. As we learned from the First and Second Fundamental Theorems, maximizing profits is good. In the language of this chapter, a business firm is a capital cooperative, owned by the contributors of capital, and distributes its surplus to the capital-supplier owners in proportion to the share of capital they provided. The greatest threat to a business firm is that it might operate in a way that fails to maximize profits. This problem can be solved by making the capital suppliers, to whom the profits go and who have a personal interest in getting the best return they can from it, the firm's owners.

Sellers Cooperative. Now consider a not-for-profit dairy cooperative. Milk is not easily stored and transportation is costly. This makes the milk market less than perfect. The threat in a rural Minnesota milk-producing county is that the farmers will have to sell their milk at a low price. Depending on how high the transactions costs are, sellers might even have to face a monopsonist.[3] The response is to set up a VPO, in this case a farmer owned dairy cooperative such as Land O' Lakes. Stakeholders of the VPO include its suppliers of capital (milk), but also vendors of inputs to Land O' Lakes, the final consumers of milk, and others. In this case, the seller cooperative's basic operation is to gather milk,[4] sell it at a good price, and at the end of the year distribute any residual to its members according to their share of the cooperative's milk they supplied. Who controls the VPO? The suppliers of milk do, who agree that they want the best possible price. The arrangement is the best response to the stated threat.

Buyers Cooperative. I have never been a milk seller, but I have been a buyer of college books and materials. Consider then a buyer's cooperative like the Harvard Cooperative Society ("The Coop," founded by students in 1882) in which at one time I was a member. The threat in this case is that students, confined to

---

[3] A monopsonist is a single buyer of a good with many sellers who can influence the market price to its advantage.

[4] This can be done several ways. One is to buy at a predetermined fixed price that is low enough that the VPO is virtually guaranteed to create a surplus, which is then distributed at the end of the year.

campus and their studies, will be forced to pay exorbitant prices for the books and educational items they need. A buyers cooperative is controlled by its members, but this time they are its buyers. At the end of the year, members are sent a check for their share of the VPO's surplus in proportion to the purchases they made from it.

Not-for-Profit Charity. Let's consider a third example, Samaritan's Purse, which is a humanitarian and disaster relief VPO. Samaritan's purse, like The Red Cross, Oxfam, and others, is a not-for-profit. What are the threats for a charity? A for-profit firm might have an incentive to take donations but not make the promised distributions or skimp on quality. Meaningful patron ownership is not a possibility because there are too many donors, they are dispersed, hard to consult and so on. The least-cost solution to get honest charity seems to be a not-for-profit controlled by a board who may not distribute any surplus to themselves.

What do the sellers' coop, the buyers' coop, and the charity engaging in third party purchases and distribution have in common? In each case they deal with a market imperfection, friction, transaction cost or deficiency of some kind in the best way possible to accomplish the purpose and overcome or defeat the impediment. Sometimes one patron is the best class of stakeholder to control the VPO, sometimes another. By trial and error through time people have learned what works and what does not. Less good structures eventually are replaced by better ones. Survivability, agents together working in their self interest, and the hard knocks of experience find resolution.

Here are a few more examples.

1. **Performing Arts**. The threat is that ticket proceeds at the prices tickets can be sold will not cover the full costs of providing the performance. A performing arts VPO in which wealthy patrons are publicly recognized and rewarded for their gifts to the performing arts provides them a bundled product (guaranteed seats at performances plus public recognition) for which they will pay more, while average income attenders pay ticket prices only for available seats.

2. **Nursing home for the elderly**. Before they died, my grandmother and later my mother-in-law required nursing home care. Many people face this situation. The threat is that

it is costly to monitor a nursing home's treatment of its elderly, nursing home operators may be dishonest, and care depends on the motivation of those providing the care. If care is a ministry the situation is different. Profit is not the goal, the probability that God monitors your work is high, and the threatened punishment of Hell is great. In my grandmother's case she was a lifelong Methodist who was delighted with the care she received in the Walker Methodist Home in Minneapolis.

3. **Higher education**. When a college degree is an investment (payment today in return for greater future income that recovers with interest the original costs) the market deficiency is that college students cannot "sell stock in themselves" as a business firm can, and borrowing alone does not solve the problem. The response is to set up higher education as an education not-for-profit VPO. This allows graduates who attain great wealth later in life to donate to their college and everyone else to pay tuition only.

4. **Public radio**. Free riders in radio can hear the broadcasts without paying. The response is to create a radio not-for-profit VPO that can accept gifts on a tax-preferred basis and provide recognition and various "fringes" to donors.

5. **Hospitals**. Many hospitals at the end of the 1900s were set up as not-for-profit charities to aid the poor who needed care and could not pay. With the advent of modern treatments, better market circumstances, higher ability to pay, better ability to monitor, and the changing nature of medical practice for doctors in general, we would expect to see the rise of for-profit hospital structures. This is the case.

8.3 A Few Legal Distinctions

Here we mention a few of the common legal distinctions between a business firm and not-for-profit VPO. VPOs differ in how authority and control are assigned, the benefits they are granted, and in the restrictions on compensation, distribution, and termination rules they face.

Authority-Determined Distinctions.

1. Voting rights: For-profit business assigns voting control by shares: one share one vote. Not-for-profit VPOs tend to assign voting control on the basis of one member one vote, with some forms designed to limit votes by one individual.
2. Organizational law: Corporations usually operate under state law rather than federal: business corporation statutes, cooperative statutes, nonprofit statutes. Generally a cooperative VPO distributes surplus.
3. Not-for-Profits cannot distribute surplus. In particular, persons who control cannot receive distribution of net earnings. NFPs cannot issue equity, cannot excess-compensate their directors.
4. Articles of incorporation remove personal liability of directors. Requirements are placed on bylaws, an IRS tax exemption letter is needed, and so on.

Benefits Distinctions.

1. NFPs do not pay taxes.
2. Gifts to NFPs are tax deductible.
3. NFPs are permitted to raise tax-free bond issues.
4. NFPs are exempt from some states' sales tax.

Compensation, Assets, and Termination.

1. NFPs may not lend to, compensate, provide services to, buy from, or divert income to creators of the organization on preferential terms.[5]
2. NFPs must comply with reporting requirements.
3. NFPs must comply with rules about appropriate director compensation, and operation.
4. NFPs are not allowed to raise capital thru equity finance.
5. NFPs may engage in charity.

Among the advantages and disadvantages claimed for not-for-profit VPOs is that donors may be more willing to give to them. Not-for-profits may be better situated to engage in charity because of information advantages and their contact with the needy targeted group. We have already talked about honesty. Patrons may believe NFPs are less likely to engage in fraud or to lie about the quality

---

[5]For example, a pastor and his board of friends and family members may not start a church, receive millions in donations, build a campus and then terminate the enterprise, distributing the residual to himself, friends and family.

offered. NFPs may foster experimentation with extreme ideologies. The absence of owner-investors is good for pursuing niche positions. On the other hand, NFPs may have no incentive to be efficient since no group has claim to residual earnings.

8.4 A Special Word on Charity and VPOs

It should not be lost that there is a natural and strong connection between VPOs and charity. The reason is deductive. Markets, government, and VPOs are the means of collective action. After eliminating markets and government, VPOs remain as the solely viable collective agent for charity. To collective action, of course, we can add the "agents of personal action"—individuals.

1. Markets produce and distribute private goods effectively and efficiently based on the profit motive, which Pareto Optimality and the First and Second Fundamental Theorems of Welfare Economics endorse as necessary to human flourishing. Markets are not designed for charity and do not do it well. A corporation—we are discussing honest business—that fails to maximize profits (even if it does so for alleged charity purposes) fails in its mission and fails to do the social good that Pareto Optimality requires. Maximize the ability to help, then maximize the help.[6]

   Thus the modern movement for "corporate social responsibility" is a misunderstanding. Adam Smith knew this in 1776. His quote on page 48 continues, "Nor is it always the worse for the society that it was not part of it. By pursuing his

---

[6]What if the business is a sole proprietorship? Can the owner do as he wishes? Yes, but the answer remains the same: The owner does the *most social good* by maximizing profits—honestly—and from those maximized profits giving the most charitably. Deviation from profit maximization reduces the good that can be done. We are the sole proprietors of ourselves. Think of a whip-smart lawyer or brain surgeon who gives up his position where he earns millions a year from which he charitably donates 10% or more, to instead ladle soup several days a week in a kitchen for the poor. Soup kitchen ladling needs to be done, but the lawyer or surgeon has the ability to do the most good in a different way. We come at this from an economic perspective, but the same conclusion comes from a moral or religious source. For example, the three points of John Wesley's famous 1789 sermon "The Use of Money" provided this advice: earn all you can, save all you can, and give all you can.

own interest he frequently promotes that of the society more effectually than when he really intends to promote it. I have never known much good done by those who affected to trade for the public good. It is an affectation, indeed, not very common among merchants, and very few words need be employed in dissuading them from it."[7]

2. <u>Government</u> has no money of its own. It can give "charitably" only what it taxes and therefore takes by force. Many view charity possible only if the giving comes from the giver's own resources. Thus, forced charity is theft. Government charity violates the Golden Rule.[8]

3. <u>Voluntary Private Organizations</u> exist to deal with transactions costs, market imperfections, and frictions. Among VPOs are institutions devoted to charity. VPOs are voluntary and do not violate the Golden Rule. To the contrary, VPOs exemplify the Golden Rule in action.

4. <u>Individuals</u> always have the freedom (and obligation) to personally help their fellow man by balancing the needs of their dependents against the needs of others. Often these circumstances are known only to themselves. Ten percent of income is an oft-discussed norm for personal charitable giving. Personal charity does not violate the Golden Rule.

8.5   Conclusion

Business firms and not-for-profit VPOs are a collection of operating arrangements that link stakeholders in a nexus of contracts. The group that controls the VPO and the form that it takes is the best suited to respond to the particular objectives, market imperfections, transactions costs, and frictions that the VPO faces. A buyers co-operative (e.g. of books and college equipment) is controlled by the patron buyers because owners of a monopoly do not monopolize themselves. The same is true of a sellers co-operative, patron suppliers, and monopsony. Charities or nursing homes for the elderly are

---

[7]The intellectual errors involved in corporate social responsibility, "to trade for the public good" in Adam Smith's terminology, are also explained in Nobel Laureate Milton Friedman (1970).

[8]The chronically ill and needy *will* be helped. This is explained in Chapters 10 and 13.

not well suited to for-profit enterprises if monitoring limitations and the incentives of the firm to mis-represent what it does are great.

We should never forget that VPOs are voluntary. Unhappy patrons and stakeholders can walk away. In the long run, forms that work better than other forms for the same task will survive and be emulated. Forms that are less effective or ineffective will eventually not survive or be replaced.

References

Coase, Ronald H. (1937). "The Nature of the Firm," *Economica*, 4, 16, November, 386-405.

_____. (1988). "The Nature of the Firm; Origin," *Journal of Law, Economics, & Organization*, 4, 1, Spring, 3-17.

_____. (1990). *The Firm, the Market, and the Law*, Chicago: University of Chicago Press.

Friedman, Milton. (1970). "The Social Responsibility of Business is to Increase its Profits," *The New York Times Magazine*, September 13.

Hansmann, Henry. (1996). *The Ownership of Enterprise*, Cambridge, MA: Harvard University Press.

Chapter 9

Voluntary Private Organization Failure

> *The IRS advises taxpayers to be on the lookout for scammers who set up fake organizations to take advantage of the public's generosity.*

U.S. Internal Revenue Service[1]

Chapter 8 explained Voluntary Private Organizations as the means agents use to respond to a perceived need given the existence of "deficiencies" elsewhere in the economy, meaning transactions costs, market frictions and imperfections. From this perspective VPOs do not "fail." They may be incomplete therapy, but as long as they provide some degree of remedy they succeed. To talk of VPO failure we must look to their mis-use, identify what they are incapable of, and recognize what they are not designed to do.

9.1 VPO Failure

To the uncritical eye, VPOs may seem more virtuous than corporations and for-profit businesses. It seems that not-for-profits are

---

[1]Internal Revenue Service (2021). "IRS 'Dirty Dozen' List Warns People to Watch Out for Tax-related Scams Involving Fake Charities, Ghost Preparers and Other Schemes," Online at. https://www.irs.gov/newsroom/irs-dirty-dozen-list-warns-people-to-watch-out-for-tax-related-scams-involving-fake-charities-ghost-preparers-and-other-schemes, 3 July.

others-oriented, more caring, more loving, more altruistic. The counter view is that they are selfish, run for insiders, are social non-contributors that do not do their fair share because they pay no taxes to the community. They are inefficient and slothful because they have no reason not to be. The truth is, a case can be made on either side, and some VPOs are better than others.

To the extent that some people are dishonest and monitoring every VPO is impossible, there will be mis-use of VPOs. The foundation that collects donations, extravagantly rewards its directors, provides its board lush considerations, resides in gold-plated accommodations, but never seems to get around to very much charity work may nevertheless be very difficult to prosecute in a court of law. The so-called Police Fraternity that solicits telephone donations, never telling that ten cents or less of every dollar given actually goes to the police, the bulk being used to pay "operating costs," or the televangelist asking for donations while living a personal lifestyle reserved for the highest ranking and fabulously wealthy captains and kings of industry, are examples of personal failings rather than structural inevitabilities pointing to intrinsic flaws of VPOs. Corruption can appear in markets, in government, in VPOs. For this reason we first turn to the question of what VPOs are not designed to do before taking up the issue of their questionable use and fraud.

9.2   VPO Design Limitations

If the task is to produce and distribute private goods, no organization or structure, including VPOs, can do a better job than competitive markets. Competitive markets, on the other hand, are designed for selling, not making charitable gifts. If a charitable gift is the task, the VPO has no better. But the strength of the VPO, its voluntary nature and the total freedom it has to work toward any goal that attracts a willing group is a sure weakness if coercion is needed. A VPO cannot define and enforce property rights, for example.

A VPO can provide club goods and even a public good if costs are small enough that a subset of the population is willing and able to pay for it. However, it is easy to imagine a public good that is

1. necessary,
2. provides immense widespread benefits,

3. is too costly to be paid for by willing subscribers only, and
4. is not able to be accomplished by VPO.

National defense probably comes to mind. While a small security force might be created for a gated community and paid for by those who benefit from its work, a true modern military at the national level is almost surely too large, too costly for a VPO to underwrite. Yet national defense might be life threateningly necessary. In accomplishing the necessary task in cases like these, a government is probably needed.

9.3 Questionable Use, Mis-use, and Fraud

The most obvious fraud involving a VPO portraying itself as a charity is to gather funds, give the impression that they will be used in one way, but instead use them in another way that the donors would not have supported if they knew about it. The other "way" generally involves spending the donations with little or no accountability or oversight on the person, projects, perks, travel, salaries and overhead of the charity's "public face" (often the charity's founding person or couple), its board, favored insiders, or managers. Sometimes the collected funds are coerced in some way. Often, if not always, deceit is engaged in to disguise and hide the fraud and abuse so that it never rises to the level of legal prosecution and conviction.

Fully honest charities exist. Dishonest charities engage in some degree of good, if only to divert suspicion. Neither fact alters the third fact that charities have been, can be, and will unfortunately continue to be used for improper purposes.

Regardless of court action or its absence, sometimes where there is smoke there is fire, but sometimes where there is smoke there is no fire. Likewise, regardless of court action or its absence, sometimes charges against foundations are politically motivated and not valid, sometimes charges are not politically motivated and are valid, and sometimes they are both politically motivated and valid. The recommendation? Do not take things at face value; look beyond the obvious.

Virtually an unlimited number of examples of VPO failure could be garnered from almost any era of history and sound very much modern in their description of human nature. Readers can form their own opinion.

Numbers Are Hard to Hide.

Hillary Clinton, First Lady to husband President Bill Clinton, U.S. Senator from New York, Secretary of State, and candidate herself for U.S. President in 2008 and 2016 had a long political career with periodic recurring allegations of financial mis-deeds that have never been proved or disproved in a court of law. In the 1990s the claim

> "that she beat four-trillion-to-one odds in parlaying a $1,000 investment into a $100,000 payoff in less than a year on the cattle futures market was absurd. More absurd was suggesting that she had learned to become such a sophisticated speculator by making trades herself and reading financial newspapers. Most absurd was not paying taxes on her profits."[2]

One of the charges, however, involved *The Clinton Foundation* which was established in 1997 as the William J. Clinton Foundation. Critics allege a suspicious pattern of gifts to the foundation and say it was used to pry money from high political office in "pay-for-play" fashion. For example, while Hillary was Secretary of State with oversight of negotiations concerning the disposition of U.S. uranium deposits involving Uranium One corporation owned by Russian-related interests, Russians with ties to the Kremlin "mysteriously had given multi-million-dollar gifts to the Clinton Foundation, and an exorbitant honorarium of $500,000 to Bill Clinton to speak just once in Moscow."[3] Clinton had a net worth of near zero in 2001, one year after her husband left the presidency, but after just ten years in political office she had a net worth of $50 million. The Clinton Foundation raised over $2 billion by 2016, receipts to which fell noticeably after Hillary failed to become president despite expectations.

---

[2] Hanson (2019) p. 241.
[3] Ibid., p. 425.

United Homeless Organization.

According to the legal filing by the governor of New York, United Homeless Organization appeared to be a nonprofit organization to help feed and house the homeless, but instead

> "does not operate a single shelter, soup kitchen or food pantry. It does not provide food or clothing to the homeless. It does not even donate money to other charities that do.

> Most of those coins and bills, Mr. Cuomo contended, end up in the pockets of those working the donation tables, who pay a daily fee to the group's founder and president, Stephen Riley, and its director, Myra Walker, for the right to use the U.H.O. tables, jugs and aprons. The rest of the money, Mr. Cuomo charged, is kept by Mr. Riley and Ms. Walker, and has been used for a variety of expenses not related to U.H.O. business, including expenditures at Weightwatchers.com,..., Bed, Bath & Beyond, and premium cable and electricity bills at their homes."[4]

In this case a court took action. By court order on June 18, 2010, United Homeless Organization was permanently shut down. Riley and Walker were banned from engaging in non-profit work.[5]

---

[4] Confessore, (2009).
[5] DeJesus, (2010).

America's Worst Charities.

Occasionally, news organizations investigate.[6] Research by the *Tampa Bay Times* resulted in their list of America's 50 worst charities. Factors that they checked included what percentage of donated dollars went to fund-raising costs and what percentage went to direct cash aid. According to the *Times*, "the best charities spend no more than 35 cents of every dollar raised on fund-raising costs," while the "worst charities spend more than 80 cents of every dollar on fundraising."[7] According to information posted by the *Times*, for example, the *American Association of the Deaf & Blind*, the *Defeat Diabetes Foundation* and the *Disabled Police Officers Counseling Center* gave only one tenth of one percent of donations to direct cash aid. As bad as that sounds, six others gave *zero*.[8]

[6]Hundley and Taggart (2017).
[7]Tampa Bay Times, https://www.tampabay.com/resources/topics/specials/worst-charities/worst-charities.pdf, accessed July 2021.
[8] Ibid.

Churches: Moral Convictions, Not Legal Convictions

A person's spiritual health and eternal destiny would seem just as important to maintain as one's physical and psychological health, which are temporary. Does it need to be said that religious VPOs should always exemplify the highest and best moral standards?

Most probably do, but while countless examples over centuries of the utmost integrity by men of God such as that of evangelist Billy Graham (1918-2018) are available, religious leaders, like political leaders, are not immune to human nature. Indeed, the Protestant Reformation was initiated by Catholic Church abuses involving the selling of indulgences, *de facto* "get-out-of-purgatory-free" cards that would be purchased by sincere but less sophisticated Christians. Needless to say, the Bible describes no such practice involving purchasing ways to shorten the stay of one's relatives in purgatory.

We know that Billy Graham intentionally limited his personal lifestyle so as not to set an example of questionably lavish living. He and his wife returned gifts. He instituted independent boards to which he made himself accountable. Nevertheless, some religious VPOs have sunk to abuses that any search of the internet can uncover. For example, the title of a 2014 *Christianity Today* article reads, "Founder of World's Largest Megachurch Convicted of Embezzling $12 Million."[9] We could catalogue worse failures in non-religious as well as religious institutions, but that is not our purpose.

VPOs can be mis-used and abused, just as other human constructions.

[9]Moon (2014).

9.4 Conclusion

Voluntary Private Organizations are the often overlooked power-house work horses of economies. The good they do is legion. As one of the three means of collective action, the VPO is better suited to many tasks than markets, less suited for others. The same statement applies to government, which does not know and probably can never be expected to know the information it needs to be effective at the detailed level of VPOs. On the other hand, VPOs cannot do as well as competitive markets what competitive markets do, and VPOs cannot do at all some of the things governments do.

The "failures" of VPOs are not truly failures, but statements about what their strengths and weaknesses are.

References

Confessore, Nicholas (2009). "Homeless Organization is Called a Fraud," *The New York Times*, City Room, 24 November 2009. https://cityroom. blogs.nytimes.com/2009/11/24/homeless-org anization-called-fraud/

DeJesus, Juan (2010). "Judge Orders Homeless Organization to Disband," *NBC News*, New York, 24 June 2010. https://www.nbc newyork.com/news/ local/judge-orders-uho-to-disband/1914728/

Hanson, Victor Davis. *The Case for Trump*, New York: Basic Books, 2019.

Hundley, Kris and Kendall Taggart (2017). "America's 50 Worst Charities Rake in Nearly $1 Billion for Corporate Fundraisers," *Tampa Bay Times*, 2 October 2017, https://www.tampabay.com/ news/nation/americas-50-worst-charities-rake-in-nearly-1-billion-for-corporate/2339540/

Moon, Ruth. "Founder of World's Largest Megachurch Convicted of Embezzling $12 Million." *Christianity Today*, 24 February 2014. https://www.christianitytoday.com/news/2014/february/founder-of-worlds-largest-megachurch-convicted-cho-yoido.html

Tampa Bay Times. "America's Worst Charities," Tampa Bay Times, https://www. tampabay.com/resources/topics/specials/worst-charities/worst-charities.pdf, accessed July 2021.

Vincent, Isabel. "Tax filings reveal Biden cancer charity spent millions on salaries, zero on research," *New York Post*, 14 November 2020. https://nypost.com/2020/11/14/biden-cancer-initiative-spent-millions-on-payroll-zero-on-research-report/

Chapter 10

Government

*Power may justly be compared to a great river. While
kept within its due bounds it is both beautiful and useful.
But when it overflows its banks, it is then too impetuous
to be stemmed; it bears down all before it, and brings
destruction and desolation wherever it comes.*

Andrew Hamilton, 1735
Summation to Jury in Trial of Printer John Peter Zenger
Involving Freedom of the Press

It is commonplace to parody the failings and silliness of selfish politicians and bureaucrat officeholders in their public characters, but forget to acknowledge the necessary and very real need for government
in some form. How much government there should be and what kind
of government is a Goldilocks-and-the-Three-Bears type question:
What is too little, what is too much, and what is just right? The
rapaciousness of criminals, the aggression of foreign powers, and the
disagreements arising from simple misunderstandings among men of
good will all demonstrate that the state of "no government" is too
little.

In this chapter we review the functions of and prior conditions
needed for an economy and from them deduce what good government is. Bad government is taken up in Chapter 11 when we consider
government failure.

10.1 "Good" Not "Limited"

Discussion is often framed in terms of limited government and how limited it should be. The economic logic is somewhat different. Human flourishing requires material flourishing, which requires economic flourishing, which implies Pareto Optimality. Pareto Optimality implies the First and Second Fundamental Theorems of Welfare Economics, which imply competitive markets for private goods, Lindahl equilibria for public goods, allocations in the Core (see page 77), and taxes in proportion to marginal benefits received by the payer. Club goods require other conditions and so on.

But upon reflection, the First and Second Fundamental Theorems of Welfare Economics are pointless unless the conditions for decent commerce are in place, people are safe, property is acknowledged, and so on. Prior conditions must apply.

We begin government in this chapter, therefore, by putting together a list of tasks that *any* economy must perform and prior conditions that must be present if human flourishing is to result. Such a list is not unique because certain descriptions can vary, but its basic ingredients are familiar and universal. We then proceed in Sherlock Holmes fashion. He solved mysteries using the principle that "when you have eliminated the impossible, whatever remains, however improbable, must be the truth."[1] We follow a similar path. After assigning an agent to each task based on what we have learned of Pareto Optimality and the Golden Rule, whatever is not done by markets, VPOs, and individuals, "however improbable," is reserved for government, with the caveat that government not use its assignment as a beachhead for unsanctioned expansion.

National Defense and Safety: The First Prior Condition. At its core, individuals form government through social compacts to secure safety, without which little else matters. National defense against external aggression would probably top everyone's list of objectives, followed by safety from internal threats from sources such as criminal activity, social instability, corrupt government, and other threats to liberty and domestic tranquility.

Property Rights. Just as little else matters if one is not safe

---

[1]Sherlock Holmes to Watson in *The Sign of the Four*, ch. 6, (1890).

and has no liberty, likewise being safe and free has little meaning if property—the source of how one lives—is not recognized and protected. Having property generally means that one has the right to use, trade, and dispose of it as one chooses, of course, but providing for property rights also involves deciding what those rights are.

In the past, leaving one cell phone service provider for another could mean giving up one's cell phone number and needing to get a new one from the new phone carrier. Naturally, no one wants to force all his friends, contacts, and customers to lose his phone number. Losing your phone number was a serious restraint of trade until the Federal Communications Commission guaranteed your right to keep your telephone number even if you switch carriers. The process is known as porting.

The right to keep your mobile telephone number even if you switch carriers is an example of a property right. Failure to determine property rights is an impediment to markets and Pareto Optimality. Chapter 6 showed that the existence of an externality implies the absence of a market, and the absence of a market is caused by the absence of an enforceable property right. We found that one solution for externalities, when it is possible, is for government to create the needed enforceable property right.

Stable Money: Means of Commerce. Money is a medium of exchange, unit of account, and store of value. It is true that barter is theoretically possible, but practical experience shows that barter is not feasible on a wide scale. An ordered list of prior conditions that must be present for a well functioning economy would include a stable money.

Produce and Distribute Private Goods. Included in producing and distributing private goods is the decision about *which* private goods will be produced and distributed. A similar statement applies to the other two classes of goods, club goods, and public goods.

Produce and Distribute Club Goods. Club goods represent an intermediate case between private goods and public goods. Club goods are excludable (like private goods) and can be consumed by more than one consumer (like public goods) but exhibit congestion: consumption of the good by many consumers beyond a certain number begins to diminish the ability of others to consume the good.

The size of the consuming "club" then matters. A movie theater is an example of a club good, or a golf course. Club goods tend to be the domain of voluntary private organizations that manage the club size for the best outcome for the consumers. A movie theater, for example, sells tickets for a showing until the theater seats are filled and not beyond.

Produce and Distribute Public Goods. Public goods are non-rival in consumption and non-excludable. One person's consumption of a public good does not prevent others from consuming the same good (an example we have used of such a public good is the safety provided by national defense), and it is not possible to prevent some-one from consuming the good even if they have not paid for it (if your house is safe, mine next door will be safe too, whether I have paid or not). Nevertheless, like national defense, public goods are often incredibly important to human flourishing. Public goods there-fore tend to be the domain of government because non-excludability makes it difficult for markets or voluntary organizations to provide the good.

Competition.   At one time, in the robber baron era, it was thought that free markets, meaning *laissez faire* markets, were the ideal.   Cartels, monopolies, business combinations and trusts of every type were the result. We now know that Pareto Optimality requires *competitive* markets. Competition is the policeman of the marketplace; the policeman must be present. Pareto Optimality and competition, of course, carry within themselves even more meaning. For example, individuals must see the same prices for the prod-ucts they buy. Otherwise they will have different marginal rates of substitution and *distributive efficiency* will fail (Chapter 5). When universities charge different tuition rates to their students without using prior-gathered fully-funded scholarship money to pay for it, they violate distributive efficiency.[2] We know from our study that

---

[2]Fully funded scholarships do not violate distributive efficiency. These are gifts (transfers) made to students from pools of money previously collected to be handed out to individuals who meet the scholarship's previously stated stan-dards and who are charged the same previously announced price that every other student getting the same educational product is charged. Unfunded "aid" is dif-ferent. It is the practice of varying the prices charged for the same educational product to different students and their families.

it would be possible to make some or all households in the economy better off—including those associated with the university, its administration, and so on—without harming anyone in the process. A similar conclusion applies to airlines that charge different prices for air tickets to identical seats on the same plane.

Property Rights and Competition

A single seller in a market for a good with no close substitutes defines a monopoly. Because there are no competitors, the monopolist can charge a price higher than the true cost needed to make the item being sold. By referring to true cost, we mean the cost that enters into the calculation of what economists call "economic profit." Economic profit allows for a normal rate of return to the business firm. The true cost of making the item sold is the marginal cost derived from the cost that enters into the calculation of economic profit. Price higher than marginal cost is objectionable. Recall the hospital on page 59 charging a price more than 1,000 percent of the true cost of provision.

Because competition is so important to holding prices down, economists expended effort describe its features. Free entry into and exit from markets (**contestability** is the term that describes competition *for* the market, as distinct from competition *in* the market), inability to influence price (**pricetaking** by firms), availability of substitutes in the market (perfect competition means perfect substitutes or a **standardized product**), and free flow of information (**perfect information** includes knowledge about the product's availability and the market's common price) define perfect competition, the opposite extreme to monopoly.

Property rights are also important to fostering competition and need to keep pace as new technologies are introduced. Recall our discussion that the right to retain your mobile phone number if you switched to another service provider was a property right that encouraged competition. (Allowing your phone service provider to keep your number if you went to another provider, forcing you to start over with a new number, would act to limit switching and therefore work against competition.) Property rights to information are important in other ways. Were Congress to establish, for example, that information collected on or provided by individuals about themselves to an entity like Facebook is their personal property and they have the right of its return, meaning upon request Facebook must cease using and provide to them in a useable form all data collected on them, their postings, pictures, and information, people could easily move between platforms and have more control over information that is about them.

Property rights would enhance competition by encouraging rivals and new entrants. Facebook would be less able to censor its users' postings, and would be more careful about users' rights and concerns.

Externalities. Chapter 6 explained the work of Ronald Coase as it related to externalities, which were presented as a form of market failure. Acknowledging externalities is to acknowledge that they need to be dealt with or responded to in some fashion if human flourishing is the goal. If markets, individuals, and voluntary private organizations cannot, government must.

Equipping. We have noted hitherto that mathematical models of economies and economics tend to assume worlds peopled by individuals who sell labor and other assets they may own, buy commodities, and thereby maximize their utility, about which we can make inferences using revealed preference and other tools. This is because the economics engaged in by these mathematical "people" is the focus.

Humans do not realistically enter the world as full blown adults, however. Like me, you started out as a young child or even a baby! Unless your mouth was filled with a silver spoon at birth, your greatest asset as an adult is probably your human capital. Education, training, equipping, making ready for adulthood are therefore necessary tasks.

No one would deem to be good parents a couple who gave birth to a child, arranged for it to be taught nothing until adulthood—even if basic food, clothing, and shelter were granted—and then sent it out into the world: Since there *are* children, there must be the endowing of them with sufficient attention, love, and assets to viably enter independent adulthood.

Charity. We have intentionally reserved charity, which we define as aid given from one's own money and resources to those in need, last. A realistic social system must recognize that among a large enough number of adults there will inevitably be some who are incapable of providing for themselves and incapable of being brought to the state of providing for themselves. Some may be temporarily in need. We have tentatively reserved the care and equipping of infants and children for the "Equipping" task, though there is obvious overlap and no clear dividing line.

The ancient Greeks were known on occasion to leave babies, who cannot care for themselves, on hillsides to die. Adolf Hitler's National Socialist regime was known to use the term "useless eaters" *(Unnütze Esser)* to describe people with serious medical problems and disabilities. As we would not want to be abandoned to die or suffer, so the Golden Rule requires us not to allow others to die or suffer. Charity is therefore included in the list of tasks the economy must engage in to honor the requirements of Pareto Optimality and morality.

10.2 Assigning Tasks

The previous section compiled a list, more or less exhaustive, of ten functions or tasks that any economy must perform. Some cannot be performed by markets, VPOs, or individuals and are immediately assigned to government. Pareto Optimality and the Golden Rule associate others with markets, VPOs, or individuals and are so assigned. What remains is reserved to government. We have already studied some of the necessary conditions for Pareto Optimality and the Golden Rule. Table 10.1 applies what we know, adding brief commentary.

It should be obvious that national defense, property rights, and the support of stable money are things that individuals, private markets, and VPOs do poorly or not at all. We can immediately assign them to government. Producing and distributing private goods is assigned by the First and Second Fundamental Theorems to competitive private markets. No other mechanism can do better. Competition is needed by the First and Second Fundamental Theorems, however, and this is not guaranteed. We have abundant examples where *laissez faire* does not result in competition. Thus enforcing competition is a government task. The First and Second Fundamental Theorems also require the existence of working markets. By definition, externalities are market failures that are not cured by VPOs or individuals. Government must be the responding agent. Public goods imply Lindahl equilibria and benefits-principle taxation, which is also implied by the Golden Rule (taxes that provide no benefits to the payer violate the Golden Rule). Because club goods are excludable, they are handled by markets and VPOs.

Table 10.1: **Assignment of Economy Tasks Implied by Pareto Optimality and the Golden Rule**

TASK	Comment	Mkt	VPO	Gov't	Individual/ Parents
National Defense; Safety; Law & Order; Protect Life & Property; Criminal Judicial System.	Necessary first condition for honest commerce.			X	
Property Rights; Civil Law	Establish, Define, Enforce Contracts; Tort Law.			X	
Stable Money	Necessary for commerce. Medium of exchange; unit of account; store of value.			X	
Produce and Distribute Private Goods	Firms and households operating in competitive private markets cannot be improved on for the production and distribution of private goods.	X			
Produce and Distribute Public Goods	Nonrival nonexcludable goods such as national defense face challenges requiring non-market forms of provision.			X	

Produce and Distribute Club Goods	Club goods, being excludable, can be produced and paid for by those who use them and benefit from them.	X	X		
Enforce Competition.	Competition is necessary to Pareto Optimality, which is necessary to human flourishing. $1st$ and 2nd FTWE and Lindahl Equilibria apply.			X	
Externalities.	When markets fail intervention theory (Coase, Pigou, corrective taxes, property rights, etc.) applies.			X	
Equipping; Education; Training.	Children are dependent on their parents whose responsibility it is to raise them.[3] If not able to be provided for by their family they may be assigned to the charity function. See also the comments on VPOs, scholarships, interest free loans and other arrangements in the text.				X
Charity	It is everyone's duty to be personally charitable. Since taxes providing no benefits to the payer violate the Golden Rule and should be zero, charity is essential. Forced charity is theft.		X		X

This leaves equipping and charity. At a civilly useful level (e.g. literacy, reading, writing, grammar, standard mathematics, civics and representative government) education probably provides true externalities, meaning it generates benefits that accrue to those who

---

[3]Education, training, instruction and equipping are part of raising children. Just as parents should see that the child is clothed and fed, parents should see that the child is equipped. In doing this, most parents do not grow their own food or sew their own clothes in isolation, of course. The same is true of education. Scholarships, VPOs, interest free loans, charity, and other arrangements can all play a part.

do not themselves get the education.[4] I feel I benefit when I am able to drive on the same roads as people who can read road signs, for example. A case can be made for a fraction of the cost of initial education that has true externalities to be paid by the general public to the extent that a member of the general public *personally* benefits from education of another's child.

Before taking up further aspects of government in the next section, we can re-organize Table 10.1. Because the vast majority of what an economy does is produce and distribute private goods, the vast majority of the economy is assigned to competitive markets.

Summary of Assignments by Agent
1. **Markets:** Produce and distribute private goods. Produce and distribute club goods (in conjunction with VPOs).
2. **VPOs:** Produce and distribute club goods (in conjunction with markets). Aid in dispensing charity.
3. **Government:** Provide national defense, law and order, property rights, legal system, stable money. Produce and distribute public goods. Enforce competition and respond to externalities.
4. **Individuals/Parents:** Equip one's children. Provide charity, balancing the needs of others against the needs of those dependent on you. The information needed to balance is not known to government.

10.3 Organismic Versus Individualistic Government

A wide philosophical and psychological divide exists between two competing conceptions of government. Nobel prizewinning economist James Buchanan identified these alternatives as the organismic approach to government and the individualistic approach.[5] Much dis-

---

[4]The education thus described goes beyond the familiar "three R's" (reading, writing, arithmetic), but because we are habituated to what we are accustomed and because parents naturally want to feel entitled to "free" benefits for their child, the threat is not imagining too few externalities for student-specific higher forms of education when they are present, but imagining too many when they are absent.

[5]Buchanan, *The Journal of Political Economy,* 1949.

satisfaction and misunderstanding about government derives from those who consciously or unconsciously have adopted one viewpoint, often without even realizing that an alternative exists.

A simple analogy is to the role of a referee in a season of sporting contests. In the individualistic approach, the referee's interest is that individuals of all teams succeed at the highest level of which they are capable. The referee sees that games take place on a level field according to rules of fair play that apply equally to all teams. The referee is careful not to intervene in the outcome of games by making bad calls or applying the rules un-equally. He has done his job if over the season all members of all teams display their best performance.

In the organismic approach, the analogy might be to a family. Mom and Dad are the government and their interest is that each of the children receives his share of food at the table. They succeed if the family's overall operation is maintained. If the oldest child, teenage Kaitlyn, makes a pie (even from ingredients bought by her own money earned from babysitting) Mom and Dad still step in to decide how it is divided at the dinner table that night and that little Chad, who is a toddler, gets his piece.

Each analogy breaks down at some point. In an economy all people have equal freedom to produce their own wealth and everybody can simultaneously be a winner. That is why we talked about a *season* of games. A single sporting contest is focused not so much on everyone winning and playing his or her best as in declaring a single winner, in zero-sum fashion.[6]

The second analogy breaks down because Mom and Dad sacrifice for their family. Government brings nothing to the table and produces no wealth or income of its own as a Mom and Dad do when they care for their children.

In the organismic approach, government is an over-arching decision maker for society taken as a whole. It maximizes the value of a social utility function, which combines the utility of everyone in society to produce a single number. In the organismic conception of government the value of social utility rises if the utility of any single member of society rises, all other utilities held constant.

---

[6]A zero-sum game is one in which the winnings of one party equal the losses to other parties so that the net winnings are always zero. What one wins, others lose.

Other than this requirement, the social utility function can take any form whatever. Specifically, the social utility function can decide how harming one group to help another group affects social utility. In the organismic framework, harming one group is acceptable if it raises social utility.

It is easy to show that the organismic approach violates the principles we have derived from our study of property, the right to own one's self, the Golden Rule, and taxes deriving from Pareto Optimality and Lindahl equilibria. In the organismic framework private property (this could be tangible property, income, or purchasing power) can be transferred from group A to group B followed by the economy settling down at a Pareto Optimum subject to the newly assigned ownerships. Pareto Optimality would be honored, but morality and the Golden Rule violated. For example, let group A and group B be known to one another and living on the same street in close proximity. Let taxes taken from group B be transferred to group A, providing no benefits to group B. By revealed preference we know that group B is harmed since they have not voluntarily chosen to give their money or property to group A, yet such a transfer is acceptable in the organismic approach because social utility has risen. As long as the value of social utility rises compared to the counterfactual where no transfer was made and a different social outcome adopted, the change in ownerships is justified in the organismic approach. Since morality implies the Golden Rule, which we accept axiomatically, it should go without saying that we reject any approach that fails to honor it.

Organismic Government at Work

The Indian Removal Act is an example of what James Buchanan would call organismic government redistributing wealth for the national good. Signed on May 28, 1830, it authorized the president to remove American Indian tribes to federal territory west of the Mississippi River in exchange for their lands. The forcible taking of Indian lands to benefit dis-advantaged others is widely condemned today. It is important to recognize that the Act was not the policy of the the nation as a whole, but of the newly formed Democrat Party. The Whig Party resisted the Act, as did the Indian tribes, as did

Figure 10.1: **Andrew Jackson**

Christian missionaries (e.g. see Supreme Court Case Worcester v. Georgia brought by Christian missionaries protecting Indians), and as did Congressman David Crockett, and many others. The act was enforced by Presidents Andrew Jackson and Martin Van Buren.

The Cherokee worked to stop relocation, but were unsuccessful. They were eventually forced to march west in what later became known as the Trail of Tears. Majorities in places such as Georgia which benefited from redistribution supported the Act.

As already noted, few today view the forced removal of American Indians by Jacksonian Democrats as moral. It is an example of re-distribution, in this case from rich Indians on large tracts of land, to poor whites. Incredibly, the policy was described to the nation by Jackson as praiseworthy for the public good of *both* Indians and whites. He said,

> "It gives me pleasure to announce to Congress that the benevolent policy of the government, steadily pursued for nearly thirty years, in relation to the removal of the Indians beyond the white settlements is approaching to a happy consummation. Two important tribes have ac-cepted the provision made for their removal...and it is

believed that their example will induce the remaining tribes also to seek the same obvious advantage.

The consequences of a speedy removal will be important to the United States, to individual States, and to the Indians themselves....It puts an end to all possible danger of collision between the authorities of the General and State governments on account of the Indians. It will place a dense and civilized population in large tracts of country now occupied by a few savage hunters. By opening the whole territory between Tennessee on the north and Louisiana on the south to the settlement of the whites it will incalculably strengthen the southwestern frontier and render the adjacent States strong enough to repel future invasions without remote aid. It will relieve the whole State of Mississippi and the western part of Alabama of Indian occupancy, and enable those States to advance rapidly in population, wealth and power. It will separate the Indians from immediate contact with settlements of whites; free them from the power of the States; enable them to pursue happiness in their own way and under their own rude institutions; will retard the progress of decay, which is lessening their numbers, and perhaps cause them gradually...to cast off their savage habits and become an interesting, civilized, and Christian community....

Toward the aborigines of the country no one can indulge a more friendly feeling than myself, or would go further to reclaim them from their wandering habits and make them a happy, prosperous people....

Doubtless it will be painful to leave the graves of their fathers; but what do they more than our ancestors did or than our children are now doing? To better their condition in an unknown land our forefathers left all that was dear in earthly object....Can it be cruel in this Government when, by events which it can not control, the Indian is made discontented in his ancient home, to purchase his lands, to give him a new and extensive territory, to pay the expense of his removal, and support him a year in his new abode? How many thousands of our own people would gladly embrace the opportunity of removing to the West on such conditions!"

Several problems of the organismic approach to government were highlighted by Buchanan.[7] "A major difficulty," he said, "is apparent in the determination of what is to be maximized." Who gets to decide which group is favored and which group is disfavored? Another issue is that "the maximizing process consists of a simultaneous determination of all the variables on both sides" of the fiscal system, taxes and expenditures. It is not possible, for example, to say what the taxes for everyone should be until the uses to which the taxes are put is known. "Only if individual shares of the aggregate benefit from public services are held to be roughly equal can the concentration of analysis on the allocation of tax burden alone be theoretically justified (p. 500)." The United States is a large system to have to analyze simultaneously. Buchanan noted that " 'social utility' and 'social welfare,' are of little use in discussion of policy problems. The theoretical steps in the maximizing of social utility offer little or no direct guidance to governmental fiscal authorities."

Another Problem with Organismic Redistribution
In the Bill of Rights the US Constitution says, "No person shall be...deprived of...property, without due process of law; nor shall private property be taken for public use, without just compensation." For example, presume that an individual's land is taken so a highway can pass through that benefits the rest of the public but not the individual. The individual's land cannot simply be taxed from him or her and put to public use. He or she must be given "just compensation." This means that the individual must be paid an appropriate dollar value for what was taken, generally the market price.

In Chapter 6's treatment of public goods we saw that Pareto

---

[7]Ibid., p. 496.

Optimality likewise requires government to compensate the taxpayer by providing the public good to him or her in an amount that exactly compensates for what was taken.

Chapter 3 explains that justly acquired wealth in financial or other form is "property."

A conundrum is thus created: if government takes money (financial property) from the taxpayer "for public use" that does not in any way benefit the taxpayer, what does it give to the taxpayer for "just compensation?" A taxed dollar that does not benefit the taxpayer, like land for the public road, requires making compensation of one dollar. But if taking a dollar for this type of use requires paying a dollar, the tax is zero.

By this reasoning, the Bill of Rights supports the finding of Chapter 6 that taxes for public use that provide no benefit to the taxpayer should be zero and the finding of Chapter 7 that taxes that provide no benefit to the taxpayer are moral *only if* they are zero.

The individualistic conception of government is different. Since the individual replaces the state as the basic unit, disagreement with the organismic approach is not over what government objectives should be, but recognition that government *should have no objectives* beyond satisfying the functions listed for it in Table 10.1. For example, in U.S. discussions of health care, it is sometimes said that government should lower the cost of health care to rural communities. Why is this a government objective? Everyone is free to choose where they live and health care is a private good, meaning it should be produced and distributed in competitive private markets. Government has no interest other than to insure health care markets operate on a competitive basis everywhere.[8]

> **Disagreement with the organismic approach is not over what government objectives should be, but recognition that government should have no objectives beyond satisfying the functions listed for it in Table 10.1.**

---

[8] A full discussion of health care is provided in Part 2 Chapter 10.

Since the early 1800s organismic governments have been associated with socialist, centrally planned, communist, fascist, and Nazi regimes. Some expositors of social utility functions such as Nobel prize winning economist Paul Samuelson would add "mixed market economies" to the list, referring to systems where private markets are allowed to retain a prominent but still managed role.

10.3.1 Optimal Tax Theory

Assume that the utility (wellbeing, degree of happiness, or satisfaction level) of every household could be quantified and that the list of all the resulting numbers in turn could be aggregated in some way to produce a single number called *social utility* or social welfare that measures how well off all of society is. This is the organismic approach. Engaging in a Trail-of-Tears-type change would lower some people's utility and raise others', but the total effect on society could be known. Policy becomes an engineering question of doing whatever produces the highest social utility number.

Optimal tax theory asks a similar engineering question of how a set amount of taxes (purchasing power, tax dollars, real resources—the problem is varied in different contexts) can be removed from the economy with social utility remaining as high as possible. There are three objections to this approach that we explain here. The first is that optimal tax theory places no importance on honoring the Golden Rule. In his optimal tax example, for example, Nobel prizewinning economist Joseph Stiglitz explains that "the revenues raised by taxes on one group are redistributed as lump-sum payments to the other group (Stiglitz, 1987, p. 994)." In other words, the setting allows taxes to be levied on one individual, used in a way that provides no benefits to that taxpayer, and distributed directly to another. Chapter 7 in Part 2 explains that such taxes violate the Golden Rule. For us, this objection is definitive in rejecting the optimal tax theory framework. Instead, we derive taxes consistent with the Golden Rule and Pareto Optimality.

The second objection is that optimal tax theory ignores the requirement we have already noted that the maximizing process must consist "of a simultaneous determination of all the variables on both sides (Buchanan (1949) p. 496)" of the system, taxes and expenditures. This, too, is a fatal objection.

The third objection is the obvious one that optimal tax theory provides no guidance on who gets to decide how everybody's utility numbers are aggregated into a single number. Even in optimal tax modeling cases where there *is* simultaneous determination of all variables (taxes and expenditures), the objection remains that the social utility function introduces redistribution. If government provides public goods, for example, Lindahl equilibria are the result (see the section on public goods and taxes in Chapter 6), not redistribution. Applying the Golden Rule rejects the entire exercise.

Organismic Optimal Tax Theory and Animal Husbandry

When a farmer has a flock of chickens from which he wants to get the most eggs, the tools available might include such things as how much food to allow each hen, how much nesting space to give each one, how much roaming time to allow, and so on. The farmer makes decisions for each member of the flock based on the eggs he wants to get. Rather than treat them the same, he might want to reduce feed for one bird and raise it for another or to make one bird work harder than another. How he treats his most valuable bird might need to be different from how he treats the least valuable one. It is possible he may not even know which bird is the innately more valuable one and so might need to make decisions based on secondary observations or measurements.

The problem of optimal taxation for organismic government is logically similar. *Government becomes animal husbandry* and citizens are the "herd." Organismic government sets itself up to extract taxes from the herd for the purpose of paying for government and transferring some of what it takes to other members, knowing that it needs to rely as much as possible on the most productive workers, while trying to leave them no option except to keep working hard. One would not want to take so much from the highly productive worker that he or she finds it to his or her advantage to adopt the ways and appearance of the less productive, for example. Government intentions are degraded.

Individualistic government faces no such problems because it maximizes no such number, operating instead from principles of efficiency, fairness, justice, benefits-principle taxation and morality.

What do we conclude from optimal tax theory? Just as early pioneers of flying like Wilbur Wright and Glenn Curtiss observed the flight of birds but quickly understood that controlled, powered flight for humans depended on different principles, so we can observe and appreciate optimal tax theory but recognize in Buchanan's already-cited words, that it offers "little or no direct guidance to govern-mental fiscal authorities."

10.3.2 "Tax Deductions" from Pareto Optimality and Morality

Taxes pay for government operations. They are collected because they must be. We said that human flourishing implies Pareto Opti-mality and morality implies the Golden Rule. Section 6.3 described what Pareto Optimality implies for government provision of public goods. Willing participation, unanimity, outcomes that are in the Core, benefits-principle taxation, and reaching the outcome in a way that respects individuals and their ownership of property describe the implied arrangements to pay for public goods.

All of these can be interpreted as safeguard conditions. For example, the condition that government production of public goods and taxes must lead to outcomes that are in the Core protects groups because no distinguishable group of individuals can be found that would be better off if it did not participate, in this case paid no taxes and received none of the publicly provided good.[9] The benefits principle of taxation must apply and there must be agreement about the quantity of government provision. In the special case where someone receives zero benefits then they pay zero taxes.

Working from a different starting point, Chapter 7 found that collecting taxes from individuals who receive no benefits from how the taxes are used violates the Golden Rule. In other words, morality also rules out redistributive taxes and forced charity. We take up the provision of charity in the next section. Once taxes to pay for public goods are described, all that remains is to describe taxes in the case

---

[9]Any time a counterfactual is involved in a comparison, it must be carefully described as in Foley, 1970. The basic idea is that the group could use the technology available to it and its own resources to do better for itself than being forced to participate in the government operation.

where government provides goods whose quantity is selected by the individual involved.

Unlike public goods, which by definition are supplied to every consumer in equal quantity, many goods supplied by government are provided in different quantities to different users. When the quantity used is determined by the user himself or herself, that user should pay user fees in proportion to his or her quantity choice. For example, courthouses contain courtrooms that benefit everyone more or less equally when they are used in the criminal justice system, but they also archive deeds and records of property transactions. When a real estate developer records 143 deeds in a year, he or she is using more clerk time and resources than the retired grandmother who lives in her house whose deed was recorded once 35 years ago. Each should pay a user fee for the costs of the specific service that the county provides them, and the user fee, acting like a price would in a private market, would require the developer to pay for each recorded transaction. It is right that the developer pays more because he or she uses more.

In earlier chapters we pointed out that interstate highway use works the same way. Modern technology allows user fees to be applied just to those who drive on them without preventing the high speed travel that the highways are designed to deliver. You and I decide how many miles we drive on high speed interstate highways. Whenever a service is provided by government and the quantity of its use is determined by the user, that user should pay a user fee that covers the cost of the additional thing provided. Like a price, the user fee should reflect the marginal cost of providing the item in question. The US Postal Service is an example of a publicly provided private good (delivery of mail) that is paid for through user fees (stamps). It is a good example (bad example) if the price one pays for each item reflects (does not reflect) its true cost of delivery. One shudders to contemplate the consequences if mail were made "free" by using general taxes to cover its cost.

In summary, the following deductions about taxes emerge. Presuming government engages in the tasks assigned by Table 10.1, as much as possible should be paid for by user fees. When public goods are involved, the benefits-principle of taxation and Lindahl equilibria should apply.

10.4 Charity

We defined charity as the provision of help from one's own money and resources to the needy. Since government has no provisions to give away except what it taxes from others, it is not the moral agent of charity. By definition, markets are competitive because firms produce and sell products to consumers to maximize their profits, an action the First and Second Theorems say we want, and the trade between the two balances in any commodity. Competitive markets, therefore, by definition and design cannot be the agent of charity. By elimination, individuals and voluntary private organizations must be the agents of charity.

In the next chapter we explain types of government failure, including reasons that politicians handing out other people's money for charitable purposes, even under the cover of law, lacks safeguards that naturally apply when individuals, operating as independent agents and through Voluntary Private Organizations, use their own money to engage in charity.

How much charity is the right amount? If each person balances his personal needs and the needs of those who are dependent on him such as his family, against the needs of others and decides how much charity he should give, then the total of all such decisions is the right amount of charity. Of course, it is necessary that people know about the needs of others. Knowledge is a public good since knowledge is non-rival (you learning does not require me to unlearn; you becoming smarter does not require me to become less smart), and an appropriate government function is the provision of public goods. Government could therefore aid the charity function by certifying and making available information about needs, urging citizens to be generous, and perhaps even using mechanisms it may have that are more efficient to enable charity, without itself being the agent of charity.[10] Government can never be as knowledgeable about the circumstances of individuals as the individuals themselves and so cannot make these decisions.

---

[10] Readers can probably provide any number of examples such as the following: Currently people file federal taxes annually. A nearly costless change might be to provide tax forms with check-off boxes about where voluntary additional payments of a charitable nature might go. Since federal taxes are filed annually anyway, the private sector probably has no more efficient or superior mechanism.

Figure 10.2: **William McKinley**

William McKinley and Help for the Hocking Valley Miners

People are habituated to think that whatever the need or problem, government is the answer: the U.S. motto might as well be "In Government We Trust." Many believe this mindset is a consequence of the entitlement program approach adopted by the administration of Franklin Roosevelt and its continued expansion ever since. Examples of the late 1800s demonstrate a different attitude.

William McKinley served in the Union Army during the Civil War, seeing action at Antietam and the Shenandoah Valley, rising to the rank of major by its end, and returned home to Ohio to learn the practice of law. In March 1876, Tuscarawas Valley coal miners went on strike for higher pay and better working conditions. Strike-breakers were called in, leading to violence and injuries on both sides and troops being called in. Then 33-year-old McKinley, sympathetic to the miners' poverty and their poor working conditions, took the miners' legal case *pro bono*. Without excusing the violence, McKinley argued that it could have been averted if the mine owners had been more reasonable. All but one miner were acquitted of any charges.

Twenty years later he was governor of Ohio and the need for charity arose from different quarters. McKinley, though he was governor, did not turn to tax money, but did personally provide help from other sources. In January 1895 with little money, Hocking Valley Miners were destitute. Representatives approached McKinley who quickly asked local authorities to investigate and report back. Just before midnight January 9, they telegraphed, "Immediate relief needed." Here is biographer Olcott's *(The Life of William McKinley)* description of what happened next.

> By five o'clock in the morning a [railroad] car had been loaded with provisions and by nine o'clock it was in Nelsonville, and the work of distribution begun. The governor **personally ordered the supplies and agreed to pay for them,** but when his friends heard of it they insisted upon bearing their share of the obligation. The governor gave instructions that every appeal was to be met and that nobody should be allowed to go hungry. He wrote to the chambers of commerce of the principal cities and through them made an inquiry into the exact conditions.
>
> Finding many families in destitute circumstances, he made a statewide appeal for charity, with the result that he was able to distribute enough money, food, clothing and other necessities to relieve the distress of 2722 miners and their families, representing at least 10,000 persons. (Emphasis added)

What do we learn from this type of man? Though he was in public office, when William McKinley heard of a desperate need he first verified its truth after which, as noted, he did not immediately turn to handing out other people's money to be taken from them as taxes. He acted swiftly by responding with his own personal money. He then used his public position to make the need known

and induced willing charity from *his own group of political support-*
ers and business leaders who came alongside him and emulated his
leadership by example.

Amazingly, this same man was nevertheless later falsely carica-
tured by cartoonists as an uncaring string-puppet of "cruel capitalism."

10.5   Conclusion

Pareto Optimality, through the First and Second Fundamental Theorems of Welfare Economics, and morality, through the Golden Rule,
provide clues about how society should be arranged for human flourishing.   Ten tasks can be identified that any economy must perform.
In addition to individuals, three means of collective action (markets,
VPOs, government) can be identified to which tasks can be assigned.
Pareto Optimality assigns the production and distribution of private
goods to competitive markets because no other assignment can do
better. Working deductively, tasks that individuals, markets, and
VPOs cannot perform are assigned to government. Some assignments are prohibited to one or more means of action because the
means is incapable of the task or the Golden Rule would be violated.
The final arrangement of tasks with agents is therefore a deductive
exercise, summarized in Table 10.1.

References

Buchanan, James M. "The Pure Theory of Government Finance,"
    The Journal of Political Economy, 57, 6, December 1949, 496-
    505.

Graff, Henry F. *Grover Cleveland*, New York: Times Books, 2002,
    p. 19.

Mankiw, N. Gregory, Matthew Weinzierl, and Danny Yagan, "Op-
    timal Taxation in Theory and Practice," *Journal of Economic
    Perspectives*, 23, 4, Fall 2009, 147-174.

Mintz, Steven, ed. *Andrew Jackson, Messages and Papers of the Presidents, Vol. 2, in Native American Voices: A History and Anthology,* St. James, New York: Brandywine Press, 1995, 115-116.

Olcott, Charles S., *The Life of William McKinley,* 2 vols. Boston: Houghton Mifflin, 1916. pp. 281-282.

Stiglitz, Joseph E. "Pareto Efficient and Optimal Taxation and the New New Welfare Economics," Ch. 15 in *Handbook of Public Economics,* Vol. 2, New York: Elsevier, 1987, 991-1042

Chapter 11

Government Failure

*It is the highest impertinence and presumption, there-
fore, in Kings and ministers, to pretend to watch over
the economy of private people.*
— Adam Smith, 1776, Author, *Wealth of Nations*

*"Public bodies feel no personal responsibility and give
full play to intrigues and cabal. Rhode Island is a full il-
lustration of the insensibility to character produced by a
participation of numbers in dishonorable measures and
the length to which a public body may carry wicked-
ness..."*
— Nathaniel Gorham, 1787, Delegate from Massachusetts
to the US Confederation Congress

*"There is nowhere to be found knaves more designing
than at a legislature, where designing scoundrels lurk
and with specious words and demure looks they calcu-
late to entrap the unwary and like blood-suckers leech
and suck the public."*
— Ephraim Cutler, 1816, Ohio Legislator[1]

*"There are people who think that plunder loses all its
immorality as soon as it becomes legalized. Personally,
I cannot imagine a more alarming situation."*

---

[1]Written from Columbus, McCullough, p. 198.

— Federic Bastiat, 1801-1850, Economist, Member of French National Assembly

The solution is always the same: More taxes, more government, more control. So they take a crisis, whether it's fabricated or real, and then they come up with all these solutions that have nothing to do with actually solving the crisis. And when government figures out that they have unlimited power in a crisis, the number of crises become unlimited.
— Jason Chaffetz, 2021, US Congressman

It is easier to think things up than to think things through.
— Anonymous, Commenting on Government

Formally described, economics has been depicted as primarily the study of three things:

1. *optimization*—how consumers make choices to maximize their happiness; how producers make decisions about hiring, firing, production, and selling to maximize their profits; what government should do to enable the best social outcomes;
2. *equilibrium*—how the choices of consumers, producers, VPOs, and government combine to generate the outcomes for the entire economy; and
3. *incentives*—how arrangements and structures in the economy produce incentives that people respond to and how those responses are determined.

Chapter 10 described what government should *be* (through what it does) when it is governed by the implications of human flourishing and morality.[2] This chapter focuses on government failure. Because government is not an organismic agent (we rejected that approach), but rather a "placeholder" equally protecting the individual interests of all the people, we begin by considering what motivates those who make up government. It is a simple matter thereafter to catalogue the mis-uses to which government has routinely been put through the centuries—drearily been put, many would say—and explain the abuse by the motivation.

---

[2]Deductions about the economy derive from Pareto Optimality and the Golden Rule, our working tools, which are implied by them.

Unlike some of the earlier chapters, this one is all too easy to write. A large book, an entire encyclopedia, could be written about government failure. Nevertheless, we will try to be brief and use examples to buttress points wherever possible.

Before we start, a disclaimer is obligatory: A *statesman* is an individual in government office who does what he does for the good of others. A *politician* is a government office-holder who does what he does for himself. We acknowledge decent and honest government officials dedicated to their appropriate stations and task, but this chapter is about government failure. There is plenty of blame to go around, even if not equally to all participants.

11.1 Human Motivators

Because we are dealing with economics in this book rather than poetry or another topic, money is the first "people motivator" that comes to mind. Money serves as a unit of account, a measuring rod for success so to speak, so it is appropriate that firms and households are incentivized by it. A mother and father that want to get ahead for themselves so they can do good to their children can measure their progress toward this goal in money terms. A firm that meets the needs of the people in society measures its success in serving them by profit. Hard work and honest business thus yield good results, goals met. It is the excessive love of money for "me and mine" acquired by inappropriate means *other* than hard work and honest business that is harmful. To make a distinction, therefore, *greed* is the first motivator we list.

If we define greed as excessive love of money and the improper acquisition or attempted acquisition of it, then excessive desire for the basic human needs (food, attire, residence) defines the next obvious motivator. Greedy people sometimes accumulate money for its own sake, sometimes for excessive indulgence in food, clothing, and shelter. This defines gluttony.

People are also motivated by power (defined as control, authority and influence over others) and fame (popular acclaim and recognition). Rarely, one might conceive that a desire for power could be motivated by an innocent and sincere wish to help others, but it is hard to describe the desire for fame the same way. Most often, the desire for power and fame is associated with pride. People who seek power and fame for reasons of pride often believe that government should be the means to their ends.

Sadly, people can be motivated by a disinclination to labor, and an overly strong desire for leisure, inactivity, and indolence. Even if one does not use government or government employment as a means to sloth, providing *others* with sinecures may be the means to secure for oneself other items in the list.

The last three motivators on our list probably have little to do with systematic government failure but certainly are part of the government experience: undue seeking of bodily gratification (sex, drugs, pleasure), envy, and even wrath or revenge. For example, a government official, misusing his or her office, can engage in vengeful and angry actions against a citizen under his or her authority. A state legal authority, such as an attorney general, might use her position to wrongfully attack the person of a political opponent. Two other examples are given starting on page 173. In cases of lust, envy, and wrath, we see government conceit, arrogance, and overreach come into play.

Considering the billions of people now alive, the billions more that have previously lived, and the labyrinthine nature of human psychology and pathology, it is surely the case that our list of motivations associated with government mis-use and failure could be augmented and adjusted. Historically, however, **greed, gluttony, pride, sloth, lust, envy**, and **wrath**—commonly known as the Seven Deadly Sins—is a good start.[3] The astute reader probably guessed where we were heading all along.

11.2   The Failures

Government failures can be organized into groupings with similar features. One could group by motivation, or by the tools and types of actions used, or by another grid. At one time I thought it might be right to put in one place government failures that were forms of *Demand for Graft* and in another those that represented the *Supply of Graft*, recognizing that companies and private citizens go begging

---

[3]Also known by the Catholic Church as the Cardinal Sins, they are usually listed in order as Lust, Gluttony, Greed, Sloth, Wrath, Envy, Pride.

to government for secret contracts, special deals, and personal favors. Politicians mis-use their authority to respond to these requests, hence government failure. If it is easier to have government tax your foreign competitor's product than to compete with it, lobbying for a tariff on its import makes total sense. On the politician's side it is easy to make a law look general and appear to apply equally to everyone, when it doesn't.[4]

I now think there are multiple ways to usefully classify government failure. We begin with the common failures and list them with others that have similarities. The reader can probably identify his or her own patterns. When a government failure has been studied for its economic content, however, as is the case with Directly Unproductive Profit-Seeking, this will be noted. The following list of government failures or misuses can be considered both a beginning taxonomy and a glossary of terms.

11.2.1   Crony Capitalism (Corporate Welfare)

"Cronyism" is questionable enhancement of the fortunes of political hangers-on, sycophants, and lobbyists without regard to merit or deservingness. "Crony capitalism" is improper advancement of a business's interests through cronyism.

As we have noted several times, government can be exploited for personal purposes that are opposed to the public interest. The Teapot Dome Scandal of over a century ago involved private companies bribing government officials and government officials leasing public oil lands at below competitive prices. War profiteers selling substandard products to the US Government for military use during

---

[4]Humorous historical examples exist as when Germany passed trade legislation applying to brown or dappled cows "reared at least 300 meters above sea level" and "which have had at least one month's grazing each year at a spot at least 800 meters above sea level." They could just as well have said the cows were Swiss. Pettiness and pride also lead to comedy. In February 2021 U.S. Democrats introduced legislation to prevent federal funds being spent to honor or commemorate any former presidents who "have been twice impeached by the House," and to prohibit them from being buried in Arlington National Cemetery (Chapman, 2021, CNS News). Since only once in history were two such impeachments conducted, and these were initiated by themselves, they would have known that there was only one president who was "twice impeached" by the House of Representatives, and who was also twice acquitted.

the Civil War is an older example.[5]

A curious current example involves the mystery surrounding continued use of the penny, which is worth less than the half cent, a coin that was discontinued *in 1857*! The penny has even less value than the mill (the mill is one-thousandths of a dollar), a denomination that was *never* minted as an actual coin because of its low value. In January 1940 the smallest coin was the penny. A January 1940 penny would be worth more than an 18 cent piece today! Why does the government continue to mint such worthless coins? The answer is crony capitalism, lobbying from the industry that supplies the metal used in pennies. Why would a metal supplier spend about $140,000 each year in lobbying expenses? The answer might be because it was awarded a $48 million government contract.[6] Crony capitalism gets uglier than this, and it is real.

> **"An elected official provides whatever some particular private interest wants, and the private interest provides the elected official with votes and reelection. However, a disturbing trend in recent years has been a growing nexus among crony deals, campaign contributions, and lobbying (Committee for Economic Development, p. 6.)"**

Crony capitalism is also sometimes called corporate welfare. Often what the firm wants is to be babied by government. Nobel prizewinner Joseph Stiglitz, quoted earlier in Chapter 10, writes,

> "It's one thing to win a 'fair' game. It's quite another to be able to write the rules of the game—and to write them in ways that enhance one's prospects of winning. And it's even worse if you can choose your own referee."[7]

Consider the case described by another respected economist, Jeffrey Sachs,

---

[5]References abound. Huntington (2006) quotes historian Shelby Foote describing shoddy cloth in uniforms, "merchants and manufacturers who supplied the government with such cloth became suddenly and fantastically rich in the course of their scramble for contracts alongside others of their kind, the purveyors of tainted beef and weevily grain, the sellers of cardboard haversacks and leaky tents."

[6]Hopper, 2016.

[7]Stiglitz, 2012, p. 59.

"a judge approved the settlement with SAC Capital, a $602 million fine for civil insider trading...the same day we had the story that the owner and CEO of SAC Capital personally took home $1.4 billion last year in compensation. So the company is paying a $602 million fine and at the same time, Steven A. Cohen takes home $1.4 billion in personal compensation for his management of the company. If we go back just a few days, his top trader was arrested and led off in handcuffs from his apartment on Park Avenue.

This is what is called the American financial system at the moment. It's really mind-boggling to me, and it is an unregulated, essentially lawless environment that is not getting any more lawful.

I checked Steven A. Cohen's political engagement this past year, and he gave $217,000 in campaign contributions. And this is a pittance from the point of view of his wealth, obviously, as a share of a $1.4 billion paycheck. But $217,000 with our cheapskate politicians actually goes a long way to making sure that Mr. Cohen will be very well treated by his senators and by others who are giving ample protection to all of this."[8]

Sachs continues, showing that the incidents he documents are anything but isolated.

"Look at the political linkages of all of this. Daniel Loeb, who gets only $380 million of compensation, gave $551,000 in campaign contributions last year. Ken Griffin, who took $900 million for Citadel, gave $2.7 million in campaign contributions; David Tepper of Appaloosa gave $601,000 in campaign contributions; and so forth. Many of these companies are involved in these civil lawsuits—payments for fraudulent behavior that is neither admitted nor denied (p. 139)....Where is the Fed? Because this is about basic regulatory practice. It seems to me in truth that we have a system that is out

---
[8]Sachs, 2014, p. 137, 138.

> of control right now (p. 139)....But the point is, very
> soon after the financial crisis hit, there was a call, even
> from the free-market right, for bailouts."[9]

Bailouts and protection from government for crony capitalists, money
for office holders.

Agricultural Subsidies

American farmers like to think of themselves as the bedrock of self-
reliance, individualism, and the rugged American Way. In the 1930s
a series of years of dry weather conditions, as periodically can occur, was experienced in the Great Plains. The attempt to farm in
this region had been encouraged by the United States government
decades earlier and itself could be considered a form of government
failure.[10] Followed by the Great Depression, the Dust Bowl created
by the weather conditions caused true hardship for many American farmers and ranchers. Looking to buy political support Franklin
Roosevelt began agricultural support programs designed, essentially,
to hand tax money to farmers. The "sons" of these programs, and
now the "sons of the sons" and even the massive "sons of the sons
of the sons" of these programs, still exist nearly a century later. If
the real reason for the programs was simply to enable Americans'
compassion for farmers, it would have been possible to set up programs under government auspices where citizens could choose to
send their money for that purpose.

Because of artificial agricultural price support programs American farmers are not so independent and self-reliant as they imagine
themselves to be. Wanting to buy the votes of farmers, it is today the Republican party that is more associated with perpetuating
agricultural support programs.

So what can we say based on principles? Farming *is* risky business. But consider this, if I plant seeds on a given plot of ground I
do so because I hope at harvest to get those seeds back plus more
and be able sell the increase at a market price that covers my costs
and gives me profit. If I buy a share of company stock, I likewise
"plant" my money and do so because I hope to receive back what

---

[9]Ibid., p. 142.

I planted plus a share of the company's production of product into the future at a market price that covers my investment and gives me a profit. Both activities are risky. Agricultural support programs are designed to prop up the prices farmers receives so they cannot fall below a certain level.

Crony Capitalism, cited earlier, writes

> "Ever since the New Deal, a highly organized agricultural lobbying effort has succeeded in obtaining a wide variety of farm subsidies and import tariffs for agriculture that have distorted markets and that have benefited the agricultural sector at the expense of the general public....ten percent of the recipients of farm subsidies collect almost three quarters of the subsidies, **which in the mid-2000s amounted to around \$90,000 per farm** (p. 10, emphasis added)."

Why does government not prop up prices of the *risky* "plantings" of all stock market investors?

---

[10]Farming as envisioned by the Homestead Act (1862 and 1866) is not sustainable on much of this dry area, which originally was home to vast grasslands and herds of American Buffalo. The Kinkaid Amendment of 1904 recognized that 160 acres was not able to support a family as it could in other parts of the country and granted tracts of up to 640 acres. Many agricultural experts conclude that farming, even dry land farming and ranching, should never have been begun in large portions of this area. They advocate dropping all agricultural subsidies and letting the land naturally return to non-agricultural uses in those areas where it is unsustainable without government propping up.

11.2.2   Pension-Seeking

Corporations are not the only ones who think government should be their supply of easy money and free programs. Pension-seeking needs little explanation: the examples below illustrate the creative efforts some people will use to try to secure money they did not earn.

Figure 11.1: **Grover Cleveland**

Government Pension Corruption

As noted in Chapter 3, the Republican Party was founded in 1854. Post-Civil-War Republicans were in the ascendancy. They had pressed the fight to free the slaves and won the war. They had been opposed in their efforts by Democrats in the South and by "Copperheads" or "Peace" Democrats in the North.

The following lists the dates of American presidents from 1868-1913. Note the names.

Ulysses Grant	1869-1877
Rutherford Hayes	1877-1881
James Garfield	1881-1881
Chester Arthur	1881-1885
	1885-1889
Benjamin Harrison	1889-1893
	1893-1897
William McKinley	1897-1901
Theodore Roosevelt	1901-1909
William Taft	1909-1913

Every one is a Republican. So dominant had Republicans become that the single missing name from this list is Democrat Grover Cleveland. "Power tends to corrupt, and absolute power corrupts absolutely," Lord Action said. It took Grover Cleveland to stand against the Republican strategy in this era to give away the public's money to keep themselves in power.

The Grand Army of the Republic (GAR) was a Union veteran group that had effectively transformed itself into a political lobbying organization. The GAR wanted government money. Money would be in the form of service pensions, which naturally would go to themselves. Here is historian and presidential scholar McClanahan's account.

> "Following the war, a Union Army veteran could apply to the Federal Bureau of Pensions for financial relief. If the Bureau rejected the claim, the veteran could appeal to his congressman to present a bill overriding the bureau's decision. This happened with such regularity that when Cleveland assumed office in 1885, the Congress was setting aside one day a week during the legislative session for pension bills. It had become a form of open corruption, a way for congressman to buy votes...Cleveland considered fraudulent pension bills to be a form of government welfare
>
> ...he vetoed over two hundred pension bills...that accounted for nearly half of his total number of vetoes while in office (McClanahan, 2018, p. 242)."

One involved,

> "A man who took the fee to serve as a substitute in March 1865, only three weeks before the war ended, contracted measles, spent the next month in a hospital, and then was mustered out of service in May 1865."

Others were for deserters,

> "One of which was filed for by a family after their son drowned in a canal while trying to make it back home."

Another was by a widow,

"Because her husband had fallen off a ladder in 1881...Cleveland could not ascertain how this accident was related to his war injury."

When we cover the American ethical base in Chapter 13 we will reference Cleveland's position that while the people should support the government, its duties do not include supporting the people. Even Cleveland, whose final words before his death were "I have tried so hard to do right," failed to put an end to all such bills.

11.2.3   Directly Unproductive Profit-Seeking

Directly Unproductive Profit-Seeking (DUP) is ways of making a profit (i.e. income) by undertaking activities which are directly (i.e. immediately, in their primary impact) unproductive. DUP constitutes demand for graft (special favors, money, programs) by businesses or citizens.

Directly Unproductive Profit-Seeking has been extensively studied by economists. Sometimes called rent-seeking, it is associated with the work of Jagdish Bhagwati, Anne Krueger, and Gordon Tullock, among others. Chapter 11 in Part 2 explains the economics involved. What caught the attention of economists was that even though an activity like lobbying produced nothing of direct value, it did waste resources that could have been productively employed in some other way. Directly unproductive lobbying might nevertheless be valuable to the firm if it causes the government to act in some manner to benefit the firm.

Consider the example of a small country that has no influence over world prices or the terms at which it trades. Lobbying by a domestic firm to have the government impose a tariff on imports of competing goods would be an example of DUP. The tariff is harmful because it diminishes the country's gains from trade, on top of which the lobbying uses resources. Yet DUP is worthwhile to the firm if it gets the tariff.

11.2.4 Vote Buying and Politician Public Troughing

Politician Public Troughing (Polittroughing) is a form of political abuse whereby a politician creates or promises to create programs that benefit some constituents who then "feed from the public trough" and to pay for them through taxes on other constituents. The purpose of Polittroughing is to buy votes and political support. Polittroughers seek personal advantages, power, and continued time in public office.[11]

Giving away the public's money to your constituents through programs paid for by others to buy votes may be the most prevalent form of government failure unless it is guarded against or prevented in some way. Many politicians who intentionally engage in Polittroughing do not even hide their intentions. They consider themselves politically clever and use it as a device to stay in office: "Vote for me, and you will receive [[fill in the blank]]." Sometimes Polittroughers seek to separate the electorate into indentifiable groups to find a way to buy the votes from chosen groups until they have exceeded the 50 percent of the votes plus one that they need to win election. E.G. West's observation explains why such banal and distasteful practices can be successful to the corrupted politician adopting them, "People would have been irrational indeed if, believing that they could really obtain something free merely by voting for it, they did not in fact do so."[12]

> **"People would have been irrational indeed if, believing that they could really obtain something free merely by voting for it, they did not in fact do so."**

This form of politicking is consistent with the organismic ap-

---

[11]Polittroughing is discussed in Grinols and Henderson (2009).

[12]West (1967), p. 113. Inefficient or sub-optimal ways of doing things are wasteful. We get more education by not wasting it. West was speaking about education in the United States, using it to explain how *not* to proceed. We have already looked at education in Chapter 10 and found it to be primarily a private good, therefore something that the beneficiaries properly should pay for. The public element likewise was discussed in Chapter 6. Public goods and publicly provided private goods should be paid for by fees and taxes that represent the benefits received, as in user fees and Lindahl equilibria. This will lead to more education, less waste, and better outcomes.

proach to government (willingness to artificially intervene in the economy to help one group, even at the possible expense of others), but it violates the Golden Rule (is therefore immoral) and violates the requirements of Pareto Optimality for publicly provided private goods and the requirements of Lindahl Equilibria for publicly provided public goods. Moral government does not seek to advantage one group (the voter constituency of politician X) at the expense of another (the non-constituency of politician X).

11.2.5   Planned Dependency

Planned dependency refers to politicians creating programs *intended* to keep individuals and voter blocks dependent on government handouts and entitlements for the purpose of controlling them and their votes.

Figure 11.2: **Planned Dependency**

(a) **James Meredith**   (b) **Dick Morris**

(c) **Thomas Sowell**

If you have been put into a position so that voting a particular way is the only way to keep your immediate life support flowing, you will certainly vote that way.

Planned dependency was used used against American Blacks in the post civil rights era. The evidence is provided by both black and white experts and authorities. James Meredith was the first black student at the University of Mississippi. He faced down great opposition and demonstrated great personal courage to break through racial barriers to attend. He is mentioned by name in Dr. Martin Luther King Jr.'s historic *Letter from a Birmingham Jail (16 April 1963)*, "One day the South will recognize its real heroes. They will be the James Merediths, with the noble sense of purpose that enables them to face jeering and hostile mobs, and with the agonizing loneliness that characterizes the life of the pioneer." Meredith demonstrated courage to go against the tide to promote truth. He demonstrated the same courage later. He says this about post civil rights era American political liberals.

> However, somewhere along the line, someone in power decided that the proud black race, a people who built cultures in Africa and built many of the physical structures of this nation, could not survive without a host of federal programs and giveaways. Thus the "participatory" goals, which united blacks and white behind black Americans, were abandoned and replaced by programs that divided us. A "dependency mentality" was created and fostered by black and white liberals **looking to buy power** (emphasis added). (Meredith, 1997)

Dick Morris, pollster, political insider, and campaign consultant to President Bill Clinton said about President Obama:

> "Everything he's doing is designed to give his party and his faction and his ideology political dominance. If he were doing it by persuading people that he's right, that would be understandable, that would be fine, but he's using dirty pool to do it.... the most insidious is that he's trying to extend his program of entitlements to everybody so they all have skin in the game **to vote for his people**....then he'll **have functional control** over

people throughout the country and add to that those who are into entitlements and food stamps, disability." (Coren, 2014, emphasis added).

Thomas Sowell, legendary Stanford economist, social theorist, and author:

> "The blacks in the West Indies had all sorts of experiences growing their own food, selling the surplus in the market, and, in fact, being responsible for budgeting what they had. Black [slaves] in the United States were deliberately kept from having that. **Dependence was seen as the key to holding the slaves down.** It's ironic that that same principle comes up in the welfare state 100 years later.
>
> The black family survived centuries of slavery and generations of Jim Crow, but it has disintegrated in the wake of the liberals' expansion of the welfare state (emphasis added)."[13]

Perhaps the strongest indictment comes from author, commentator, and host of her own show, Candace Owens speaking to business news anchor Maria Bartiromo during the 2020 election season.

Figure 11.3: **Candace Owens**

"Black economic empowerment," those are terrifying words to the Democrat Party. They have worked tirelessly over the last six decades to insure that that never

---

[13]Hudson, (2016).

happens. **What Democrats want is a Black America that is dependent upon government policies and dependent on welfare.** This is why they love to push more handouts for Black America. They do not want to see a Black America that is actually empowered. They like Black America screaming in the streets, rioting, looting, **being pawns to help them get their officials elected** when they do nothing to serve Black communities.[14] (Emphasis added)

Planned dependency would not be embraced if its adopters did not believe it works. Writing in the 1830s, Alexis de Tocqueville (*Democracy in America*) provided an economics incentive-based theory. He said the rich in society were content with their financial status and did not feel the effect of taxes. Having money, they want "power and renown." To them, government spending is not a concern. He said the middle class "appears to me to be the most economical" because taxes on themselves are felt. The poor "have no taxable property" and therefore "no great economy of public expenditure ought to be expected" from them. He wrote,

> "Communities as well as organic bodies are subject in their formation to certain fixed rules from which they cannot depart. They are composed of certain elements that are common to them at all times and under all circumstances. The people may always be mentally divided into three classes. The first of these classes consists of the wealthy, the second, of those who are in easy circumstances; and the third is composed of those who have little or no property...

> It is evident that each of these classes will exercise an influence peculiar to its own instincts upon the administration of the finances of the state. If the first of the three exclusively possesses the legislative power, it is probable that it will not be sparing of the public funds, because **the taxes which are levied on a large fortune only diminish the sum of superfluities and are, in**

---
[14]Bartiromo (2020).

fact, but little felt. If the second class has the power of making the laws, it will certainly not be lavish of taxes, because nothing is so onerous as a large impost levied upon a small income. The government of **the middle classes appears to me the most economical**...

Let us now suppose that the legislative authority is vested in the lowest order: there are two striking reasons which show that the tendency of the expenditures will be to increase, not to diminish.

As the great majority of those who create the laws have no taxable property, **all the money that is spent for the community appears to be spent to their advantage, at no cost of their own**....

When an aristocracy governs, those who conduct the affairs of state are exempted, by their very station in society, from any want: **content with their lot, power and renown are the only objects for which they strive**...(Emphasis added).

11.2.6   Paternalism

Paternalism is the twin sister of planned dependency. A dictionary definition is "usurping a subordinate's responsibility and liberty in the manner of a father acting to manage the affairs for a child." In other words, paternalism is interference in the decision-making of an autonomous person that is not asked for and agreed to in advance. Of course, the father claims that everything he does is for the benefit of the child. Why would state or government officials want to engage in paternalism? The question could better be phrased, Why would state or government officials want power and control?

The Officeholder's Externality

Why do officeholders so often prefer to do nothing, choosing the *status quo* and failing to intercede, even when change is needed and they have the assigned authority and responsibility to act?

A possible answer is found by considering their incentives. The official retains the *status quo*, even when it imposes *huge* costs on the public, because the personally felt costs for inaction are low compared to the imagined risks of taking the initiative. Doing what has always been done seems personally safe so selfish interest wins over the massively larger, but unfelt, public interest.

The paternalist claims that there is a need. Philosophers find this insufficient, "It is not enough to show that individual reasoning is inadequate, one must also show that the intervener, or its agents, can and will do better. Clearly, interveners may be unable or unwilling (or both) to do better (Leonard, et al., 2000, p. 324)." We will not delve into the many and varied issues that one can imagine with respect to paternalism such as whether it can be justified, when is intervention not paternalism, and so on. The reader can distinguish from paternalism valid government functions that are described in Chapter 10 such as interventions to correct market failure or to prevent criminal activity. Instead, we return to de Tocqueville who worried how paternalism would lead to despotism.

"I want to imagine with what new features despotism could be produced in the world. I see an innumerable crowd of like and equal men who revolve on themselves without repose, procuring the small and vulgar pleasure with which they fill their souls. Each of them, withdrawn and apart, is like a stranger to the destiny of all the others: his children and his particular friends form the whole human species for him; as for dwelling with his fellow citizens, he is beside them, but he does not see them; he touches them and does not feel them; he exists only in himself and for himself alone, and if a family still remains for him, one can at least say that he no longer has a native country.

Above all these an immense tutelary power is elevated, which alone takes charge of assuring their enjoyments and watching over their fates. It is absolute, detailed, regular, far-seeing, and mild. It would resemble paternal power if, like that, it had for its object to prepare men for manhood; but on the contrary, it seeks only to keep them fixed irrevocably in childhood; it likes citizens to enjoy themselves provided that they think only of enjoying themselves. It willingly works for their happiness; but it wants to be the unique agent and sole arbiter of that; it **provides for their security, foresees and secures their needs, facilitates their pleasures, conducts their principal affairs, directs their industry, regulates their estates, divides their inheritances;** can it not take away from them entirely the trouble of thinking and the pain of living? Subjection in small affairs manifests itself every day and makes itself felt without distinction by all citizens. It does not make them desperate, but it constantly thwarts them and brings them to renounce the use of their wills. Thus little by little, it extinguishes their spirits and enervates their souls (de Tocqueville, *Democracy in America*, p. 663, emphasis added)."

11.2.7   Legalized Plunder

As earlier noted, government has no wealth of its own to distribute. Whatever it gives away must first come by taking it from others. Frederic Bastiat, whom we will see again when we discuss planning failure, writing in 1850 described self-preservation and self-advancement as "common aspirations of people." These are unfortunately paired to another tendency that he noted, the desire "to live and prosper at the expense of others." He called the resulting government failure "legalized plunder":

> "The government, I say, not only turned from its proper purpose but made to follow an entirely contrary purpose! The government become the weapon of every kind of greed! Instead of checking crime, the government itself guilty of the evils it is supposed to punish ...
>
> But how is this legalized plunder to be identified? Quite simply. See if the government takes from some persons what belongs to them, and gives it to other persons to whom it does not belong. **See if the government benefits one citizen at the expense of another by**

doing what the citizen himself cannot do without committing a crime (Bastiat, 1850, emphasis added).

Bastiat greatly opposed legalized plunder and explained one of its consequences. When government is organismic and socialist, it quickly expands into controlling nearly every aspect of life. In that case it becomes critical to political factions that they must control government in order to protect themselves. Politics becomes vicious and foul. Under the section heading **Perverted Government Causes Conflict** Bastiat writes,

> As long as it is admitted that the government may be diverted from its true purpose—that it may violate property instead of protecting it—then everyone will want to participate in making the law, either to protect himself against plunder or to use it for plunder. Political questions will always be prejudicial, dominant, and all-absorbing. There will be fighting at the door of the Legislative Palace, and the struggle within will be no less furious. To know this, it is hardly necessary to examine what transpires in the French and English legislatures; merely to understand the issue is to know the answer.
> Is there any need to offer proof that this odious perversion of the government is a perpetual source of hatred and discord; that it tends to destroy society itself? (Bastiat, 1850.)

No government official or politician who settles on legalized plunder to further his personal ambitions would be realistically expected to acknowledge in those terms what he is doing. It is far easier to provide smooth sound-bite justifications. The recipients of legalized plunder, of course, will consider the plunder they receive their proper due. As long as those who are plundered are a minority, such as the American Indians in the Trail of Tears, their voices do not carry weight in organismic democracy.

11.2.8 Government Planning Failure

Government planning failure refers to harm imposed on the economy by government planners.

It may seem thus far in a chapter on government failure that we have been too hard on government minions, politicos, and bureaucrats. Perhaps not. Those who look to government for their exalted status and lifetime employment often portray themselves as the action heroes and saviors of those they "serve" from the public sector. Many of them come to truly believe themselves equivalent to their public declarations.

Figure 11.4: **Capacity of Government Errors to Harm the Entire Economy Significantly**

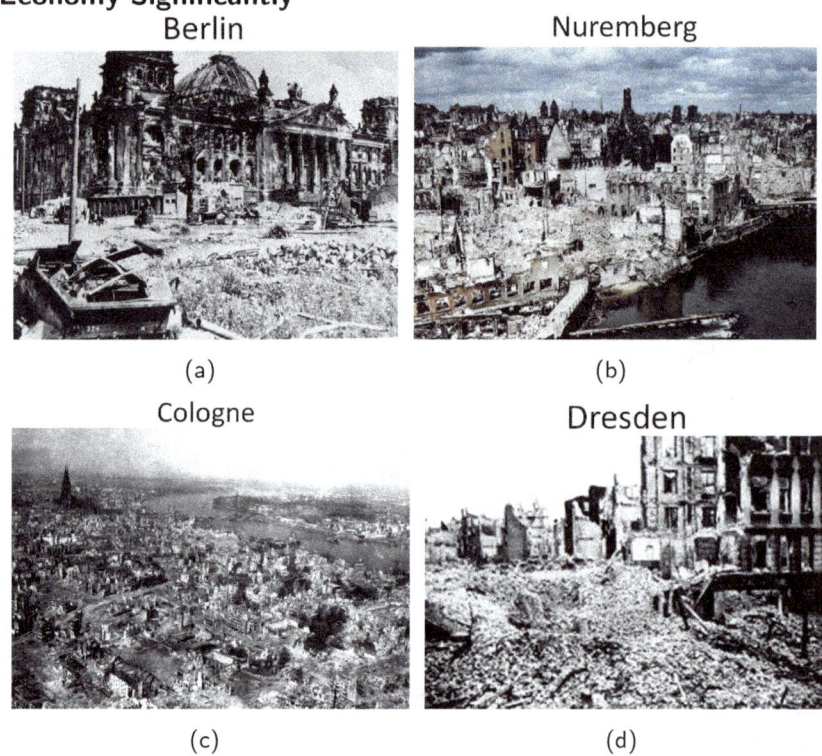

The problem is this. When a sincere but inept private sector firm messes up, it is but one of thousands or even scores of thousands. While the inept or deluded firm may die an agonizing death of bankruptcy, it does not take with it the fortunes of a large portion of the economy. I may be the worst wheat farmer in Kansas, but my stupidity is my own and falls on me and mine. There will be wheat from other sources.

It is not so when someone in government is captured by a foolish or delusional idea that is then able to be forced onto the entire economy through government. When government fails, its stupidity no longer falls on itself alone. Consider thoughtfully the Figure 11.4 pictures of Germany in 1945. What these pictures show was not caused by the bad business decisions or bankruptcies of a few business firms, or the poor spending decisions of some household. When *government* planning goes off the rails, it can take the entire economy with it.[15]

In fact, it is a proper government function to guarantee that competition prevails in the marketplace. This prevents the operation of monopolies, monopsonies, cartels, and harmful business combinations in restraint of trade. The existence of a business entity that is "too big to fail" (i.e whose demise might bring down a significantly large portion of the entire economy) probably indicates a government failure to engage its Chapter 10 duties.

Examples of government planning failure are easy to produce. The people of the United States endured extreme hardships during the Great Depression in the 1930s. Modern scholars have gone to great lengths to understand its causes and sources that point to government such as the Smoot-Hawley tariff (see page 166) and actions by the Federal Reserve. One of the bigger sources of harm was Franklin Roosevelt and his government planning. "The New Deal is widely perceived to have ended the Great Depression," scholars Cole and Ohanian write[16] but "the facts do not support the perception that FDR's policies shortened the Depression." Instead New Deal policies "choked off powerful recovery forces that would have plausibly returned the economy back to trend by the mid-1930s." Far from helping the economy, Roosevelt's planning *prolonged* the Depression by seven years. In other words, "employment and invest-

---

[15]In this book, we have avoided taking the position that small government is intrinsically "good" government. However, if there is an argument that small government is intrinsically better, this might be it: that small government is less likely to take the whole economy with it if government delusionally should go off the rails.

[16]Cole and Ohanian 2004, and Cole and Ohanian 2009. This quote is from Cole-Ohanian 2009.

ment should have been back to normal levels by 1936."[17] Economist Nobel laureate Robert Lucas and co-author Leonard Rapping report that it could have been back to normal by 1935.[18] A large literature from other respected scholars like Nobel laureate Milton Friedman likewise place blame on government. The following is from Amity Schlaes:

> Consider the centerpiece of the New Deal's first 100 days, the National Recovery Administration (NRA), which was in effect an enormous multi-sector mechanism calibrated to manage the business cycle through industrial codes that, among other things, regulated prices. **The principles on which its codes were based appear risible from the perspective of microeconomics and common sense.** They included the idea that prices needed to be pushed up to make recovery possible, whereas competition constrained recovery by driving prices down (emphasis added).[19]

Again, planning failure is a shame when engaged in by a private sector firm or household, but it can become a *national disaster* when engaged in by government. One countermeasure to government failure, therefore, is not to have government engage in planning activities at all (planning is done in the private sector) unless they are grounded in appropriate functions (see Chapter 10).

Government planning failure does not require that government planners tend to be bad people, bad planners, or fools, though in view of the applicable incentives at work in government this often may be the case. The claim is different. The claim is that certain features and circumstances that relate to government *always* work against it. The first has to do with information. There always will be important detailed information known only to individuals that government cannot know and for which its actions work at cross purposes.

Nobel Prizewinner Friedrich Hayek:

---

[17]Cole and Ohanian, 2009.

[18]Ibid.

[19]Schlaes, 2010. That NRA "management" would be considered comically laughable is a serious charge of government planning failure.

"if we judge measures of economic policy solely by their immediate and concretely foreseeable effects, we ... shall be certain progressively to extinguish freedom and thereby prevent more good than our measures will produce. Freedom is important in order that all the different individuals can make **full use of the particular circumstances of which only they know.** We therefore never know what beneficial actions we prevent if we restrict their freedom to serve their fellows in whatever manner they wish. All acts of interference, however, amount to such restrictions (emphasis added)."

Franklin Roosevelt did not know "what beneficial actions" he prevented. By inhibiting prices, he held back recovery.

A second reason has to do with the natural rewards to shortsightedness in the political cycle. The instigator of a bad plan often escapes its consequences and can be long gone from political office when the harmful effects appear. Often only the immediate effects matter to a politician, or indeed are known. Frederic Bastiat:

In the economics sphere an act, a habit, an institution, a law produces not only one effect, but a series of effects. Of these effects, the first alone is immediate; it appears simultaneously with its cause; it is seen. **The other effects emerge only subsequently; they are not seen; we are fortunate if we foresee them.**

There is only one difference between a bad economist and a good one: the bad economist confines himself to the visible effect; the good economist take into account both the effect that can be seen and those effects that must be foreseen.

Yet this difference is tremendous; for it almost always happens that when the immediate consequence is favorable, the later consequences are disastrous, and vice versa. Whence, it follows that the bad economist pursues a small present good that will be followed by a great evil to come, while the good economist pursues a great good to come, at the risk of a small present evil (emphasis added).

Bastiat might as well have said, politicians do not risk a small present evil to pursue a great good to come. Rather, they look to the immediate effect almost always and are rewarded to pursue a small present good, even when followed by a great evil to come.

Figure 11.5: **Government Planning Mis-Alignment**

A third explanation follows from the description of Figure 11.5. The American Indian developed an effective way to hunt American Buffalo that involved stampeding them over a cliff. Several of these famous locations are tourist sites today. The technique worked because Buffalo in the front of the herd knew they needed to stop but had no ability to do so. Buffalo in the rear had the ability to stop, but did not know they needed to. Because the decision maker was separated from the consequences and lacked knowledge, Buffalo perished. Figure 11.5 is a picture of government planning failure.

Now consider the same story from the perspective of one of my most useful classes, seventh grade wood shop. On the first day the instructor pointed out wide bright yellow lines on the floor surrounding the band-saw, the drill press, and the other power tools.

No one was allowed to be inside the yellow line except the one working the piece of equipment. He was very strict about enforcing that rule. "If you are helping your friend to cut a piece of wood," he said, "he can cut your hand or finger entirely off, and he won't feel a thing. If you are cutting your own finger, you might notice in time before you finish the job."

Exactly the Wrong Policy by Government
Franklin Roosevelt likely extended the Great Depression by 7 years but he was not the only source of harm. The Federal Reserve, a government entity, bears blame for mishandling the money supply according to modern consensus, and so does Congress for mishandling trade law.

By passing the Smoot-Hawley Tariff in 1930, named for sponsors Senator Reed Smoot in the Senate and Representative Willis C. Hawley in the House, Congress raised tariffs to a previously unknown height of 60 percent on average. More than 1,000 economists sent a petition urging President Hoover not to sign the legislation, but he ignored them. The effect on the system was immediate and understandable, competing protectionist tariffs by trading partners and a long run calamitous decline in world trade. Instead of helping the situation, or standing aside and letting markets correct, government made matters truly dire.

Figure 11.6 shows the outcome in one of the most famous diagrams in the field of international trade (Monthly value of total imports of 75 countries in terms of millions of old U.S. gold dollars. League of Nations, *World Economic Survey, 1932-33*).

If government planning means officials in Washington, D.C. making decisions and rules for the rest of the country we have a Buffalo or band-saw situation. I am cautious, careful, and concerned when I invest my own money because I can lose real dollars. Private investment is also just: the one paying for the investment makes the decision and gets the gain or loss. When some employee sitting in some building in Washington invests as part of the government, he or she feels no pain if it fails. Buffalo over the cliff. A finger lost. No problem to the decision maker.

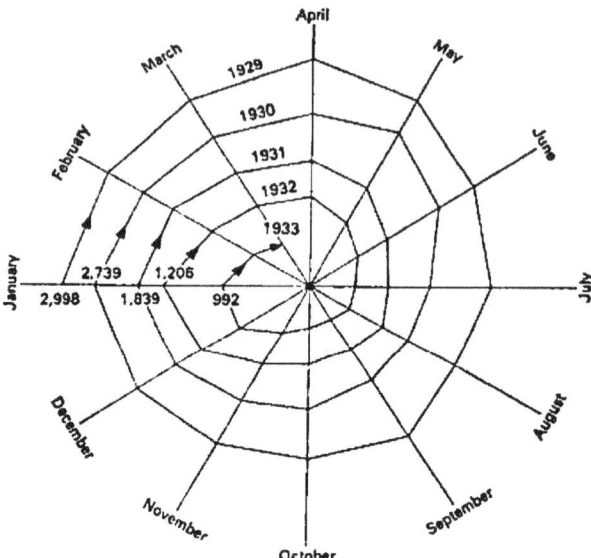

Figure 11.6: **The Spiral of Declining World Trade: 1929–1933.**

Government is not the valid location for investment in private ventures.

11.2.9   Friedman's Law

Milton Friedman, referenced many times in this volume, never stated *Friedman's Law* in theorem-proof format, but did refer to it in almost these terms:

> *Take a government program and write down its stated objectives. Then write down the opposite of its stated objectives. The program will often more nearly accomplish the opposite of its stated objective than its stated objective.*

He says in *Capitalism and Freedom*:[20]

> Which if any of the great "reforms" of past decades has achieved its objectives? Have the good intentions

---

[20]Friedman, 1962, pp. 197-200.

of the proponents of these reforms been realized? ... If a balance be struck, there can be little doubt that the record is dismal. The greater part of the new ventures undertaken by government in the past few decades have failed to achieve their objectives. The United States has continued to progress; its citizens have become better fed, better clothed, better housed, and better transported; class and social distinctions have narrowed; minority groups have become less disadvantaged; popular culture has advanced by leaps and bounds. All this has been the product of the initiative and drive of individuals co-operating through the free market. Government measures have hampered not helped this development. We have been able to afford and surmount these measures only because of the extraordinary fecundity of the market. The invisible hand has been more potent for progress than the visible hand for retrogression.

Is it an accident that so many of the governmental reforms of recent decades have gone awry, that the bright hopes have turned to ashes? Is it simply because the programs are faulty in detail?

I believe the answer is clearly in the negative. **The central defect of these measures is that they seek through government to force people to act against their own immediate interests in order to promote a supposedly general interest** ... These measures are therefore countered by one of the strongest and most creative forces known to man—the attempt by millions of individuals to promote their own interests, to live their lives by their own values. This is the major reason why the measures have so often had the opposite of the effects intended (emphasis added).

The government tendency to fail to accomplish its objectives is fundamental. The reason has to do with incentives, the "central defect" imbedded in many of the programs' designs. Good intentions are no substitute. Compassion does not compensate for ignorance.

Example 1: The state of California wanted to insure that women received a greater share of the joint estate in divorce settlements. A law to the effect that women should be paid no less than half the estate was passed.

The result? Women were harmed by the law and eventually came to oppose it. Why? Requiring the divorce settlement to provide wives with half of the assets often required that the couple's house be sold. Previously, the wife would have been allowed to live in the home while the man would be made to seek shelter elsewhere. Ignorantly seeking to do good, the law did the reverse.

Example 2: In Sudan, in recent years slavery was still practiced. Young girls were often the slaves. An international organization decided that they must help as many women as they could. They raised money to buy slaves and set them free.

The result? They caused greater harm. Why? By offering to buy slaves, the organization unwittingly increased the demand for slaves. They created an incentive for slave traders to abduct even more young girls and sell them.

Example 3: The Americans with Disabilities Act (ADA) was designed to end discrimination against disabled workers and help the job prospects of Americans with disabilities. It did the opposite? Why?

Figure 11.7: **Gary Becker**

No better person is better suited to answer this question than Gary Becker, yet another Nobel laureate. Instead of help, "this act has generated lawsuits that have benefited trial lawyers more than the disabled (Becker, 1999)." He continues,

> it is not surprising that the principal "disabilitys" litigated under the ADA involve workers who charge discrimination over difficulties in coping with stress, drug addiction, alcoholism, obesity, or back problems that are impossible to verify. Lawyers see an opportunity to gamble before sympathetic juries with often ridiculous types of "disability" claims.

The *truly* disabled, he says, are likely the principal victims of the act, the very group its promoters thought they would help. According to Becker, "Truly disabled workers might be better off if the ADA were scrapped altogether."

Example 4: The government seeks to preserve endangered species. Congress passed the endangered species act requiring that land that harbored selected species could not be altered in ways that would endanger the animals.

The result? Species on private land were unnecessarily put *more* at risk. Why? Faced with the effective confiscation, stealing, of their personal property should an endangered species be identified on their land, landowners naturally did not want that to happen. They took a "shoot, shovel, and shut up" response. Whereas they might have been cooperative under the right arrangements, exterminating the animal was far preferable to the hardships that awaited them if its existence became known.

How might good incentives that support the principles of Pareto Optimality (which implies markets), morality, and property have created good policy? This can be a test case. If particular parcels of land are essential to preserve a species, then interested parties should *buy* such land (possibly aided by government to publicize the need and gather the donated funds) and devote it to the species preservation that those involved purport to care about. Land that is especially valuable for certain purposes should have this reflected in its price. Federal law might even provide for a premium to be paid above market value for such purchases if eminent domain became absolutely essential. Landowners might come to welcome finding endangered species on their land and selling. A current example where private parties are working together is the American Prairie Reserve, which does exactly this, buying land for conservation goals.

11.2.10   Ordinary Graft & Corruption

Graft is the acquisition of money, gain, or advantage by dishonest or illegal means, especially through the misuse of one's position or influence in politics. A judge that accepts a bribe in return for a particular verdict is engaging in graft. An office holder that accepts money in return for being on a particular side of an issue that comes before government is engaging in graft.

Among my interactions with elected officials in over half of the U.S. states having to do with my professional expertise in the economics of casino gambling comes this first-hand story.[21] The individual, a member of the senate of one of our U.S. states went to his senate mailbox one day to discover an envelope containing $5,000.00 in cash. Inquiry eventually revealed that the source was a gambling interest. Coming before his committee later that year would be legislation regarding legalizing gambling opportunities in his state. The attempted bribe did not succeed. In fact, in this case it had the opposite effect, which is why the senator told me his story. The state senator was so incensed at the brazen attempt to buy his honesty that, after studying the issue closely, he ultimately became an opponent of expanded gambling in his state and the methods that they used. The respected state senator from a different state, a former president *pro tempore* of his senate, told me that I could quote him when he said, "The gambling industry *owns* the legislature" in his state. In yet another state that I visited as an expert witness on gambling matters I learned that a major proponent in the legislature for the industry expected to be offered a well-paid and lucrative position on the board of a gambling company once he left office. Graft can be dishonest, unfair, or illegal, and the difference in shade between the three is often hard to discern.

---

[21] Grinols, *Gambling in America: Costs and Benefits*, 2009.

Graft and Crony Capitalism Joined: Two Farmers' Markets
*The tendency is not to understand how hugely damaging govern-
ment failure can be. In the case explained here, a "little" graft and
attempt at crony capitalism destroyed an entire market for an entire
county.*[22]

Steward County, a small rural county with a population of about
40,000, has one large village which serves as the county seat. Just
outside the village is a county-owned field of approximately 3 acres
that the county uses for occasional municipal activities, such as a
yearly auction of abandoned vehicles and other items. The county
clerk is responsible for supervising the use of all public properties,
including the field.

For several years, local farmers and artisans have used the field
for a "farmers' market," Saturdays from July through October. The
county clerk authorizes 60 spots 10' x 15' for a fee of $5.00 per
week, the location chosen by the user, first come, first served. All of
the funds received are used to offset the cost of some port-o-johns
and weekly trash collection.

Depending on the day and the season, there is a wide variety of
items available—fresh fruits and vegetables, honey, jams and jellies,
leather products, hand made clothing and other items. The market
is very popular with many Steward County folks, rain or shine, and
with many "out-of-towners" who come regularly.

Multiple sellers have similar items, but since no two tomatoes
are the same, customers can shop for the best quality and prices.
As it turns out, some vendors develop great reputations and usually
sell out, but those with inferior products don't do so well, and they
generally stop coming. As the season goes on, there is a festive at-
mosphere and many satisfied vendors and customers at the Steward
County Farmers' Market.

Forty-five miles away is Baker County, remarkably similar to
Steward County in size, population and character, right down to
a popular Farmers' Market in a 3 acre field managed by the county
clerk. However, only two years ago a new clerk was elected, and he
began to rule with an iron hand.

New rules were instituted: applications for "spots" were required
two weeks in advance, together with a non-refundable fee of $10.00

per week. Spots were assigned by the clerk, and vendors soon learned that a ten dollar bill in addition to the official fee prevented being assigned a spot in an undesirable location.

Complaints that the port-o-johns were not serviced regularly went unheeded, and trash pick up was spotty. Both services were under contract with relatives of the clerk.

Worst was a decision by the clerk that he would set maximum prices for some items. (It turns out that one vendor did not grow anything, but would buy fruits and vegetables from a large wholesaler. The quality of those items was often sub-standard, but the price low.) Local farmers did not know that the vendor was paying the clerk to set requested prices, but soon realized that they couldn't be profitable for their high quality produce at the clerk's prices.

After three years the Baker County Farmers' Market folded. Local vendors stopped coming, many choosing to sell from stands in front of their homes, and, without a variety of quality items, customers lost interest.

Actually, many had been going to Steward County. (Like the saying goes, "if you have a better product, the world will beat a path to your door.") With the influx of new customers from out of town, restaurant business in Steward County picked up on Saturdays, and other local businesses saw an increase as well.

Only a few Baker County folks ever realized what went wrong.

---

22 Provided by a resident of one of the affected counties, whose names are changed.

How many ways are there to use one's public office to engage in graft? The reader should have no trouble producing examples.

11.2.11   Government Arrogance, Conceit

Presumptious overbearing by a government official involving disregard of citizens and their rights. Use of government office as a weapon against citizens in callous disregard.

What happens when a government official comes to dislike you personally, or to hold a grudge against you? Did you not show proper deference? Did you unknowingly inconvenience the official? Your building permit or business approval may be in trouble. Maybe the office holder is not particularly against you, just selfish and enormously lazy. It is easier ignore you. Even if you are in the right, the government office holds all the power. When the wrong person wields that power, he or she can arrogantly abuse it, going to egregious lengths to defend himself or herself. Conceit and arrogance become a problem.

Warren and Henny Lent bought their house in Malibu in 2002. It came with a side yard containing a narrow stairway that provided emergency exit with steps that led down to a landing. The landing covered a county-owned storm-water pipe that had been placed on their land by a county easement 36 years earlier. Prior owners had installed a gate to protect the public. "It had a gate barring entry from the street to ensure passersby did not fall onto the wooden landing, which was a dangerous six-to-seven feet lower than the street and another 14 feet above the beach (Unruh, 2019)."

Five years after the Lents bought their house the California Coastal Commission informed them that the protective features were "unpermitted and blocked the easement." The Lents' alleged wrongdoing was leaving the gate and stairway in place. Now the couple's legal team was needed. The team found that the original easement had been illegal. Moreover, the county easement was non-exclusive, meaning the homeowners had every right to continue to use their property as they chose as long as such use did not interfere with the commission's use, in this case a pipe. The commission had not developed or done anything with its easement for 41 years. The couple offered to remove the fence and gate whenever the county easement was to be prepared for any development. An important hearing was scheduled. The agency opposed the Lents in the hearing and also decided to issue a fine of $4.185 million! Who did the Lents think they were to engage legal counsel to find the truth about an easement or defend themselves against the exalted California Coast Commission? The reason the commission gave for the arbitrary and capricious fine of $4.1 million? "The couple spent 'too much time' trying to find a solution (ibid)."

Cliven Bundy grazed cattle in Nevada. In the American West the fact that a dispute arose between him and the Bureau of Land

Figure 11.8: **Armed Agents Come for Bundy's Cattle, Citizens Protect Them**

Management (BLM) over grazing rights is not as remarkable as the fact that BLM claims contained issues left unfinished going as far back as the early 1990s. In 2014 the federal government decided to take Bundy's cattle from him by force to impound them. This resulted in an armed standoff between weapon-carrying BLM agents, the Bundy family, ranchers, and armed supporters who were prepared with high powered rifles to shoot federal agents if they fired on civilians. Violence was avoided, but Bundy and his sons were arrested and charged with various offenses. The case went to court. In 2018 the federal judge said she was throwing out of court the government's charges against the Nevada rancher. Further, "the case could not be tried again due to the actions of the prosecution, which she said had been 'outrageous' (Stepman, 2018)." What would cause citizens to take up arms against the BLM and what would cause a federal judge to throw out the government agents' case with such strong words?

The answer is simple. Investigation, including by Bureau of Land Management watchdogs, found that the agents (at least one of whom subsequently lost his job) had personally

- acted maliciously toward the Bundys,
- acted "with incredible bias,"
- withheld key facts,

- "likely broke the law,"
- "showed clear prejudice toward 'the defendants, their supporters, and Mormons,' "
- engaged in a " 'punitive' and 'ego-driven' campaign against the ranchers" in "an effort to 'command the most intrusive, oppressive, large scale, and militaristic trespass cattle impound possible.' "

The internal investigation concluded,

> "The ridiculousness of the conduct, unprofessional amateurish carnival atmosphere, openly made statements, and electronic communications tended to mitigate the defendant's culpability and cast a shadow of a doubt of inexcusable bias, unprofessionalism, and embarrassment of our agency (Stepman, 2018, emphasis added)."

None of the above is to suggest that Cliven Bundy was in the right, nor to suggest what proper actions by the government agents would have led to. Rather, "the **attitude and ambition of Bureau of Land Management agents led them to inappropriately militarize the operation against the Bundys,** even after the FBI had conducted a threat assessment and concluded that the Bundys weren't dangerous (Stepman, op cit., emphasis added)."

Gretchen Whitmer was governor of Michigan in 2020. That year the novel corona virus Covid19 emerged from China to infect millions of people worldwide including in Michigan. Whitmer responded by imposing some of the strictest lock down regulations in the country (Sheehy, 2020), issuing no fewer than 182 executive orders from January through September. So what is the problem? Arrogance is one. First, recall that the executive branch does not have authority to make law. That is reserved to the legislature. Executive orders are like instructions an office manager gives to his or her staff telling them how the office will function. Theodore Roosevelt's first executive order, for example, instructed that the open position in his executive branch for a person to sign checks in the pension agency in Philadelphia could be filled without a civil-service examination.[23] Anything that applies to the public at large must be specifically authorized by previous law. Executive orders may not

---

[23] "An appointment to the vacancy now existing in the position of the clerk

Figure 11.9: **Gretchen Whitmer**

violate existing law, may not attempt to create law, may not violate a state's constitution, and may not violate the federal constitution. Orders that do are null and void and can be ignored. With this in mind, the First Amendment of the US Constitution protects "the right of the people peaceably to assemble" against which many of Whitmer's restrictions were directed. A government servant needs to exhibit humility and care here. First Amendment protections are unconditional.

Second, Whitmer demonstrated that she considered herself above following her own rules. Just before Memorial Day she relaxed some restrictions on certain parts of the state that included Traverse City, an area near where she had her own vacation property, but told those living in other parts of the state not to travel there: "A small spike could put the hospital system in dire straits pretty quickly. That's precisely why we're asking everyone to continue doing their part. Don't descend on Traverse City from all regions of the state."[24] Here is what happened next.

> Three days later, a marina owner wrote on Facebook that the governor's husband, Marc Mallory, had asked its workers to get their nearby boat in the water before

---

designated to sign checks for the pension agent at the pension agency at Philadelphia, Pa., may be made without examination under the civil-service rules." Executive Order 141, 31 October 1901.

[24]Olohan (2020).

Memorial Day, the Detroit News said Monday. The vacation property that the governor and her husband own is about 25 minutes from Traverse City, the News said. The couple's main residence is in Lansing.

"This morning, I was out working when the office called me, there was a gentleman on hold who wanted his boat in the water before the weekend," NorthShore Dock LLC owner Tad Dowker wrote Thursday on Facebook, according to the News, which said the posting has since been made private.

"Being Memorial weekend and the fact that we started working three weeks late means there is no chance this is going to happen," Dowker wrote, the paper said.

"Well our office personnel had explained this to the man and he replied, 'I am the husband to the governor, will this make a difference?' "[25]

Just days later on June 5 Whitmer ignored her own rules again. Another reporter asked,

"Oh, Governor Gretchen Whitmer. Is she aware of her hypocrisy? Does she even know how bad it looks when she orders her draconian mandates, then defies them for the sake of a photo op?"

...

"She swore the coronavirus was so serious it wasn't worth doing anything whatsoever that could possibly allow people to be exposed to it. Then, she hopped on the first opportunity...The Democrat was filmed during the photo opportunity leaning on her fellow demonstrators and removing her mask to speak to the cameras in violation of the guidelines she insisted on maintaining for her state amid the continued presence of COVID-19."[26]

By the end of the year, the Michigan Supreme Court had been alerted to Whitmer's overreach and her scores of executive orders.

---

[25]Ibid.
[26]Wimble, (2020).

They found that "The Democratic governor's directives were an 'unlawful delegation of legislative power to the executive branch in violation of the Michigan Constitution.' "[27]

Figure 11.10: **Crown "Governor-in-Chief" William Cosby**

Governor Failure

Misuse of power can appear in any era. Appointed by the British Crown in 1732 to be Provincial Governor-in-Chief of New York, William Cosby owed little to nothing to those he was supposed to serve. This is what modern historians say about him:

> Cosby quickly developed a reputation as "a rogue governor." It is almost impossible to find a positive adjective among the many used by historians to describe the new governor: "spiteful," "greedy," "jealous," "quick-tempered," "dull," "unlettered," and "haughty" are a sample of those that have been applied.[28]

Cosby is the governor that within a year began to persecute the free press of New York City, leading to the trial of John Peter Zenger and his defense by Andrew Hamilton, quoted at the begining of Chapter 10.

---

[28] *Linder (2021).*

---

[27]Binion, (2020).

Gavin Newsom. Accounts of county officials and petty health department bureaucrats smirking and laughing at the citizens they were accosting to enforce Covid19 restrictions were not uncommon in 2020.

(a) Patrol Boat Enforces State Rules on Lone Paddle Boarder

(b) Afterward In Handcuffs

(c) Governor Newsom (Highlighted) Ignores State Rules

Figure 11.11: **Government Arrogance**

Lest we think such behavior is a statement only about the individuals involved, it is an important question whether the concentration of power itself is an "attractive nuisance" that will lead to arrogance and vindictiveness in the same way the law recognizes that an "attractive nuisance" leads to dangerous behavior by children.[29] The pictures in Figure 11.11 are from California that year. The first

---

[29]Leaving a dangerous open pit on public property bordering where children play is an example of an attractive nuisance.

shows a lone paddle boarder as a patrol boat converges on him. (There were actually two patrol boats at the scene.) The second picture shows him being taken away in handcuffs. The issue was enforcement of new rules announced by the state explained to be for the purpose of preventing viral spread. Science at the time said six feet social distancing was a sufficient countermeasure. The third picture shows Governor Gavin Newsom later in the same year of restrictions, ignoring the state rules and enjoying a party with friends and health department officials at an elite and expensive restaurant. *He* was not handcuffed and removed.

11.2.12   Governmentalism

Conversion of an action better handled by individuals, markets, or voluntary private organizations into a government function with worse or harmful results.

Theoretical ability to execute a task is not a reliable guide to how something should be done in the real world. Government is capable of producing private goods in competition with private producers. But when the government firm starts to founder, will it be allowed to die, even if that is the right outcome, or will it be subsidized from taxes? Will it exhibit the same push for excellence and profit as a private firm? Why should it?

Behold The Politician!
As a species, why are politicians mostly disappointing? Consider their own political jest: *In politics sincerity is everything. If you can fake that, the rest is easy.*

The answer must rest in the options available to the types of people politics attracts and to their incentives. What would you think of the sort described here?
* No occupation except permanent public office holder.
* No special body of knowledge mastered such as medicine, engineering, public finance, business, physics, chemistry, or music.
* Good at speaking and speechmaking. No other particular skills.

- Public office is the best job they will ever have.
- Main pre-occupation is staying in public office.
- If out of power, no profession to return to.

This type would feel overwhelming urgency to do everything to maintain themselves. They would consider cheating if they could get away with it. They would masquerade as needed to divert suspicion. They would enthusiastically support spending public money on giveaways to buy votes, put people onto public programs to be able to describe it as their good works, uncaringly enlarge government taxes and spending as long as their personal interests were helped, encourage greater dependency on such programs, treat the dependent class like chattel ("If you are **X** you must vote for me and my party, because we do more for you."), and consider rigging elections if it helped and could be gotten away with.

Since members of this group have oratorical ability, they often suffer from the "Big Hat, No Cattle" disease. This is the political mis-belief that speaking is same thing as doing. The politician says, "I have worked my whole life on behalf of children" whether they have done anything for children or not. What they mean is, **I have made speeches that mention this topic.**

A second reason government needs to stand apart—not be engaged in actions it should not be engaged in—is the following. Business creates wealth. That is its proper purpose. The nature of business is to relentlessly pursue opportunities for reward. From profits the captains and kings of industry reward themselves. When the patriotic citizen or civic minded group needs to oppose business corruption the struggle is unequal. The firm makes money by its activities, but the civic-minded citizen gains nothing by stopping it. One party makes money from winning, the other earns nothing by opposing. That is a recipe for social failure in repeated confrontations, especially when corruption needs to win just once and is able to hold the *status quo* ever after.

When business needs to be opposed is when people need government and the law to turn to. When they do, what will they find? If compromised government is linked to compromised business, where can the citizen turn?

Behold The Useful Idiot!

Why do people fail to condemn, fail to recognize, and worse, aid and abet government failure? The best explanation seems to be a collection of reasons. The first one is that they personally benefit from the money, programs, and graft that come their way and rationalize that it is justified. Another is existence of the selfish, unaware and indolent wight (see the person described by de Tocqueville on p. 157) but there are others.

Useful Idiots. Communists in the 1950s developed the term "useful idiots" and used it among themselves to describe uninformed, naive, and mentally adolescent supporters who thought they were doing good but did not really understand the policies they worked for.[30] Anarchists, whose goal is *Solve et Coagula* ("dissolve and re-configure") present their idealized new world as the antidote alternative to the flawed real world we inhabit. They do not compare real with real, or idealized with idealized. The credulous are drawn in on the belief that they are helping to create the idealized future described to them, which certainly sounds better than the present real world.

The Self-Seeking. Useful idiots tend to be outside government and (mostly) others-oriented, but there is a second group that causes government failures. Winston Churchill, apparently no admirer, described Prime Minister William Gladstone's policy as, "Keep the peace, stay in office, and let the years roll by." This might be the motto of the caretaker public office holder or administrator-bureaucrat. The objectionable sorts of politicians that we have already described on page 180 want lifetime public office and will do whatever they need to to attain it, because they are not particularly talented or principled, and such office, elected or appointed, is the best job they can get. Staying is their "life." They go along to get along. If this means supporting and participating in government mis-use when it is safe to do so, so be it. The primary difference between the Self-Seeker and the Puppetmasters described next is self-awareness and motivation.

The Puppetmasters. Finally, there are those who seek position, fame, worldly power, and wealth who *intend* to manipulate and subvert as needed. Their actions, often taken covertly to hide their ambition and motives, are knowingly directed to using government and others as they can in false and even wicked ways. The useful idiots and the self-seeking tag-alongs are tools in their plans.

---

[30]Roche, John P. (1984). *The History and Impact of Marxist-Leninist Organizational Theory: "Useful Idiots," "Innocents' Clubs," and "Transmission Belts,"* Cambridge, MA: Institute for Foreign Policy Analysis, January.

11.3 Countermeasures to Government Failure

In this life there never will be perfect government, just as there never will be perfect politicians, but there are measures that emerge from the study of human flourishing and morality that provide guidance about how to moderate government failure. We present a few here.

11.3.1 Honor Tasks Assigned by the Implications of Human Flourishing plus Morality

The first and best countermeasure to government failure is to restrict government to its Pareto-Optimality-and-morality-identified tasks (see Chapter 10 and Table 10.1 on page 120, also the summary on page 122), and to reject the organismic conception (see Section 10.3 on page 122). A review of nearly every government failure reveals that the government is engaged in governmentalism and/or something that is not authorized. In other words, let government do only what it should do, and let other means of collective action do what they should do.

An incomplete list of the most significant ways to prevent government failure that are implications of what we have already learned follows.

11.3.2 Enforce the Core: Every Pot Sits on its Own Base!

Crony capitalism, pension-seeking, polittroughing, vote buying, planned dependency, legalized plunder all have in common that they involve a violation of the Core. Recall that the notion of the Core protects groups in society from harm imposed on them by the rest of society. Essentially, being in the Core means a program "sits on its own base." A program in the Core is supported solely from the taxes of those who benefit from the program, and if a program is in the core no group can withdraw from the program (receive no benefits from it and pay no taxes toward it) and do better for itself by such withdrawal. A group is one or more individuals.

For example, social insurance programs can be established so that *everyone* is better off by participating in the program compared to not participating in it, due to the advantages that insurance and risk-spreading provide. No one group subsidizes the benefits of another group or is subsidized by the taxes on another. If someone does not want to participate, that should be their choice. Freedom to participate or not participate in government programs (we are not talking about public goods) is an important safeguard. Since Ponzi schemes fail to enforce the Core, no government program can be a Ponzi scheme where the payouts to early participants are not covered by their own contributions, but by the contributions of later participants.

Much more can be said about the importance of protecting groups within society using the concept of the Core. It is an overlooked and important concept.

11.3.3   The Intervention Principle

Even when restricted to the tasks identified by the requirements of human flourishing plus morality, and even with every program sitting on its own base, there will be government policy interventions from time to time that government will want to do. By definition, a government policy intervention involves government being unhappy with the level of some quantity and taking some action to cause the quantity to take on a preferred value. If 2,000 tons of pollutant are being dropped into the river, and I want the number to be 0 (or 10, or 100, or 250) then there are multiple ways to accomplish that objective, among which we want to select the best way. Showing what that best way is requires an involved mathematical process that nevertheless leads to a conclusion that can be simply described. We have already touched on this principle in Chapter 6 (see page 82). The following is from Grinols and Henderson, p. 27-28:

The intervention principle states that the most efficient way to accomplish a desired objective in a wide range of circumstances is to identify the margin to be influenced and impose a tax or subsidy narrowly at that margin at the minimal level needed to accomplish the objective.

For example, if the federal government wants all uninsured individuals living east of the Mississippi River to purchase health insurance, it should subsidize insurance purchase for individuals living east of the Mississippi who do not currently purchase it. The intervention should apply only to insurance purchase, only to households east of the Mississippi, only to those households who do not now purchase it, and at the minimum level to achieve the objective.

Notice that the intervention should be *narrowly* targeted to the objective desired. It would be wrong in this example to establish a nationwide program of health care entitlements if the objective is limited. Scatterguns are not the best tool unless a scattergun outcome is the objective. Applying the principle also acts as discipline on the thinking of politicians. Grinols and Henderson continue,

In the early 1970s America faced its first oil crisis, caused by an embargo of Middle East oil producers. Many citizens and political leaders called for less dependence on foreign oil. Various options were suggested, including a tax on gasoline at the pump (reducing consumption of gasoline), subsidies to domestic oil production (increasing domestic oil production), and a tariff on imported oil (reducing import levels). Was our goal to reduce gasoline consumption, increase domestic production, decrease domestic production, reduce imports, or accomplish something else altogether? In reality, the different policy options lead to different outcomes. Some suggested that "independence" meant using foreign oil first, and thereby conserving domestic stocks. The overall objective of "limiting dependence on foreign oil" was too vague to provide much direction. Worse, achieving

one objective in the least cost manner was incompat-
ible with achieving others at least cost. The lesson is
that the path to success involves carefully choosing the
appropriate goals and selecting policies that accomplish
them at least cost to citizens.

If You Cannot Be an Example, You Can Be a Warning

This book differs from most other treatments of economics because
it reaches its conclusions deductively from the principles of human
flourishing and the principles of morality. Chapter 7, for example,
explained that natural law contains the view that humans innately
know certain things are wrong—such as stealing, murder, lying—
and others are right—such as not doing to others what you do not
want them to do to you. Some things, however, must be thought
through carefully.

One of these is the sometimes-made claim that "the principles
of Christianity and Socialism go hand in hand." We have shown
in this book that this cannot be true, if only because socialism is
based on the notion of redistribution, benefitting "one citizen at the
expense of another by doing what the citizen himself cannot do without committing a crime (Bastiat, p. 159)." The socialist principle
"from each according to his ability, to each according to his need"
violates the Golden Rule. Helping one's fellow man through personal
charitable giving does not. (Chapters 8 and 10 discuss individuals,
voluntary private organizations, and assignment of economy tasks).
So why do people say Christianity and Socialism go "hand in hand?"

The Book of Acts records events in the early Christian church.
It is now considered canonical, meaning it is inspired Holy Scrip-
ture. In Acts it says that the members of the early church in
Jerusalem "shared everything they had (Acts 4:32)." Presuming
that this therefore provides an example that we are meant to follow
fails to recall that much of the Bible is simply recorded history, not
meant as an example, but meant as a warning. For a good number
of years after the events of Acts 4, the Bible also records that the
new Christians in Greece and Macedonia were constantly needing
to send charity to Jerusalem, which they willingly and generously
did. There is no presumption that sharing everything in common is

a good idea or a Christian norm.

Those who know the history of the Pilgrims in Plymouth Colony after they arrived in what is now Massachusetts in 1620 likewise know that they came for religious freedom to follow the true dictates of Christianity. They tried socialist farming in their first years, but abandoned it. Their governor William Bradford's history describes what they did and why they ultimately decided against it.

Bradford's own words selected from his personal history *Of Plymouth Plantation*, now an American classic, report what they found. Originally the Pilgrims were to

> have their meat, drink, apparel, and all provisions out of the common stock and goods of the said colony.

This

> was found to breed much confusion and discontent and retard much employment that would have been to the benefit and comfort. For the young men, that were most able and fit for labour and service, did repine that they should spend their time and strength to work for other men's wives and children without any recompense...

They decided to look to other arrangements that

> they might raise as much corn as they could, and obtain a better crop than they had done, that they might not still thus languish in misery,

The new arrangements

> assigned to every family a parcel of land, according to the proportion of their number, for that end.

Bradford reports that,

> This had very good success, for it made all hands very industrious, so as much more corn was planted than otherwise would have been by any means the Governor...could use, and saved him a great deal of trouble,

> and gave far better content. The women now went willingly into the field, and took their little ones with them to set corn; which before would allege weakness and inability; whom to have compelled would have been thought great tyranny and oppression.
>
> ... Instead of famine now God gave them plenty, and the face of things was changed, to the rejoicing of the hearts of many, for which they blessed God.

11.4   Conclusion

The facts of government force onto it a unique position in the economy. Government's primary obligation is to provide safety to its citizens through an army of national defense and through domestic policing and criminal courts. These are public goods and public goods require taxes.

The special position that government enjoys means that people will try to use government to satisfy the motivations that drive them. These can be honorable, but we would be naive not to recognize that greed, gluttony, pride, sloth, lust, envy, and wrath are also present. This chapter, therefore, documented some of the government failures that result from mis-use of government: Crony Capitalism, Pension-Seeking, Directly Unproductive Profit-Seeking, Vote Buying and Polittroughing, Planned Dependency, Paternalism, Legalized Plunder, Government Planning Failure, Friedman's Law, Graft and Corruption, Arrogance and Conceit, and Governmentalism. One could say that demand for graft is naturally to be expected in the private sector, and that supply of graft is naturally to be expected in the public sector.

In some cases, such as Directly Unproductive Profit-Seeking, Government Planning Failure, and Friedman's Law, we can discern economic reasons why the information available to government, the options available to it, and the incentives that apply to it incline government to certain kinds of failure.

So what can be done? We ended with important counter measures to government failure. Chapters 12, 14 and Chapter 11 of Part 2 should also be consulted.

Last, in view of the many examples of government failure, it is right to recall our disclaimer at the outset that there are and have been "statesmen" in government. Government has no money of its own and no people of its own, just offices that are occupied by individuals. Our point has been that some government failure is inherent to the institution of government, but some is the failure of particular kinds of people who hold offices, who public office attracts, and who misuse the power they have. This is why we do not grant too much. Throughout history there have been good people in national government—George Washington, Abraham Lincoln, Grover Cleveland, William McKinley, Calvin Coolidge, John Kennedy, and Ronald Reagan make my list—perhaps you would add others. There is probably also a long list of high quality office holders and officials whose names we will never know.

REFERENCES

Bartiromo, Maria (2020). "Candace Owens: Democrats Want Black Americans Dependent on Government Policies," *Sunday Morning Futures with Maria Bartiromo*, 'The Candace Owens Show' host reacts to the president's Black economic empowerment plan on 'Sunday Morning Futures', Fox News Channel, September 27. Online at https://video.foxnews.com/v/6195035834001#sp=show-clips.

Bastiat, Frederic. *The Government.* The title of this piece is usually translated from the French as *The Law*, but more accurately describes what modern usage would call the government.

_____. "What is Seen and What is Not Seen," reprinted in *Selected Essays on Political Economy I*, George B. de Huszar, ed., 1995.

Becker, Gary S. "Are We Hurting or Helping the Disabled?" *Business Week*, 2 August 1999, 21.

Bhagwati, Jagdish. "Directly Unproductive, Profit-Seeking (DUP) Activities," *The Journal of Political Economy*, 90, 5, October 1982, 988-1002.

Binion, B. (2020) "Michigan Supreme Court Strikes Down Gov. Gretchen Whitmer's COVID-19 Executive Orders," *Reason* news, 5 October. Online at: https://reason.com/2020/10/05/michigan-supreme-court-strikes-down-gov-gretchen-whitmers-covid-19-executive-orders/.

Bradford, William (1651). *Of Plymouth Plantation*. Boston: Commonwealth of Massachusetts, 1998. (Many modern editions have been published.)

Cole, Harold L. and Lee E. Ohanian. "New Deal Policies and the Persistance of the Great Depression: A General Equilibrium Analysis," *Journal of Political Economy,* 112, 41, 2004, 779-816.

_____. "How Government Prolonged the Depression," *Wall Street Journal*, 2 February 2009, online at https://www.wsj.com/articles/SB123353276749137485.

Chapman, Michael W. "Democrats Introduce Bill to Prevent Trump From Being Buried at Arlington," *CNS News*, 18 February 2021. https://cnsnews .com/ article/washington/michael-w-chapman/ democrats-introduce-bill-prevent-trump-being-buried-arlington

Committee for Economic Development. *Crony Capitalism: Unhealthy Relations Between Business and Government*, A White Paper by the Committee for Economic Development of The Conference Board, Arlington, VA: CED, October 2015, pp. 1-44.

Coren, Courtney. "Dick Morris: Obama Wants to Turn US Into Japan, Mexico." *Newsmax*, 24 September 2014.

de Tocqueville, Alexis, "Government of the Democracy in America," Chapter 13 in *Democracy in America*, 1835, 1840.

_____. *Democracy in America*, Harvey Mansfield and Delba Winthrop, trans. Chicago: University of Chicago Press, 2000, p. 663.

Foley, Duncan. "Lindahl's Solution and the Core of an Economy with Public Goods," *Econometrica*, 38, 1, January 1970, 66-71.

Friedman, Milton. *Capitalism and Freedom*. Chicago: University of Chicago Press,1962.

Grinols, Earl L. *Gambling in America: Costs and Benefits.* New York: Cambridge University Press, 2009.

Grinols, Earl L. and James W. Henderson. *Health Care for Us All: Getting More for Our Investment.* New York: Cambridge University Press, 2009.

Hayek, Friedrich. "Preface," *The Road to Serfdom,* Fiftieth Anniversary Edition, Chicago: University of Chicago Press, 1994.

Hopper, Mike. "Pennies are Useless, Here's Why the Government Keeps Making Them," *Economy,* Generation Opportunity, 21 February 2016, https://generationopportunity.org/articles/2016/02/21/pennies-are-useless-heres-why-the-government-keeps-making-them/.

Hudson, Jerome. (2016) "Eleven Great Thomas Sowell Quotes," *Breitbart News,* 28 December. Online at: https://www.breitbart.com/politics/2016/12/28/11-great-thomas-sowell-quotes/.

Huntington, Tom (2006). "The Profiteers of the Civil War," Originally published in the February 2006 issue of Civil War Times. Online: https://www.historynet.com/the-profiteers-of-the-civil-war.htm.

Leonard, Thomas C., Robert S. Goldfarb, Steven M. Suranovic. "[Wm.] New on Paternalism and Public Policy," *Economics and Philosophy,* 16, 2000, pp. 323-331.

King, Martin Luther. "Letter from a Birmingham Jail," 16 April 1963.

Kroll, Emily. "My Take: Hypocricy is the Word of the Day," *Sentinel,* Holland City, 27 May 2020. https://www.hollandsentinel.com/opinion/20200527/ my-take-hypocrisy-is-word-of-day

Krueger, Anne. (1974) "The Political Economy of the Rent-Seeking Society," *American Economic Review,* 64, April/May, 291-303.

Linder, Douglas O. (2021). "The Trial of John Peter Zenger: An Account," *Famous Trials,* Online: https://famous-trials.com/zenger/87-home.

McClanahan, B. *9 Presidents who Screwed Up America and Four Who Tried to Save Her,* Washington: Regnery History, 2018, pp.242-42.

McCullough, David. *The Pioneers.* New York: Simon & Schuster, 2019.

Meredith, James. "A Challenge to Change," *Newsweek*, 6 October 1997, p. 18.

Olohan, Mary M. "Whitmer Does Not Deny That Her Husband Sought Special Treatment Over Boating On Memorial Day Weekend," *Daily Caller*, 26 May 2020. https://dailycaller.com/2020/ 05/26/ gretchen-whitmer-husband-special-treatment-boat-memorial-day-coronavirus/

Sachs, Jeffrey. *The Next Money Crash*, Bloomington, IN: iUniverse, 2014.

Schlaes, Amity. "The Rules of the Game and Economic Recovery," *Imprimis*, 39, 9, September 2010.

Sheehy, Kate. "Embattled Michigan Governor in Hot Water Over Hubby's Boat Request," *New York Post* 25 May 2020. https:// nypost.com/ 2020/05/25/ michigan-gov-gretchen-whitmer -in-hot-water- over-husbands- boat-request/

Stepman, Jarrett. "This Case Against Western Ranchers Shows Why Americans Are Right to Fear Government," *The Daily Signal*, 8 January 2018, https://www.dailysignal.com/2018/01/08/ unprofessional-case- western-ranchers-shows-americans-right-fear-government/.

Stiglitz, Joseph. *The Price of Inequality*, New York: W. W. Norton and Company, 2012.

Traverse City Eagle. "There Can't Be Two Standards," Editorial: Traverse City Eagle. 2 August 2020. https://www.record-eagle.com/ opinion/ editorial-there-cant-be-two-standards/ article_74eb3450-d414 -11ea-8693- 9798eb7932b2.html

Tullock, Gordon. "Efficient Rent-Seeking," in *Toward a Theory of the Rent-seeking Society,* edited by James M. Buchanan, Robert D. Tollison, and Gordon Tullock. College Station: Texas A & M University Press, 1980.

Unruh, Bob. "State Fines Couple $4.1 million for Gate on Own Property," *World Net Daily,* https://

www.wnd.com/2019/02/state-fines-couple-4-1-million-for-gate-on-own-property/, 17 February 2019.

West, E. G. (1967). "The Political Economy of American Public School Legislation," *The Journal of Law and Economics*, October, 101-128.

Wimble, Lorie. "Gretchen Whitmer's lockdown hypocricy is the modern Democratic Party in a nutshel," TextitNOQ Report, 5 June 2020. https:// noqreport.com/2020/06/05/ gretchen-whitmers-lockdown-hypocrisy- is-the-modern-democratic- party-in-a- nutshell/

Chapter 12

"The Rules"

Follow the rules, or follow the fools.

Tupac Shakur, American Rapper

In this book's terminology, *essential economics* are the instructions that tell society how it should organize its economic affairs to produce greatest human flourishing. This code of essential economics needs to be augmented by morality if it is to offer a complete guide.

Restated, economics *without* morality is incapable of providing a complete guide to social organization. A necessary condition for morality is the Golden Rule, which has been our working principle and starting point for deductions about morality.[1]

In this chapter we summarize what we have learned. We emulate Naval Criminal Investigative Service (NCIS) field agent, Leroy Jethro Gibbs who created for himself a list of straightforward rules that he followed ardently in his life and work.

12.1 Gibbs Rules

The television series *NCIS: Naval Criminal Investigative Service* follows the actions of a team of NCIS special agents led by the charismatic Leroy Jethro Gibbs. Gibbs is like a modern Sherlock Holmes

---

[1]Recall our terminology. If proposition A implies proposition B ($A \Rightarrow B$) we say that B is a *necessary* condition for A. A implies B is logically equivalent to *Not B* implies *Not A* ($\sim B \Rightarrow \sim A$). If A implies B, and B implies A, then B is a *necessary and sufficient* condition for A ($A \Leftrightarrow B$).

Figure 12.1: **Mark Harmon as NCIS Agent Leroy Jethro Gibbs**

figure. By the tenth season NCIS was the most watched television series in the United States and later became one of the longest running and most successful in history. *"Give it to me in English"* is Gibbs' response to receiving technical information about complex subject matter "forcing the expert to get to the point, as well as making it easy for the audience to understand."[2]

> Gibbs follows a series of at least 51 rules, which he appears to have memorized, that apply to life situations and casework....

His rules were like Rule 9: "Never go anywhere without a knife" or Rule 1 "Never screw over your partner."[3] We need only a baker's dozen. Section 12.3 shows how the 13 rules apply to an unresolved real world policy issue. Another application to real world policy is found in Chapter 10 of Part 2.

---

[2]Television character Leroy Jethro Gibbs even has his own Wikipedia page, from which the information above was taken: https://en.wikipedia.org/wiki/Leroy_Jethro_Gibbs

[3]Emulating Gibbs seems appropriate. "Leroy" is Gibbs' unused name. It is my unused name. Gibbs was born on May 2. I was born on May 2. Gibbs likes being direct. I like being direct. Gibbs knows his craft.

12.2 The Rules of Essential Economics ("The Rules")

Rules are in bold. The additions underneath are explanations.

1. You own yourself.
You own the product of your own labor.

2. Pay fully for what you take from society. Be fully paid for what you provide.
Competitive prices apply. Competitive markets enforce natural justice: If you take double, you pay double. If you take half, you pay half. If you take nothing, you pay nothing. Similar justice applies to work supplied and pay.

3. Not paying one's debt is stealing.
If you take now and pay now, that is a spot transaction. If you pay now and receive later, that is a futures transaction. If you take now, but do not pay now, you have incurred a debt.

4. Private goods are best produced and distributed in competitive private markets.
The First and Second Fundamental Theorems of Welfare Economics apply. No other method is superior.

5. Competition is the only reliable way to keep prices as low as possible.
Competition is the policeman of the marketplace. The policeman is needed to keep prices low.

6. Markets muddle from time to time. It takes government to massively mess up for long term misery.
Competition means that individual firms and households are not large enough to do massive sustained damage to the entire system.

7. The larger government is relative to the economy, the more harm it can do and the larger the push to use it for corruption.

8. Good policy is in the Core.

The Core (see pages 77 and 183 in Part 1 and 333 and 334 in Part 2) protects the group against unjust social arrangements, just as voluntary exchange protects the individual. No group, able to be identified in advance, should be in a position that by withdrawing from society or a government program it can do better for itself by such withdrawal.

9. Pareto Optimality and morality imply benefits-principle taxes.

The easiest case to identify is when the individual's tax is used in a way that provides the payer zero benefits. In that case, the tax is zero. Another implication is that in principle the total tax paid by an individual is determined by the sum of benefits received by that individual from government activity.

10. It is government's job to enforce appropriate property rights.

Property rights protect the individual, markets, and the economy. Absence of appropriate property rights can cause the absence of a market and lead to externalities.

11. Business investment is not a government job.

Investment by government leads to Crony Capitalism. Citizens forced to feel the pain of a bad choice by government are not the ones who chose it. Government, who made the bad choice, does not feel the pain of it.

12. Government should not engage in theft. Forced charity is theft.

The Golden Rule and the Core require voluntary charity. Every individual should engage in charity and has unlimited freedom to give to charity as much as he or she wants plus unlimited freedom to join with others in Voluntary Private Organizations to get more done. The right amount of charity is the total that informed individuals choose to give. Everyone has a personal duty to be generous with his or her money, labor, and time. Government may appropriately facilitate and inform about needs if economic efficiency is improved thereby.

13. Society consists of individuals. No organismic overarching government objective exists.

Attempting to implement an overarching organismic objective is inconsistent with the joint implications of Pareto Optimality and morality.

12.3 Property Rights in Yourself and Paying for College

Paying for college can be expensive. Nearly every father and mother do not have enough money to pay for their childrens' college. This has caused some to want to violate Rules 1 and 2. Rule 2 is violated because they want to vote themselves a free college education that they do not pay for, and Rule 1 is violated because they want to take the fruit of someone else's labor to pay for it, thus denying that the other person owns himself or herself. There is, however, a proper way to pay for college that the Rules support.

At the college level, education is a rival good that benefits the recipient, has no externalities,[4] and is therefore a private good. To the extent that college is a consumption good (a time to enjoy and learn from campus life with other college students), it benefits the person who consumes it and is a private good. To the extent that it is an investment good, it again benefits the person whose human capital is augmented and is still a private good. How should an expensive private good be paid for?

When a business enterprise needs outside money for expansion, the firm can issue debt or equity. Issuing debt amounts to borrowing the needed money and repaying it to the lender with interest on a fixed schedule. The lender is given priority to be paid from the firm's future stream of earnings. Issuing equity means giving the provider

---

[4]We have already debunked the false view, for example, that a college educated engineer is more valuable to a firm and the firm therefore has an obligation to help pay for the engineer's education. The firm already pays more for the engineer in the form of the higher market wage that engineers earn, and since the engineer benefits from the higher wage that his or her degree leads to, and no one else, the engineer should fully pay for the investment in the engineering degree. No externality is present, so no side payments are called for.

of money a share of the company's returns (its future profits if there are any, nothing if there are none[5]) where the size of the share is determined by the share of the firm's total capital (money used for set up) that the equity holder provided.

Students now can borrow to pay for college (issue debt) but the threat is that the fixed amount and interest on it will saddle them with unacceptable payments into an endless future. What if the student's future jobs are bad or he is laid off? Instead of "issuing debt," why can't the student issue equity? The answer is that an equity market for college education does not exist. Why does it not exist?

Figure 12.2: **Dr. Ben Carson**

From Chapter 6 we know that the existence of externalities indicates the absence of a market, and that the absence of a market indicates the absence of enforceable property rights. Rule 9 says it

---

[5]If there are negative future earnings, the modern limited liability corporation is capable of going bankrupt, but the shareholders' private assets are shielded. Why has this arrangement arisen? Because the shareholder is not the decision maker whose choices result in the bankruptcy. The corporation knows what it is doing (or should), and those dealing with the corporation know what the risks of dealing with the corporation are (or should). Therefore the parties with the best ability to take right actions bear the burden of their own decisions. No Buffalo over the cliff problem (page 164).

is government's job to enforce appropriate property rights. We are nearly done with respect to knowing what to do about the high cost of college education. To find that answer consider the life story of Dr. Ben Carson.

Ben Carson grew up in poverty in Detroit, became a neurosurgeon, ran for president, and later became Secretary of Housing and Urban Development. Why was he unable to offer to a lender a fixed share of his future high income as a brain surgeon in return for money now to pay tuition? No legal ability to write such a contract, called an *Income Sharing Arrangement (ISA)*, existed. In an ISA the lender would verify Carson's academic ability and prospects, pay the tuition, and get paid an agreed share of Carson's future income for an agreed period of time. *The benefit to Carson would be that after the specified passage of time, he would know with certainty that his college is paid off.* Medical school is hugely expensive. If Carson slipped on a banana peel after graduation, broke both hands and never became a surgeon, his college *still* would be paid off at the pre-specified time. With ISAs, any smart Ben Carson would be able to attend college and pay for it himself. College funding would then come from funded scholarships, interest-free loans, loans, and ISAs. Parents' income no longer matters.

Property Rights in Yourself
Making it possible to pay for college using income sharing arrangements through establishing appropriate property rights is just one way that government helps the economy. As noted on page 115, changing one's cell phone service once required losing your phone number. Since people did not want all their friends, business partners, and others to lose their phone number this fact acted to restrain competition until the law was changed to let consumers retain their phone numbers.

Free flow of information is a fundamental requirement of competition and therefore the responsibility of government to maintain. Congress did not always understand the obligation to maintain the conditions for competition. In the Robber Baron era of the late 1800s cartels, combinations, and monopolies ruled over vast parts of the economic landscape.

In the modern era of online activities and the internet, the Robber Baron threat takes a different form. Tech Giants, Facebook, Twitter, Amazon, Google, and other information purveyors that engage in surveillance of private electronic devices act in restraint of trade when they censor and mis-use the free flow of information. Once again it is government's job to guarantee freedom of information and lack of censorship.[6] As long as speech— even if it is misguided, unpleasant, mocking, satirical, self-serving, and wrong—does not specifically call for sedition it is a First-Amendment-protected right of everyone.

Do you own your own postings and data? We have asked these questions before. Do you own the information that is about yourself? Can you force a company to send you whatever data it may have collected that involves you personally, do so in a form that can be used by you or otherwise serve your interests and the interests of competition, and prohibit its further use if you so choose? It is the obligation of government to establish and support property rights.

---

[6] See Josh Hawley, *The Tyranny of Big Tech*, (2021).

There are naturally many details that government will have to decide when it sets the needed property rights for ISA markets. What do lenders want? They need to know that contracts are enforceable in the courts and be able to provide themselves assurance that they will be repaid. For example, they need to be able to verify the income on which future payments depend, ISA recipients need to be trackable after graduation, and so on. What do students want? They want tuition in return for future payments that bear a fair proportion of future earnings and on terms that guarantee they are free of debt at the agreed future date. This ISAs will do.

We do not envision a student selling 100 percent of future income for 100 percent of future life since that sounds like a form of slavery. Also, who pays the taxes on the stream of income once it has been sold? These are property rights details, which government needs to settle to establish the ISA college market.

12.4 Conclusion

The Rules of Essential Economics say in simple English what human flourishing and morality require to be true of society's social structures. Human flourishing implies Pareto Optimality and morality implies the Golden Rule. Pareto Optimality and the Golden Rule imply the rules.

The logical sequence that leads to the rules bears repeating: Human Flourishing requires economic flourishing, which implies Pareto Optimality, which is equivalent to competitive equilibrium, which implies necessary conditions. From these we get descriptions of consumers, producers, private goods, public goods, club goods, prices, taxes that must apply, and assignments for markets, VPOs, and government. Fairness and equality of opportunity emerge from competitive equilibria and Pareto Optimality. In the case of taxes for publicly provided public goods, Pareto Optimality implies benefits-principle taxes. The payment is determined by the benefits the payer receives from the public good. These are the connections pursued in Chapters 1 through 11.

Morality enters in its own right, primarily in describing one's right to the fruits of one's own labor. One's property is that which one has mixed one's labor with to produce something of greater value. Taking another's property by force is stealing and violates the Golden Rule. Forcing another's wealth or income down to a level one's actions show by revealed preference one does not want for oneself also violates the Golden Rule. Taxes used in a way that provides no benefits to the payer violate the Golden Rule. This last conclusion is proved in Chapter 7 of Part 2.

References

Hawley, Josh (2021). *The Tyranny of Big Tech*, Washington, D.C.: Regnery Publishing.

Chapter 13

Charity and the American Ethical Base

While the people should patriotically and cheerfully support their Government its functions do not include the support of the people.

Grover Cleveland, Second Inaugural Address

This chapter extends our study of morality from the historical perspective. Specifically, we consider the ethical base of the United States in the 18th, 19th and 20th centuries through 1929. 1929 is a pivotal year economically. Why it is also pivotal ethically will be made evident before we finish this chapter.

Though we take an historical approach, our purpose is to shed light on an economic problem, which is how needy economic individuals, including those who may not have the physical capability of providing for themselves as fully autonomous adults, should fare. It is important to note at the outset that with rare exceptions throughout history, this group tends to be exceedingly small, one percent or less of the population. Even if the number is much less than one percent, however, we want to avoid two mistakes. The first mistake would be failure to recognize that this can be a lot of people. The incapable needy will be among us in any reasonably-sized society and need to be accounted for in any description of social

205

arrangements.[1] The second mistake would be to think that national policy for the 99 must be dictated by the 1. For example, it violates the intervention principle to construct a national entitlement system of universal health care and health care insurance because a needy 1 percent cannot pay for the true cost of the health care they take from society. We take up this question specifically in Part 2 Chapter 10.

A major divide hinges on the organismic versus the individualistic approach to government described by Nobel laureate James Buchanan and first introduced on page 122. Our position has been that actions violating morality and the Golden Rule are failures of the individual, but system design can encourage or discourage such violations. Historically, the Jeffersonian, Whig and later the Republican Parties in the United States have been individualistic, while Democrats have been organismic. What systemic moral failures have been associated with each? We provide a short list in Part 2 Section 11.1 and explain our assignments. But first, we take up the problem of needy individuals and the historical way in which they have been regarded.

13.1   The Irreducible Problem of the Needy

We proceed by producing a taxonomy of the needy. The first description we consider, of course, is the state itself of being needy or unneedy. By describing someone as "needy," we mean an individual who is unable to pay for the goods and services he or she takes from society. Needy individuals are the object of this chapter's interest. Related to the state of being needy or unneedy, however, are other factors. One is whether the individual is *capable* of taking action to exit the state of being needy. An individual capable of leaving the needy state by his or her own exertions has the volition to leave the needy state. We may thus wish to limit attention to the incapable needy.

We continue with two more factors. In non-agrarian settings, education is important to one's ability to provide for oneself. We therefore ask if an individual has been educated to some threshhold

---

[1]Moreover, no matter what we do for needy economic people, the credible information available to us is that we will have them with us always.

standard.[2] Has he or she been *equipped*, in the terminology of Chapter 10?

Finally, is the individual *deserving* to be the recipient of aid from the system? Some readers may say the "needy undeserving" category is an empty set. Others may disagree. We leave any thought of defining deserving and undeserving, or removing them from the screening grid entirely, to others.

The following list displays our resulting groups.

1. **Unneedy-needy:** These are outcomes, the presence or absence of being economically independent.
2. **Capable-incapable:** These refer to ability, the state of being able to be economically independent.
3. **Equipped-unequipped:** These are treatments, the endowing of an individual with the tools of economic independence.
4. **Deserving-undeserving:** This involves the decision to grant unearned *systemic* aid (aid from the system). It is an unemotional final screen. The terminology is not pejorative and does not mean classified individuals are unworthy of compassion or private charity.

Four bilateral classifications—and there obviously can be variations on how the screen is described—result in $2 \times 2 \times 2 \times 2 = 16$ categories. Figure 13.1 arranges these to produce a decision tree. We dispense with the unequipped category first. Developing economies and many less advanced societies do not adequately provide for the equipping of children prior to adulthood. In this book we have explained that education at some standardized level probably has true positive externalities, though these have never been measured and current arrangements probably greatly over compensate for them.[3] Members of society at large, to the extent that they personally benefit from the education of another family's child, should pay the

---

[2]In agrarian economies, ownership of land is the key ingredient to providing for oneself. Land plus personal exertion implies being able to provide for oneself. Absence of land, or absence of personal exertion, or both, implies neediness. Education serves a similar role: Education plus personal exertion implies non-neediness.

[3]Providing free education at no cost to the parents and student is certainly overcompensation, since positive educational benefits accrue to the student himself or herself, and the presence of externalities implies only that others contribute toward *some* of the total costs.

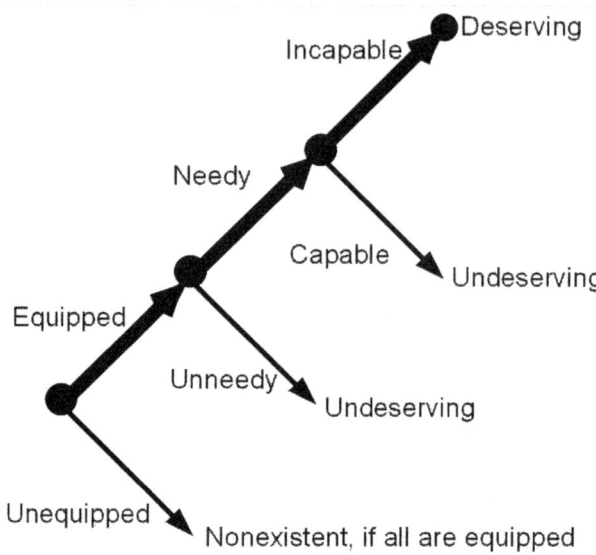

Figure 13.1: **Charity Screening**

appropriate (probably relatively small) portion of that level of education. The rest of the costs and the costs of education beyond that level is a private good that can be financed by the individual receiving the education. For these discussions see page 121 in Chapter 10 and page 199 in Chapter 12. Money from parents, interest-free loans,[4] private scholarship funds, debt, and equity, and earnings from the student himself or herself are the list of sources of the money from which *every* individual's private-good component of education can be paid. Whether his or her parents are rich or poor, *every* individual can get the education he or she needs to whatever level their desire, ability, and initiative take them. Anyone who wants more to be done for the education of others' children is always free to contribute to the appropriate scholarship funds of their choice. In view of this list of arrangements, we presume in what follows that *everyone* is equipped.[5]

---

[4]If interest-free loans are made available, correction for price-level changes between time of receipt and time of repayment are not interest.

[5]Because the economic science that we have been pursuing is at variance with longstanding practice, the following point cannot be over emphasized. Removing waste in the current system means more is available to spend. In addition

In Figure 13.1, therefore, we proceed up the "Equipped" arrow of the decision tree to consider the state of being needy or unneedy. By definition, we presume that an unneedy individual is "undeserving," by which we mean is granted no systemic aid beyond what other individuals might voluntarily choose to provide. We therefore proceed up the "Needy" arrow of the decision tree.

The next filter has to do with equipped-needy-capable individuals or equipped-needy-incapable individuals. Since equipped-needy-capable individuals can leave the needy state on their own volition, we again presume they are "undeserving." We therefore move up the "Incapable" arrow.

Of the sixteen groups, only the equipped-needy-incapable-deserving remain, and they should be granted aid from the system. Whose responsibility, consistent with Pareto Optimality and morality, is it to provide the identified aid? Markets? Government? Individuals? VPOs? Before answering in Section 13.5, we turn to history.

13.2 New World Advancements in Thinking

The United States was founded on July 4, 1776 when the Continental Congress issued the Declaration of Independence. The political break from Great Britain also represented an exceptional break from old world thinking about class structure, rule by oligarchs, nobles, tyranny and monarchy. The physical separation of Americans on a distant continent produced in them the need for self-governance, self-defense, and self-reliance that caused their founders to maintain a different and peculiar perspective. We consider that perspective in Chapter 14 as it relates to how well or how poorly the provisions of the original US Constitution provided for and supported the *essential economics* and morality treated in this book. In this section we investigate documents that describe the American ethical base as it relates to the needy.

---

to having more to spend, better allocating what *is* spent further improves the educational outcome. An enormously better educational outcome is possible, but going half way in the right direction is as good as wrong. Any half-way partial fix to education funding that fails to make it possible *for every* individual, as an individual, rich or poor, regardless of family background, to obtain education appropriate to his or her wants, abilities, and motivation is not fix enough. We have explained in several places what the full fix entails.

13.2.1   The Founding Generation to 1929

We start with the founding generation, meaning those that wrote the Constitution, include early presidents some of whom were also founders, add individuals such as Congressman Davy Crockett, and augment these with selected material. Clearly a nearly unlimited number of prominent and widely recognized individuals for their time could be selected, but these are sufficient for our purposes to show the existence of a particular style of American thinking.

Benjamin Franklin

Present at the signing of the Declaration of Independence and the US Constitution was the polymath Benjamin Franklin (1706-1790). At age 70, he was the oldest leader present at the Declaration's signing. Among his many pursuits, Franklin was a printer and a writer. In 1766 he published in the *London Chronicle* an article titled, "On the Price of Corn and the Management of the Poor."[6] Our interest is his views on the management of the poor. Great Britain had recently imposed restrictions that included embargoes on the export of wheat or wheat flour for the purpose of reducing its price internally. The policy obviously violates the intervention principle (it is not narrowly targeted to the objective, relief of the poor), harms farmers, mis-aligns price incentives for production, and is overly costly by "wasting" help through lowering prices to the unneedy. Franklin wisely comments on the misguided incentives it creates. The entire document is recommended for what it reveals about Franklin's genius and understanding of economics. It is only five pages in its entirety so easy to read, but the key statement is the following:

> For my own part, I am not so well satisfied of the good-
> ness of this thing. I am for doing good to the poor, but
> I differ in opinion about the means. I think the best
> way of doing good to the poor, is, not making them
> *easy in* poverty, but leading or driving them *out* of it. In
> my youth I travelled much, and I observed in different
> countries, that the more public provisions were made for

---

[6]Franklin, 1766, p. 355.

the poor, the less they provided for themselves, and of course became poorer. And, on the contrary, the less was done for them, the more they did for themselves, and became richer. (Emphasis in original).

Presidents

Familiar with Locke, the founding generation understood the importance of property rights to the individual and groups, and were protective of them. To take from one individual or group for the purpose of giving to another violated the laws of property, and was wrong. They believed in aid to the needy *and* in the rights of property. Morality explicitly entered into their thinking. Historians consider President John Adams to be a Father of the Constitution:

> The moment the idea is admitted into society that property is not as sacred as the laws of God, and that there is not a force of law and public justice to protect it, anarchy and tyranny commence.

> If "Thou shalt not covet" and "Thou shalt not steal" were not commandments of Heaven, they must be made inviolable precepts in every society before it can be civilized or made free.[7]

Thomas Jefferson, first president in the 19th century of the still-young republic, wrote the Declaration of Independence, and was minister to France at the signing of the Constitution in 1787. His vision of the federal government was circumscribed.

> **Congress has not unlimited powers to provide for the general welfare,** but only those specifically enumerated. (Emphasis added.)

> A wise and frugal government ... shall restrain men from injuring one another, shall leave them otherwise free to regulate their own pursuits of industry and improvement, and **shall not take from the mouth of**

---

[7]Adams, 1787.

> **labor the bread it has earned.** This is the sum of good government. (Emphasis added.)[8]

> To take from one ... to spare [give] to others ... is to **violate arbitrarily the first principle of association,** the guarantee to everyone the free exercise of his industry and the fruits acquired by it. (Emphasis added.)[9]

James Madison, more than any other individual, deserves the title *Father of the US Constitution.* He took daily notes of debates and produced the only complete history of the constitutional convention. He authored (with Alexander Hamilton and John Jay) *The Federalist Papers,* writing 29 out of 85, which have become the standard commentary authority on the Constitution. John Marshall, Chief Justice of the Supreme Court, said that if eloquence included "persuasion by convincing, Mr. Madison was the most eloquent man I ever heard."

> "The government of the United States is a definite government, confined to specified objects. It is not like state governments, whose powers are more general. **Charity is no part of the legislative duty of the government.**" (Emphasis added.)[10]

In 1794, Congress appropriated $15,000 for relief of French refugees who fled from insurrection in San Domingo to Baltimore and Philadelphia, Madison spoke on the floor to object saying,

> **I cannot undertake to lay my finger on that article of the Constitution which granted a right to Congress of expending, on the objects of benevolence, the money of their constituents.**[11]

He was consistent on other occasions and after becoming president.

> **If Congress can do whatever in their discretion** can be done by money, and will promote the general welfare,

---

[8] Jefferson, 1801.
[9] Jefferson, 1816.
[10] Madison, 1794a.
[11] Madison, 1794b.

the **government is no longer a limited one possessing enumerated powers,** but an indefinite one subject
to particular exceptions. (Emphasis added.)[12]

With respect to the two words "general welfare," I have
always regarded them as **qualified by the detail of
powers connected with them.** To take them in a
literal and unlimited sense would be a metamorphosis of
the Constitution into a character which there is a host of
proofs was not contemplated by its creators. (Emphasis
added.)[13]

For the remainder of the century various presidents periodically rejected the use of federal tax monies for anything that was not general
welfare (a topic to which we return in Chapter 14) for the same reason they rejected federal spending for charity. James K. Polk was
the 11th president:

To the House of Representatives: I have considered the
bill entitled "An act making appropriations for the improvement of certain harbors and rivers" ... many of
them of a local character ...

**The Constitution has not, in my judgment, con-
ferred upon the Federal Government the power to
construct works of internal improvement within the
States**...

**the deliberately expressed judgment of the people
have denied the existence of such a power under
the Constitution.**...

**my predecessors have denied its existence in the
most solemn forms.** (Emphasis added.)[14]

Franklin Pierce was the 14th president:

The question presented, therefore, clearly is ... that of
providing for the care and support of all those among

---

[12]Madison, 1792.
[13]Madison, 1831.
[14]Polk, 1846.

the people of the United States who by any form of calamity become fit objects of public philanthropy.

I readily and, I trust, feelingly acknowledge the duty incumbent on us all as men and citizens, and as among the highest and holiest of our duties, to provide for those who, in the mysterious order of Providence, are subject to want and to disease of body or mind; but **I can not find any authority in the Constitution for making the Federal Government the great almoner of public charity throughout the United States.** To do so would, in my judgment, be contrary to the letter and spirit of the Constitution and subversive of the whole theory upon which the Union of these States is founded. (Emphasis added.)[15]

Grover Cleveland (1885-89, 1893-97), quoted at the heading of this chapter, was the 22nd president. We explained his opposition to unearned government pensions on page 147. On the occasion of the Texas Seed Bill, which Cleveland vetoed in 1887, he did not let sympathy or emotionalism override justice. His message to Congress explained,

I can find no warrant for such an appropriation in the Constitution; and I do not believe that the power and duty of the General Government ought to be extended to the **relief of individual suffering which is in no manner properly related to the public service or benefit.**...

the lesson should be constantly enforced that, though **the people support the Government, the Government should not support the people.** (Emphasis added.)[16]

Cleveland was not against charity. In fact the opposite was true. According to historian Robert Higgs, "he suggested that if members of Congress really wanted to send seed to the suffering Texans, the congressmen might personally carry out this charitable transfer by

---

[15]Pierce, 1854.

[16]*Cleveland, 1875*

using the seed routinely provided to all members for distribution to their constituents (at an expense of $100,000 in that fiscal year).[17]

Congressman David Crockett, discussed in the next section, likewise thought congressmen had the right to distribute their own money in personal charity and offered to join with them to do so, but they did not have the right to hand out others' money for that use.

In 1896 Democrat candidate for President, William Jennings Bryan, expressed his views in a pamphlet prepared in conjunction with the National Convention in Chicago. Bryan described himself as a man who "denies the right of any government to take from any man by means of taxation any money not needed for government expenses or to tax one man to enrich another."[18]

Examples can be added, but they tend to diminish after our watershed year of 1929. Perhaps the most famous is the well known inaugural address injunction by President John Kennedy in 1961 "Ask *not* what your country can do for you, ask what *you* can do for your country."

By the era of President Calvin Coolidge (1923-29), a man who strongly believed in charity, "the big-government horse was already out of the barn."[19] President Franklin Roosevelt thereafter ushered in the era of big government and entitlement programs, a topic relevant to the content of Chapter 14.

Davy Crockett

A remarkable story comes to us that describes the opinions and personal integrity of David Crockett[20] in his service to the nation as a US Congressman. Better known for service to his country at the Alamo in 1836, a lesser known contribution has to do with his three terms in Congress (1827-35) and his views about the public's money. Here is the story.

In the House of Representatives where Crockett served, a bill appropriating money to go to the widow of a naval officer from the

---

[17] Ibid.

[18] Bryan, 1896.

[19] Higgs, 2003.

[20] Though he is known to history as Davy Crockett, he himself never used the name "Davy."

Figure 13.2: **Congressman David Crockett, 1834**

War of 1812 was taken up. Speeches had been made in its support more "because it afforded the speakers a fine opportunity for display than from the necessity of convincing anybody, for it seemed to me that everybody favored it."[21] The Speaker was about to call the vote when Crockett rose. "Everybody expected, of course, that he was going to make one of his characteristic speeches in support of the bill." Instead, he said,

> Mr. Speaker—I have as much respect for the memory of the deceased, and as much sympathy for the sufferings of the living, if suffering there be, as any man in this House, but we must not permit our respect for the dead or our sympathy for a part of the living to lead us into an act of injustice to the balance of the living....**Some eloquent appeals have been made to us upon the ground that it is a debt due the deceased.** Mr. Speaker, the deceased lived long after the close of the war; he was in office to the day of his death, and I have never heard that the Government was in arrears to him. This Government can owe no debts but for services rendered, and at a stipulated price....**I do not**

---

[21]Ellis, 1884, p. 138.

wish to be rude, but I must be plain. Every man in this House knows it is not a debt. We cannot, without the grossest corruption, appropriate this money as the payment of a debt. We have not the semblance of authority to appropriate it as a charity. (Emphasis added)

Crockett was not against charity. He went on to explain that because it was not a government debt and could not be granted as charity, he personally would give.

Mr. Speaker, I have said we have the right to give as much money of our own as we please. I am the poorest man on this floor. I cannot vote for this bill, but I will give one week's pay to the object, and if every member of Congress will do the same, it will amount to more than the bill asks.

13.3 Give Others' Money or Give Your Own?

This book is not about psychology, but where money is concerned we cannot help but touch on incentives and the human condition. The following three stories show people to want to imagine themselves sympathetic and helpful, but to rely on other people's money when possible.

Story 1: At mid-career a group typically ranging from eight to a dozen and a half regularly met from time to time in my home for Bible study. At this phase of my career, my four children ranged in age with some in elementary school and my youngest still a toddler. Answering my home phone one Saturday I received a call from a recent addition to the group, let's call him Jamie, who was in his late twenties and drove a taxi. He had taken a fare on board his taxi who was a young mother who he said was not being treated well by her husband and needed a place to stay with her baby for "just a few weeks" until she could decide what she wanted to do next. He volunteered the downstairs room in my house that was near a full bathroom, but wanted to check with me. After swiftly reviewing possibilities in my mind, I said that my first God-given responsibility had to be to the welfare and safety of my small children and wife;

that I was worried about "hiding" a mother and baby from her husband, who I did not know, had not talked to, and who might not like the situation. What if he arrived unannounced at my front door one day, perhaps waiving a gun and demanding entrance to see his wife, who he said I could not keep him from? Thus, I did not immediately agree, but offered an alternative. I explained that we should set up a meeting with the pastor at our church who handled benevolence, that I would attend, he could attend, and together we would quickly work out something for this dire situation. We ended the call. I immediately called the pastor in question and explained I was willing to help. He suggested, however, he first meet privately with the mother on Monday or Tuesday, then immediately follow through with the rest of us. I got back to Jamie, who said this would be okay, was timely enough help, and who seemed now to be calmer. He could get the mother to the meeting if she needed transportation. The meeting was set. The day came. The mother never showed.

Story 2: A little later in my career, I was asked to run for the board of a small private Christian school and was elected. On or about my first board meeting, the issue was raised that the school had been in deficit the previous year, had raised its tuition significantly, but was still insolvent and needed more revenue. Among other things, we began an advertising campaign and also decided on a program whereby pastors of local churches could send their children for half the usual tuition. We knew that many classes were less than full. Added students added very little operating cost depending on what classes they would be in. If the program raised other enrollment as anticipated, it would pay for itself. I reminded the board that we were NOT doing this to be kind to pastors, but as a business decision to advertise the school to members of churches whose pastor was sending his own children and induce them to enroll.

Months later around November a board member, let's call him "Rick," explained that a missionary to Africa had returned for a year of furlough, had several children of school age and, since a missionary was "like a pastor," would we not extend the tuition break to him? Rick wanted us to be generous, benevolent benefactors. My position was that the missionary had no congregation and would not draw in other students. There would be no offsetting gain. I pointed out that it would not be right as board members to hand out other parents' money, many of whom were sacrificing greatly and could barely afford what they were already paying, to cover costs related to the missionary's children knowing that we would not gain anything for the school. We could, however, volunteer our *own* money if we so chose, and this was the honest course. Rick resisted, asserting that we *would* get the needed money in additional enrollment numbers by the next semester. I doubted this. I suggested that I would agree to the arrangement only if (1) we committed that if the promised enrollment projections did not materialize by February (after which the next term would be well underway) we seven board members would personally cover the $9,000 of cost, and (2) that our commitment to do so would be written into the official board minutes. This was done and the courtesy granted to the missionary. February arrived, the promised projections did not materialize, but no one on the board took action. At the next board meeting I brought my check for $1285.71 and explained that we needed to honor our commitment. In the next week or two, all of the other board members did—except one: Rick.[22]

Story 3: The previous firsthand accounts show that people want to be helpful, especially if it can be done with other people's money. This last story adds an additional feature, which is government "other money." It is from writer, observer of the human condition, and greatest novelist of his time Charles Dickens, his story *A Christmas Carol*, and the life of Ebenezer Scrooge.

We all know that early in the story Scrooge is unlikeable and selfish. He did not give to the poor. But why was he selfish? His position was that helping was the *government's* job, not his. He paid taxes and that was enough. From Dickens' story:

> "The Treadmill and the Poor Law are in full vigour, then?" said Scrooge.

---

[22] During my time of board service for this type of school, I had to be unwavering if it were to be preserved for everyone's benefit. Modern hospital administrators have a saying that makes the point, "No margin, No mission." In the case of a school, God loves the little children of paying parents just as much as he loves the little children of poor parents. Filling the school with students who didn't cover the costs of their education and were not covered by true scholarship funds, risked killing the entire operation for everyone. Funded scholarships are the way both to preserve the viability of the mission and to help all children.

"Both very busy, sir."

"Oh! I was afraid, from what you said at first, that something had occurred to stop them in their useful course," said Scrooge. "I'm very glad to hear it..."

"I help to support the establishments I have mentioned— they cost enough: and those who are badly off must go there."

The entire exchange is in *A Christmas Carol*. In other words, Scrooge believed that government should take care of the poor and that by him agreeing to this, he had done enough. "I do not need to be generous. I voted for the government." The point in Dickens story is that *personal* charity is needed, and pushing it off to government is selfish. Often this aspect is misunderstood about Scrooge. Even Nobel laureate Paul Krugman got it wrong, thinking that those who favor government charity can think of themselves as generous and those who don't are like Scrooge.

Here is economist David Henderson,[23]

> Krugman has misstated the point of Charles Dickens's classic, *A Christmas Carol*. The Scrooge whom Krugman and I dislike at the beginning of the story is the Scrooge who actually defended the welfare state and, because he thought it was working so effectively, refused to give his own money to charity. The Scrooge whom I (and, I assume, Paul Krugman) like at the end of the story is the one who gives his own money to charity....
>
> I also point out (now referring to the Alistair Sim movie version):
>
> In my favorite scene in the movie, Scrooge dances around in his nightshirt like a kid in a candy store, celebrating his power to change. And what is the change? Does he say, "Oh, boy, now I'll support a politician who will tax me, as well as other people less rich than me, to help poor people?" Of course not. An author or a movie producer who tried to set up such a scene would have produced

---

[23]Henderson, 2010.

a much less compelling novel or movie. Scrooge is excited because now he can change, now he can get pleasure from helping others who are worse off. **In other words, the lesson of** *A Christmas Carol* **is the importance of being generous, not the importance of supporting higher taxes on oneself and others.**

So here's my modest suggestion. Next time you hear someone advocating a coercively financed government program to help those in need, call him a "Scrooge." I guarantee that you'll catch him off guard. Moreover, he'll likely ask why you called him that. Then you can tell him the truth about Ebenezer Scrooge and *A Christmas Carol*. (Emphasis added.)

What have we learned? Taxi driver Jamie, school board member Rick, and Ebenezer Scrooge all wanted good things to be done for the poor and needy, they just didn't want to provide it themselves. Now recall the Black-Tie event and story of the university vice president and her college dean husband on page 87 of Chapter 7. The vice president wanted more to be done for those in poverty; she just didn't want to do it herself. Nathan the prophet's story of the rich man on page 88 is similar. The rich man wanted to provide a meal for the traveler, he just didn't want to use his own lamb. The economics of revealed preference and the Golden Rule work this way: If by revealed preference these individuals show by their own unwillingness to give voluntarily, that they did not want the desired help taken from their assets, then by the Golden Rule neither can they desire that the help be taken from other people's assets unless the others reveal by their actions that they so choose. Our thoughts about Scrooge were correct. In his original state, he was violating the Golden Rule and was therefore immoral.

This brings us to the next question.

13.4 Who is Generous?

Why would anyone give away his or her money to another, or forego their goods for another's benefit? Love for a child or family member is certainly one reason. In fact, the family is so well established in nature, custom, and law that we place the obligation to provide for children to adulthood on their mother and father. The person who provides for his or her own child is often also generous in general.

To the economist, revealed preference is really all we can go on. People apparently give because it raises their utility. The underlying motivation may be religious—Christians, for example, are instructed under the New Testament to be cheerful givers—or the willingness to give may be innately present in people deriving from natural law. So how do people become cheerful givers with respect to the needs of others? When people know the needs of others, plus know their own family's needs, they can decide from their assets what should go to those directly depending on them and what should go to the needs of others. Presuming people are informed about their own and others' needs, the sum of all such giving must by definition be the moral total. Notice, the right amount of total giving is not the decision of a government body. It is a disaggregated collective decision.

We tend to focus more on selfish givers, but obviously there can be selfish askers as well as selfish givers. According to celebrated and renowned theologians such as Thomas Chalmers the Golden Rule places one into the shoes of the other. The Golden Rule "prescribes *moderation to our desires of good from others,* as well as generosity to our doings in behalf of others; and makes the first the measure of obligation to the second (emphasis added)."[24] In other words, you are limited to ask no more than you would give, and are obligated to give no more than you would ask.[25]

Rule No. 2 from Chapter 12 says to pay fully for what you take from society. In the present context therefore, one reason to work is to "be dependent on no one,"[26] but the second reason is to "have something to give him who has need."[27] We return to John Wesley's words, "Having first, gained all you can, and, secondly saved all you can, then give all you can."[28]

---

[24] Chalmers, 1850.

[25] This understanding solves the problem of always feeling that more should be done and, since you are limited, others therefore should be forced to contribute (thus violating the Golden Rule and morality).

[26] I Thessalonians 4: 11-12.

[27] Ephesians 4:28.

[28] Wesley, 1872.

Who Really Cares?

Ebenezer Scrooge thought government should take care of charity and he personally should do nothing. Arthur Brooks, *Who Really Cares?* New York: Perseus Books, 2006 provides research on the relative generosity of those who favor government charity. Several findings stand out.

1. "A significant number of Americans (and Europeans as well) consider themselves charitable simply because they support policies of income redistribution through taxation. And this affects their private giving (p. 54)."

   "For many people, the desire to **donate other people's money** displaces the act of giving one's own (p.55, emphasis added)."

2. "Religion, skepticism about the government in economic life, strong families, and personal entrepreneurism (p. 11)" describe generous people. For example, religious individuals give more charitably than non-religious, **even after subtracting giving to religious causes.**

   "Religious people do not outperform secularists in charity simply because of their gifts to houses of worship. Religious people are, inarguably, more charitable **in every measurable way** (Emphasis in original, p. 40)."

3. Conservatives are more charitable than liberals. **"Conservative principles are most congenial to the four forces of charity (p. 12)."**

   "Liberals, who often claim to care more about others than conservatives do, are personally less charitable (p. 70)."

4. "People who have children are more generous than people who don't. Perhaps the act of having children stimulated giving, or givers are more likely to have kids (p. 98)."

5. "Statistically it is nearly impossible to disentangle welfare, single parenting, and antisocial behavior—including selfishness (p. 108)."

6. Giving charitably is associated with success. "For example, imagine two people who are identical with respect to education, age, religion, politics, sex, and race. The only difference is that one person gives money and volunteers his or her time annually, but the other does not. The data tell us that the charitable person will earn, on average, about $14,000 more per year than the uncharitable person (p. 145)."

"Low-income working people who are exceptionally generous also tend to have high levels of income mobility (p. 147)."

13.5   Who Should Give?: The Era Ending in 1929

John Calvin Coolidge, Jr. was born in Plymouth, Vermont on the 4th of July, 1872.[29] Publicly devout, Calvin Coolidge achieved prominence as Governor of Massachusetts and later as President of the United States. His term ended in January 1929, a year famous for

Figure 13.3: **Calvin Coolidge 1923**

---

[29]Another "Jr.," also named eponymously, was Martin Luther King, Jr. who we cited in Chapter 7.

the October stock market crash, first year of Herbert Hoover's presidency, and the beginning era of big government.[30] Coolidge could have stayed president longer, but chose not to saying, "If I take another term, I will be in the White House until 1933....Ten years in Washington is longer than any other man has had it — too long!" Coolidge died in 1933 having confided to a friend, "I feel I no longer fit in with these times."

His speeches insisted on personal charity, duty to religious moral obligations,[31] use of the private sector and business for Americans' advancement, budgeting and wise use of government. Coolidge frequently explained his beliefs about government, the private sector, economics and morality. He evidently would be comfortable with Locke, the Rules of Essential Economics, morality based on religion, the Golden Rule, individualistic and not organismic government, and personal responsibility.

Coolidge's Economics: We provide Coolidge's own words that compare to Rules 1, 2, 12, and 13.

> When service is performed, the individual performing it is entitled to the compensation for it. **His creation becomes a part of himself. It is his property.** To attempt to deal with persons or with property in a communistic or socialistic way is to deny what seems to me to be this plain fact. Liberty and equality require that equal compensation shall be paid for equal service to the individual who performs it. Socialism and communism cannot be reconciled with the principles which our institutions represent. They are entirely foreign, entirely un-American. We

---

[30] Coolidge is reported to have once said about his successor, "for six years that man has given me unsolicited advice—all of it bad (Ferrell, 1998, p. 195)." Hoover served as Secretary of Commerce under Coolidge.

[31] Coolidge was member of the Congregational Church. See also Coolidge biographer Amity Shlaes, "Calvin Coolidge's faith was the secret to his success," Fox News, March 10, 2013, updated May 11, 2015, https://www.foxnews.com/opinion/calvin-coolidges-faith-was-the-secret-to-his-success ').

stand wholly committed to the policy that what the individual produces belongs entirely to him to be used by him for the benefit of himself, to provide for his own family and to enable him to serve his fellow men.

Of course we are all aware that the recognition of brotherhood brings in the requirement of charity. But it is only on the basis of individual property that there can be any charity. Our very conception of the term means that we deny ourselves of what belongs to us, in order to give it to another. If that which we give is not really our own, but belongs to the person to whom we give it, such an act may rightfully be called justice, but it cannot be regarded as charity. (Address Delivered to the Holy Name Society, Washington, DC, September 21, 1924. Emphasis added.)

The Government can do much, but it can never supply the personal relationship that comes from the ministrations of a **private charity** of that kind. (Emphasis added.)

No person was ever honored for what he received. Honor has been the reward for **what he gave.** (Emphasis added.)

The collection of taxes which are not absolutely required, which do not beyond reasonable doubt contribute to the public welfare, is only a species of **legalized larceny.** (Emphasis added.)

Coolidge's requirement "that we deny ourselves of what belongs to us, in order to give it to another," of course, rules out voting to give another's property. Coolidge's labeling taxes beyond "absolutely required" as "legalized larceny" is reminiscent of William Jennings Bryan (p. 215) and Frederic Bastiat (p. 158).

Moral Foundations: Section 13.4 suggested that revealed preference cannot tell us the deepest underlying reasons why a person chooses to give, though we know that people do give and respond to the needs of others. For Calvin Coolidge it was obvious that religious truths were foundational, without which society and government were at risk.

Our doctrine of equality and liberty, of humanity and charity, comes from our belief in the brotherhood of man through the fatherhood of God. The whole foundation of enlightened civilization, in government, in society, and in business, rests on religion. Unless our people are thoroughly instructed in its great truths they are not fitted either to understand our institutions or provide them with adequate support.

America seeks no earthly empire...The higher state to which she seeks the allegiance of all mankind is not of human, but of divine origin. She cherishes no purpose save to merit the favor of Almighty God (Inaugural Address, 1924).

The foundations of our society and our government rest so much on the teachings of the Bible that it would be difficult to support them if faith in these teaching would cease to be practically universal in our country.

Organized government and organized society [VPOs] have done much and can do much. Their efforts will always be necessary, but without the inspiration of faith, without devotion to religion, they are inadequate to serve the needs of mankind. It is in that direction [devotion to religion] that we must look for the permanent sources of the ministrations of charity, the kindness of brotherly love, and the renunciation of consecrated lives. (Calvin Coolidge, "Address of President Coolidge before the General Convention of the Episcopal Church," Washington, D.C., October 10, 1928.)

Private Sector Sourcing: Coolidge did not turn to government when charity was involved. Government could be helpful, such as when another country needed humanitarian aid, but even then his first source for help was to consider "business" solutions, such as loans to allow purchase of American grain. Rules No. 2 and 3 were again being honored. If something is granted you that you cannot pay for now, you have been given a loan and incurred a debt. Coolidge believed in private means such as personal charity and loans for providing help.

Figure 13.4: **President and Mrs.   Coolidge Exit Church on Thanksgiving Day**

An inquiry as to whether this proposal could be carried out by the War Finance Corporation under its powers at the present time: I think **it has powers at the present time to engage in financing** a legitimate and sound business enterprise for the export of grain. Of course, **it hasn't any powers to engage in anything like charity,** and I shouldn't want to have it engaged in any unsound business enterprise. (Press Conference, Washington, D.C., October 26, 1923. Emphasis added.)

Question: Mr. President, would you care to discuss any opinion on Senator Lenroot's proposal to appropriate $20,000,000 of Treasury funds for German relief?

I haven't seen that proposal. **I very much prefer that it be a matter of business,** and I don't know that I have before me at the present time such information that would lead me to a conviction that it was necessary to proceed in the way of charity. (Press Conference, Washington, D.C., December 7, 1923. Emphasis added.)

Whether any decision has been reached regarding food aid to Germany by the United States, the general decision that I have already indicated, is that **we want that done as a business proposition if possible,** and investigations are now being made and proposals are being considered, and negotiations are in process for the purpose of making a loan to the German Government, as I understand it, the proceeds of which would be spent in this country by the loans made, part here and part, I think, in Great Britain, for the purpose of buying food stuffs for Germany, if that is accomplished. I have great hopes it may be. I do not think it may be so necessary to resort to charity. **Now don't say anything in the paper that would result in drying up the private charity that is being encouraged.** I am speaking now of Government charity. It is very desirable that the private charity that is being organized should go on. It is under the direction of such men as Mr. Allen and I believe General Dawes, who is the Director of it in his region, and other men of like calibre, and of course we are very much desirous that it should go on." (Press Conference, Washington, D.C., December 11, 1923. Emphasis added.)

This is the end of our historical inquiry. The analysis in Chapter 7, Rule 12, the U.S. Constitution supported by the Father of the Constitution James Madison plus other presidents, William Jennings Bryan, Davy Crockett plus others, and Calvin Coolidge agree that government cannot be the source of charity. Likewise, markets cannot be the source of charity since their function depends on the profit motive and is lost if the profit motive is lost. This leaves individuals and VPOs to be the agents of charity. Table 10.1 on page 120 already reflects this conclusion as well.

> **The real question is this. Are we personally going to budget for a regular program of serious charitable giving or be like the man during the Civil War: "What do you mean? I am a huge supporter of the cause. I already have sacrificed an Uncle, two cousins, and a nephew, plus now I am willing to sacrifice my wife's brother."**

13.6   Conclusion

The American ethical base from founding of the nation to 1929 contained a strong understanding of and commitment to both charity and to Rule 2, "Pay fully for what you take from society. Be fully paid for what you provide." If payment is not possible now, you have incurred a debt to be paid later. Government and the private sector can be the source of emergency loans on generous terms, but the individual and the individual working through voluntary private organizations is the source of charity. Calvin Coolidge applied this principle in his presidency to public dealings. When he said that he "very much preferred that it be a matter of business," he meant that Russia and Germany should be offered loans as emergency help, and the U.S. was "to engage in financing." He did not believe that private charity should be discouraged, but government was not its source. Charity is our personal obligation.

We also learned that the natural desire to give other people's money and consider oneself generous is a strong tendency. This is written into experience and the story of Ebenezer Scrooge, who fortunately changed his ways after he was shown the truth by the appropriate spirit and learned personal giving.

Seeing that "forced charity is theft" and "government should not engage in theft," is *not* forthwith an endorsement of uncharitableness or selfishness. It is a conclusion about the *source* of systemic help, a point emphasized in the conclusion to Chapter 7 (p. 91). Information is a public good, and it is a proper government function to provide efficiency-enhancing, human-flourishing enhancing public goods. If providing information about the needs of others raises efficiency of the economy in support of the charitable function, this is a valid contribution that government can make. The modern internet makes available innumerable ways that government can aid individuals and VPOs informationally as they engage in charitable giving.[32] In Part 2 Chapter 10 we apply what we have learned to health care.

References

Adams, John (1787). "A Defense of the Constitutions of Government of the United States of America."

Brooks, Arthur (2006). *Who Really Cares?* New York: Perseus Books.

Bryan, William Jennings (1896). Quoted in *Wall Street Journal*, "The Cross of NAIRU." Editorial, 20 June 1996, A18. [Non-Accelerating Inflation Rate of Unemployment, NAIRU, refers to a theoretical level of unemployment below which inflation would be expected to rise.]

Chalmers, Thomas (1850). "On The Great Christian Law of Reciprocity Between Man and Man," Discourse V, in *Sermons and*

---

[32]For example, many of us are familiar with Crowdfunding sites like GoFundMe that make it possible with little effort to direct funds to specific purposes. Since information is a public good, and government is appropriately tasked with providing public goods, it could aid in efforts to publicize and certify certain needs, certify the honesty of funding options and internet sites, possibly run certain sites itself, and in other ways facilitate the flow of charitable giving. Individuals who want more to be done charitably should always find it easy to do so as well as being helped and encouraged in that direction.

Discourses, Vol. II, New York: Robert Carter & Brothers, 1850, 147-153. Available online.

Cleveland, Grover (1887). *Congressional Record*, 49 Cong., 2d Sess., Vol. XVIII, Pt. II, p. 1875.

Coolidge, Calvin. (1890)–(1929) *Coolidge Speech Full Archive*, Calvin Coolidge Presidential Foundation. Available online at https://www.coolidgefoundation.org/coolidge-speech-full-archive/

Ellis, Edward S. "A Sensible and Timely View of a Certain Constitutional Question." Chapter XIII in *The Life of Colonel David Crockett*. Philadelphia: Porter and Coates, 1884.

Ferrell, Robert H. (1998). *The Presidency of Calvin Coolidge.* University Press of Kansas. ISBN 978-0-7006-0892-8.

Franklin, Benjamin (1766). "On the Price of Corn and the Management of the Poor," *The London Chronicle, 1766*, reprinted in *The Works of Benjamin Franklin*, Vol. II, Jared Sparks, ed. Chicago: Townsend Mac Coun., 1882, 355-360.

Grinols, Earl (2007). Review of Arthur Brooks, *Who Really Cares?: The Surprising Truth About Compassionate Conservatism–America's Charity Divide, Who Gives, Who Doesn't, and Why It Matters* in *Faith and Economics*, 49, Spring, pp. 50-55.

Henderson, David (2010). "Krugman Misstates Dickens's Point," 24 December, http://econlog. econlib.org/archives/2010/12/krugman_misstat_1.html

Higgs, Robert (2003). "Why Grover Cleveland Vetoed the Texas Seed Bill," *Independent Institute*, Research Article, 1 July. https://www.independent.org/publications/article.asp?id=1329

Jefferson, Thomas (1801). First Inaugural Address, 4 March.

Jefferson, Thomas (1816). Letter to Joseph Milligan, 6 April.

Madison, James (1792). Letter to Edmund Pendleton, 21 January, in *The Papers of James Madison,* vol. 14, Robert A Rutland et. al., eds. Charlottesvile: University Press of Virginia,1984.

Madison, James (1794a). Speech to the US House of Representatives, January.

Madison, James (1798b). *(Annals of Congress 179.*

Madison, James (1831). Letter to James Robertson, 20 April

Pierce, Franklin (1854). Veto of measure to help the mentally ill.

Polk, James K. Polk (1846), Veto of "An act making appropriations for the improvement of certain harbors and rivers," 3 August.

Shlaes, Amity (2013). "Calvin Coolidge's faith was the secret to his success," Fox News, March 10, 2013, updated May 11, 2015, https://www.foxnews.com/opinion/calvin-coolidges-faith-was-the-secret-to-his-success

Wesley, John Wesley (1872). Sermon "The Use of Money," available online, http://www. umcmission.org/Find-Resources/John-Wesley-Sermons/ Sermon-50-The-Use-of-Money

Chapter 14

Essential Economics of the US Constitution

If America sticks by its moral guns, if the American president articulates what America stands for, those words resonate.

—History Channel Documentary, "Presidents at War," Release: 17 February 2019

America was founded on liberty and independence—not government coercion, domination, and control. We are born free, and we will stay free. Tonight, we renew our resolve that America will never be a socialist country.

—Donald Trump, *State of the Union*, 2019.

Do not move the ancient landmark that your fathers have set.

—Proverbs 22:28

The U.S. Constitution forms the oldest single constitutional document continuously in force in the world. It and the first ten amendments, the Bill of Rights placed into force the following year in 1789, are the subject of this chapter. Our question is, How well did the economic provisions as envisioned in the original Constitution and the Bill of Rights do in supporting the conditions derived in this volume from both human flourishing and morality? The simple answer is that they did remarkably well. In this chapter we briefly explain how.

Rather than delve far into details, however, we take a 10,000 foot view, just enough to explain why the United States has done as well as it has for its first 2.5 centuries. Much is familiar, but much has a particular economics twist.

14.1   Spending for General Welfare Only

An important finding for us is that the government tasks identified in Table 10.1 (p. 120)—national defense, establishing property rights, stable money, enforcing competition, and dealing with externalities—all relate to the functioning of the entire "system" and to "society-wide" matters. The remaining task shown in Table 10.1, which was to produce public goods, was associated with agreement by everyone that the scale of government activity was beneficial to them (see the discussion of Lindahl Equilibria beginning on page 74). The focus on promoting society-wide matters is so prominent in the U.S. Constitution that we consider it in this stand-alone section.

At the outset, the Preamble to the Constitution says that it was ordained to "promote the general welfare." In Article 8 the federal government is granted "Power To lay and collect Taxes, Duties, Imposts and Excises," but for the purpose "to pay the Debts and provide for the common Defence and general Welfare of the United States." Thus, the only two times the word "welfare" is used in the Constitution, it is joined to the word "general." It was not *any* welfare that Congress was granted power to promote through its expenditures, but only general welfare. Anything that was not general welfare was excluded from expenditures. Federal money could not be used to promote "a person's welfare," for example, or "a special interest group's welfare," or "New York's or North Carolina's welfare." How can we know more precisely what the founders meant by "general welfare?" How is general welfare distinguished? Fortunately, there is a way to check.

Apart from new words and slang, the English language has changed little since 1788. It changed even less in the 40 years between 1788 and 1828 when *An American Dictionary of the English Language* was published by Daniel Webster, author of the first American dictionary. Webster tells us there were only two meanings for the word "welfare," one applying to persons, one applying to states. The entire entry is:

> WELFARE, n. [well and fare, a good faring; G.] 1. Exemption from misfortune, sickness, calamity or evil; the enjoyment of health and the common blessings of life; prosperity; happiness; **applied to persons.** 2. Exemption from any unusual evil or calamity; the enjoyment of peace and prosperity, or the ordinary blessings of society and civil government; **applied to states.** (Emphasis added.)

The Constitution's limitation to "general welfare" rules out the first meaning, leaving only the second, which applies to political states.

The same dictionary also defines the word "general" to mean "1. Properly, relating to a whole genus or kind; and hence, relating to a whole class or order.... 4. Public; common; **relating to or comprehending the whole community; as the general interest or safety of a nation**.... 6. Not directed to a single object. (Emphasis added)"

Webster's definition would render Article 8 as

> "The Congress shall have Power To lay and collect Taxes, Duties, Imposts and Excises, to pay the Debts and provide for the common Defence and <u>enjoyment of peace, prosperity, and the ordinary blessings of society and civil government</u>; but all Duties, Imposts and Excises shall be uniform throughout the United States."

Taxing A and B to give to C or to pay for a program that benefits only C may promote *special* welfare but not general welfare because A's and B's welfare has been harmed and C's helped.

Many do not like this spending limitation. Chapter 11 explained that sometimes it can be beneficial to one's personal political ambitions to give out public money or programs to a group whose votes you want to buy. Some have tried to argue that the phrase "provide

for the common defense and general welfare of the United States"
represents an all-purpose grant of power that is over and above the
specifically enumerated authority given in the Constitution. This
view was anticipated in the Federalist papers. It "amounts to an
unlimited commission to exercise every power which may be alleged
to be necessary for the common defense or general welfare," as described in Federalist Paper #41. Federalist Paper #41 refutes this
claim. Such an interpretation was rejected early on, including by
James Madison in the cited Federalist Paper. Madison calls the
argument "a misconstruction." He writes,

> But what color can the objection have, when a specifica-
> tion of the objects alluded to by these general terms im-
> mediately follows, and is not even separated by a longer
> pause than a semicolon?...For what purpose could the
> enumeration of particular powers be inserted, if these
> and all others were meant to be included in the preced-
> ing general power? Nothing is more natural nor common
> than first to use a general phrase, and then to explain
> and qualify it by a recital of particulars. But the idea
> of an enumeration of particulars which neither explain
> nor qualify the general meaning, and can have no other
> effect than to confound and mislead, is an absurdity...

The absurdity, Madison said, had its origins in those who claim
that the clause amounts to an unlimited commission to exercise
every power alleged to be for the general welfare. In his Report of
1800, Madison wrote:

> Money cannot be applied to the General Welfare, oth-
> erwise than by an application of it to some particular
> measure conducive to the General Welfare. Whenever,
> therefore, money has been raised by the general Au-
> thority, and is to be applied to a particular measure, a
> question arises whether the particular measure be within
> the enumerated authorities vested in Congress. If it be,
> the money requisite for it may be applied to it; if it be
> not, no such application can be made.

Thomas Jefferson affirmed this view:

> [O]ur tenet ever was, and, indeed, it is almost the only
> landmark which now divides the federalists from the re-
> publicans, that Congress has not unlimited powers to
> provide for the general welfare, but were to those specif-
> ically enumerated; and that, as it was never meant they
> should raise money for purposes which the enumeration
> did not place under their action; consequently, that the
> specification of powers is a limitation of the purposes
> for which they may raise money.[1]

Safeguards in the original Constitution about the purpose of federal government spending matter. An Ayers-McHenry poll asked a
large group of Americans, "Overall, would you prefer larger government with more services and higher taxes, or smaller government
with fewer services and lower taxes?" 79% did not favor larger
government and higher taxes. Unsurprisingly, polls that leave out
reference to the taxes receive higher support.

The Maysville Road and Special Welfare
The Maysville road was intended to link Maysville, Kentucky to
Lexington, Kentucky, a distance of about 65 miles. Congress passed
legislation in 1830 to spend $150,000 of federal money on the project
by purchasing stock in the Maysville, Washington, Paris, and Lexington Turnpike Road Company. Martin Van Buren, later himself to
succeed Jackson as president, advised against federal involvement.
Unconstitutionality of the bill was at issue, and Van Buren argued
that it wrongly encouraged logrolling and pork barrel projects that
would be injurious to the federal government and its finances. On
27 May 1830 Jackson vetoed the bill as unconstitutional, saying it
was entirely within a single state and had no connection to a larger
interstate transport system.[2]
Funds for continued construction of the interstate Cumberland
Road, however, connecting Cumberland, Maryland with Illinois was
approved by Jackson four days after the Maysville Road veto. Jackson's enforcement of the Constitution's restriction that spending be

---

[1]Thomas Jefferson, letter to Albert Gallatin, second Treasury Secretary, 16
June 1817.

for general welfare only, and the example he established for later spending is considered to be one of the major positive achievements of his presidency.

_____

[2] Commager 1963, p. 253.

14.2   Taxes and Other Provisions

The Constitution tells us what kind of society the founders of the United States had in mind. We identify those particular features here that touch on essential economics and use Section 14.3 to evaluate whether the Rules are satisfied or not.

Taxation

In this book, our approach regarding taxation was to limit ourselves to taxes that are consistent with Pareto Optimality and morality in all circumstances. If there are circumstances where only one such method exists, that is our selection. The benefits principle of taxes satisfies the requirement that it is consistent with Pareto Optimality and morality in all circumstances, and in the case of an economy with public goods present (see discussion of Lindahl and Foley, p. 74), Lindahl equilibrium is the unique tax description that applies.

> **Our approach regarding taxation was to limit ourselves to taxes that are consistent with Pareto Optimality and morality in all circumstances.**

The writers of the Constitution, of course, knew nothing of taxes implied by Lindahl equilibria and were limited in the kind of taxes technologically available to them. They did consider that taxes to pay for general welfare should not be levied on some and omit others. Thus, Congress provided for uniform taxation in two ways. First, the taxing authority granted in Article 8 had to be uniform,

but all Duties, Imposts and Excises **shall be uniform**

throughout the United States; (Emphasis added.)[3]

and

> No Tax or Duty shall be laid on Articles exported from any State. No Preference shall be given by any Regulation of Commerce or Revenue to the Ports of one State over those of another: nor shall Vessels bound to, or from, one State, be obliged to enter, clear, or pay Duties in another. (Article I, Section 9)

Second, if it were a direct tax on persons, it must be paid equally based on actual enumeration. Article I, Section 2 reads,

> direct Taxes shall be apportioned among the several States which may be included within this Union, according to their respective Numbers, which shall be determined by adding to the whole Number of free Persons, including those bound to Service for a Term of Years, and excluding Indians not taxed, three fifths of all other Persons. The actual Enumeration shall be made within three Years after the first Meeting of the Congress of the United States...

and Article I, Section 9, reads

> No Capitation, or other direct, Tax shall be laid, unless in Proportion to the Census or enumeration herein before directed to be taken.

The uniform duties and excises envisioned were on commercial transactions,

> The Congress shall have Power To lay and collect Taxes, Duties, Imposts and Excises, to pay the Debts and provide for the common Defence and general Welfare of the United States...." (Article I, Section 8, Clause 1)

---

[3]The right to set laws of bankruptcy likewise were restricted to be uniform: "The Congress shall have Power....To establish...uniform Laws on the subject of Bankruptcies throughout the United States;..."

had to be spent to benefit everyone and were limited to three uses only,

1. debts,
2. common defense, and
3. general welfare.

The debts on the mind of the founders in 1788 had to do with the Revolutionary War, so were general welfare in nature.[4]

The Federal System

We have already noted that today we are so accustomed to thinking in terms of progressive taxation that we forget that progressive taxes are not the outcome of any economic theory, that they violate the conditions for Pareto Optimality in economies with public goods present, and if used for charity purposes that they violate the conditions of morality discussed in Chapter 7.[5] Return to the example that we first introduced in Section 6.3, page 78. The rich New York banker in Manhattan has, we presume, immensely more money that the modest laborer living next door to the city park in Indianapolis, yet the rules of essential economics and morality require that the banker pays nothing for the park because he will *never* benefit from it. A federal system whereby individual states, and beneath them individual counties, and beneath them smaller jurisdictions collect taxes for local public goods (public goods that provide benefits to everyone within a "local" region) ensures that no taxes will be collected from the Manhattan banker for the Indianapolis park.

> **We are so accustomed to thinking in terms of progressive taxation that we forget that progressive taxes are not the outcome of any economic theory.**

In this case Federalism supports good economics.

---

[4] "All Debts contracted and Engagements entered into, before the Adoption of this Constitution, shall be as valid against the United States under this Constitution, as under the Confederation (Article VI)."

[5] See Chapter 7 in Parts 1 and 2.

Property Rights

Rule 10 says it is government's job to enforce appropriate property rights. Property law, of course, forms a massive portion of the legal system in this country, or any country. The Constitution unquestionably supports property rights. Article I, Section 10, Clause 1 reads

> No State shall...pass any...Law impairing the Obligation of Contracts....

It also prohibits any *ex post facto* law[6] as this could threaten property and contracts. Amendment V reads in full

> No person shall be held to answer for a capital, or otherwise infamous crime, unless on a presentment or indictment of a grand jury, except in cases arising in the land or naval forces, or in the militia, when in actual service in time of war or public danger; nor shall any person be subject for the same offense to be twice put in jeopardy of life or limb; nor shall be compelled in any criminal case to be a witness against himself, nor be deprived of life, liberty, or property, without due process of law; **nor shall private property be taken for public use, without just compensation.** (Emphasis added.)

also protecting private property against even public use.

Safeguards are needed. A simple example suffices. Half of my career was spent at a particular state university where the sole retirement program required payment by the employee into a fund, augmented by payment by the state, from which a specified dollar amount of pension was to be granted in the employee's period of retirement. Following the example of the federal Constitution, the state constitution stipulated that retirement plans for state employees were contracts. Having chosen not to fund its pensions appropriately for many years the state legislature understandably created for itself a budget problem.[7] The legislature decided the easiest way

---

[6]Article I, Section 9: "No Bill of Attainder or ex post facto Law shall be passed."

[7]In the chapter on government failure we explained using incentives why funding a retirement plan might take low priority for a legislator compared to voting

to solve its budget problem was to vote not to honor the promises it had made. "Legal" changes (reductions) to its pensioners was the legislators' preferred answer. (Should this have been a surprise?) The same approach was attempted for the state's retiree health care plan.

Fortunately, the state supreme court upheld the rule of law. It decided that the state could not legally change the terms of a contract after the contract had been made and completed. Many legislators believe they may vote into existence anything they choose. Had the state constitution not contained is contract clause, the state legislature *still* could have been charged under the federal constitution with passing a "law impairing the obligation of contracts" in violation of its protections.

Support for Competition

By the prominent role it gives to the rights of private property and free trade, such as the prohibition on the kinds of taxes that limit trade such as taxes on exports and trade between states, the Constitution encourages competition. Another way that it does the same is by its insistence on the free flow of information: freedom of the press, freedom of speech, and the freedom to peaceably assemble, in addition to freedom of religion.

Checks and Balances

The establishment of checks and balances may be the U.S. Constitution's greatest contribution to promoting essential economics and morality. By keeping government *out* of what was not its business, they may have provided their greatest support for human flourishing. The founders were not just promoting idle theory. They knew the rapacious seizing for plunder, the single-mindedness, and the intensity of factions that would want to turn government to their own ends. They knew the intensity of fights that would result if one group were made to pay for the financial errors of another. Preventing the mis-use of government and the incessant political warfare

---

for other ways state money could be used that would provide greater immediate personal benefits to the legislator in popularity, re-election, and accretion of power.

that came with it was on their mind. Checks and balances may also
be the Constitution's most written about and best known aspect.
Instead of trying to better what has already been said, or even to
equal it, we devote a small amount of space to the motivations and
origins of this feature.

The American founders were predominantly Christian.[8] They
certainly came from the Christian culture and had a Christian world-
view that was incorporated into the Constitution. For example, the
Christian day of worship and gathering is Sunday. For Jews it is
Saturday. For Moslems it is Friday. The words Friday and Saturday
appear nowhere in the Constitution. The word Sunday does appear.
In what context? Article I, Section 7 says,

> If any Bill shall not be returned by the President within
> ten Days **(Sundays excepted)** after it shall have been
> presented to him, the Same shall be a Law, in like Man-
> ner as if he had signed it, unless the Congress by their
> Adjournment prevent its Return, in which Case it shall
> not be a Law. (Emphasis added.)

thus respecting Sunday by exempting it from legislative calculations.
Isaiah 33:22 reads,

> For the Lord is our **Judge,** the Lord is our **Lawgiver,**
> the Lord is our **King;** he will save us.

---

[8]The influence of Christianity and Christians among those present at the
Constitutional convention has been well studied. Those who dispute the influence
of Christianity make various arguments. For example, the view that president of
the convention, George Washington, was merely a deist is often put forward, but
this position is contradicted by letters and statements from those who knew him
personally and intimately, including members of his family. Thomas Jefferson
is reported to have produced a Bible that removed all the miracles from it, but
retained the moral precepts, because he was not a believing Christian himself.
Removal of miracles did take place, but it was to produce a work that could be
used to teach morality to the American Indians then confronting the young nation
on its frontiers as hostile elements. Jefferson, who died on the fiftieth anniversary
to the day of the nation's founding, July 4th 1826, is reported to have asked, "Is
it the Fourth? I resign my spirit to God, my daughter, and my country." John
Adams, an undoubted Christian, died on the identical day. Benjamin Franklin,
who perhaps presents the strongest case for having a complicated view of religion
was the individual who asked for daily prayer at the Constitutional convention.
Did Deism not hold that God was inactive in human affairs? Why did Franklin
ask for prayers to God if he believed they would accomplish nothing?

This verse is acknowledged by James Madison, "Father of the U.S. Constitution," as the inspiration for the three branches of our government, judicial, legislative, and executive.

The founders had just experienced firsthand the excesses of monarchy documented in the Declaration of Independence. They were determined to separate the government functions and through checks and balances prevent any one branch from dominating the other two. Federalist Papers 51, written by James Madison (or possibly Alexander Hamilton) says,

> But the great security against a gradual concentration of the several powers in the same department, consists in giving to those who administer each department, the necessary constitutional means, and personal motives, to resist encroachments of the others. The provision for defense must in this, as in all other cases, be made commensurate to the danger of attack. **Ambition must be made to counteract ambition.** The interest of the man must be connected with the constitutional rights of the place. It may be a reflection on human nature, that such devices should be necessary to control the abuses of government. But what is government itself but the greatest of all reflections on human nature? If men were angels, no government would be necessary. **If angels were to govern men, neither external nor internal controls on government would be necessary.** In framing a government which is to be administered by men over men, the great difficulty lies in this: You must first enable the government to control the governed; and in the next place, oblige it to control itself. A dependence on the people is no doubt the primary control on the government; but experience has taught mankind the necessity of auxiliary precautions. (Emphasis added.)

Because we have Federalist 51, we know that the founders reflected "on human nature" to guide their plans. And what was that guidance? While some people and religions espouse the view that man is, at core, good, Christian doctrine says the reverse. "As it is written: 'There is no one righteous, not even one (Romans 3:10),' " "all have sinned and fall short of the glory of God (Romans 3:23)," "All we like sheep have gone astray; we have turned—every one—to his own way (Isaiah 53: 6)" "The heart is deceitful above all things, and desperately sick. Who can understand it (Jeremiah 17:9)?" The King James Version, which is the translation the founders would have been familiar with, says "the heart is deceitful above all things, And desperately wicked."

The separation of powers, the use of checks and balances, the limitation of government to specified duties comes out of and is more consistent with the Christian world view about humans than other views.

Educated in Greek history and Thucydides, the founders were also realists, accepting the historical judgment that states and the politicians that peopled them operated from emotions, self-interest, and fear. The founders wanted to avoid a democracy, which they had read the failures of, and selected instead a Constitutional Republic that would avoid eventual mob rule and the tyranny of usurper politicians gathering to themselves all authority and control.

> Democracies have ever been spectacles of turbulence and contention; have ever been found incompatible with personal security or the rights of property and have in general been as short in their lives as they have been violent in their deaths.
> **(James Madison)**

> We are a republican government. Real liberty is never found in despotism or in the extremes of democracy.
> **(Alexander Hamilton)**

> Democracy never lasts long. It soon wastes, exhausts and murders itself.
> **(Samuel Adams,** signer of Declaration of Independence.)

Article IV, Section 4 of the Constitution reads,

The United States shall guarantee to every State in this Union a Republican Form of Government.

The Bill of Rights, really the "Bill of Limitations on Government," begins with the protection of religious freedom, even before free speech, press, and the right of people peaceably to assemble. We have already noted the influence of the Christian world view. Why did the founders turn first to protect religion? Our first three presidents:

> Let us with caution indulge the supposition that morality can be maintained without religion. Reason and experience both forbid us to expect that national morality can prevail in exclusion of religious principle.
>
> **George Washington**
>
> Our Constitution was made only for a moral and religious people. It is wholly inadequate to the government of any other.
>
> **John Adams**
>
> Religion is a matter which lies solely between Man & his God ... I contemplate with sovereign reverence that act of the whole American people which declared that their legislature should "make no law respecting an establishment of religion, or prohibiting the free exercise thereof," thus building a wall of separation between Church & State.†
>
> **Thomas Jefferson**

† The original draft of Jefferson's letter in his own hand, which still exists and from which the quote comes, explains that his concern was not to remove religion from public life, but to protect religion from state legislation:

> "be assured that your religious rights shall never be infringed by any act of mine..." (Jefferson, 1802.)

The operative language of Bill of Rights Amendments 1 – 9 shows their intent to limit federal government.

1. "shall make no law"
2. "shall not be infringed"
3. "no soldier shall"
4. "shall not be violated, and no warrants shall issue"
5. "no person shall be held ... nor shall private property be taken"

6. "the accused shall enjoy the right to..."
7. "trial by jury shall be preserved, and no fact tried by a jury, shall..."
8. "shall not be required, nor excessive fines imposed"
9. "shall not be construed to deny or disparage"

The remarkable Tenth Amendment makes acknowledging this intention unavoidable. The federal government has only those powers specifically listed for it and no others.

10. The powers not delegated to the United States by the Constitution, nor prohibited by it to the States, are reserved to the States respectively, or to the people.

14.3 Are The Rules Satisfied?

Table 14.1 is the most direct way to assess the 1788 Constitution and Bill of Rights satisfaction of "The Rules."

Table 14.1: **Constitutional Satisfaction of the Rules**

	Rule	**Met**	**Comment**
1	**You own yourself.**	*	Yes, but qualified. The Declaration of Independence says that all men are endowed with the inalienable right to liberty. The Constitution anticipated eliminating slavery, but had to compromise with southern sentiments to move forward. Sadly, it took the Republican Party (see page 42) and the Civil War to end slavery.
2	**Pay fully for what you take from society. Be fully paid for what you provide.**	Yes	Government was limited to general welfare duties. It was not anticipated that persons or groups would receive anything from government except participating in the general welfare. Regarding other sources, persons and groups would receive from their fellow citizens only what they bought from them or received from them as voluntary charity.
3	**Not paying one's debt is stealing.**	Yes	The framers provided for strong protections of property rights, contract enforcement, and the rule of law in general.

4	Private goods are best produced and distributed in competitive private markets.	Yes	The framers, of course, did not have modern economics or its terminology. By limiting government to its appropriate role, markets and VPOs were left free to compete. *Laissez faire* competition, whether wittingly supported or not, worked remarkably well until the era of the Robber Barons in the late 1800s.
5	Competition is the only way to reliably keep prices as low as possible.	Yes	See comment to Rule 4.
6	Markets muddle from time to time. It takes government to massively mess up for long term misery.	Yes	The framers were worried about the tendency toward government tyranny, which they believed politicians would inevitably gravitate to. By limiting government to narrowly specified duties, however, they avoided all of the problems and misery that could be caused by government as, for example, when it worsened and extended the Great Depression. By setting up checks and balances they limited the damage that an all-powerful branch of government could do by embracing dangerous delusion and forcing it on the entire economy.
7	The larger government is relative to the economy, the more harm it can do and the larger the push to use it for corruption.	Yes	The framers did all they could to limit the size of government just to its needed functions by enumerating its limited powers and prohibiting to it any others in the Tenth Amendment. See also comments 3 and 4.
8	Good policy is in the Core.	Yes	See comment 2. The Table 10.1 duties—national defense, establishing property rights, stable money, enforcing competition, and dealing with externalities—are "society-wide" objectives that benefit everyone. Production of public goods also benefits everyone and is in the Core if proper taxes are adhered to. By adopting Federalism and rejecting direct taxes except in proportion to population, the framers came as close as possible in their time to supporting the Core. In the world created by the Constitution it would be very hard for government to do anything except benefit everyone equally by means of regionally and sectionally uniform taxes.

9	Pareto Optimality and Morality imply benefits-principle taxes.	*	Yes, but qualified. See comments 2 and 7. It is unrealistic to expect that the founders could do any better subject to the knowledge they had (benefits-principle taxation was unknown as an economic concept as we have discussed it here) and the limited forms of taxes available to them. They prevented re-distributional taxes by requiring direct taxes to be in proportion to states' populations and requiring spending to be for general welfare only.[9] As was understood by the founders, ruling out spending for special welfare purposes did not stop pressure for such spending. One way was to (falsely) claim that any spending one wanted provided general benefits. Presidential vetoes frequently had to re-iterate that spending to benefit special welfare was unconstitutional.
10	**It is government's job to enforce appropriate property rights.**	Yes	The framers were acutely aware of the importance of property and property rights to human flourishing. They did everything they could to enforce appropriate property rights, knowing that a subsequent body of laws would arise to work out the details. The federal government was prevented from infringing contracts, forceably taking property for public uses, taxing except for the general welfare, and in other smaller ways protecting property rights. They went as far as they could with the economics knowledge available to them.
11	**Business investment is not a government job.**	Yes	Business investment and crony capitalism are not "general welfare" activities of government. To the extent that the founders were suspicious of politicians and what they would do, their attempts to provide checks and balances, rule of law and not rule of men, show their intention to prevent graft, crony capitalism, and the like.

---

[9]In 2021 the specific criticism was raised against federal legislation signed early in the year that taxes originating in states that had fiscally prudent budgets were being given to other states that had budget deficits, and this was being done as a political reward for affiliation with the party in power. Regardless of how justified or unjustified one takes the complaint to be, the founders were aware of the threat posed to the nation of taxing one state for the purpose of supporting another and tried to prevent it.

12	Government should not engage in theft. Forced charity is theft.	Yes	See comment 2.
13	Society consists of individuals. No organismic overarching government objective exists.	Yes	The founders did not begin to entertain the view that it might be government's policy to help one group to the harm of another. The federal government they created was to promote the general welfare only, was limited to a specifically identified list of functions, and was prohibited from doing anything else. They were as clear about this as they knew how to be.

Notes: * See qualification of the answer in right hand column.

A thoughtful review of Table 14.1 cannot help but lead to an astonishing conclusion about how close to fulfilling the requirements of human flourishing and the Golden Rule the founders came. Rules 1–3 cover a host of potential sins. The case can be made that had the founders known what today we know about Pareto Optimality and its equivalence to competitive markets; the nature of pollution, externalities, absence of markets, and associated property rights; the distinction between public goods and private goods; Lindahl equilibrium; and organismic versus individualistic conceptions of government, they would have come much, much closer.

14.4   Renegade Government

What happens when government no longer promotes the general welfare, arrogates more and more power to itself, arrogantly decides it is permitted to harm some people to help others, acts arbitrarily, and in fact fails to the point of haughtily going "over to the dark side?" In *Second Treatise of Civil Government* John Locke described that when government leaves its proper station and all the political and individual methods of resisting tyranny are exhausted, then by its actions government has thrown the citizens back into a state of nature where an "appeal to heaven" remains.

Chapter 14 explains:

> where the body of the people, or any single man, is deprived of their right, or is under the exercise of a power

without right, and have no appeal on earth, then **they have a liberty to appeal to heaven,** whenever they judge the cause of sufficient moment. And therefore, though the people cannot be judge, so as to have, by the constitution of that society, any superior power to determine and give effective sentence in the case; yet they have, by a law antecedent and paramount to all positive laws of men, reserved that ultimate determination to themselves which belongs to all mankind, where there lies no appeal on earth, viz. to judge, whether they have just cause to make their **appeal to heaven.** (Emphasis added.)

If "by a law antecedent and paramount to all positive laws of men" the "ultimate determination" is reserved to themselves "to judge whether they have just cause to make their appeal to heaven," then inalienable natural rights transcend the political process.

Figure 14.1: **The "An Appeal to Heaven" flag, long familiar to Revolutionary War historians.**

The "appeal to heaven" motto, referring to John Locke's *Second Treatise of Government*, was used in one of the earliest patriot flags.

More that just an artistic creation, it was stating the basis for the rights of colonists when their government failed to govern justly. Sometimes known as the "Pine Tree Flag," it flew over a squadron of six cruisers serving George Washington. Massachusetts also used it on naval vessels. Since "God governs in the affairs of men," as Benjamin Franklin famously remarked in the Philadelphia convention that adopted the US Constitution, Americans saw this message as more than a mere motto.

When the people have been thrown back into a state of nature by government overreach and appeal to heaven is all that remains, what can the people do? Our best clue comes from the Constitution and the Bill of Rights itself. The colonists wanted to protect first the freedom of religion, but then the rights of free speech, free press, and freedom of assembly, in that order. What was the next right they protected? The second Amendment protects the right of the people to bear arms. Had the citizens of the colonies not had arms, often superior weapons to the arms wielded against them by England's mercenary troops and British regulars, the Constitution and the Bill of Rights would never have risen to human attention.

In the rear view of history, the *Trail of Tears* suffered by the Cherokee and Choctaw is easy to select as an abhorrent example of organismic government deciding to help one group at the expense of another. What seems arbitrary today did not seem arbitrary to the subset of Americans enforcing it then. The Trail of Tears *killed* people. Had the American Indians involved understood the impact of what was coming, been able on a widespread basis and fiercely willing to defend their lives and rights, it is likely that forced removal would never have been contemplated by a calculating man like Andrew Jackson, and never tried on them. The ability to defend one's rights, and the public knowledge that one will do so, ironically, often makes the need unnecessary.

The Swiss and the Americans

In addition to lessons learned by the Cherokee and Choctaw, there are other indications that groups able to defend themselves might fare better than defenseless ones in many circumstances.

Switzerland encourages an armed citizenry as an added national

Figure 14.2: **Swiss President Ueli Maurer with His Weapon at a Shooting Exercise**

deterrent with its military. Every year in Switzerland, Zurich holds its *Knaben-Schiessen* ("Boy shooting"), a shooting contest for 13 to 17 year olds that dates back to the 1600s. Swiss military service is mandatory for men, after which they typically keep their service weapons, resulting in about half of the privately owned guns being military firearms. Switzerland has the third highest civilian ratio of guns per resident in the world, a murder rate near zero—and it has not fought in an international conflict since 1816.[10]

The US has the highest civilian ratio of guns per resident in the world. The following story comes from 1960. On board the USS Constellation just fifteen years after World War II had ended, ranking Japanese Defense Force officers were asked by their US counterparts why the Japanese did not plan to invade the US west coast after their success at Pearl Harbor. It is reported that a Japanese admiral answered:

> We knew that probably every second home in your country contained firearms. We knew that your country actually had state championships for private citizens shooting military rifles. We were not fools to set foot in such

quicksand.[11]

[10]Brueck, Hilary. (2019). "Switzerland Has a Stunningly High Rate of Gun Ownership," *Business Insider*, 5 August. Online at: https://www. businessinsider.com/switzerland-gun-laws- rates-of-gun- deaths-2018-2?op=1, accessed 23 January 2021.
[11]Eidsmoe, John A. (2009). "The Militia: In History and Today," *The New American* 5 March. Online: https://thenewamerican.com/the-militia-in-history-and-today/, accessed 21January 2021. This story is reported by several sources. The earliest found was in the Lutheran journal: *Christian News*, New Haven, Missouri, Feb. 4, 2002.

Presume that we accept the conclusion that the Constitution did unusually well, perhaps better than any previous attempt, at supporting the conditions for human flourishing and morality. We know that it has been altered in critical ways, most notably by the 16th Amendment that admitted the income tax. The natural question is, Were those changes for good or ill? After all, the further the Constitution moves from helpful principles, the less well it will do.

This topic is more extensive that we can address. We can, however, provide food for thought in the form of a late 19th century perspective. *Pollock v. Farmers' Loan and Trust Company* is a landmark case decided by the U.S. Supreme Court in 1895 ruling that an income tax was unconstitutional. Here is what the judges said,

> Whenever a distinction is made in the burdens a law imposes or in the benefits it confers on any citizens by reason of their birth, or wealth, or religion, it is class legislation, and **leads inevitably to oppression** and abuses, and to general unrest and disturbance in society.

The justices explain,

> "If the court sanctions the power of discriminating taxation, and nullifies the uniformity mandate of the Constitution," as said by one who has been all his life a student of our institutions, **"it will mark the hour when the sure decadence of our present government will commence."** If the purely arbitrary limitation of $4,000

in the present law can be sustained, none having less than that amount of income being assessed or taxed for the support of the government, the limitation of future Congresses may be fixed at a much larger sum, at five or ten or twenty thousand dollars, parties possessing an income of that amount alone being bound to bear the burdens of government... Unless the rule of the Constitution governs, a majority may fix the limitation at such rate as will not include any of their own number. (Emphasis added.)

The Supreme Court's warnings are reminiscent of Bastiat (page 159) half a century earlier who argued that when government is too prominent a part of society, "Political questions will always be prejudicial, dominant, and all-absorbing. There will be fighting at the door of the Legislative Palace, and the struggle within will be no less furious." If government is everything, then you and your group must control government or you have nothing. Some fight to protect themselves from legalized theft, others fight to engage in legalized theft. One might even predict that political factions would begin to promote themselves by offering money and programs to their supporters, promising to arrange the burden of paying for them "as will not include any of their own number."

> **If government is everything, then you and your group must control government or you have nothing.**

The relevant question might be, not when such "sure decadence" will begin, but when will it end.

14.5 Conclusion

The U.S. Constitution of 1788 and the Bill of Rights of 1789 are sympathetic to modern requirements of Pareto Optimality and the Golden Rule, hence to human flourishing and morality. The framers did remarkably well by establishing a government limited to promoting the general welfare, protecting property and property rights, establishing the rule of law, relying on uniform taxes, and prohibiting direct taxes except in proportion to population.

It should be evident by now that the twentieth century concept of the entitlement program, if it means giving money or in-kind private goods to one group (that does not pay for what it receives) and paying for them by taxing another group (that does not receive what it pays for), does not promote the general welfare, is not charity, fails the requirements of morality, fails the requirements of Pareto Optimality, and would have been prohibited by the original U.S. Constitution.

Lest we allow emotion and not science to cause us to drift in our thinking or mis-construe what this means, the comment highlighted at the end of Chapter 7 is helpful to repeat: **Finding that tax supported charity is immoral does not endorse selfishness or say there should be no charity. It says to use proper means.**

References

Brueck, Hilary. (2019). "Switzerland Has a Stunningly High Rate of Gun Ownership," *Business Insider*, 5 August. Online at: https://www. businessinsider.com/ switzerland-gun- laws-rates-of-gun- deaths-2018-2?op=1, accessed 23 January 2021.

Commager, Henry Steele (1963).   "Jackson's Veto of Maysville Road Bill," *Documents of American History*, 7th ed., New York: Meredith Publishing Company.

Eidsmoe, John A. (2009). "The Militia: In History and Today," *The New American* 5 March. Online: https://thenewamerican.com/ the-militia-in-history-and-today/. This story is reported in several sources. The earliest appearance seems to be in the Lutheran journal: *Christian News*, New Haven, Missouri, Feb. 4, 2002.

Jefferson, Thomas (1802). Letter to Danbury Baptists Association in the state of Connecticut, 1 January.

Jefferson, Thomas (1817). Letter to Albert Gallatin, second Treasury Secretary, 16 June.

Pollock v. Farmers' Loan & Trust Co. No. 893. Supreme Court of the United States, 157 U.S. 429 (1895); Argued March 7, 8, 11, 12, 13, 1895. Decided April 8, 1895.

Epilogue to Part 1

What is the bottom line for how the most good can be done in the best possible way? The answer is not contained in poring over policy details and minutia—though some special cases and specifics can be sketched out[1]—but in the implications of efficiency plus morality.

Inevitably, for some there might be lingering uneasiness. "Theory is well and good, but I don't see how it gets the job done; we need to move beyond mere principles." This is like the man on the fourth floor of a burning building who needs to make his way to the ground deciding "Your theory about gravity and acceleration is all well and good, but this is a fire, so I am jumping."

There are other ways to jump. Ebenezer Scrooge wanted government to take care of the poor, pretending not to recognize that whatever tax money he felt he was willing to pay was always in his voluntary power to give to a charity organization for that purpose. There are valid theoretical reasons why a VPO does a better job than government does in certain tasks. Why did Ebenezer Scrooge think a tax system was necessary for him to give to charity?

Here we have emphasized that especially when it acts outside its sphere, government introduces imbedded problems of its own. Sometimes the greatest fallacy appears as the syllogism:

> Something must be done.
> This is something.

---

[1]In Part 1 we returned several times to talking about what the theory has to say about the difference between public goods and private goods and what this implies about paying for college education. Certainly, providing tax-raised dollars for frat boys to goof off with their friends on a college campus while they decide whether they want to complete their degree or not is *not* what most people would consider the right use of funds. In Part 2 Chapter 11 contains an extensive discussion of health care.

This must be done.

It sounds pretty silly, but politicians fall into it. We have explained why politicians are so often loathe to change, even when theory and circumstances say change is needed.[2] Some of us have lived so long in the imperfect that we scarcely can imagine anything better. The comedy movie character Evil Roy Slade was advised that he needed to start over, change his name, begin afresh. He had never thought like this! What new name should he choose?

Evil John Ferguson? Evil Fred Knowlan? Evil Lee Rich?

Let us imagine instead a world where individuals, voluntary private organizations, and government truly are engaged solely in the tasks assigned to them in Table 10.1 of Chapter 10. Rather than federal spending exceeding 20 percent of GDP and more, a number closer to 6 percent would apply. From the difference, 10 percent or more would go to charitable, foundational, scholarship and similar civic ends, still leaving money to spare. Rough agreement on the size of government provision of public goods would apply, and no one would pay taxes except those that provided them benefits in return. On average, health care would cost 40 percent of what it does today, and for young people even less, making it affordable to many who cannot now afford it. Everyone who needs care would get it. Anyone who could not pay would receive interest-free loans that they could repay later so the help they received could be re-cycled to help others. Competitive prices would apply. No longer would absurdly high and out-of-touch surprise billing exist.

Other changes would be evident. Those who need to work will be able to find jobs. With greatly lower taxes, those who work will keep nearly all of their money. The requirements that today act as barriers to workers getting jobs easily and quickly (and to employers hiring employees easily and quickly) would be gone. If you want to start a small business, for example, your decision to hire would be just the decision to hire. No longer would your choice to hire be converted into a mandate to require you to act as if you were the parent and your worker the adolescently irresponsible accountability shirker by taking on the planning of your workers' insurance decisions, their saving and retirement decisions, withholding their pay from them for

---

[2]See *The Officeholder's Externality* on page 156.

umpteen purposes and in other ways assuming the duty to manage their private choices and lives.

Neither do workers want to be treated like babies. From the worker's point of view, employment will be easier. The compensation that the worker earns will be fully under his or her own control to spend as he or she personally decides. Why should it be different? Government would still be needed to insure honesty by businesses and workers in their dealings with one another, but by removing the accumulated tangled mass of governmental intrusions everyone would be better off. Firms that want to provide pay in in-kind goods could do so, but there would no longer be reason to because government's unwarranted interventions and false incentives would be gone. Workers would have the right to take all of their compensation as cash. Life insurance, health insurance, car insurance, retirement accounts, education accounts, food, clothing, shelter would all be the personal property and domain of the employee, not controlled by the employer nor controlled by the government. In short, with harmful encumbrances cleared out, economic participants—employer and employee, worker and retiree, young and old, every human being in the economy—would again be freed to control their own affairs as they themselves decide, pursue their dreams and lives as they themselves choose, and create and reap the benefits that economics generates in an economy arranged to further human flourishing and the Golden Rule.

PART 2

Part 2: Chapter 1

Essential Economics

Everything in the study of economic efficiency, or simply "efficiency," starts from the assumption that it is a necessary condition for human flourishing. Without it we have inefficiency. By *inefficiency* we mean a situation where it is possible to improve the circumstances of some one or more individuals without harming anyone in the process. We take as self-evident that if something better is possible humans cannot be said to flourish. Necessary conditions for flourishing might include the presence of justice, the ability to enjoy beauty, being safe in one's person, giving and receiving love, and so on. Here we are interested in the *economic* aspects of human flourishing and their supporting social arrangements.

1.1   Efficiency in an Economy

To learn about efficiency it is convenient to think in terms of a miniature economy having two goods, two types of productive inputs (sometimes just "inputs" or factors of production), two individuals, some resource endowments, and some technological know how. We will refer to such a $2 \times 2 \times 2$ example in the next section. Understanding this small economy means we can understand a big one.

There is really no distinction between a good and a factor of production. When something is consumed we call it a good. When something is used in the production of some other thing, we call it an input or factor of production, but there is no intrinsic difference.

Definition: An *economy* is a collection of
- *individuals,* quantities of
- *available endowments* (goods, factors of production), and the
- *available technology* for converting some goods into other goods.

Definition: An *allocation* is a listing of the consumption of each individual and the production of each producer. If voluntary private organizations and government are present, their consumption and production is included. By consumption we mean to include all goods that matter to the consumer's utility such as hours of labor supplied and by production we mean to include a listing of all the goods and services produced plus goods and services used in production.

Definition: An allocation is said to be *Pareto Optimal* or *efficient* if replacing it by any feasible allocation harms one or more individuals, or leaves all individuals indifferent. "Efficiency" and "Pareto Optimality" are terms we will use synonymously.

In other words, optimality rules out just one possibility: that it is possible to improve one or more individuals's wellbeing without hurting anyone in the process of doing so. Pareto Optimality is sometimes equivalently defined, therefore, as an allocation from which it is impossible to improve anyone's wellbeing without harming another. If an allocation is one from which it *is possible* to improve someone's wellbeing and harm no one in the process, then that allocation is *Inefficient* or *Pareto Suboptimal.*

Figure 1.1 displays five alternatives. On the horizontal axis we show the utility of individual 1 and on the vertical axis the utility of individual 2. Points a − e represent this economy's hypothetical attainable utility combinations. Point b is efficient because no achievable alternative exists in the shaded region to the northeast. Raising the utility of one individual without harming the other is impossible. Equivalently, any move from point b to another point lowers the utility of individual 1 or of individual 2 or of both. Applying the same logic to points a, c, d, and e reveals that points a and c are also efficient, but points d and e are not. Moving from point d to point b, for example, raises the utility of individual 1 and raises the utility of individual 2. Moving from point e to point

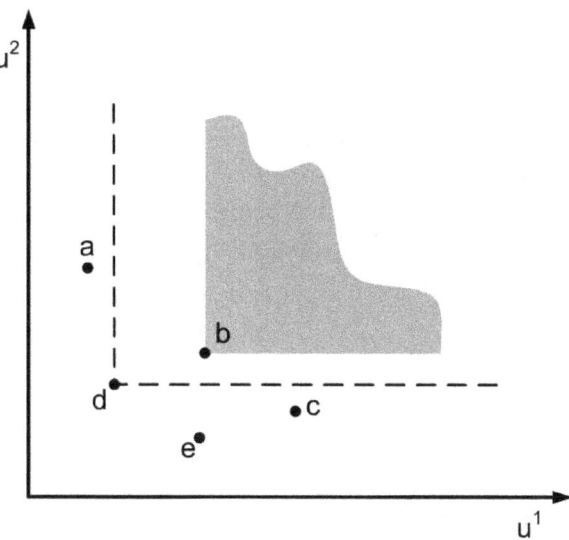

Figure 1.1: **Only Undominated Utility Arrangements are Pareto Optimal**

b, which lies directly above it, raises the utility of individual 2 and leaves individual 1 indifferent.

In defining Pareto Optimality as we have, two aspects are important. First, Pareto Optimality is evaluated in terms of *individuals*. The glory of the state, or even the glory of the emperor who might embody the state, is *not* how we measure efficiency. Society is made up of people. All people are our interest. Later we may talk of the decision-making unit as being the household in recognition of the existence of dependent children below the age of reason and self-sufficiency. But for the moment, the elements of society are *individuals* and it is in *individuals'* terms that we measure human flourishing and efficiency.

Second, the wellbeing of the individual is what the *individual himself or herself* says it is. No one but the individual decides for the individual.

This means that we assume individuals are rational. That is, they have stable preferences capable of choosing between available consumption bundles and their preferences are transitive: If bundle A_1 is preferred to bundle A_2 is preferred to bundle A_3 all the way to bundle A_n, then A_1 is preferred to A_n. More complicated descriptions are possible, but let us assume that goods x_1, x_2 and leisure L_e are such that utility always rises with greater quantities. Since the consumer supplies labor x_L, which is the endowment of total available time (E) less leisure $(x_L = E - x_{L_e})$, we can display the utility of individual 1 and 2 being plotted in Figure 1.1 as the numbers given by the utility functions

$$
\begin{aligned}
u^1 &= u^1[x_1^1, x_2^1, x_{L_e}^1] = u^1[x_1^1, x_2^1, E - x_L^1] \\
u^2 &= u^2[x_1^2, x_2^2, x_{L_e}^2] = u^2[x_1^2, x_2^2, E - x_L^2].
\end{aligned}
$$

The individual generally is able to make the choice of how much to consume and how much labor to supply, all three variables of which are thus displayed in the utility function.

Economists make a great demonstration of pointing out that utility need only matter in relative size. Preferred bundles have higher numbers. We don't say that a preferred bundle is twice as good or 2.34 times as good as a less preferred bundle, for example. That would imply a cardinal utility measure, which we do not need.

1.2   Production Possibilities

It is scarcely possible to think about economic efficiency without discussion of the production of final goods and services. Efficiency naturally carries over to requirements on production.

Economics as a discipline is generally regarded to have begun with the publishing of Adam Smith's *An Inquiry into the Nature and Causes of the Wealth of Nations* in 1776, apparently an auspicious year for other reasons, as well. The most famous passage from Smith's *Wealth of Nations* deals with the value of national production. He says,

> the annual revenue of every society is always precisely equal to the exchangeable value of the whole annual produce of its industry, or rather is precisely the same thing with that exchangeable value. As every individual, therefore, endeavours as much as he can both to employ his capital in the support of domestic industry, and so to direct that industry that its produce may be of the

greatest value; every individual necessarily labours to render the annual revenue of the society as great as he can. (*Wealth of Nations*, Book IV, Chapter II)

Smith goes on to say, "he intends only his own gain, and he is in in this, as in many other cases, led by an invisible hand to promote and end which was no part of his intention," rendering "the annual revenue of the society as great" as it can be. It is a remarkable passage and justly celebrated.

Just as efficiency is necessary for human flourishing, so rendering the annual revenue of the society as great as it can be is necessary for efficiency. Dealing with production cannot be avoided.

Figure 1.2 helps explain Smith's point. The horizontal axis measures the production of the first good as y_1 and the vertical axis measures the other good y_2. The combinations of the two goods that society is capable of producing is represented by the shaded set. Point a, for example, is doable and point b is doable. Point a, however, contains both a smaller quantity of good 1 and a smaller quantity of good 2 than point b. Gross Domestic Product (GDP), the value of all final goods produced domestically by the society is $p_1 y_1 + p_2 y_2$, where prices for the two goods are p_1 and p_2. At point a GDP is obviously less than it would be at point b. The line through point a shows other combinations of y_1, y_2 that have the same value of y_1, y_2 as at point a. Similarly for the line through point b and its higher value of production. Points on the same line have the same value. Smith's claim is that each agent, by maximizing the value of what he or she does individually, contributes to a *total* that is maximized.

Only a point like b, where no alternative production lies to the northeast, can have maximum value, because value increases for lines to the northeast. For the prices shown, Smith's world would never produce at point a, but *would* produce at point b. Given prices p_1, p_2, therefore, value-maximizing production leads to efficient output at a point on the frontier. This is because the line showing GDP lies above the GDP of all alternatives. Except for frontiers with non-smooth edges or production on an edge, selected production will be at a tangent as at point b.

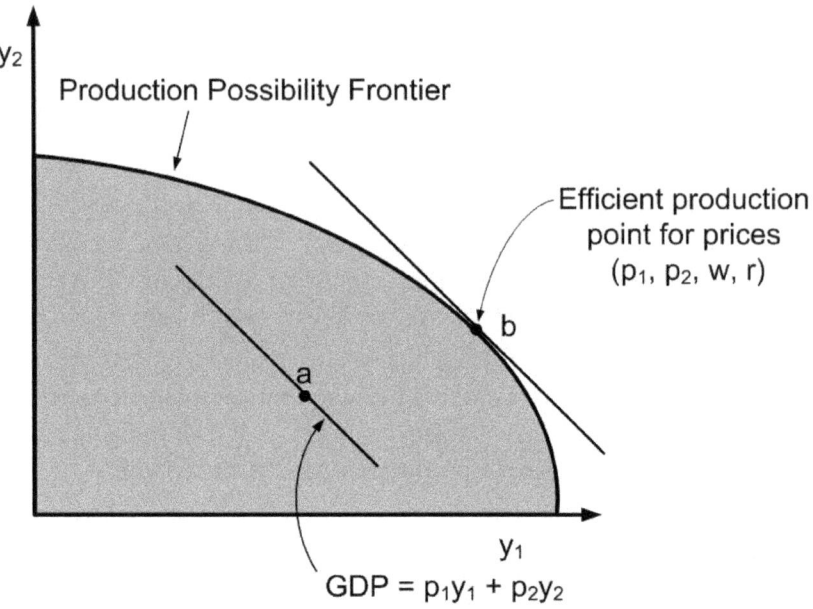

Figure 1.2: **Adam Smith's Invisible Hand Demonstrated**

1.3 The Two-Good, Two-Factor Case

In this section we provide an example showing that individuals who maximize the value of their individual activity cause the value of GDP to be maximized for all of society.

There are two goods consumed y_1, y_2 and two factors of production available in total supply K, L. We will refer to these as capital and labor. Both can be used in production of goods 1 and 2. Thus $K = K_1 + K_2$ and $L = L_1 + L_2$.

With four goods in all, there are four prices p_1, p_2, r, w, which we display in the vertical list,

$$p = \begin{pmatrix} p_1 \\ p_2 \\ r \\ w \end{pmatrix}$$

Price r can be thought of as the rental rate on an hour of machine time and price w as the price paid for an hour of the input L. We use letter y_1 to denote production of good 1 and y_2 for production of good 2. The profits of the two firms are therefore revenue minus costs of inputs

$$\pi_1 = p_1 y_1 - r K_1 - w L_1$$
$$\pi_2 = p_2 y_2 - r K_2 - w L_2$$

Gross domestic product can be measured either in income or the value of all final goods. In our economy,

$$
\begin{aligned}
\text{GDP} \ &= \ \text{Value of all Income} \\
&= \ \pi_1 + \pi_2 + rK + wL \\
&= \ (p_1 y_1 - r K_1 - w L_1) + (p_2 y_2 - r K_2 - w L_2) + rK + wL \\
&= \ p_1 y_1 + p_2 y_2 + r(K - K_1 - K_2) + w(L - L_1 - L_2) \\
&= \ p_1 y_1 + p_2 y_2 \\
&= \ \text{Value of all Final Goods and Services}
\end{aligned}
$$

Look now at the second line. Since prices are given, and K, L are fixed numbers, maximizing π_1 and π_2 causes GDP to be maximized and hence the value of all final goods is maximized. As in Figure 1.2 society must be producing on the production possibility frontier where the line measuring GDP is greatest. Note that this also implies it is impossible to raise the output of one good without lowering the output of another. Logically, being efficient means that moving from an efficient production allocation to any other lowers the output of one or more or all goods.

1.4 Conclusion

In this chapter we defined *an economy*, an *allocation* within that economy, and *Pareto Optimality* to describe the allocations that we like best. We know what *utility* is, and we have a diagram (Figure 1.2) to discuss for society "the exchangeable value of the whole annual produce of its industry," in Adam Smith's words. It turns out that this annual value, Gross Domestic Product (GDP), equals the sum of all incomes in the economy, which is the same as the value of all final goods and services produced. If GDP is as large as possible, production must be at a point like b in Figure 1.2 that is on the surface of the frontier (not the interior), and firms must be maximizing profit.

There are connections between those particular allocations that are Pareto Optimal and firms maximizing profit that we take up in the next chapter.

Part 2: Chapter 2

The Fundamental Theorems of Welfare Economics

In the previous chapter, we defined efficiency as a concept and set up the elements of an economy. The purpose of this chapter is to operationalize Pareto Optimality and make it into a working tool by distinguishing what a "healthy" economy looks like as opposed to an "unhealthy" one. This is what the First and Second Fundamental Theorems of Welfare Economics (FTWEs) do. These results are called fundamental for a reason. They interpret efficiency and also provide an organizational device.

At its simplest, the concept of efficient social arrangement is about how best to convert goods of little value into things of greater value—where value is measured by how well the improved "thing" serves people's needs—and get these converted things to the right people. The more that people are helped, the greater is the value created. The greater the value created, the greater economic profit must be and the more that wealth is added to. Profit is a flow concept, wealth is a stock concept. Our first job, therefore, is to start from our measure of profit for all of society, after which we can move to the First and Second Fundamental Theorems.

As we have heretofore, we use the words individual, consumer, and household interchangeably. Similarly we use the words firm and producer interchangeably.

273

2.1   National Wellbeing

Recall the elements of our 2 good $\times$ 2 factor example economy.
- Goods: 1, 2.
- Inputs: K, L.
- Consumers i $= 1, ..., $ m. Their choices: x^i, i $= 1, ...,$m.
- Producers j $= 1, ..., $ n.   Their choices: y^j, j $= 1, ...,$ n.
- 4 Prices: p_1, p_2, r, w.
- Endowments (goods available for use from nature or the past) denoted by elements in the list w.
- *Outputs are positive* numbers; *inputs are negative* numbers by convention.

Placing our information about the economy into an array shows how quantities inter-relate. Superscripts identify consumers and firms, subscripts identify goods or factors. Presume that firm 1 produces good 1 and firm 2 produces good 2. Then, market clearing is

$$
\begin{array}{ccccccc}
\text{Consumption} & & = & \text{Production} & + & \text{Endowments} \\
x & & = & y & + & w \\
x^1 \quad + \cdots + \quad x^m & & = & y^1 \quad + \quad y^2 & + & w \\
\end{array}
$$

$$
\begin{pmatrix} x_1^1 \\ x_2^1 \\ 0 \\ -x_L^1 \end{pmatrix} + \cdots + \begin{pmatrix} x_1^m \\ x_2^m \\ 0 \\ -x_L^m \end{pmatrix} = \begin{pmatrix} y_1^1 \\ 0 \\ -K^1 \\ -L^1 \end{pmatrix} + \begin{pmatrix} 0 \\ y_2^2 \\ -K^2 \\ -L^2 \end{pmatrix} + \begin{pmatrix} 0 \\ 0 \\ K \\ 0 \end{pmatrix}
$$

Row by row this means demand equals supply, market by market, across our four markets:

$$x_1^1 + x_1^2 + \cdots + x_1^m = y_1^1$$

$$x_2^1 + x_2^2 + \cdots + x_2^m = y_2^2$$

$$0 = -K^1 - K^2 + K$$

$$x_L^1 + x_L^2 + \cdots + x_L^m = L^1 + L^2$$

2.2   Putting Values on the Quantities

Social value means applying prices to the quantity actions of firms and households. The previous chapter listed prices as the vertical list

$$p = \begin{pmatrix} p_1 \\ p_2 \\ r \\ w \end{pmatrix}$$

When prices value a firm's choices such as those of the first firm, y^1, and household choices such as those of the first household, x^1, they generate the firm's *profit* and the household's *expenditure*. These are dollar numbers that can be summed to the national level. The best notation uses the *inner products* $p \cdot y^1$ and $p \cdot x^1$ defined as follows

$$p \cdot y^1 = \begin{pmatrix} p_1 \\ p_2 \\ r \\ w \end{pmatrix} \cdot \begin{pmatrix} y_1^1 \\ 0 \\ -K^1 \\ -L^1 \end{pmatrix} = p_1 y_1^1 - rK^1 - wL^1$$

$$\equiv \quad \pi^1 = \text{Profit of Firm 1}$$

$$p \cdot x^1 = \begin{pmatrix} p_1 \\ p_2 \\ r \\ w \end{pmatrix} \cdot \begin{pmatrix} x_1^1 \\ x_2^1 \\ 0 \\ -x_L^1 \end{pmatrix} = p_1 x_1^1 + p_2 x_2^1 - wx_L^1$$

$$\equiv \quad I^1 = \text{Expenditure of Household 1}$$

In other words, inner product adds the first price times the first quantity to the second price times the second quantity to the next times the next until the end of the price list is reached. Inner product is defined only if the number of prices matches the number of quantities in the associated list. Using the triple equality $\equiv$ as we did here, means that the equality *defines* the term being introduced. E.g., the Profit of Firm 1 is *defined* as the value of the firm's output less the cost of inputs used to produce that output.

It follows that $p \cdot y = p \cdot (y^1 + y^2 + \cdots + y^n) = p \cdot y^1 + p \cdot y^2 + \cdots + p \cdot y^n$ is the profit of all firms, just as $p \cdot x$ is the expenditure of all households in the economy. $p \cdot y$ and $p \cdot x$ are a whole lot easier to write than some of the horrendous lists and lists of price times quantities! We will see that they also can be succinctly used to analyze efficiency.

Where does the income that households spend come from? In our 2×2 example economy, $p \cdot x = p \cdot y + p \cdot w$ tells us that individuals are deciding how much labor to supply (this is one of the elements in their choice of x^i), plus receiving their share of firm profits and their share of the earnings of the capital stock $(p \cdot w = rK)$.[1]

---

[1] $p \cdot x^i$ equals $p_1 x_1^i + p_2 x_2^i - wx_L^i$, which says the sum of spending by the household equals the "lump sum" income of household i, meaning that income whose value is not determined by the household's current choices. $p \cdot x^i$ equals the household's income from non-labor sources such as share of firm profits and share of the economy's income from capital stock rK.

2.3   Competitive Equilibrium

We are continuing with preliminaries. Because markets are closely linked to optimality, we need to say what we mean by a competitive market equilibrium. We have already verified that market clearing for all of the quantities in the economy implies that profits and payments for capital stock are spent by the households. That is, all income is properly present and accounted for.

A competitive market equilibrium means pretty much what we think it should: It is a situation in which households are maximizing their utility subject to the available income they have to spend, firms are maximizing profits, and the quantity demanded equals the quantity supplied in all markets.

Allocation Labeling.

Referencing individuals $i = 1, ..., m$; firms $j = 1, ..., n$; and goods $k = 1, ..., K$ needs little change, even for large economies. $\sum_{i=1}^{m} A^i$ means to sum whatever "A^i" is over all its terms 1, ..., m.

- If individual i consumes goods $k = 1, ..., K$ in quantities $(x_1^i, x_2^i, ..., x_k^i, ..., x_K^i)$ we can represent his or her consumption as x^i. Things consumed by i are positive numbers and things supplied are negative numbers. Summing over individuals 1 to m item by item produces $(\sum_{i=1}^{m} x_1^i, \sum_{i=1}^{m} x_2^i, ..., \sum_{i=1}^{m} x_K^i) = (x_1, x_2, ..., x_K) = \sum_{i=1}^{m} x^i = x$, where $\sum_{i=1}^{m} x_k^i = x_k^1 + x_k^2 + ... + x_k^m$.

- As we did in the 2×2 example, lists can be displayed vertically.

$$x = \sum_{i=1}^{m} x^i = \sum_{i=1}^{m} \begin{pmatrix} x_1^i \\ x_2^i \\ \vdots \\ x_K^i \end{pmatrix} = \begin{pmatrix} \sum_{i=1}^{m} x_1^i \\ \sum_{i=1}^{m} x_2^i \\ \vdots \\ \sum_{i=1}^{m} x_K^i \end{pmatrix} = \begin{pmatrix} x_1 \\ x_2 \\ \vdots \\ x_K \end{pmatrix}$$

- To multiply two lists of equal length we multiply the first item by the first, add to it the second by the second, and so on to the end of the list. The result of this process is an **inner product**. It is denoted by a dot between the two lists being multiplied. If p is a list of prices and x is a list of consumption quantities,

$$p \cdot x = \begin{pmatrix} p_1 \\ p_2 \\ \vdots \\ p_K \end{pmatrix} \cdot \begin{pmatrix} x_1 \\ x_2 \\ \vdots \\ x_K \end{pmatrix} = p_1 x_1 + \cdots + p_K x_K$$

- Goods that are not produced during the current period because they are inherited from nature or the past are called **endowments.** We use ω to be the list of endowment quantities.

We add the word "competitive" to our definition of market equilibrium to clarify that firms and households take prices as given. This rules out a firm monopoly, for example, because a monopolistic firm can set its own price subject to the demand it faces. We also assume that preferred bundles exist. Theory can handle cases of satiated consumers—an ascetic who argues that nothing beyond his self-imposed minimum can make him happier, for example, is satiated—but the cost of doing so is not worth the effort here. We have bigger fish to fry.[2]

Competitive Equilibrium
A market is defined to be in competitive equilibrium if for the prices p that apply
- firms maximize profits,
- consumers maximize utility subject to their budget constraints, and

---

[2]Throughout the study of welfare economics there will be places where additional details—some would call them rabbit trails—could be pursued. In this book we are not producing an encyclopedia, and in any event, no model will represent every possible tiny feature of life. When rabbit trails appear, we remind ourselves that a map on a scale of one to one is useless. The economies we study *are* detailed enough that they could be a full blown economy. Any universal principles, therefore, must apply and be derivable in the settings we cover.

- demand equals supply in all markets.

2.4   Rationality and Revealed Preference

The essence of our treatment of welfare is that consumers *themselves* decide how well off or not well off they are. On page 27 we provided the four rules that are typically used to define rationality. The first four requirements seem to be good enough to define rationality, but they also can describe preferences that, while rational, would not reflect human behavior. We give one example relating to lexicographic preferences in the boxed material here. Assumption 5 rules this out. The next two requirements added to the first four are standard in the literature. Think of them as "axioms for *human* rationality."

5. for any bundle the set of alternatives in the *better-than set* (bundles that the individual ranks higher than a given bundle, or are indifferent to it) satisfies two properties
    a. if a series of bundles in the set can get arbitrarily close to a bundle A, then bundle A is in the set, and
    b. if bundles B and C are different bundles in the better-than set, then a bundle that is a weighted average of B and C is in the set,[3] and
    the above are true for the *worse-than set*, too.
6. for any bundle ranked by the consumer, there is another nearby bundle that the consumer would strictly prefer (i.e. no satiation),

One implication is that consumers who satisfy 1–6 can assign numbers to bundles such that a bundle with a higher number is preferred to a bundle with a lower number. Bundles with the same number are indifferent to one another. *What* numbers are used doesn't really matter as long as they preserve the ranking between bundles. Henceforth, we will call this number the consumer's *utility*.

---

[3]If x and y are numbers, then $tx + (1 - t)y$ where t is between 0 and 1, is a weighted average of them. A weighted average of two *bundles* is another bundle whose amounts are a weighted average, component by component, of the original two.

Lexicographic Preferences

A consumer who orders bundles the way a lexicographer orders words in a dictionary is said to have *lexicographic preferences.* Bundle A is strictly preferred to bundle B if A's first component exceeds the first component in B. If the first components are the same, then the bundle with the higher second component is strictly preferred. If the first and second components are equal, then the process proceeds to the third, and so on.

While rational according to the requirements of completeness, transitivity, and reflexivity, such preferences would trade away everything to reach a best possible state where only the quantity of the first good is maximized and valued. To see why this does not work to represent humans imagine a two-year-old who thinks he wants nothing but macaroni and cheese and is willing to trade away all other food, clothing, shelter, warmth, and even water. Adults know this is not viable.

Even without knowing a consumer's entire description of preferences we can use the consumer's actions to reveal facts about his or her preferences. For example, if we observe a consumer buying bundle of goods A when another bundle B was affordable because it cost less than the purchased bundle, then we know that the consumer must prefer bundle A to bundle B or be indifferent between them.

Let a particular set of prices p^0 be given and let bundle $x^{i,0}$ be the bundle chosen by household i when those prices prevailed. Let $x^{i,1}$ be some other bundle. Revealed preference tells us that the following must be true if consumers choose the best for themselves and have stable preferences:

Revealed Preference Rules

1. If $p^0 \cdot x^{i,0} \geq p^0 \cdot x^{i,1}$, it implies that bundle $x^{i,0}$ is preferred or indifferent to bundle $x^{i,1}$ (If both bundles are affordable, a strictly worse one will not be chosen).
2. If $x^{i,1}$ is strictly preferred to bundle $x^{i,0}$, then $p^0 \cdot x^{i,1} > p^0 \cdot x^{i,0}$ (If the strictly better bundle was not chosen, it must have been too expensive).

It is amazing, in some sense, that revealed preference and competitive market equilibrium are all that are needed to generate efficiency. In fact, they are not merely sufficient for efficiency, *they are efficiency.*

2.5 First & Second Fundamental Theorems of Welfare Economics

We are ready to state our two theorems. The First and Second Fundamental Theorems of Welfare Economics (FTWE) operationalize efficiency and provide us with a tool to organize discussions in other chapters.

2.5.1 Theorem One

Theorem 1: First Fundamental Theorem of Welfare Economics
Let $\{x^{1,0}, x^{2,0}, \ldots, x^{i,0}, \ldots, x^{m,0}\}, \{y^{1,0}, y^{2,0}, \ldots, y^{j,0}, \ldots, y^{n,0}\}$
be an allocation describing consumers $i = 1, \ldots, m$ and producers $j = 1, \ldots, n$ in some situation "0" in a competitive market economy where
  1) firms maximize profits,
  2) consumers maximize utility subject to their budget constraints,
  3) demand equals supply in all markets,
and consumers' utility rises for a bundle that contains a greater quantity of one or more goods and no less of any. Then the allocation in situation 0 is Pareto Optimal.

Proof: Because consumers value bundles with larger quantities of one or more goods, prices in situation 0 must be positive. Were a price negative or zero, more of the good would be demanded at the existing price by one or more consumers, implying excess demand and contradicting the assumption that demand equals supply in the initial equilibrium.

   Next, the allocation in 0 must be efficient, since if it were not there would then be some alternative feasible arrangement for the economy, call it "1", with quantities described by

$$\{x^{1,1}, x^{2,1}, \ldots, x^{m,1}\}, \{y^{1,1}, y^{2,1}, \ldots, y^{j,1}, \ldots, y^{n,1}\}$$

such that $x^{i,1}$ is preferred or indifferent to $x^{i,0}$ for all consumers and at least one consumer strictly prefers $x^{i,1}$.

By revealed preference, it must be that $p^0 \cdot x^{i,1} \geq p^0 \cdot x^{i,0} = I^{i,0}$ for every consumer where $I^{i,0}$ is the spendable money of household i in situation 0, and $p^0 \cdot x^{i,1} > p^0 \cdot x^{i,0}$ for at least one. Summing to the economy level, $\sum_{i=1}^{m} p^0 \cdot x^{i,1} = p^0 \cdot x^1 > p^0 \cdot x^0 = I^0 = \sum_{i=1}^{m} p^0 \cdot x^{i,0}$. Hence

$$p^0 \cdot x^1 > I^0.$$

But, x^1 can be no greater than production $y^1 + \omega$, hence $y^1 + \omega - x^1 \geq 0$ and $p^0 \cdot (y^1 + \omega) \geq p^0 \cdot x^1$ since prices p are positive. Likewise income I^0 must be derived from production $y^0 + \omega$.

Putting this all together,

$$p^0 \cdot (y^1 + \omega) \geq p^0 \cdot x^1 > I^0 = p^0 \cdot (y^0 + \omega)$$

which says that

$$p^0 \cdot y^1 > p^0 \cdot y^0.$$

This, however, contradicts the fact that firms maximize profits, and $p^0 \cdot y^0 \geq p^0 \cdot y$, for any choice of y including y^1. Thus, no such preferred allocation exists. This ends the proof. □

Waste and Excess Supply

It would seem obvious that if an equilibrium is to be efficient, there can be no "waste" or "extra" goods present in it. Consider for example a hypothetical wealthy consumer who buys an extra dress shirt that he leaves in its package at home never worn. Having an extra shirt in its package may provide him satisfaction nevertheless. Who are we to say that it does not?

Were it truly to be the case that this consumer was satiated, however, (no bundle could provide greater satisfaction than the one he is currently consuming), we could imagine another allocation where everything was identical except that this shirt was assigned to another consumer who would wear it and receive strictly greater utility. Obviously, then, the original allocation could not have been Pareto Optimal.

The mathematics of efficiency forces us to consider details like this. How can we rule out waste or excess goods? Our proof assumed that a consumer would always choose the bundle with one or more larger components present. In terms of our example, the rich man's shirt in the drawer provides satisfaction. Other ways economists have dealt with these kinds of particulars include simply assuming that equilibrium prices are positive; assuming that preferences satisfy certain convexity requirements (if bundle A is strictly preferred to bundle B, then a bundle equal to their average gives greater satisfaction than A); assuming that consumption equals available production ($x = y + \omega$) and so on.

How these and similar assumptions work to imply that competitive equilibria are efficient are details that we don't need to cover, but they do remind us that the First Fundamental Theorem of Welfare Economics applies to more circumstances than those shown treated here.

Before collecting remarks about the First Fundamental Theorem, let's restate it in a diagram that shows what the core of the proof is. Figure 2.1 shows aggregate consumption of an economy as point x^0. It is on the production possibility frontier because firms are maximizing profit in the competitive equilibrium which we assume applies in situation 0. The income associated with this consumption point is I^0. If a better consumption possibility exists, it must be associated with some higher income according to revealed preference, and therefore lie to the northeast such as at a point like x^1. Since consumption must come from production, points x^0 and x^1 require that the income associated with $y^1 + \omega$ necessarily be greater than the income associated with $y^0 + \omega$ as shown in the two labeled budget lines. Meeting this requirement is impossible, however, because profit was maximized at y^0 and any other production must come from points below the Income = I^0 line. Since the required presence of x^1 to the northeast is impossible, no such possibility exists.

We now turn to Figure 2.2, which shows a Venn diagram, popularized in the 1800s by English mathematician John Venn to show logical relationships between sets. If the entire space is the set of feasible allocations possible for the economy, the larger circle con-

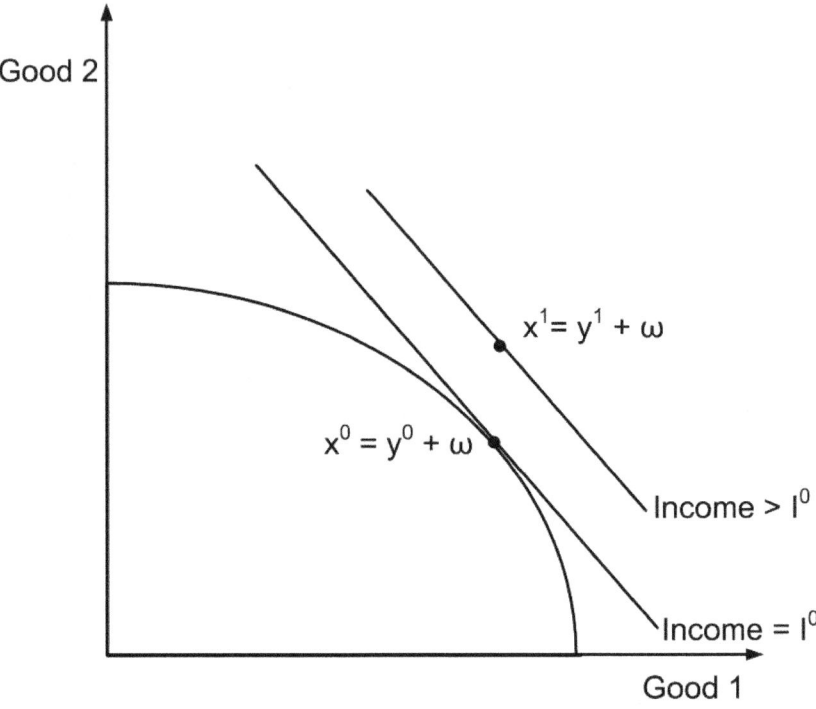

Figure 2.1: **The First Fundamental Theorem Explained**

tained therein represents all allocations that are efficient, i.e. those allocations from which is it physically impossible to alter circumstances to make one or more individuals better off without harming anyone in the process. The 1st Fundamental Theorem says that the set of allocations resulting from a competitive equilibrium is a subset of the set of efficient allocations.

No one has told anyone in a competitive equilibrium to work to organize the entire economy in a particular way, no government is even present in our discussion. Yet somehow the desire of households to maximize utility in their own best interest and the desire of firms to maximize profits in their own best interest, leads to an efficient outcome that cannot be improved on. Competitive markets produce and distribute private goods efficiently. No Pareto Superior alternative exists.

We have said little about how a competitive equilibrium might be

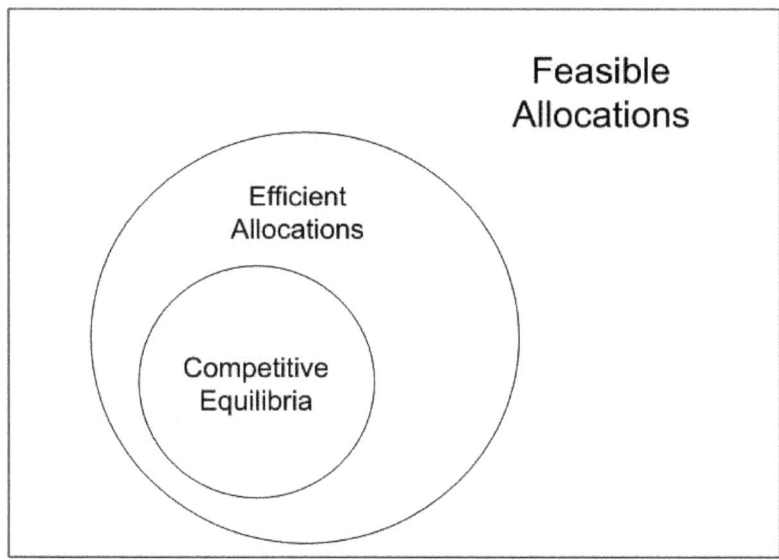

Figure 2.2: **Competitive Equilibria are Efficient Equilibria**

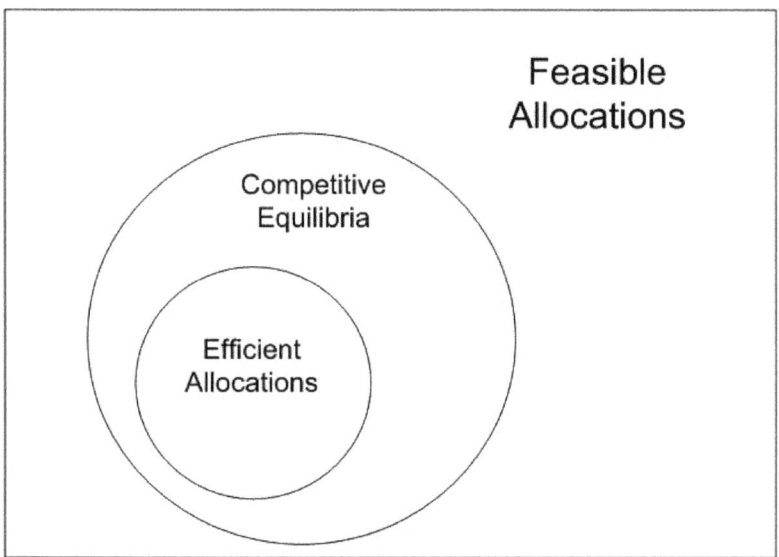

Figure 2.3: **Efficient Equilibria are Competitive Equilibria**

arrived at. In our 2×2 economy there were two firms that could have profits and the income from endowments was $p \cdot \omega = rK$. The other source of income arose as part of our description of the consumer's choice x^i. This is income derived from the sale of labor, wx_L^i. By identifying x_L^i with each consumer, the definition of competitive equilibrium automatically implied that each consumer would spend the earnings produced by his or her own labor. If we go outside the definition of competitive equilibrium, however, there is nothing in our description of the economy that says income *must be* spent by the household that earned it. If the consumer's share of income from endowments and profit were arbitrarily set to equal $-wx_L^i + A$, for example, such a consumer would have spendable income A. The model naturally leads us, therefore, to think about morality and ownership issues that go beyond efficiency.

Finally, it is possible in our economy to envision a consumer that provides no labor, has no share of profits, owns no share of the economy's endowments. Do we let this consumer starve? In the 1st Theorem, we started from the assumption of a competitive equilibrium. By assumption viable consumers were present where each spent sufficient income to support himself or herself.

2.5.2 Theorem Two

Theorem 2: Second Fundamental Theorem of Welfare Economics

Let an economy of $i = 1, \ldots, m$ consumers and $j = 1, \ldots, n$ producers satisfy standard assumptions regarding consumer preferences, production technologies, and endowments that allow a market equilibrium to exist. Then if

$$a^0 = [\{x^{1,0}, x^{2,0}, \ldots, x^{i,0}, \ldots, x^{m,0}\}, \{y^{1,0}, y^{2,0}, \ldots, y^{j,0}, \ldots, y^{n,0}\}]$$

is an efficient allocation, a^0 could be made to be the outcome of a competitive equilibrium for this economy with appropriate assignment of asset ownerships.

The need to assign appropriate prior ownership of assets is required, of course, because the efficient allocation that we might want to replicate in the market setting could involve one agent being given the bulk of the feasible consumption. In that case, the market replica would need to assign a large ownership to him. It should also be evident that in order for an efficient arrangement to be the outcome of a competitive equilibrium, situations in which no competitive equilibrium exists need to be excepted. There are odd cases, often involving agents that are on the edge of their feasible consumption set (the set of bundles which could be consumed and keep the agent alive), for example, where no competitive equilibrium will exist. The assumption that every consumer consumes a bundle that is larger than the absolute minimum needed to keep him alive might be needed to rule out the exceptions. While we are grateful that the mathematics directs us to take account of the exceptional cases, we care about more normal situations.

The proof of the second theorem, dating back to the 1950s, takes more mathematical sophistication than we wish to take the space for here. It can be found in sources referenced at the end of the chapter.

Figure 2.3 uses the same Venn diagram as Figure 2.2. The First Fundamental Theorem says that the set of allocations resulting from a competitive equilibrium is contained in the set of efficient allocations, while the Second Fundamental Theorem says that the set of efficient allocations is contained in the set of allocations resulting from a competitive equilibrium. If set A is a subset of set B, and set B is a subset of set A, the two sets must be the same.

In other words, competitive market equilibria don't just have the property of efficiency, competitive market equilibria *are the same thing as efficiency*. If you want an efficient economy, then you want an economy that is a competitive market equilibrium and the closer you get to efficiency the closer you get to that configuration.

2.6 Conclusion

The First and Second Fundamental Theorems of Welfare Economics say that efficient outcomes in the economy are the same thing as competitive equilibria. They convert the definition of Pareto Optimality into a working tool because we can discuss the requirements of markets, trade, and commerce and use them to find the required conditions for efficiency. The engineering requirements of efficiency become the economic requirements of markets and vice versa. The next chapter explores this connection.

References

The prime reference for the First and Second Fundamental Theorems of Welfare Economics is:

Debreu, Gerard. *Theory of Value: An Axiomatic Analysis of Economic Equilibrium*, Cowles Foundation for Research in Economics at Yale University, New Haven, CT: Yale University Press, 1959.

Theory of Value provides references to earlier material, nearly all of which post date World War II. There are numerous subsequent references, a few of which follow.

Arrow, Kenneth J. and F. H. Hahn, *General Competitive Analysis*, San Francisco: Holden-Day, Inc., 1971.

Quirk, James and Rubin Saposnik, *Introduction to General Equilibrium Theory and Welfare Economics*, New York: McGraw-Hill Book Company, 1968.

Malinvaud, E., *Lectures on Microeconomic Theory*, New York: American Elsevier Publishing Co., Inc., 1972.

Mas-Colell, Andreu, Michael d. Whinston, and Jerry R. Green, *Microeconomic Theory*, New York: Oxford University Press, 1995.

Starr, Ross M., *General Equilibrium Theory: An Introduction*, New York: Cambridge University Press, 1997.

Part 2: Chapter 4

Behind the Magic Curtain

Chapter 4 of Part 1 explained that human flourishing implies Pareto Optimality, which in turn implies a list of things about firm production, household consumption, and the relationship between the two. In this chapter we use first year calculus[1] and diagrams to elaborate on the meaning of this list using two goods, two factors, and two people.

We start with implications for the firm. Firms must "outdated technology despise, cost minimize, profit maximize, and hire wise." Sections 4.1–4.4 begin by sorting out the rhyme.

4.1 Step 1: "Outdated Technology Despise"

The most basic description of production is a recipe. "Take two of these, two of those, three of that, stir, and bake for 45 minutes to produce one of this." If there is more than one way, the firm must pick the best recipe. If we can understand the choice in a simple case, we can understand it in more complicated ones. Figure 4.1(a) displays a situation where 16 recipes use labor and capital (L, K) to produce one unit of output (q). The number of units of labor needed is read from the horizontal axis, the number of units of capital needed is read from the vertical axis. Recipe 15, far to the northeast, appears to need a lot of labor and a lot of capital, while recipe 4 appears to need less labor and less capital.

---

[1]Specifically, we assume familiarity with the derivative, partial derivative, and total differential.

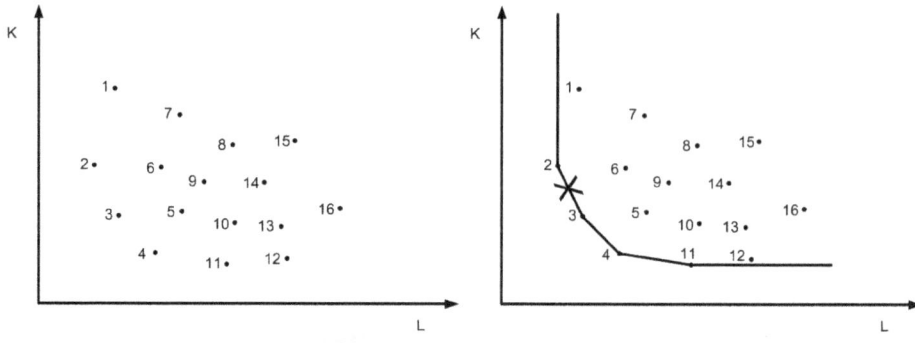

(a) **16 Recipes That Produce One Unit of Output**

(b) **Only 4 Recipes Are Efficient**

Figure 4.1: **"Outdated Recipes Despise"**

Figure 4.1(b) adds lines between recipes 2, 3, 4, and 11. A vertical line lies above recipe 2 and a horizontal line lies to the right of recipe 11. What does this boundary mean? First look at the line between recipes 2 and 3. Were half a unit of output produced using recipe 2 and half a unit produced using recipe 3, the inputs needed would be halfway between 2 and 3 (marked by an "x"). As the percentage of output produced using recipe 2 rises, the "x" moves proportionately closer to 2 until at 100% the x lies at point 2. Now notice, for any point that lies to the northeast of the boundary, there exists some point on the boundary that uses *less labor and less capital* to produce one unit of output. Any recipe to the northeast of the boundary, therefore—including recipes 1, 5 to 10, and 12 to 16—is "out of date," i.e. inefficient. It follows that the firm should produce one unit of output using points on the boundary only. The vertical line and horizontal line represent possible choices but ones that use either too much capital or too much labor. We will see why these are rejected when we talk about cost minimization.

A similar process that we could explain mathematically but could no longer draw applies when there are more inputs than 2 and more outputs than 1.

Since what we learn from Figure 4.1 suffices for our purposes, we summarize: Technology consists of society's book of recipes. If some good (say iPhones in 1955) has no recipes, it cannot be produced until knowledge increases and someone invents a way. As

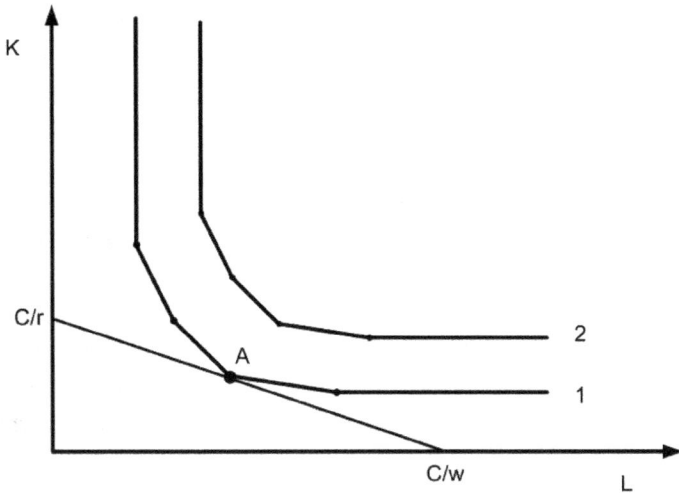

Figure 4.2: **Choosing a Point A Where Cost is Minimized**

the collection of recipes grows, the boundary for a producable good such as shown in Figure 4.1(b) moves toward the origin. The first requirement that Pareto Optimality places on a firm is to use only recipes that are efficient, i.e. on the boundary.

4.2   Step 2: "Cost Minimize"

Figure 4.1(b) can be taken a step further. Call the boundary already drawn an "isoquant" from "'iso" for same, and "quant" for quantity. Any input combination selected on the isoquant is capable of producing one unit of output. To produce 2 units of output, means there will be another isoquant that lies to the northeast, and so on for 3 units of output and up. In fact, the diagram will be filled with isoquants, all convex to the origin, that reflect the efficient (or "undominated") input choices for producing the given amount of output.

Beyond choosing to produce using an input combination on an isoquant, the firm must also choose the best place on the isoquant. If the firm pays for labor and capital, its cost is

$$C = wL + rK$$

where C is cost, w is the wage rate, L is the amount of labor hired, r is the price of capital (say the cost of an hour of machine time), and K is the amount of capital hired.[2] If all cost is devoted to labor, then $\frac{C}{w}$ is the amount of labor hired, and if all cost is devoted to capital, $\frac{C}{r}$ is the amount of capital hired. Plotting the line generated gives the downward-sloping line shown in Figure 4.2 with intercepts $\frac{C}{w}$ and $\frac{C}{r}$. Lines for lower cost spending lie below and to the left of the line drawn. Thus the lowest possible cost line that still allows a choice of inputs on the isoquant for 1 unit of output, is the line drawn. Point A is that input choice ("input mix," "recipe") that minimizes the cost of producing 1 unit of output. We can imagine moving the cost line outward (not drawn) to find the cost minimizing choice to produce 2 units of output, or 3 or 4.5 or any other quantity. We would never choose a point on the vertical line above point 2 of Figure 4.1(b) or to the right of 11 because it would mean paying for more input than needed. Higher cost, same output.

Let's summarize: Using the process just described, let L[q] and K[q] be the cost minimizing choices for producing any given quantity q. Then

$$C[q] \equiv wL[q] + rK[q]$$

defines the least cost of producing q units of output. C[q] comes from using efficient technologies only (i.e. isoquants) and selecting cost-minimizing points from them.

4.3   Step 3: "Profit Maximize"

To be efficient a firm must reject working with inefficient technology, choose the least-cost point on an iso-quant, but also pick the right iso-quant, which from the First and Second Fundamental Theorems of Welfare Economics we know it does by choosing that q which

---

[2]Unfortunately, the term "capital" is commonly used to refer both to the services of capital (a flow, or quantity per unit time) and to a stock, as in a physical machine. When capital as a stock is referred to, its price is the purchase price of the machine. When capital refers to the productive services of a machine its price is the price of the service provided, that is, a "rental rate" on the machine's time. We use variable r to emphasize that we are talking about a rental rate. For completeness, we note that financial capital is also often abbreviated and called simply "capital" because financial assets can be converted into the previous two forms of capital by purchase.

maximizes profits. Profit, $\pi[q]$, is the difference between the value of what the firm sells and the cost of making it

$$\pi[q] = pq - C[q]$$

where p is price. How is profit maximized? The answer is, in the same way that any function of a single variable that ranges from 0 to infinity is maximized. Straight engineering (or straight mathematics) tells us that if the right choice, $q*$, is positive, then

1. $\pi'[q*] = p - C'[q*] = 0$, i.e. price equals marginal cost ($C'[q*] \equiv \frac{dC}{dq}$ is marginal cost),
2. $\pi''[q*] \leq 0$, i.e. marginal cost rises at $q*$ (π'' denotes the second derivative of π), and
3. $\pi[q*] \geq \pi[0]$, i.e. price exceeds average variable cost at $q*$.[3]

Otherwise, $q*$ is zero.

All this is the subject of standard microeconomics. We have done enough, however, to highlight this connection: Pareto Optimality requires maximizing profit at market price p and this, in turn, implies that the price consumers pay will be held down to the actual cost of producing the unit being sold, which is its marginal cost of production. It is the competition in competitive equilibrium that keeps prices low.

4.4   Step 4: "Hire Wise"   (ly)

Profit maximization implies at least one other important fact. Presume Step 1. Then output is a function of inputs, $q = F[L, K]$, and $\pi[F[L, K]] = pF[L, K] - wL - rK$, since costs are $wL + rK$. Figure 4.3 explains a hiring condition that results. Since additional L results in additional output, we give it the name MP_L for "marginal product of labor."[4] If the value of the added output (pMP_L) exceeds the cost of the added labor that produced it, profit is raised and hiring should continue. The hiring process should end only when L^* is reached as in the figure. Going beyond L^* means the firm is

---

[3] $\pi[0] = C[0]$ = fixed cost by definition of fixed cost. Since $C[q*] - C[0]$ equals variable cost by definition, condition 3 becomes $q \times (p - \frac{\text{variable cost}}{q*}) \geq 0$, which is equivalent to requiring that price exceeds average variable cost.

[4] $MP_L \equiv \frac{\partial F}{\partial L}$.

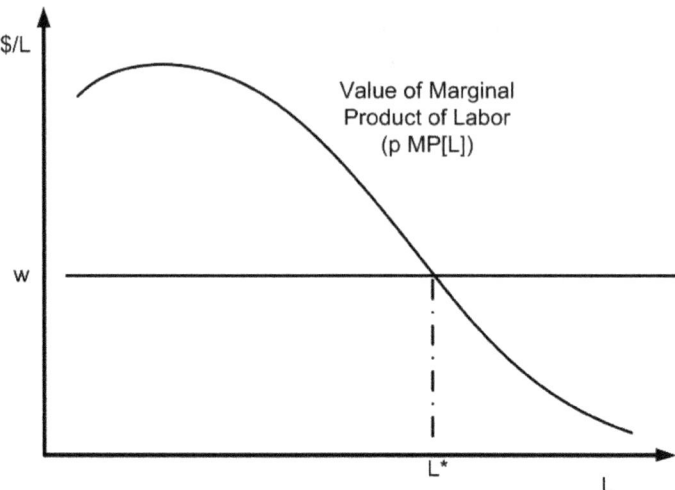

Figure 4.3: **The Hiring Condition for Input L is** $w = MP_L$

reducing its profit. We will use the resulting hiring condition

$$w = pMP_L$$

(wage equals the value of the marginal product of labor) and its counterpart for capital to discuss the essential economics of competitive markets.

4.5   The Edgeworth Box

Francis Ysidro Edgeworth (1845-1926), Oxford professor, economist and mathematician of the late nineteenth and early twentieth centuries developed a useful tool to graphically display matters relating to trade and value. The Edgeworth Box has been used ever since. It is so valuable that we take a short digression to introduce it, then use it in our discussion of the implications of Pareto Optimality. Presume a fixed stock of two goods, X and Y, owned by two individuals Blue and Green. If we create a box whose dimensions are the total quantity of X between the two of them on the horizontal axis and the total Y between the two of them on the vertical axis, we can place Blue at the lower left corner and Green at the upper right. Figure 4.4 results.

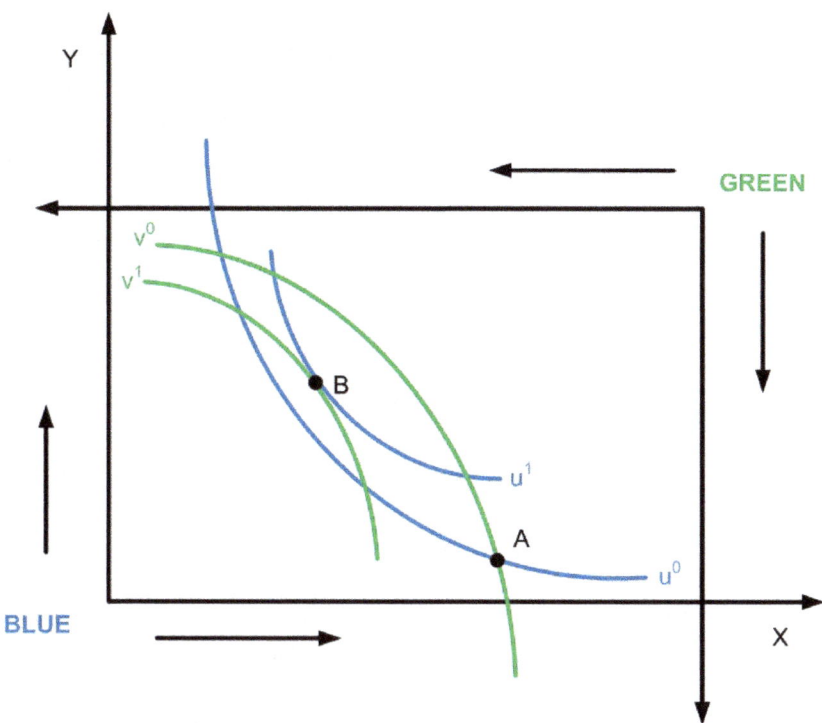

Figure 4.4: **Edgeworth Box for Consumers Blue and Green**

Now consider point A. From the Blue origin, the rightward distance to A measures how much X Blue has. Measuring upward,
point A shows how much Y Blue has. Measure *down* from the
Green origin. It shows how much Y Green has. Finally, measure to
the left from the Green origin, and it shows how much X Green has.
In other words, the location of point A in the box formed in Figure
4.4 automatically divides the total quantity of X and of Y between
the two consumers.

Next notice the curved line labeled u^0. It is the collection of all
bundles (X, Y) of the two goods that give to Blue utility equal to u^0,
which is the same utility that bundle A gives to Blue. It is called an
indifference curve because the consumer is indifferent between any
two bundles on it. A second indifference curve labeled u^1 is shown
whose bundles give higher utility. The identical explanation applies
to indifference curves v^0 and v^1 that apply to consumer Green, which
are viewed from the perspective of Green's origin. There is more that
can be said about the Edgeworth Box, but this is enough to proceed.

4.6   Distributive Efficiency

Imagine now that consumers Blue and Green have been isolated
from some economy. In other words, there might be many other
consumers and many other goods, but these two consumers happen to consume X and Y, and their holdings are given by point A.
Pareto Optimality requires that there be no opportunity for mutually
beneficial trade between Blue and Green. How do we check this?

From point A consider all bundles that would give higher utility to Blue. We can call the bundles that are better than A the
"better-than" set. These bundles lie to the northeast of indifference
curve u^0. Likewise, the better-than set to point A for Green lies
to the southwest of indifference curve v^0. These two better-than
sets overlap! Any point in the lens shaped region of overlap would
provide greater utility to Blue *and* greater utility to Green. Point B
is an example.

Since re-arranging Blue and Green's holdings to point B gives
both consumers higher utility (u^1 is greater than u^0 and v^1 is greater
than v^0) we know that the economy from which Blue and Green were
taken could not have been Pareto Optimal. In fact, the move from

point A to point B can be thought of as a trade. Blue gives up X
to gain Y, and Green does the reverse.

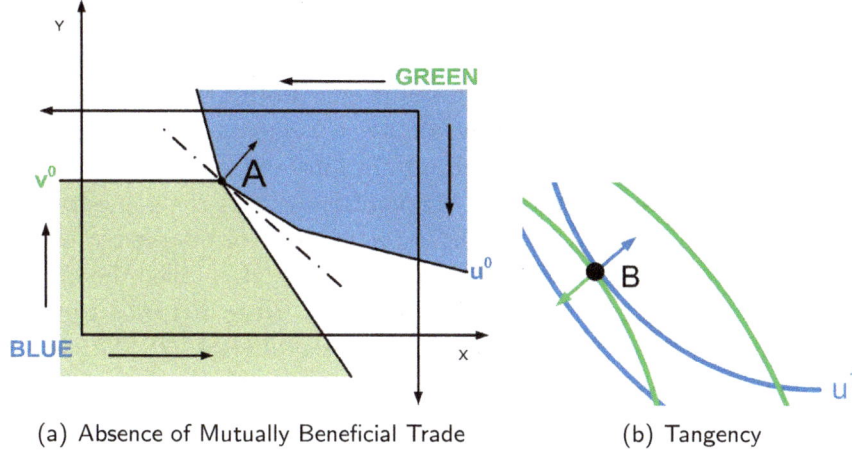

(a) Absence of Mutually Beneficial Trade   (b) Tangency

Figure 4.5: **Non-Tangencies and Tangencies**

Figure 4.5(a) produces a different diagram where the allocation
is at point A and the better-than sets of Blue and Green (shaded) do
not overlap. Whenever this happens, no further mutually beneficial
trade is possible. From the First and Second Fundamental Theorems
of Economics we know that there will exist a set of prices, call these
p_X and p_Y, such that there is a budget line such as the dashed line
that separates these sets and guarantees they lie on opposite sides.[5]

When no re-arrangement of existing goods can improve the utility of any consumer without harming some other, we say that **Distributive Efficiency** holds. Pareto Optimality implies Distributive
Efficiency. That is our main takeaway. The second has to do with
prices. For any budget line it is the case that plotting its prices
as a vector (p_X, p_Y) in a Cartesiaon coordinate system produces a
direction (from the origin to the plotted point) that is perpendicular
to the budget line. Placing these direction arrows at point B as is
done in Figure 4.5(b) produces the blue and green arrows. In three
dimensions the direction is perpendicular to the budge plane, and in
higher dimensions the same result applies.

---

[5]Blue would have a budget line where $p_X X^{Blue} + p_Y Y^{Blue}$ is the amount
spent and likewise Green would spend $p_X X^{Green} + p_Y Y^{Green}$.

Point B in Figure 4.5(b) is at a tangency of indifference curves and further mutually beneficial trades are impossible. Were Blue to do better, point B would have to move to the northeast of indifference curve u^1, and for Green to do better, point B would have to move to the southwest of the green indifference curve passing through B. It cannot simultaneously do both. Because of smooth curves and interior B, we get a tangency where only one budget line can pass through B that doesn't cut into either better-than set.

If we were to ask Blue, "At point B, what is the value to you of having a bit more X?" the answer would have to be given in terms of Y given in trade. This trade-off has a name. It is called the marginal rate of substitution of X for Y, $MRS_{X,Y}$. Since it is *Blue's* personal internal value placed on good X, we designate it $MRS_{X,Y}^{Blue}$. Green's private internal value for X would be $MRS_{X,Y}^{Green}$. We will give the calculus and geometrical meaning shortly.

When mutually beneficial trade remains, these two personal values are unequal, e.g. $MRS_{X,Y}^{Blue} > MRS_{X,Y}^{Green}$ would indicate that Blue should acquire X from Green in a trade. When the values have become equal, no further trade is mutually beneficial.

There is a geometrical interpretation, too. In Figure 4.5(a) if A is the origin, we have already said that the arrow pointing northeast from A can be plotted as (p_X, p_Y). As is the case in Figure 4.5(b), when a differentiable utility function, $u = u[X, Y]$, gives an indifference curve as all (X, Y) that generate a common utility value,[6] it is the case that the same direction can be plotted as (MU_X, MU_Y) where $MU_X = \frac{\partial u}{\partial X}$ and $MU_Y = \frac{\partial u}{\partial Y}$.

Last, because directions (i.e. the arrows in Figures 4.5(a) and 4.5(b)) do not change when multiplied by a fixed number, all of the following point in the same direction,

$$(p_X, p_Y), \ (MU_X, MU_Y), \ (MRS_{X,Y}, 1), \ (\frac{p_X}{p_Y}, 1),$$

and the last two are numerically equal, i.e. $(MRS_{X,Y}, 1) = (\frac{p_X}{p_Y}, 1)$. Thus,

$$MRS_{X,Y} = \frac{p_X}{p_Y} \qquad (4.1)$$

---

[6]That is, $u[X, Y] = 4$ gives the indifference curve for utility equal to 4. $u[X, Y] = 12$ gives the indifference curve for utility equal to 12.

is the mnemomic equation we use to remind us of Distributive Efficiency.

Conclusion: When goods are distributed in such a way that redistribution of the available totals cannot improve anyone's utility without harming another we say that we have Distributive Efficiency. Distributive Efficiency means further mutually beneficial trade is impossible. In the typical case, the mnemonic that applies is equation (4.1).

4.7   Input Efficiency

Having done the hard work of creating the Edgeworth Box and explaining Distributive Efficiency, we reap the benefit in Input Efficiency. **Input Efficiency** applies if by re-arranging the use of the fixed supply of inputs it is impossible to increase the output of any good without lowering the output of any other. Figure 4.6 shows the

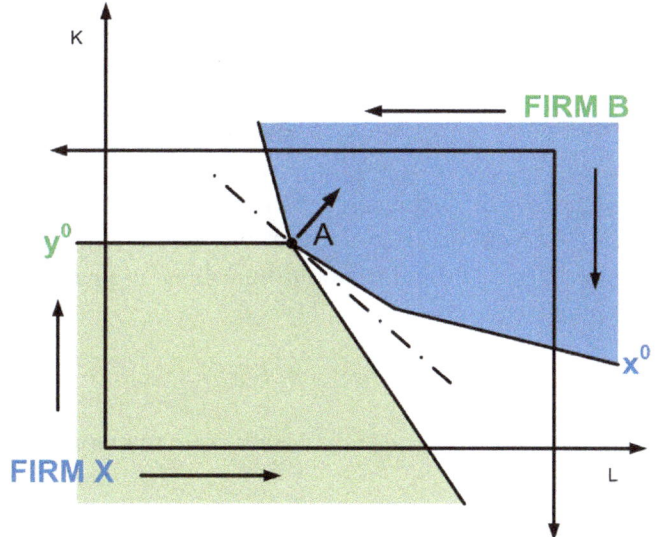

Figure 4.6: **Input Efficiency**

production of two firms, Firm X and Firm Y, that we imagine have been isolated from the rest of the economy along with their inputs of L and K. If the economy is Pareto Optimal then Input Efficiency must hold. Since the diagram is identical to a relabeling of Figure 4.5(a) we apply the identical arguments.

From the First and Second Fundamental Theorems of Welfare Economics there exist prices for inputs L and K, plus prices of outputs X and Y such that at point A any way to produce more X lies to the northeast of the iso-quant labeled X^0 and any way to produce more Y lies to the southwest of the iso-quant labeled Y^0. There is no way to simultaneously move into both regions, so there is no way to increase X without lowering Y. In this diagram cost is determined by the expenditure on inputs used, say $wL^X + rK^X$ in the case of Firm X which produces good X,[7] and the direction given by (w, r) is perpendicular to the dashed cost line shown in Figure 4.6.

We intentionally drew a case where the iso-quants are not smooth, because the conclusions about Pareto Optimality and Input Efficiency apply in general. However, as was true in the case of Distributive Efficiency, when smooth iso-quants apply and A is an interior point we can produce a mnemonic to summarize the main conclusions about efficient use of inputs. Let $X = F[L^X, K^X]$, $Y = G[L^Y, K^Y]$ be the production functions that generate iso-quants as level curves.[8] In analogy to the case of consumption, define

$$MP_L \equiv \frac{\partial F}{\partial L}, \ MP_K \equiv \frac{\partial F}{\partial K}, \ \text{and} \ MRTS_{L,K} \equiv \frac{MP_L}{MP_K}.$$

The Marginal Rate of Technical Substitution of L for K, $MRTS_{L,K}$, is the private internal value to the firm of an additional unit of labor measured in units of capital it would be willing to give up for labor. All of the following

$$(w, r), \ (MP_L, MP_K), \ (MRTS_{L,K}, 1), \ \left(\frac{w}{r}, 1\right)$$

point in the same direction and the last two are numerically identical. Thus,

$$MRTS_{L,K} = \frac{w}{r} \tag{4.2}$$

is the mnemonic equation we use to remind us of Input Efficiency.

---

[7]w is the wage rate for labor, r is the price of capital input, L^X and K^X are labor and capital inputs used, and X is the firm's output.

[8]That is, $F[L^X, K^X] = 32$ gives the iso-quant for 32 units of output, $F[L^X, K^X] = 120$ gives the iso-quant for 125 units of output, and so on.

4.8 Sector Allocation Efficiency

If Pareto Optimality holds, then **Sector Allocation Efficiency** must also hold. That is, it must be impossible to increase the output of any good by re-assigning output levels of two sectors.[9] Consider two

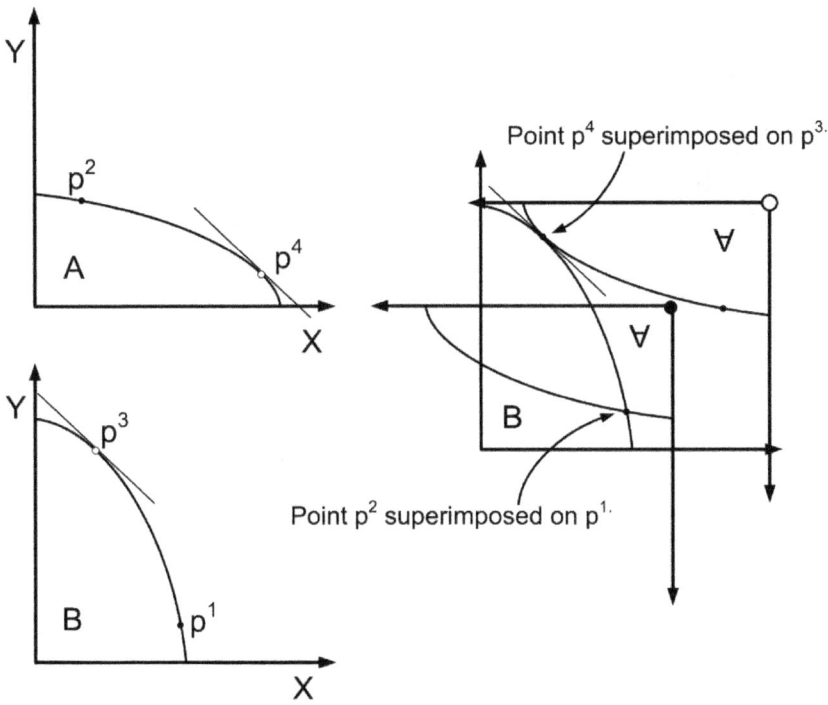

Figure 4.7: **Sector Allocation Efficiency**

regions, A and B, that produce two goods X and Y. Presume that each sector is producing on its frontier, given by points p^1 and p^2 in Figure 4.7. Total output of the two sectors is shown to the right were we have inverted the diagram for sector A and superimposed point p^2 on point p^1. In the right diagram the origin of inverted sector A (solid circle) and the origin of sector B identify a box, the dimensions of which give total X and total Y produced. Now try having sector B produce at point p^3 and sector A at point p^4. In the rightmost diagram, invert sector A as before, superimpose p^4 onto p^3

---

[9]A sector is defined on page 61.

and consider the larger box that is produced. No re-arrangement of sector outputs can produce combined output that lies to the northeast of the open circle. In other words, sector assignment p^3, p^4 is Pareto Optimal and the other assignment is not. Sector Allocation Efficiency requires that the marginal rate of transformation of sectors be equalized, $MRT^A_{X,Y} = MRT^B_{X,Y}$ as it is at points p_3 and p_4.[10] Consider again sector A. $MRT^A_{X,Y}$ is the cost in sector A of producing more good X in terms of good Y that has to be given up.[11] As long as $MRT^B_{X,Y} > MRT^A_{X,Y}$, which is the case in the original assignment, it makes sense to have the lower-cost sector do more of the X production. This re-assignment stops only when the two costs become the same $MRT^B_{X,Y} = MRT^A_{X,Y}$. In Figure 4.7 equality $MRT^B_{X,Y} = MRT^A_{X,Y}$ is shown by identical slopes of the sector frontiers at p^3 and p^4.

Conclusion: Presuming a smooth frontier so slope is defined, the slope of the sector frontier is given by the applicable prices p_X/p_Y,[12] hence if Pareto Optimality holds,

$$MRT^A_{X,Y} = \frac{p_X}{p_Y} = MRT^B_{X,Y}$$

.

Marginal Rates of Substitution and Transformation
If $MRS_{X,Y}$ is being considered, think of this term as the "value" of the first item showing in the subscript. If $MRT_{X,Y}$ is being considered, think of it as the "cost" of producing the first item in

---

[10]The marginal rate of transformation of X for Y, $MRT_{X,Y} = -\frac{dY}{dX}$, where the derivative $\frac{dY}{dX}$ is taken on the production frontier. For example, at point p^4 for sector A, $MRT^A_{X,Y} = -\frac{dY}{dX}$ where $\frac{dY}{dX}$ is the slope of the line passing through p^4.

[11]Sector A's inputs must be re-directed to generate more X, meaning less Y.

[12]The First and Second Fundamental Theorems do not depend on smooth frontier. Presuming differentiability, however, let $X = F[L^X, K^X], Y = G[L^Y, K^Y]$ for a given sector. Since labor and capital are fixed in the sector, adjustments between them must add to zero ($dL^X + dL^Y = 0$, $dK^X + dK^Y = 0$), and the hiring conditions $p_X MP^X_L = w$, $p_X MP^X_K = r$; $p_Y MP^Y_L = w$, $p_Y MP^Y_K = r$ apply. Then $MRT_{X,Y} = -\frac{dY}{dX} = \frac{MP^Y_L dL^Y + MP^Y_K dK^Y}{MP^X_L(-dL^X) + MP^X_K(-dK^X)} = \frac{\frac{w}{p_Y}dL^Y + \frac{r}{p_Y}dK^Y}{\frac{w}{p_X}dL^Y + \frac{r}{p_X}dK^Y} = \frac{p_X}{p_Y}$.

the subscript. If "'value" exceeds "cost," for example, the item is worth producing. If not, then not.

4.9 Full Employment

Pareto Optimality requires there to be full employment. The discussion of BigGears electricity on page 61 explains that if at the end of the production period usable inputs were never used, it would have been possible to put them to work, produce more of some good without lowering the output of any other, and from the increased output raise utility. We use this section, therefore, to expand our discussion. For example, what does full employment mean for a productive input such as labor whose provision lowers utility? How do competitive markets lead to full employment? Finally, what about renewable and non-renewable natural resources?

Labor. There are many kinds of inputs. We have already noted that in most people's minds the most important input probably would be labor. Just because I offer myself to be lead opera singer at New York City's Metropolitan Opera and am never chosen, does that mean I am unemployed? Or, I offer myself for the lead quarterback position for the coming season of last year's National Football League Superbowl team. I will suit up hour for hour, I will be at practice hour for hour, I will play games hour for hour just like the team's current quarterback. Am I an unemployed Superbowl quarterback?

Not quite. To be unemployed a factor of production must be fully suited to the job, willing to work at the available rate, and not be employed, while buyers who are willing to pay the available rate for such a fully suited input simultaneously go wanting. Pareto Optimality implies market clearing and market clearing guarantees this situation does not happen.

Figure 4.8 uses one of the most familiar diagrams in all of economics to show demand and supply in a market for skilled labor that involves high risk. Perhaps this involves dangerous high altitude work on skyscrapers under construction. Below wage w^0 no one is willing to do such risky work, but at wage w^1 willing buyers want

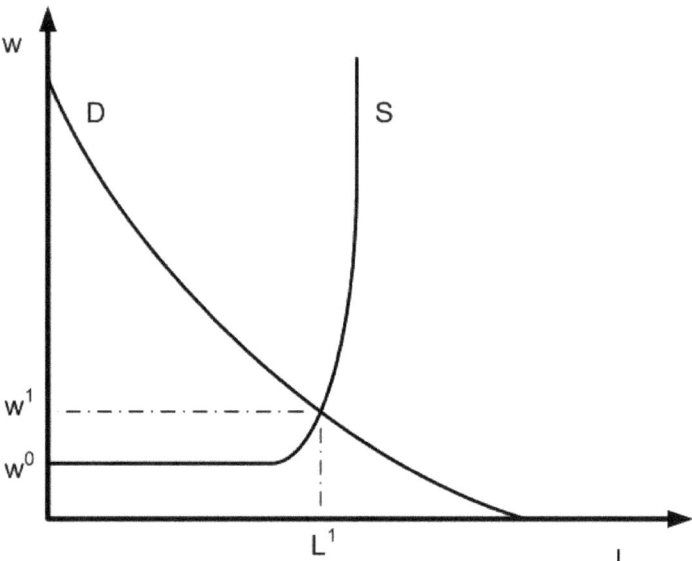

Figure 4.8: **Market Clearing in Labor**

to hire L^1 units of labor that willing sellers want to provide. Because Pareto Optimality implies that markets clear, unemployment is zero. In this example the supply curve becomes vertical as one moves to the right, meaning that there is a limited number of people willing to work in this market at any wage. The risk, unpleasantness, and other working conditions may determine features of the supply curve, but do not affect the conclusion about full employment. The same arguments apply to supplying the services of other inputs such as a physical machine whose use does not enter directly into utility as it does for labor.

Time. Now consider a different hypothetical example having to do with a non-renewable input such as oil. Figure 4.9 shows stocks of oil on the vertical axis and time on the horizontal. There obviously should be no oil left whenever the sun burns out 5 to 6 billion years from now and human life, at least on this earth, must end. But should the path of usage be Path A, B, or C? If we choose Path A we are using almost no oil today, leaving it for our descendants who may, in fact, be far richer than we are and not need it. Path C is the reverse, using it all up today and perhaps leaving our children to freeze in the dark tomorrow. Path B is intermediate, but it too may or may not be right. Full employment has to do with knowing how

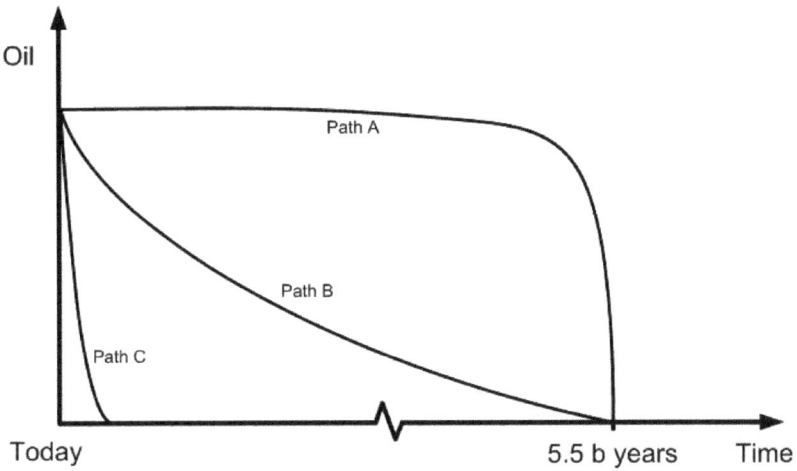

Figure 4.9: **Non-Renewal Input Use**

fast a renewable or non-renewable resource should be used over time, the study of which constitutes an entire sub-discipline in economics and about which entire books have been devoted.[13] This is beyond our intentions and interest here to cover, but we provide one result that shows the flavor of what can be done.

Figure 4.10 breaks the timing decision about whether to use now or later into two periods. Let Q be the quantity of the non-renewable (oil) in hand today. It can either be used now (sold today) or stored (sold tomorrow). If it is sold today at the current price P^0 it garners P^0Q dollars that can be put into the bank at i interest making $(1 + i)P^0Q$ available tomorrow.

To compare like with like, let's find out what selling tomorrow does for spending tomorrow. Tomorrow's price by definition is $P^1 = P^0 + \Delta P$. If the oil is stored and sold tomorrow it generates $(P^0 + \Delta P)Q$. Thus, if $(1 + i)P^0Q > (P^0 + \Delta P)Q$ it implies all oil will be sold today and the reverse inequality implies none will be sold today. Only if equality holds is oil available in both periods. After

---

[13]A renewable natural resource might be a forest that is left to grow over many years. When to cut its trees becomes the subject of study.

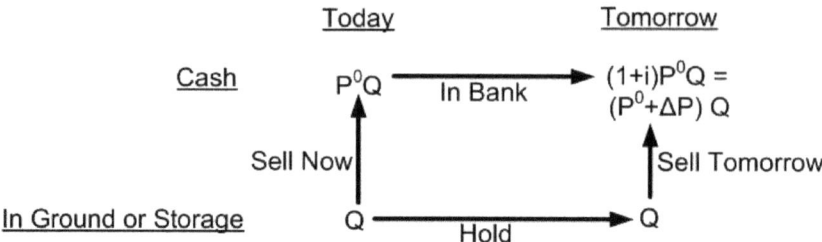

Figure 4.10: **Non-Renewable Asset**

a little algebra we find that

$$\frac{\Delta P}{P^0} = i$$

must be true. In other words, *ceterus paribus* the price of the non-renewable input should rise with the rate of interest, a result that ties the rate of usage to economic conditions.

4.10   Consumer Sovereignty

We have already seen that Pareto Optimality implies Distributive Efficiency and that equalized marginal rates of substitution means no re-distribution of existing goods and can improve anyone's utility without harming another.   In this section, we start by assuming equality of MRS's and show that Pareto Optimality implies a fifth condition, equality of $MRS^i_{X,Y}$ with $MRT_{X,Y}$. This new condition, **Consumer Sovereignty**, says that it is impossible by changing the mix of goods produced to improve anyone's utility without harming another.

We demonstrate this condition by showing that if $MRS^1_{X,Y} = MRS^2_{X,Y} = ... = MRS^m_{X,Y} > MRT_{X,Y}$ it is possible to make everyone better off by producing more X, less Y, and re-assigning allocations.

Let C_X and C_Y denote consumption of two goods X and Y. Subscripts on the functions $u^i[C^i_X, C^i_Y]$ (utility) and $F[X, Y]$ (country production frontier) denote partial derivatives. For example,

$$\frac{\partial F}{\partial X} = F_X = MP_X \qquad\qquad \frac{\partial u^i}{\partial C^i_X} = u^i_X = MU^i_X$$

We use the following facts (displayed here for convenience). For $i = 1, ..., m,$

$$du^i = u^i_X dC^i_X + u^i_Y dC^i_Y \quad \text{[Change in } u^i\text{.]} \quad (4.3)$$
$$0 = F_X dX + F_Y dY \quad \text{[Movement on frontier.]}(4.4)$$

Thus,

$$dY = -MRT_{X,Y} \, dX \quad (4.5)$$

where by definition

$$MRT_{X,Y} \equiv \frac{F_X}{F_Y}. \quad \text{Also define} \quad MRS^i_{X,Y} \equiv \frac{u^i_X}{u^i_Y}.$$

Now consider this re-allocation:

$$dC^i_X = \frac{1}{m} dX \qquad dC^i_Y = \frac{1}{m} dY \quad (4.6)$$

By (4.3), (4.5), (4.6), and the definition of MRS we have,

$$du^i = u^i_Y \left(MRS^i_{X,Y} (\frac{1}{m} dX) + (\frac{1}{m} dY) \right)$$
$$= \frac{u^i_Y}{m} \left(MRS^i_{X,Y} \, dX - MRT_{X,Y} \, dX \right)$$
$$= \left(\frac{u^i_Y}{m} \right) dX \left(MRS^i_{X,Y} - MRT_{X,Y} \right) \quad (4.7)$$

Hence, if

$$\left(MRS^i_{X,Y} - MRT_{X,Y} \right) > 0,$$

it follows from (4.7) that utility rises if $dX > 0$ since m and u^i_y are each positive. This is true for all individuals i. Hence the result follows.

4.10.1   Consumer Sovereignty for Public Goods

An interesting fact is that with private goods, Pareto Optimality implies everyone pays the same price but can consume different quantities. With public goods the reverse is true: everyone consumes the same quantity but can pay different prices. The reverse parallelism is less real than apparent because with both types of goods the consumer pays a price that reflects the benefits received from the good.

Since a public good is consumed by everyone, its benefits are the summation of everyone's benefits. Since a private good is consumed by just one person, its benefits are that single person's benefits.

It follows that the Consumer Sovereignty condition for public goods looks as it should when compared to the Consumer Sovereignty condition for a private good. To show this, let X be a private good, G be a public good, Y be some other private good, and $i = 1, \cdots, m$ be the list of consumers in the economy. Equation 4.8 is the Consumer Sovereignty condition for private good X. Equation 4.9 is the Consumer Sovereignty condition for public good G.

$$MRS^i_{X,Y} \quad = \quad MRT_{X,Y} \qquad (4.8)$$

$\underbrace{\qquad\qquad}$ Benefit of i from X $\qquad$ Cost of X $\qquad$ (Private Good X)

$$\sum_{i=1}^{m} MRS^i_{G,Y} \quad = \quad MRT_{G,Y} \qquad (4.9)$$

Benefit of all i from G $\qquad$ Cost of G $\qquad$ (Public Good G)

In either case, as long as the marginal benefits (left side above) exceed the marginal cost of provision, more of the good should be made available for consumption (i.e. purchased in the case of a private good, produced in the case of a public good).

Table 4.1 collects all the conditions just given, provides the associated mnemonic equation and adds a summary comment. Because Pareto Optimality implies that these conditions must hold, if any one or more of them is violated, the economy cannot be Pareto Optimal and human flourishing in the economic realm is thwarted.

Our discussion of public goods in Chapter 6 of Part 1 and the corresponding Chapter 6 in Part 2 allows us to add the sixth necessary condition relating to public goods. Just as Consumer Sovereignty means that a private good must be supplied in such a way that the value placed on it by the consumer matches the cost of producing it (for private goods X and Y and any consumer i this is the condition that $MRS^i_{X,Y} = MRT_{X,Y}$), so Consumer Sovereignty for a public good requires that the value placed on the good by those who consume it (this is all consumers $i = 1, ..., m$ by definition) must equal the cost of producing it. If it were more or less, then more or less of the public good should be produced. Equality implies that for any public good G and private good X, $MRS^1_{G,X} + ... + MRS^m_{G,X} = MRT_{G,X}$.

We hasten to add that if human flourishing implies Pareto Optimality, other conditions are implied as well. One, for example, would be the condition that households agree about the quantity of public good supplied and that public activity leads to outcomes in the Core. In Chapter 6 of Part 2 we discuss the testable and conceivably falsifiable implication that any two groups of citizens would answer a particular survey question with identical, or roughly identical, proportions of yes and no.

Table 4.1: **Six Necessary Conditions for Pareto Optimality**

	Mnemonic	Comment
Distributive Efficiency	$MRS^I_{X,Y} = MRS^{II}_{X,Y}$ for any two consumers I, II and any two private goods X, Y.	No further mutually beneficial trade is possible between consumers.
Input Efficiency	$MRTS^j_{L,K} = MRTS^h_{L,K}$ for any two firms j, h and inputs L, K.	No further mutually beneficial re-arrangement of inputs is possible between firms, raising output of any good without lowering output of another.
Sector Allocation Efficiency	$MRT^A_{X,Y} = MRT^B_{X,Y}$ for any two sectors A, B and any two private goods X, Y.	No re-assignment of sectoral production can raise the output of one good without lowering the output of any other.
Full Employment	$L_A + \cdots + L_Z = L^{Supplied}$	There are no unemployed factors of production. (I.e. demand for factors across all firms $A, ..., Z$ equals supply of factors.)
Consumer Sovereignty	$MRS^i_{X,Y} = MRT_{X,Y}$ for any consumer i and any two private goods X, Y.	No change in the goods produced can improve the welfare of any consumer without harming another.
Consumer Sovereignty for Public Goods	$MRS^1_{G,x} + ... + MRS^m_{G,x} = MRT_{G,x}$	No change in the quantity of public good G produced can improve the welfare of any consumer without harming another.

4.11 Conclusion

Pareto Optimality implies a number of conditions that apply to firms. Firms must reject outdated and inferior recipes for their production, produce at least cost, and choose their quantity and inputs to profit maximize. Among the necessary conditions that apply to the economy as a whole are Distributive Efficiency, Input Efficiency, Sector Allocation Efficiency, Full Employment, and Consumer Sovereignty. The presence of public goods implies yet other conditions that must be satisfied including Consumer Sovereignty for Public Goods. The provision of public goods is a topic taken up greater detail in Part 2, Chapter 6.

Part 2: Chapter 6

Market Failure

This chapter augments Chapter 6 of Part I in three ways. First, when prices fail we know that one or more of the necessary conditions for Pareto Optimality (we have documented Distributive Efficiency, Input Efficiency, Sector Allocation Efficiency, Full Employment, Consumer Sovereignty, Consumer Sovereignty for Public Goods) will be violated. Starting with monopoly, Section 6.1 provides five examples where market failure leads to failure of one of these conditions and shows how that failure occurs. Second, Section 6.2 provides a numerical example in a mathematical economy of Lindahl Equilibrium that displays the benefits principle of taxation and allows comparison to US real world data. Last, Section 6.3 expands the treatment of Lindahl Equilibrium for an economy with public goods present using technical descriptions omitted from Part I.

6.1 Failures to Satisfy Necessary Conditions

We start with some facts that are familiar from microeconomics producer theory and consumer theory.[1] If the firm producing good x is competitive $p_x = MC^x$. In that case these four equalities follow from profit maximization and the firm hiring conditions for labor and

---

[1]Our terminology and labeling are standard. As stated in the beginning of Part 2, we assume familiarity with first-year calculus.

capital.[2]

$$p_x \cdot MP_L^x = MC^x \cdot MP_L^x \;\; = \;\; w \tag{6.1}$$
$$p_x \cdot MP_K^x = MC^x \cdot MP_K^x \;\; = \;\; r \tag{6.2}$$

If the firm producing good x is a monopoly, then $MR^x = MC^x$, where MR is marginal revenue,[3] and these conditions follow from profit maximization by the monopoly.

$$MR^x \cdot MP_L^x = MC^x \cdot MP_L^x \;\; = \;\; w \tag{6.3}$$
$$MR^x \cdot MP_K^x = MC^x \cdot MP_K^x \;\; = \;\; r \tag{6.4}$$

where $p_x > MC^x = MR^x$ (value of good x to the consumer exceeds its cost of production, which in turn we know will be set equal to marginal revenue to the monopolist).

If the consumer is maximizing utility at prices p_x, p_y then[4]

$$\frac{MU_x}{MU_y} = \frac{p_x}{p_y}. \tag{6.5}$$

Last, because we consider adjustments in a "freeze-dried" or frozen economy when we evaluate Pareto Optimality through checking the ability to improve through making adjustments, increase in input use in one place must come from reduction somewhere else. With just two goods present,

$$dL_x + dL_y = 0 \tag{6.6}$$
$$dK_x + dK_y = 0 \tag{6.7}$$

We will make use of equations (6.1)-(6.7) in the examples that follow.

---

[2] Recall that if $x = F[K, L]$ and the total cost of production is $C[x]$, then $MP_L^x \equiv \frac{\partial F}{\partial L}$, $MP_K^x \equiv \frac{\partial F}{\partial K}$, $MC^x \equiv \frac{\partial C}{\partial x}$.

[3] $MR \equiv$ Marginal Revenue $= \frac{\partial(p_x x)}{\partial x}$ is the marginal revenue of the firm from producing and selling an additional unit of output x. Revenue is $R[x] = p[x]x$ where price, p[x], is determined as a function of quantity by the demand curve. Then the derivative of revenue is $MR[x] = R'[x] = p + x\frac{dp}{dx}$.

[4] If $u = u[x, y]$ then $MU_x \equiv \frac{\partial u}{\partial s}$, $MU_y \equiv \frac{\partial u}{\partial y}$.

6.1.1 Monopoly Violates Consumer Sovereignty

If monopoly is present, competition is absent, and market failure occurs. Which necessary condition for Pareto Optimality is violated? If we consider consumer i,

$$MRS^i_{x,y} \equiv \frac{MU^i_x}{MU^i_y} = \frac{p_x}{p_y} > \frac{MC^x}{MC^y}.$$

Because x is a monopoly $p_x > MC^x$. Because y is competitive $p_y = MC^y$. Continuing,

$$
\begin{aligned}
&= \frac{MC^x}{MC^y}\left(\frac{wdL_x + rdK_x}{wdL_x + rdK_x}\right) \\
&= \frac{MC^x}{MC^y}\left(\frac{w(-dL_y) + r(-dK_y)}{w\,dL_x + r\,dK_x}\right) \\
&= -\frac{\frac{w}{MC^y}\,dL_y + \frac{r}{MC^y}\,dK_y}{\frac{w}{MC^x}\,dL_x + \frac{r}{MC^x}\,dK_x} \\
&= -\frac{MP^y_L\,dL_y + MP^y_K\,dK_y}{MP^x_L\,dL_x + MP^x_K\,dK_x} = -\frac{dy}{dx} = MRT_{x,y}
\end{aligned}
$$

$$(6.8)$$

Inequality (6.8) tells us that Consumer Sovereignty is violated by monopoly. The monopolist lowers its output to get a higher price, thereby producing too little output. The indicator of market failure is that price is higher than the true cost of producing the additional unit involved $p_x > MC^x$.

6.1.2 Differential Factor Costs Violate Input Efficiency

When firms are taxed differentially the ability of prices to function is destroyed. An example would be situations where large firms are mandated to provide some benefit to workers that small firms are not required to provide with the result that hourly costs are higher to the large firm. For example, if large firms are required to pay unemployment insurance taxes on their worker's wages that small firms are not required to pay, the following situation can result. Distinguish between buyer (demander) and seller prices, in this case, of labor. Since laborers see the wage received by the seller of labor, w^S, this must be the same to them in whatever employment they find themselves. Firms demanding labor, on the other hand must pay the price paid by demanders, $w^D = w^S + t$, where t is the differential tax if the firm is large. Assume firm x is large and firm y small. Then

$$MRTS^x_{L,K} = \frac{w^S + t}{r} > \frac{w^S}{r} = MRTS^y_{L,K}. \tag{6.9}$$

It follows from (6.9) that Input Efficiency is violated.

6.1.3 Import Duties Violate Sector Allocation Efficiency

Viewed from one perspective, international trade is merely commerce between sectors of the world economy. When countries impose tariffs (import duties) these taxes cause violation of Sector Allocation Efficiency. A similar conclusion applies internally to a country. The US Constitution wisely prohibited one state from taxing imports from another state. Assume two sectors, Home and World. Then

$$MRT^{HOME}_{x,y} = \frac{p^{WORLD}_x + \text{tariff}}{p^{WORLD}_y} > \frac{p^{WORLD}_x}{p^{WORLD}_y} = MRT^{FOREIGN}_{x,y} \tag{6.10}$$

(6.10) demonstrates that the marginal rate of transformation differs between sectors due to the tariff. Hence Sector Allocation Efficiency is violated.

6.1.4 Commodity Taxes Violate Consumer Sovereignty

As noted, taxes destroy the ability of prices to do their job of allocating resources appropriately for optimality. Small taxes cause damage, and as the tax rate rises the degree of damage rises more than proportionately.[5] Distinguish between buyer (demander) and seller prices and consider the situation of Consumer 1.

$$MRS^1_{x,y} = \frac{p^S_x + t}{p^S_y} > \frac{p^S_x}{p^S_y} = MRT_{x,y} \tag{6.11}$$

---

[5]Public finance economists study taxes among other things. They show that starting from a zero tax, the damage of a larger tax rises approximately as the square of the size of the tax. This implies that low taxes, hence uniform near zero, are preferred.

(6.11) shows that the condition for Consumer Sovereignty is violated. Interestingly, this is the same condition that monopoly causes to be violated. By taxing a commodity, the market equilibrium is forced to a position where the price paid by the buyer exceeds the price received by the seller (the difference, the tax, goes to the government), which the selling firm sets equal to marginal cost. Consequently, the price paid by the buyer exceeds the marginal cost of providing the good and Pareto Optimality is prevented.

6.1.5   Externalities (Missing Markets) Violate Efficiency

We learned in Part 1 Chapter 6 that an externality is the consequence of a missing market. Absence of a market means there is a missing price, which in turn prevents proper resource allocation. Depending on where the externality appears, different conditions for Pareto Optimality might be violated.

Consider an example where consumption of good x imposes a negative externality. Figure 6.1 labels the demand and supply curve for x with intersection at quantity x^0 and price p_x^0.

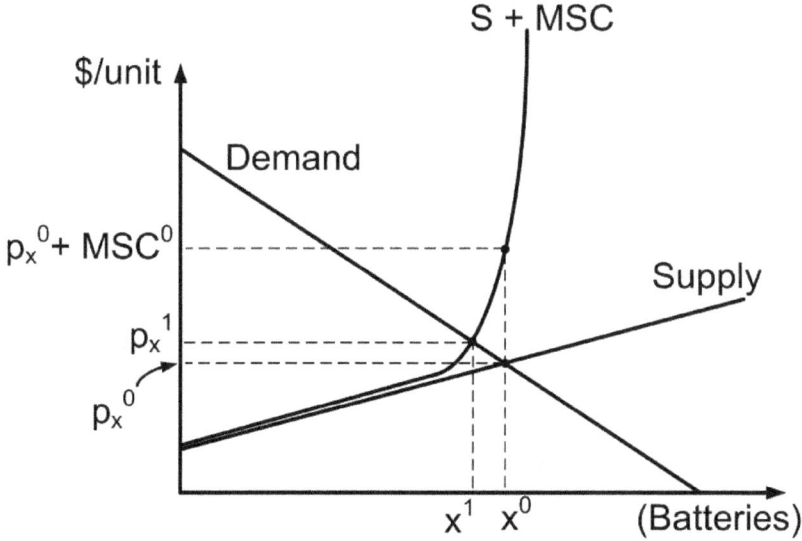

Figure 6.1: **A Negative Consumption Externality Violates Consumer Sovereignty**

So far everything is familiar. We assume, however, that consumption of good x requires additional resources for proper disposal (e.g. x might be potentially hazardous batteries). When the marginal social cost of disposal (MSC) is added to the cost of supply, curve S + MSC results, which lies above the ordinary curve labeled Supply. Were there no externality, meaning all costs are known and properly accounted for by consumers, the market price would be p_x^1 and quantity would be the smaller quantity x^1. Since by assumption there is a consumption externality present where consumers do *not* see the marginal social cost MSC^0 at the original equilibrium, we have

$$
\begin{aligned}
MRS_{x,y}^0 = \frac{p_x^0}{p_y^0} &< \frac{p_x^0 + MSC^0}{p_y^0} = \frac{MC^x + MSC^0}{MC^y} \\
&= \frac{\frac{w(dL_x^0 + dL_{MSC}^0) + r(dK_x^0 + dK_{MSC}^0)}{dx}}{\frac{wdL_y^0 + rdK_y^0}{dy}} \\
&= -\frac{dy}{dx}\frac{wdL_y^0 + rdK_y^0}{wdL_y^0 + rdK_y^0} \\
&= -\frac{dy}{dx} \\
&= MRT_{x,y}^0 \qquad\qquad (6.12)
\end{aligned}
$$

which tells us that the consumption externality violates Consumer Sovereignty. The inequality in (6.12) uses the fact that real labor and capital resources, L_{MSC}, K_{MSC}, must be expended in the disposal of x, which alter (6.6) and (6.7).

6.2   Lindahl Equilibrium and Benefits-Principle Taxes

Efficiency in an economy with public goods present is analyzed in Duncan Foley, "Lindahl's Solution and the Core of an Economy with Public Goods," *Econometrica*, 38, 1, 1970, 66-72. What we learn from his analysis is immense. To understand what Pareto Optimality (hence Lindahl Equilibrium) tells us about taxes, this section constructs a numerical example of a small economy of 100 individuals whose shares of income match the shares of household income actually observed in the US economy. We consult the economy to ask, How should the richest taxpayer pay taxes compared to the poorest according to the principles of Pareto Optimality? How does this compare to actual US taxes?

We first describe the components of this economy, then compute the Lindahl Equilibrium that applies to it, and finally use the results to look at the implied tax rates. The next few paragraphs summarize the main points already covered in Part 1 and get us to the analysis as soon as possible.

By definition, a public good is consumed in the same quantity by every individual. Because demand for the public good depends on preferences and income, we expect that the prices charged to some consumers need to be raised to bring their demanded quantity *down* to the common level, and the price charged to others might need to be lowered to bring their demand *up* to the common level.

One imagines that the rich taxpayer will need to be charged a higher price (i.e. pay higher taxes) for the public good and the poor taxpayer a lower price so that both demand the same quantity. Sometimes this is true, sometimes not. It is also possible that the public good benefits the poor taxpayer more than it does the rich taxpayer. We highlighted in Part 1, Chapter 6 the limiting case where the taxpayer receives no benefits whatever from the government program of expenditure, and therefore pays nothing. We used the example of a poor taxpayer in Indianapolis who pays to support his next-door public park but the rich taxpayer in New York City, who never visits or even knows of the park, properly pays nothing. In this case, both fairness and efficiency imply that the poor taxpayer should pay more than the rich one. The US constitutional federal system approximates to this arrangement when local decisions are made locally and paid for by the local residents who benefit from these local decisions.

Closely related to agreeing on quantity (just discussed), Pareto Optimality (i.e. Lindahl Equilibrium) requires that every consumer pay for the public good according to the benefit that he or she receives from it. Foley writes, "In the language of the 'benefit theory,' the value of public goods received by each individual is equal to the total tax he pays."

A Lindahl Equilibrium is always reachable (i.e. an equilibrium exists) that respects initial asset ownerships under certain regularity conditions. Essentially these conditions are that every consumer will be capable of earning enough money to provide for himself or herself. In the next section we will describe in more detail how this conclusion is reached when we focus on more general economies than the one in this section.

Lindahl Equilibrium is in the Core. No unhappy sub-group can do better for itself by withdrawing to establish a sub-economy.

Publicly-provided goods for which the degree of use varies by taxpayer choice are not *public goods.* A publicly-provided private good is still a private good. Thus, when publicly-provided goods are involved, the first thing that should be checked is whether user fees can be used to pay for them.

In principle, we would like all taxes to be user fees—taxes are prices paid by the user—because they would automatically implement the benefits principle. As many have noted, gasoline taxes, or windshield speed pass chips with respect to interstate highways, are nearly perfect ways to pay for roads that honor the benefits principle. Those who choose how much they use of publicly-provided goods and services should pay for them at a fixed tax rate (price) in proportion to their use. If you never use harbor yacht services because you do not own a yacht, you should pay nothing toward services for harbor yachts whether the private sector or the government provides them.

Now let's turn to the model.

U.S. income distribution is change-resistant from year to year and remarkably stable. At different times a given household may be at different parts of the distribution—college students earn little while in school but much more later in life, the retired earned much while working but less later, and so on. One's location in the distribution may change, but the distribution itself is relatively stable. Currently, the bottom 20 percent of households produces 3.1 percent of the total income generated by households. The second, third, and fourth quintiles produce 8.3, 14.1, and 22.7 percent of total household income, respectively. The next 15 percent of households produce 28.8 percent of the income, and the highest 5 percent produces 23.0 percent. For the Lindahl economy considered here,

Table 6.1: **Income in the Lindahl Economy Example**

	Members in Group	Group's Production of Income (% of Total)	Income Per Person
Top 5%	5	23.0	46.0
Rest of Top Quintile	15	28.8	19.2
4th Quintile	20	22.7	11.35
3d Quintile	20	14.1	7.05
2d Quintile	20	8.3	4.15
Bottom Quintile	20	3.1	1.55
TOTAL	100	100	10 (Avg. Per Person)

we assume that members of each group are identical and that the economy's total income is normed to 1,000. Table 6.1 summarizes what we have just said.

In the U.S., earning income below 81.7 percent of the mean income of the bottom quintile of households is considered to be poverty.[6] Applied to our economy, income equal to 1.27 is the poverty income cut off. In other words, the income earned by members of the lowest quintile is 22 percent above the poverty cut-off.

Our Lindahl economy has one private good, x, for which we can set the price to be $p_x = 1$ and one public good, g. The public good can be thought of as a composite good consisting of the court system, national defense, and similar pure public goods. One unit of g can be produced from one unit of x. How this is paid for in a Pareto Optimum is the question we ask of our exercise.

---

[6] The current poverty cut-off divided by the mean household income of the bottom quintile equals .817.

Everyone has a Stone-Geary utility function of the form

$$u[x, g] = \alpha \ln[x - A] + (1 - \alpha) \ln[g - B].$$

In other words, the 100 individuals differ only in the income they earn. Their utility function is the same. Stone-Geary utility is well used and liked by economists for several reasons. Since it depends on the logarithm, if consumption of good x were to fall below the number A, utility would drop to negative infinity. The number A, therefore, can be taken as the minimal amount of good x needed to sustain life. Likewise, if consumption of g falls below B utility goes to negative infinity. In our Lindahl economy, we set A to be 1.27, which is equivalent to the US the poverty cut-off. If $x \leq 1.27$ the consumer "dies."

How much public good is minimally needed requires thought. We set the level for B as follows. Looking back in history, the era just before World War II was the last one in which government engaged in functions costing about 6 percent of GDP. No Social Security, no Medicare, and few entitlement programs were in existence. People survived and life went on.[7] We take $B = .06\ GDP$, therefore, but will also consider the effects of half this level and double this level.

Parameter α, which is a fraction between 0 and 1, is the last number we need. We determine it as follows. Assuming income and prices (I, p_x, p_g), the Stone-Geary function has the property that the consumer first buys $x = A$ and $g = B$ then spends fraction α of the remaining income, $I - p_x A - p_g B$, on good x and the fraction $(1 - \alpha)$ on good g. If you were to get an additional $10,000 how would you spend it? If you would spend most of it on private goods for your family and yourself, say $9900, and $100 of it to expand the court system/military/public goods your α is .99. We think this split makes sense, so set $\alpha = .99$.

In summary: the distribution of income by quintile matches the actual distribution of household income by quintile in the United States. Everyone values the private good x and the public good g. Everyone will therefore end up supporting the public good in some amount. If the economy is Pareto Optimal, what should the distribution of payments be?

---

[7]We are looking for better ways to accomplish the goals of these programs.

Table 6.2 shows the results for each quintile down its columns. In the benchmark case the first quintile has income per person of 1.55, consumes 68.13 units of the public good and 1.53 units of the private good. Individuals in this quintile pay taxes at the rate of 1.41 percent of their income (very manageable!). As a group they contribute six tenths of 1 percent of the total cost of the public good. At 1.53, consumption of x is above the poverty level of 1.27, and at 68.13, consumption of the public good is above the minimally necessary level of 60. The higher income quintiles, second through fifth, are displayed in the columns to the right. We also separate out the top 5 percent in the right hand column.

Benchmark Case: $\alpha = .99$, $A = 1.27$, $B = .06$

Quintile	1st	2d	3d	4th	5th	Top 5%
Income per person	1.55	4.15	7.05	11.35	25.9	46.00
g consumed	68.13	68.13	68.13	68.13	68.13	68.13
x consumed	1.53	3.93	6.60	10.56	23.98	42.51
Tax rate (% income)	1.41	5.42	6.40	6.93	7.42	7.59
Group Income (% of total)	3.1	8.3	14.1	22.7	51.8	23.0
Implied Group Taxes (% of total)	0.6	6.6	13.2	23.1	56.4	25.6
US Actual Tax Share (%)	0	3.2	9.1	17.8	69.6	42.4
Deviation from Model	**-100%**	**-51.5%**	**-31.1%**	**-22.9%**	**+23.4%**	**+65.6%**

Low Government Case: $\alpha = .99$, $A = 1.27$, $B = .03$

g consumed	38.43	38.43	38.43	38.43	38.43	38.43
x consumed	1.54	4.02	6.80	10.91	18.41	44.03
Tax rate (% income)	0.80	3.05	3.61	3.91	4.11	4.28

High Government Case: $\alpha = .99$, $A = 1.27$, $B = .12$

g consumed	127.53	127.53	127.53	127.53	127.53	127.53
x consumed	1.51	3.73	6.21	9.88	16.58	39.47
Tax rate (% income)	2.64	10.14	11.98	12.97	13.64	14.20

Table 6.2: **Consumption of x and g, and Taxes in the Lindahl Economy Example**

We notice several things:

1. As expected, the model economy says that every consumer should contribute something to help pay for the public good. After paying taxes all consumers remain able to consume the private good at a rate above the poverty level.

2. As income rises, individuals are willing to pay more for the public good, keeping their desired quantity of it at q = 68.13, which is the same quantity desired by lower income individuals.

3. The share of income produced by each quintile is not far off the share of taxes paid by that quintile. The top 5%, for example, earns 23 percent of income as a group and pays 25.6 percent of all taxes. The middle quintile earns 14.1 percent of all income and pays 13.2 percent of all taxes. The bottom quintile earns 3.1 percent of income and pays 0.6 percent of all taxes. The tax *rate* for individuals ranges from 1.41 percent of income at the low end to 7.59 percent of income at the high end. This provides for a public sector that everyone agrees should be 6.813 percent of GDP.

4. Everyone is happy with the arrangements. Everyone pays for the public good based on the value of benefits they receive from it. No individual, no group can do better for itself.

Since we based the model on the distribution of real-world actual income, a natural question is: How does the model compare to actual? The row labeled "Deviation from Model" shows that in the real world the lowest quintile pays 0 percent of actual taxes paid,[8] which is 100% too low, while the top 5 percent pays taxes that are 65.6% too high. The deviation for the other quintiles can be seen across the row in bold. If we compare an individual in the top 5% and to an individual in the second quintile, the model says that the richer individual should pay total taxes 16 times what the second quintile member pays. As high as this is, in the actual US economy the ratio is **53 times**, not 16![9]

Finally, in addition to the cases reported in Table 6.2 we ran

---

[8] In the actual tax distribution it is possible for taxes to be negative because of government transfers to the needy.

[9] We would like to compare taxes of the highest income individual to the lowest, but cannot because in the actual U.S. data the lowest pays nothing and division by 0 is not possible.

one more experiment. In this experiment, we left all parameters as they were in the Table 6.2 benchmark case but changed just the utility of the Top 5% by altering α solely for that group to .999. In other words, the richest 5% receives less benefits from the public good than the other households. In this case, Pareto Optimality and Lindahl Equilibrium imply that the tax rate (percent of income paid for the public good) for the Top 5% should be 1.038, compared to 1.774, 6.813, 8.049, 8.719 for the 1st to 4th quintiles. As expected, even though the other quintiles have less income per household, they should pay a higher share of their income in taxes. Were α raised even further to .9999, the top 5% tax rate would fall to 0.108 compared to 1.827 for the lowest income 1st quintile. The share of taxes paid by the top 5% falls in that case to 0.38 percent of total taxes paid compared to .85 percent for the 1st quintile. Were no benefits from the public good received by the top 5%, of course, their fair share of taxes would fall to zero.

Some readers might be shocked if they were told that in the real world it is possible that the rich pay too much in taxes and the poor pay too little. They have regularly heard the reverse: Taxes on the rich should be higher and the rich should pay "their fair share." What is "their fair share"? There is no standard to say. Part 2 Chapter 7 shows that no matter how progressive taxes are, they can always be made more progressive. Only when the rich have 100% taken from them and their holdings reduced to that of the next one down in the distribution is greater progressivity impossible. From a morality perspective, *all* citizens are supposed to put their shoulder to the wheel and contribute in a significant way to the joint enterprise of government. Benefits-principle taxation tells us what is "significant" for each taxpayer.

The predicted consequence of an economy where the poor are undertaxed and the rich overtaxed is constant pressure for larger government with intense political struggles. Struggles about the size of government activity disappear in a Lindahl economy because taxes are set according to benefits received and every group pays for what it receives.

If our model were, in fact, a miniature US economy we would predict from it that we should see pressure for larger government from the lowest income quintiles who simultaneously would want higher taxes to fall on someone else. Politics being what it is, one or both political parties would be trying to get votes by promising more government and higher taxes on someone other than their voters.

What have we learned from public goods and Pareto Optimality? In practical terms, there are a number of realistic things that can be done. The reader can probably add to the following list.

1. The total tax applied to any individual should equal the sum of the separate taxes he or she owes on a benefits-principle basis for each distinct program and benefit that he or she receives from government. In the age of information and the computer implementing this is more possible than ever before. [Rule 9: Pareto Optimality and morality imply benefits-principle taxes.]

2. Surveys can be used to check whether the responses by any identifiable-in-advance group match for the following question introduced on page 76: "If government were to reduce all of its activity by 10%, at the same time reducing your taxes by 10%, would you favor such a change?" Surveys could even be contemplated on an activity-by-activity basis. If any group is found to consistently answer differently, then government taxes and expenditures should be adjusted appropriately until all groups answer the same way. [Rule 9: Pareto Optimality and morality imply benefits-principle taxes. Benefits-principle taxes and Lindahl Equilibria imply unanimity.]

3. The choice by citizens to participate in all Government activities and programs for citizens should be voluntary unless, as in the case of true public goods, this is not possible. Freedom of choice protects the individual and groups. [Rule 8: Good Policy is in the Core.]

4. All taxes should be user fees, unless this is not possible. User fees charge to each user the common fee that reflects the true cost of provision of the good being provided by government. [Rule 2: Pay fully for what you take from society. Distributive Efficiency, which implies a common price for private goods, is required by Pareto Optimality.]

5. If an individual receives no benefits from a government program or activity, then the individual's taxes for that activity should be zero. [Rules 1, 8, 9, 12 all come into play and would

be violated otherwise.]

6.3   Theory of Lindahl Equilibrium with Public Goods

So far in Part 2 we have used a $2 \times 2 \times 2$ economy (two goods, two consumers, two inputs) and the many-consumer Lindahl economy of the previous section and have learned much. More sophisticated economies are possible, however. While none will ever be as detailed as the actual US economy, they do not need to be. With respect to taxes we are looking for arrangements that work in any economy, honor the rights of property consistent with the Golden Rule (plus John Locke and the principle that you own yourself) and support Pareto Optimality. If in some circumstances these are the *unique* arrangements that support Pareto Optimality and the Golden Rule, then these are our selection.

The economy described in this section uniquely identifies Lindahl Equilibrium and benefits-principle taxes.

6.3.1   Consumer and Producer Assumptions

Assume that the economy has m consumers $i = 1, ..., m$, n private goods $x_1, ..., x_n$ and k public goods $g_1, ..., g_k$. Each consumer owns some bundle of private goods, call these bundles w^i, and has a consumption set X^i that consists of those consumption bundles that are possible and will sustain life for the consumer. Each consumer has preferences that allow him or her to choose between bundles. We assume that the consumer's preferences are stable enough and regular enough that we can consider the consumer rational. More on this below. The production that the economy is capable of is described in the set Y of all production plans ("recipes") that are technically possible. We assume these plans are regular enough and good enough that the economy won't starve, is capable of producing public goods, but can't get something from nothing, and no public good is absolutely necessary as a production input.

If A and B are consumption bundles, we say that $tA + (1 - t)B$ where t is a number taking a value between 0 and 1 is a *weighted average* of A and B. Multiplying a bundle by t means multiplying each element by t.

Consumer Assumptions

C.1 The consumer's consumption set contains its boundaries and a weighted average of any two points in the set is also in the set. If A is a bundle in the consumption set, then there is a neighborhood of points containing A and having the same quantities of public goods as A, that is also in A.

C.2 For each consumer there is a bundle whose size, component by component, is less than or equal to the size of any bundle in the consumer's consumption set.

C.3 For each consumer i, if A is in the consumption set, then there is another bundle also in the consumption set where consumption of public goods is the same and consumption of private goods is less than w^i component by component.

Consumer assumptions C.1-C.3 can be stated in more mathematical notation, but it is unnecessary for us to do this. They are made to describe viability and insure that we are talking about viable consumers.[10] Assumption C.3 says that in whatever equilibrium the consumer might find himself or herself, he or she will have the capability to sustain life because his or her holdings of private goods w^i exceeds a viable amount.

C.4. Preferences of the consumer are such that any two bundles can be ranked relative to each other and if bundle A is better than or indifferent to bundle B, which is better than or indifferent to bundle C, then bundle A is better than or indifferent to bundle C. Every bundle is indifferent to itself.

C.5 For each consumer and bundle in the consumption set, the better-than set and the worse-than sets contain their edges.

---

[10]For example, if labor is supplied as a negative number, its value cannot be unboundedly low. We rule this out.

C.6 For each consumer, if bundle A is strictly preferred to bundle B, then a bundle C consisting of $tA + (1 - t)B$ where t can be anything between 0 and 1 is strictly preferred to A or B.

C.7 For each consumer, if component by component bundle A is larger than or equal to bundle B, and they are not the same, then bundle A is strictly preferred to bundle B.

Assumptions C.4-C.7 are focused on rationality. They imply that the consumer has convex-to-the-origin indifference curves over goods and a utility function that can represent them. Indifference curves are sensible, reasonable, and natural, as is the assumption that a bundle with more in one or more of its components is strictly preferred.

The fact that even more general situations than these can be handled by the mathematical economist should not deter us in the least from considering the implications from an economy with features C.1–C.7.

Production Assumptions

P.1 If A and B are feasible production plans ("recipes" A and B are in Y) and α and β are positive numbers, then the scaled production plans αA, βB and $\alpha A + \beta B$ are also feasible.[11] The set of feasible production plans contains its edges (is closed).

P.2 Using no inputs and producing no outputs is a feasible production plan (0 is a member of Y).

P.3 A non-zero production plan requires use of at least one input.

Assumptions P.1–P.3 are just standard descriptions of what we mean by a collection of production recipes. For example, if two ways of producing output are possible then we can produce half the output using one recipe and the other half using the other recipe. This is a weighted combination using equal weights. Other weights are possible, too.

P.4 For each public good type, there is a recipe that can produce a positive quantity of that public good.

---

[11] Multiplying a recipe by α means multiplying each of its components by α.

P.5 If a production plan involving private goods and public goods is possible, then there is a way to produce the same positive quantities of private goods and public goods without using any public goods as inputs.[12]

Production assumptions P.4 and P.5 describe public goods of the type we realistically expect to encounter. They are producible (why discuss public goods that no one knows how to make?) and, at the same time, are not essential to have as inputs. Possibly one could imagine an economy where some kind of public good was essential to first have before production of other things could be done, but the economy satisfying P.1–P.5 is general enough.

6.3.2 Five Conclusions Reached from Pareto Optimality and Lindahl Equilibria

At least three theorems apply to economies with public goods present that lead to five important conclusions.[13] The first theorem says that if the economy is arranged to be Pareto Optimal, then it must be arranged as a Lindahl Equilibrium, which is described as follows. There is a common set of prices for private goods that is the same for all consumers and firms $(p_1, ..., p_n)$, and a set of prices for the public goods that can be different for each consumer $(p_{g_1}^i, ..., p_{g_k}^i)$ such that were the consumer to spend the amount given by

$$p_1(x_1^i - w_1^i) + \cdots + p_n(x_n^i - w_n^i) + p_{g_1}^i g_1^i + \cdots + p_{g_k}^i g_k^i \quad (6.13)$$

utility would be maximized. That is, any bundle of goods $(x_1^i, ..., x_n^i; g_1^i, ..., g_k^i)$ that was strictly preferred by the consumer would cost more. The quantities $x_j^i - w_j^i$ for $j = 1, ..., n$ appear in (6.13) because of net spending on each private good.[14] Since goods g are

---

[12]This is one place where the mathematical notation might be easier to follow than the word explanation. In the production plan, whenever a public good appears as a negative number (it is an input), then the same production of (positive) private goods and public goods can be accomplished where the public good inputs are replaced by a zero.

[13]This discussion is based on Foley, 1970 though other treatments are possible. See Raut, 2004 and references. One simplification that we make has to do with the Core. See page 334.

[14]Alternately, we can mentally imagine a sequential process. The consumer sells his or her holdings w^i. The resulting money is then spent on goods

public goods, it is the case in Lindahl Equilibrium that the quantity of each public good is voluntarily chosen to be the same by consumers. That is, $g_{g_1}^i = g_1, \cdots, g_{g_k}^i = g_k$ for all i. At the same time, the choice of production maximizes profits at the prices $(p_1, \cdots, p_n; p_{g_1}, \cdots, p_{g_k})$ where the price of each public good is the sum of the prices paid by all of the consumers,

$$
\begin{aligned}
p_{g_1} &= p_{g_1}^1 + \cdots + p_{g_1}^m \\
p_{g_2} &= p_{g_2}^1 + \cdots + p_{g_2}^m \\
&\vdots \\
p_{g_k} &= p_{g_k}^1 + \cdots + p_{g_k}^m
\end{aligned}
\tag{6.14}
$$

Finally, since the consumer's spending on each public good defines taxes, $T_{g_1}^i = p_{g_1}^i g_1, \cdots, T_{g_k}^i = p_{g_k}^i g_k$. If no other tax (positive or negative) is involved, we say the Lindah Equilibrium respects property holdings. The sum of all taxes T_g^i collected on each public good pays for the good,

$$
\begin{aligned}
T_1^1 + \cdots + T_1^m &= p_{g_1}^1 g_1 + \cdots + p_{g_1}^m g_1 = p_{g_1} g_1 \\
&\vdots \\
T_k^1 + \cdots + T_k^m &= p_{g_k}^1 g_k + \cdots + p_{g_k}^m g_k = p_{g_k} g_k
\end{aligned}
\tag{6.15}
$$

From the consumer's perspective, the total taxes he or she pays is the sum of the taxes collected on each public good, $T^i = T_{g_1}^i + \cdots + T_{g_k}^i$.

Theorem: *Given the assumptions C.1-C.7 and P.1-P.5, if the economy is arranged to satisfy the requirements of Pareto Optimality, then it satisfies the requirements of Lindahl Equilibrium.*

Theorem: *Given the assumptions C.1-C.7 and P.1-P.5 there exists a Lindahl Equilibrium for the economy in question that respects property holdings.*

$(x_1^i, ..., x_n^i; g_1^i, ..., g_k^i)$ at the given prices. Some of the private goods would normally be labor of some type. Labor supplied enters spending as a negative number, meaning labor supplied provides income with which to buy other goods.

Theorem: *Lindahl Equilibrium that respects property holdings is in the Core.*

In other words, Pareto Optimality in an economy with public goods present requires that there be prices such that firms maximize profits at the prices they see for the public and private goods, consumers maximize utility at the prices they see for the public and private goods, markets clear (no good is consumed at quantities greater than supplied by production), prices for the private goods are the same across all firms and households, the quantities for the public goods are the same across all households, and the implied taxes collected from each household are determined from (equivalent to) the prices they pay for the public goods. A third conclusion, to be discussed below, has to do with the Core.

Nothing in Pareto Optimality and the Golden Rule suggest that income or any necessarily progressive exaction from it governs taxes. If taxes do rise as a percentage of income, as was the case in the example economy of Section 6.2 in this chapter, it derives from entirely different considerations. The discussion there showed that other examples are just as easy to produce where taxes might *fall* with income.

We have tried to be succinct, but even so have taken a good bit of space to explain Pareto Optimality in an economy with public goods present. In the next four subsections, we call out as briefly as we can five conclusions.

1. Existence from Existing Endowments

Presuming everyone is viable, a Pareto Optimum, which implies a Lindahl Equilibrium, exists that respects existing endowments. It is always possible to contemplate taking assets from someone to whom they belong and giving them to someone else to whom they do not belong, but this is unnecessary. A Pareto Optimum exists that is reachable from existing asset holdings that respects the Golden Rule, John Locke, and the principle that you own yourself. Legalized plunder or any other form of stealing is not needed.

2. Unanimity about Size

Pareto Optimality implies that consumers agree about the quantity of each public good. Disagreement about how big the government sector should be indicates a false application of taxes. Discussion prompted by the example in the previous section suggested that when taxes are too low on one identifiable-in-advance group, and too high on another identifiable-in-advance group the former will tend to favor a larger public sector and the latter a smaller. Unanimity is a safeguard against abusing one group to benefit another.

3. Outcomes in the Core

The outcome in an economy is said to be "blocked" or "blockable" if a subset of consumers can withdraw from the economy and using their assets and the existing technology (production know how that the original economy has) generate a different outcome that is better for each of the withdrawing members. We assume for simplicity that if a different outcome can be reached that is strictly better for some of the withdrawing members, no worse for any, but indifferent for some, it is possible to reach an outcome that is strictly better for all. An economy outcome that is unblockable is said to be in the Core. Since the set of all consumers is a subset of consumers, outcomes in the Core are Pareto Optimal.

Several comments are in order. First, slightly different definitions of blocking are possible. For example, the withdrawing members may have access to a slightly different technology than the original Y or some of the withdrawing members might be indifferent, but still be willing to participate in the withdrawal. The primary point is that the Core protects the interests of a group against abuse by the rest of the economy. A group that is harmed by social arrangements should be able to withdraw from the arrangements to protect itself.

Good government should make withdrawal unnecessary. In fact, Pareto Optimality in an economy with public goods present implies Lindahl Equilibrium, which implies the outcome is in the Core.

4. Benefits Principle Taxes

The Golden Rule, John Locke, and the principle that you own your-self imply that property holdings are respected. The Golden Rule and Lindahl Equilibrium therefore imply that the benefits principle applies to taxes. In the important special case where no benefits are received, no taxes should be paid.

5. Total Taxes Equal the Sum of Taxes Owed for Each Government Activity

If the Golden Rule and Pareto Optimality apply, taxes are determined by Lindahl Equilibrium and the benefits principle. Total taxes paid by the consumer equal the sum of taxes collected on each of the public goods from which the consumer receives benefits.

6.4   Conclusion

Taxes based on the benefits principle and user fees in cases where the quantity consumed is chosen by the user work in all circumstances. The analysis of economies with public goods present shows that there are circumstances where these are the *only* type of taxes that are consistent with Pareto Optimality and the Golden Rule. They are therefore the standard of good government implied by human flourishing.

References

Foley, Duncan (1970). "Lindahl's Solution and the Core of An Economy with Public Goods," *Econometrica*, 38, 1, January, 66-72.

Raut, Lakshmi (2004). "Two-sided Altruism, Lindahl Equilibrium, and Pareto Optimality in Overlapping Generations Models," *Economic Theory*, 27, pp. 729-736.

Part 2: Chapter 7

Morality

There are at least four lines of thought that lead to the same conclusion. The older of the first two begins with John Locke's starting point that you own yourself, your work, and the product of your own giftings. It is self-evident that stealing is immoral, and that slavery in any degree is a form of stealing. No man, no group of men, no legislature, no government can forceably take from you what you own and give it to another or use it for another's benefit without your permission. Forced charity is theft.

The second line of reasoning starting from Human Flourishing and Pareto Optimality leads to the same conclusion. Government has a necessary societal role. It needs taxes to pay for what it provides. How may it tax you to provide to you what it morally owes to you as part of its function? Benefits-principle taxes are the only ones that support Pareto Optimality and apply in all circumstances. They are acceptable to the payer precisely because they satisfy a number of properties derived from optimality (see the discussions of government, Lindahl Equilibrium, and benefits-principle taxes in Part 1 Chapter 10 and Part 2 Chapter 6). When the tax payer receives zero benefits from the use to which the paid tax is put, the benefits principle dictates that the tax be zero.

The third line of reasoning is the oldest and most direct. The Golden Rule says that you may not reduce another's wealth to a level to which you are unwilling to have your own wealth reduced. This applies to any form of un-compensated taking by force without permission. The Golden Rule's implications were explained in

Chapter 7 in Part 1.

The U.S. Constitution contains the fourth argument that also leads to the inference that taxes for the public benefit that provide zero benefit to the tax payer must be zero.[1]

We expand these investigations by asking what morality has to say about progressive taxes and uncompensated takings. Our main result is contained in Theorem 7.1. Its rejection of un-compensated involuntary taking is a major departure from organismic optimal tax theory.

7.1   Gifts and Un-Compensated Takings

Let W_i, W_j represent the holdings of individuals i and j (wealth or income, whichever is the tax base), let $G_i \geq 0, G_j \geq 0$ be their charitable gifts (giving), and let lower case w_i, w_j be their respective after-gift, after-tax holdings. The respective taxes are $T_i \equiv W_i - G_i - w_i, T_j \equiv W_j - G_j - w_j$, by definition.

This notation is intended to be easy to remember. Smaller lower case letters represent the smaller after-gift, after-tax holdings. G_i and T_i are removed from W_i, leaving it as w_i.

In this chapter we are considering the case where individuals voluntarily make charitable gifts, thereafter pay non-negative taxes from which by assumption they receive no benefits in return, and are left with non-negative $w_i \geq 0$.[2] We start by clarifying terminology and listing two assumptions.

Terminology:

(i) When we say, "Assume Morality," or "Morality holds," we mean that the requirements of right conduct, justice, fairness, honesty, morality and ethical behavior are being honored in the realm of the taxes and taxation being discussed. Among other things, "Morality" implies that the Golden Rule is not violated by the tax arrangements. If a tax arrangement vio-

---

[1]This conclusion derives from the Fifth Amendment. See page 127.

[2]The usual way that an individual might receive benefits from the uses to which his or her taxes could be directed are from government programs that give to him or her cash, from private goods that might be given to him or her by government, or from public goods that might be produced by government. It is possible that none of these three benefit the payer.

lates the Golden Rule we say it is "immoral" or "Morality does not hold."

(ii) Taxes that take from the inferior (the one with lesser tax base) and not from the superior are said to match the "Nathan Pattern," $W_i > W_j$, $T_j > T_i = 0$.[3]

(iii) If pre-tax holdings satisfy $W_i > W_j$ and after-gift after-tax holdings satisfy $w_i > w_j > 0$ where $T_i, T_j > 0$, we say that the taxes match the "Black-Tie Pattern."

(iv) We assume that confiscatory taxes are immoral. For example, let $i = 1, ..., m$ be the set of taxed individuals. Taxes that imply one-hundred percent of the individual's taxable base will be taken if the individual's holding is above some bound involve 100 percent marginal tax rates above the boundary and are said to be confiscatory. In addition, we know that 100% taxes on income or wealth create harmful incentives that make them impractical and infeasible since no rational consumer will work to produce income or wealth above the bound.

(v) Finally, as we have already done, we refer to taxes that are used in ways that provide no benefits to the payer as "un-compensated takings," "involuntary takings," "forced takings," or simply "forced charity" to highlight the difference between them and benefits-principle taxes, that are used in ways that do return benefits to the payer.

Assumptions:

A.7.1 Confiscatory taxes are immoral.

A.7.2. Morality implies that the Golden Rule is not violated.

A.7.3. For individuals $i = 1, ..., m$, W_i is pre-gift, pre-tax holding of the tax base (wealth or income, whichever applies); G_i is voluntary giving (gifts); T_i is taxes paid; and w_i is post-giving, post-tax holdings, where $W_i - G_i - T_i = w_i$, $W_i \geq 0$, $G_i \geq 0$, $T_i \geq 0$, $w_i \geq 0$.

---

[3]As the wealth of the superior (richer) approaches (decreases to) the value of the inferior the limit of the Nathan Pattern is reached, $W_i = W_j$, $T_j > T_i = 0$. It is possible to treat the limiting case as part of the definition of the Nathan Pattern, i.e. $W_i \geq W_j$, $T_j > T_i = 0$, which alters the discussion somewhat but leads to essentially the same content.

7.2   Forced Charity is Immoral

Tax devotees often extol progressive taxation, the notion that higher
income or wealthier individuals should pay not only more tax but
a larger *proportion* of their income or wealth in taxes.   Nowhere
does economic theory imply progressive taxation, however.[4] We see
in Chapter 6 that the principle of taxation that *does* apply takes
account of the degree to which the payer of taxes receives benefits
from the uses to which the taxes are put. The tax base is usually
defined in terms of income or wealth so we state our definition in
terms of either.

**Definition: Progressive taxes are defined by the requirement
that when comparing two individuals the higher-income/wealthier
individual pays a larger fraction of his or her income/wealth in
taxes.**

The absence of a theoretical justification for progressive taxation has
not stopped its supporters from advocating for ever greater progressivity. With the exception of perfectly progressive taxes, no matter
what degree of progressivity exists, it is possible to ask that taxes be
made more progressive. For example, in situations when taxes are
being reduced, advocates of progressive taxation have sometimes
complained that the tax dollars are being returned to those who
paid them, and thus disproportionately returned to the rich.   Instead, they argue, through various means taxes should be returned
in a way more equal to all. This, of course, is equivalent to the
belief that the new tax structure should be more progressive, and
that some of the taxes paid by one individual should be used for the
benefit of someone other than the taxpayer, i.e. forced charity, the
subject of this investigation.

**Definition: Perfectly progressive taxes apply when individuals
are rank-ordered by the tax base (e.g. income or wealth)
and taxes are collected from the wealthiest until he or she is**

---

[4]See for example, Mankiw, Weinzierl, and Yagan (2009), pp. 147-174. Optimal marginal tax schedules could even decline at high incomes (p. 151). We
saw the same possibility in Lindahl Equilibria.

reduced to the wealth of the second wealthiest, then taxes are taken from both until they are reduced to the level of the third, and so on, until the total amount of taxes needed are collected.

The reader will recognize perfectly progressive taxes as those introduced earlier that take 100% of the tax base in question (wealth or income) above some bound B. Progressive taxation creates unavoidable tension. On one hand, there is no natural limit to tax progressivity unless perfect progressivity is achieved. On the other hand, if perfect progressivity is achieved it implies 100 percent taxation of those taxed until their holdings no longer exceed the greatest upper bound of untaxed individuals. Perfectly progressive taxes are confiscatory. It is self evident that perfectly progressive taxes are unworkable in the long term because no one chooses to work for nothing or subjects himself to confiscation.

There are reasons to be suspicious that less-than-perfectly-progressive taxes, the Golden Rule, and taxes providing no benefits to those being taxed have problems. For example, let individuals i and j be taxed to pay for something that benefits neither. Let $W_i > W_j$, $T_i > 0$, $T_j > 0$ and $W_i > w_i > W_j > w_j$. Now introduce a third individual k where $W_k = w_i$. Individual k has more than j, who was taxed, suggesting that k likewise should be taxed. On the other hand, k and after-tax i are equal, suggesting it would be wrong to treat k differently by reducing him to less than i. Taxing k cannot both be moral and immoral. Something is wrong.

We have the following theorem:

Theorem 7.1: Let assumptions A.7.1 - A.7.3 hold. Assume taxes provide no benefits to those being taxed and that positive taxes are collected from one or more individuals. Then the taxes are immoral.

Proof: Assume Morality. Then by A.7.2 the Golden Rule is not violated. Without loss of generality, arrange and label individuals so that

$$w_m \geq w_{m-1} \geq \cdots \geq w_2 \geq w_1.$$

Assume that a strict inequality exists in the arrangement just formed and, starting from the left, select the first one to create two groups of individuals labeled as follows:

$$\underbrace{w_m = w_{m-1} = \cdots = w_i}_{\text{Group A}} > \underbrace{w_j \geq \cdots \geq w_k \geq \cdots \geq w_1}_{\text{Group B}}$$

If $T_j > 0$ it implies that j has been forced down to post-gift, post-tax wealth w_j that by revealed preference we know individual i, or any member of Group A, is unwilling to go (Group A members could give until their wealth was down to w_j but do not want to). This violates the Golden Rule, contradicting the statement that the Golden Rule is not violated. Thus $T_j = 0$.

The same argument applies to individual k and all members of Group B. Thus all members of Group B pay 0 tax.

Since positive taxes are collected by assumption, at least one person, perhaps all, in Group A pay positive taxes. For members of Group A

$$W_m - (T_m + G_m) = W_{m-1} - (T_{m-1} + G_{m-1}) = \cdots = W_i - (T_i + G_i) = w_i.$$

and any member of Group A not voluntarily giving G_i sufficient to reduce post-gift wealth to w_i has 100% of the difference taxed ("Give us all your wealth above w_i or we will take it.") This is 100% taxation which is confiscatory and therefore immoral by Assumption A.7.1. This is a contradiction.

Therefore, it must be that no strict inequality exists. But if no strict inequality exists, then

$$w_m = w_{m-1} = \cdots = w_2 = w_1$$

and 100% taxation is being applied to everyone. This is confiscatory and therefore immoral, contradicting the assumption of Morality.

Thus, taxes used in a way that provides no benefits to the payer are immoral. This proves the result. □

Two remarks are in order. First, the proof shows that no one in Group B pays any tax at all. Forcing just one or a few individuals to pay taxes for everyone else can itself be considered immoral.

Second, Theorem 7.1 applies to the situation about which so many of us have wondered. We who try to give meaningful amounts charitably, decide how much we can afford and give it. For others that is not the story. They want more done, but not to do it themselves: "I have done my share, others need to do more" or "I can't afford to give. Richer people than me *can*." For whatever reason, they want government enlisted and forced taxes. Theorem 7.1 is clear: if taxes for charity collect any money, they are immoral.

> **Theorem 7.1 is clear: if taxes for charity collect any money, they are immoral.**

7.3   Conclusion

Is morality needed in the administering of taxes?

Yes, because without morality the Golden Rule can be violated, un-compensated forced takings can be imposed, legalized plunder is not prevented, and any number of other forms of government failure are encouraged.

References

Mankiw, N. Gregory, Matthew Weinzierl, and Danny Yagan, "Optimal Taxation in Theory and Practice," *Journal of Economic Perspectives*, 23, 4, Fall 2009, 147-174.

7.4 Appendix to Chapter 7

If one is willing to accept at the outset a few seemingly reasonable assumptions one can get to similar conclusions about the pattern of taxes. For the reader's benefit we provide one example here using assumptions A.7.4 - A.7.7.

Table 7.1: **Possible Tax Outcomes**

Case	Case Description				Conclusion
1.1	$W_i > W_j$	$T_i > 0$	$T_j > 0$	$w_i > w_j$	Violates A.7.5
1.2	$W_i > W_j$	$T_i > 0$	$T_j > 0$	$w_i = w_j$	
1.3	$W_i > W_j$	$T_i > 0$	$T_j > 0$	$w_i < w_j$	Violates A.7.6
2.1	$W_i > W_j$	$T_i > 0$	$T_j = 0$	$w_i > w_j$	
2.2	$W_i > W_j$	$T_i > 0$	$T_j = 0$	$w_i = w_j$	
2.3	$W_i > W_j$	$T_i > 0$	$T_j = 0$	$w_i < w_j$	Violates A.7.6
3	$W_i > W_j$	$T_i = 0$	$T_j > 0$		Violates A.7.4
4	$W_i > W_j$	$T_i = 0$	$T_j = 0$		No tax collected.
5.1	$W_i = W_j$	$T_i > 0$	$T_j > 0$	$w_i > w_j$	Violates A.7.7
5.2	$W_i = W_j$	$T_i > 0$	$T_j > 0$	$w_i = w_j$	
5.2	$W_i = W_j$	$T_i > 0$	$T_j > 0$	$w_i < w_j$	Violates A.7.7
6	$W_i = W_j$	$T_i > 0$	$T_j = 0$		Violates A.7.7
7	$W_i = W_j$	$T_i = 0$	$T_j > 0$		Violates A.7.7
8	$W_i = W_j$	$T_i = 0$	$T_j = 0$		No tax collected.

A.7.4 The Nathan Pattern Violates the Golden Rule: $W_i > W_j, T_i = 0, T_j > 0$.
A.7.5 The Black-Tie Pattern Violates the Golden Rule: $W_i > W_j, T_i > 0, T_j > 0, w_i > w_j$.
A.7.6 Punitive Taxes Violate the Golden Rule: $W_i > W_j, w_i < w_j$.
A.7.7 Equals Treated Unequally Violates the Golden Rule: $W_i = W_j, w_i \neq w_j$.

Without loss of generality, let $W_i \geq W_j$, $T_i \geq 0, T_j \geq 0, w_i > 0, w_j > 0$. Then among the patterns that collect tax, only 1.2, 2.1, 2.2, and 5.2 survive. Thus, the lesser is taxed $(T_j > 0)$ only if both are reduced to the same post-tax holdings $(w_i = w_j)$, and if the lesser is left with less $(w_i < w_j)$ the lesser is not taxed $(T_j = 0)$.

Possibly the richer only is taxed, leaving the two the same $(w_i = w_j)$. This produces the pattern of taxes for Groups A and B in the proof of Theorem 7.1.

Part 2: Chapter 10

Government

If you want something new, you have to stop doing something old.

Peter F. Drucker
Author, Educator, Management Consultant

Health care is a good place to practice our principles. It is covered in this chapter because the first issue is whether it is a government matter to be involved in supplying health care at all. Health care is a private good,[1] so according to Rule 4 is best produced and distributed in competitive private markets.

It is government's job to see that health care markets and health care insurance markets are competitive. When instead of doing this, government imagines that it can substitute for markets, it tends to force citizens to buy things they do not choose, to grossly elevate their prices, to overregulate, and to create false incentives. Good

---

[1]Health care is rival in consumption and excludable. My appendectomy benefits me, and you can be refused care if you do not pay for it. For health care—*as for virtually all goods and services*—one can imagine labyrinthine pathways to consumption externalities. For example, keeping myself fit and trim means I am less likely to get a transmittable disease and, either unknowingly or by ignorance, passing it to you. Are you responsible for part of the cost of my gymnasium membership, therefore? Hardly. In Law, effects that are minimal and trivial or negligible are classified as *de minimis* to be appropriately ignored. They are present, but not the basis for policy. A better solution is education so that everyone knows how disease is treated, is caught, is prevented and so on.

policy supports citizens choosing for themselves what is in their own interest.

The second issue, though, is that Americans want features that can be accomplished only if their deviation from normal market function is understood and additional policies crafted to these precise objectives. The intervention principle of Chapter 11 introduced on page 184 of Part 1 therefore comes into play.

Thus, this chapter shows how *The Rules* (Part 1 Chapter 12) apply to the following prominent policy question: How should health care and health care insurance be produced and distributed, presuming that we grant the apparent desires of the American people in the best way possible?

In other words, starting with a list of specifications for health care, how should they be met consistent with morality and human flourishing? We will discuss the non-market desires first, explain what ideal health insurance looks like, and then turn to applying the rules. An outline will be provided at this point in the discussion followed by elaboration of the components. When a rule is relevant, it is indicated in a boxed frame.

10.0   Two Health Care Preliminaries

The public's desire for non-market features when it comes to health care requires extra-market policies and interventions to meet them. These are susceptible to our methods, but require explanation. We start with three observations and a description of perfect health care insurance.

10.0.1   The Public's Health Care "Specs"

Many Americans believe three things about health care and health care insurance that are unrealistic:

1. **They want prices to be low, unrealistically believing this can be done in the absence of competition.**
2. **They want insurance companies to sell policies at standard premiums to individuals who**

> **the companies know in advance will have enor-
> mously above-standard claims, naively think-
> ing companies should comply.**
>
> 3. **They want citizens having the expectation of
>   receiving free insurance and free care never-
>   theless to act fairly and responsibly, believing
>   that their fellow citizens will somehow do so
>   without the discipline and accountability that
>   markets provide.**

Disregarding the fanciful (for example, prices cannot magically be made lower than the true cost of care), what Americans want for health care such as *guaranteed issue, guaranteed renewability, freedom of choice*, and *portability can* be accomplished. Good policy will do so with as little damage as possible. System-changing reforms that move the system inevitably and naturally to the more desirable new state of affairs should be introduced first. Where there are different ways to meet a particular objective, allowing the states to experiment with options has advantages as we learn what works.

Good policy uses the Intervention Principle, The Rules of Essential Economics, and knowledge of what ideal insurance looks like to make the adjustments to move current arrangements as quickly as possible to the new ones. We begin by explaining perfect insurance.

10.0.2 Perfect Insurance Explained

To illustrate perfect insurance, consider how it would be provided for a generation not yet born. Just as the military used the term "D-Day" to refer to a future day when certain events would occur, but the precise time was unknown, let "Y-Year" refer to a time four or five years into the future, before the generation we are interested in is born or is even conceived.

Consider now the cohort of all males that will be born in Y-Year. By looking ahead to Y-Year prior to when members of the cohort have any existence whatever, we are assuming that all of them are homogeneous in their medical probabilities prior to conception. That is, it may turn out that some need more care in their first year of life and some less but we cannot determine as of now which ones. Once born, each male makes identical health insurance payments throughout life into a common pool that collectively covers the group's medical expenses on a year-by-year basis. Using this self-funding arrangement, no other group contributes to this group's medical expenses and this group makes no payments to any other group's medical expenses. The cohort of males born in Year Y-Year+1 does the same for its group, and so on for cohorts Y-Year+2 and up. There are no subsidies across cohorts.

Females born in Y-Year, are likewise placed into a common pool, and females born into other years are placed into theirs.[2]

Since everyone in a given cohort pays the same premiums year by year throughout life, receives the same insurance, and had the same prospects when they entered their pool, the insurance they receive throughout life is actuarially fair. Everyone pays for what they take from the system and receives back insurance of the same value. Rules 1–5, 8, 9, and 13, relating to morality, the individual, protection of groups (the Core), and market efficiency are satisfied. If government does not interfere in the above arrangements, one can make a case that Rules 6, 10–12 are also satisfied.

So why do we not have such insurance?

1. The insurance described requires everyone to be insured each year of life. If someone does not pay premiums in any year, the arrangements are broken. In the real world, therefore, provisions must be present to enable an individual's return to good standing. Guaranteed issue becomes a concern.
2. The insurance described presumes that everyone gets the same insurance. If someone insists that they want a smaller policy or a bigger policy, a more generous policy or less generous policy, a more expensive policy or less expensive policy, the arrangements are broken. In the real world, freedom of choice and premiums that differ by the choice made and remain actuarially fair need to be present.
3. The insurance described needs design features that provide proper incentives. Just as car insurance insures against low-

---

[2]An individual's care and insurance begin at birth. Pre-natal care is care of the adult. We know in advance that males and females will have different expected medical costs. Actuarially fair insurance requires separate pools for males and females. In other words, we insure against the cost of medical events, we do not insure against the event of being one sex or the other.

probability large-expenditure accidents, and it does not cover the cost of minor routine oil changes, car washes, and maintenance, so health care insurance needs to be designed for low-probability large-expenditure medical events. If insurance foolishly stated that any care, elective or not, routine or not, was covered from the first dollar onward, such first-dollar coverage would induce massive over-use. That is why deductibles, co-insurance, co-pays, and out-of-pocket limits exist.

4. The insurance described requires that the person insured carries it wherever they go in life. If insurance is provided by one's place of employment (a peculiar feature of U.S. health insurance caused by past government actions that are universally condemned by economists for its harmful consequences[3]) and one leaves that place of employment, then insurance is lost. Insurance portability becomes an issue.

5. The insurance described requires that the insurance be actuarially fair. If persons of different ages and sexes are commingled, the arrangements are broken. Age and sex discrimination, guaranteed renewability, guaranteed issue, portability, utilization gatekeeping and a host of other problems become concerns.

6. Last, the insurance described requires that insurance be offered competitively, meaning at the lowest cost possible. If actuarial fairness is lost, and the products bought with insurance are not provided in competitive markets, high cost and un-affordable health care becomes a problem.

As the preceding list shows, when multiple things are wrong with a system they often cause inter-related problems. As promised, in the case of health care these can be sorted out. Table 10.1 on page 352 takes the issues described in the list above and places their resolution in order of importance as they will be discussed.

---

[3]Insurance offered by place of employment has it origins in "an accident of history" that we need not delve into. It nevertheless persists and has pernicious effects.

Table 10.1: **Essential Economics of Healthcare Policy**

10.1[†] Competition enforced by pro-competitive government action. [[Deals with page 348 unrealistic belief 1.]]

    A. Price transparency (public posting of prices).
    B. Most-Favored-Customer Pricing.
    C. Sale of insurance by companies to any willing buyer.

10.2 Insurance reform enforced by government actions. [[Deals with page 348 unrealistic belief 2.]]

    A. Guaranteed issue and Portability
    B. No utilization gatekeeping by insurance companies.
    C. Actuarially fair rating by age and sex.
    D. Application of rules about deductibles and co-insurance.
    E. Guaranteed renewability.
    F. Equalized tax treatment.
    G. Freedom of choice provision

10.3 Natural market incentives for individuals to buy insurance. [[Deals with page 348 unrealistic belief 3.]]

10.4 Targeted intervention on behalf of the small group of truly needy.

    A. Cash aid targeted only to those who are objects of charity, remembering that
    B. those who cannot pay premiums now may be able to pay in the future.

10.5 Transition

    C. Remove over-regulation, mandated excessive coverage, bad incentives.
    D. Move insured groups swiftly to competitive market insurance where premiums are rated for them actuarially fairly.

[†] Points labeled 10.1 through 10.5 in this list are explained in the correspondingly numbered sections of this Chapter.

10.1 Competition Enforced by Government Action

A. Price Transparency (Public Posting of Prices)

> **Application of Rule 5: Competition is the only reliable way to keep prices as low as possible.**

It is government's duty to enforce healthy competition. Transparent prices are the first requirement of competition. Government's role also involves information flows. It is therefore necessary that government mandate the posting of prices by all health care providers. Each health care provider can charge whatever prices it chooses, but they must be posted. The establishment of a government website self-supporting from dues of the providers and allowing search by service type, provider name, provider type, region, price, and volume of services performed is part of price transparency. Material+labor prices should be included in the posted information.

B. Most-Favored-Customer Pricing.

> **Application of Rule 5: Competition is the only reliable way to keep prices as low as possible.**

Most-favored-customer pricing is a second essential ingredient for government's establishment of healthy competition. There is historical precedent. The very first clause of the 1948 General Agreement on Tariffs and Trade (GATT) negotiated by the Truman administration (now subsumed in the World Trade Organization) is called the most-favored-nation clause. Nations were engaging in anti-competitive treatment of their trading partners by applying differential price schedules and keeping their schedules hard to know and non-transparent. Negotiators knew this was against the public interest. GATT sought to force healthy free market competition. Designed to change the anti-competitive way the system operated, Article I of GATT fought back. Most-favored-nation treatment became its *first* founding principle.

If we replace the words "customs duties and charges of any kind imposed on or in connection with importation or exportation or imposed on the international transfer of payments for imports or exports" with health care references "prices and charges in connection with health care products or services" and make relevant substitutions, the result is a modern Article I for restoring health care competition:

> **Article I: General Most-Favored-Health-Care Customer Treatment**
>
> 1. **With respect to prices and charges in connection with health care products or services, and**
> 2. **with respect to the method of levying such prices and charges, and**
> 3. **with respect to all rules and formalities in connection with supplying health care products or services,**
> 4. **any advantage, favor, privilege or immunity granted by any supplier of health care products or services to any buyer of health care products or services shall be accorded immediately and unconditionally to the like product or service destined for any other buyer.**

Hospitals and other health care providers often want to offer both charity and market services. If the medical charity account is fully funded prior to issue, medical "scholarships" do not violate the rule that prices be the same. Products and services described by items 1-4 that are offered through medical scholarships at zero charge therefore are exempted from the requirement to be offered to all other customers at the same price. The net effect of most-favored-customer pricing is that either $0 or only one non-zero price may be charged.

C. Sale of Insurance by Companies to any Willing Buyer

> **Application of Rule 5: Competition is the only reliable way to keep prices as low as possible.**

"Any willing buyer" applies to any consumer in the economy. A state may regulate insurance companies operating within its borders, but healthy competition requires that they may not impede the free flow of sales purchased from other states, which, after all, are already regulated by their state of origin. In the US it is a constitutional principle that neither the federal government nor a state may tax the exports from one state to another.[4]

10.2   Insurance Reform by Government Actions

A. Guaranteed Issue and Portability:

Application of Rule 4: Private goods are best produced and distributed in competitive private markets.

Rule 4 says that private goods are best produced and distributed in competitive free markets, meaning the good bought becomes the buyer's personal property. It follows that health insurance, like one's dress shoes or clothing, is property that should be personal and portable. When someone leaves one place of employment for another, the insurance policy held by the individual should travel with him or her as personal property.

Since health insurance offered at place of employment has become the norm due to federal tax interferences in the World-War-II era, we need a mechanism to allow individuals to travel from one insurance policy to another if they meet the definition of being in "good standing." Guaranteed renewability implies that an individual be able to buy coverage from a new insurance plan at the same premiums as others of his or her age and sex. Presume that good standing is defined to mean having had continuous insurance coverage. Forcing insurance companies to accept all customers who have had continuous insurance coverage to the time of application means that companies could end up with a pool of high risk insureds, needing greater claims payout than the norm for this age and sex pool.

Several ways of accommodating the risk of attracting a higher risk pool because of being forced by law to accept applications of

---

[4]Article I, Section 2, Part 9, paragraphs 5 and 6 read: "5: No Tax or Duty shall be laid on Articles exported from any State. 6: No Preference shall be given by any Regulation of Commerce or Revenue to the Ports of one State over those of another: nor shall Vessels bound to, or from, one State, be obliged to enter, clear, or pay Duties in another."

those who have continuous coverage exist.[5] A re-insurance mechanism can be set up under government auspices. Re-insurance is
"insurance for insurance companies" against the risk of getting a
high-cost pool. The re-insurance body should be self-funding from
the premiums of the insurance companies that re-insure through the
pool.

Several options exist. Re-insurance could be state-wide and done
state by state. This allows experimentation with different formats.
Alternately it could be nationwide. Payments between companies
could be ex ante or ex post. Different formats have advantages and
can work in principle.

Three exceptional types of insureds need attention. The first is
continuously-insured individuals who enter into a permanently high-
claims status and are "stranded" in a company that charges them
premiums higher than the premiums for similar age and sex offered
elsewhere, or it might be that the quality of service is worse when
compared to what can be found offered by other insurance companies. Such an individual needs to be able to move to another
company. This is not a natural market function, since the individual
has, in effect, become uninsurable through no fault of his or her
own (future claims will be high and exceed the size that competitive
premiums for others of same age and sex could cover). One method
to guarantee insurance coverage, is to require insurance companies
to accept the individual at standard rates, but apply a re-insurance
mechanism to spread the risk to the entire insurance field that insurance companies are being forced to take by such a regulation.

The second special class is the temporarily carelessly uninsured,
but who generally were careful to have continuous health insurance.
Perhaps they became uninsurable during the careless gap in cover-

---

[5]Imagine a number assigned to each individual that encodes his or her expected claims status, and is updated with changing conditions. If the number is
1, the individual is expected to incur insurance claims in the coming year equal
to 1xAvg where Avg. is the average claim for an insured of the same age and
sex (i.e. of the same cohort). If the number is different, say 1.4 then the individual is expected to incur claims in the coming year of 1.4xAvg., and so on.
All that is needed to facilitate guaranteed issue and portability is that the number be known and a mechanism for covering the expected higher claims, such
as through a re-insurance mechanism, from higher premiums on the individual,
from transfer payments by the sending company, from a high-risk pool funded
by tax money, or a combination of the above be employed.

age. Because such an individual became uninsured for some gap in time, are they forever relegated to an uninsurable pool or high risk pool, possibly threatening their financial health and safety? For these individuals, some mechanism for re-establishing good standing is needed. One could use open enrollment periods with appropriate penalties. For example, persons who carelessly became uninsured can get "back on the wagon" during an open enrollment period, pay the back premiums (the look-back period could be set at 2 years, for example), plus penalty, and be returned to the "continuously insured" group. The goal is to leave in place sufficiently strong natural incentives so that no responsible individual would choose to go uninsured, but allow the temporarily uninsured to return to good insurance standing.

> **Application of Rules 2 and 3: Pay fully for what you take from society. Be fully paid for what you provide. Not paying one's debt is stealing.**

The third group is the irresponsibly un-insured. These are un-insureds attempting to game the system or without any intention of establishing for themselves financial means. For them, health care may need to be covered by The Emergency Medical Treatment and Active Labor Act (EMTALA) regulations, interest-free loans, high risk pools, and charity, remembering the importance of individual accountability. "Accountability Accounts"—future tracking to collect payment from those able to pay back in the future—is the appropriate first response. This also allows their aid to be recycled to help others.

B. No utilization gatekeeping by insurance companies

Utilization gatekeeping is denial by health insurance companies of claims for covered healthcare services rendered. Utilization gatekeeping is an improper device used by insurance companies to increase profits. Insurance companies also increase profits through investment of excess premiums collected, and by selling access to price schedules that they negotiate with providers. None of these three schemes for raising profits are valid insurance functions. Insurance companies are firms that collect premiums, process claims paperwork, and make payments on claims. If a medical service is covered by a policy, the insurance company's sole duty is to verify that that service was provided and make payment on the claim.

Rather than attempting to create bureaucracy to regulate health insurance to its proper limited functions, establishing competition and letting competition do the job is preferred. Most-favored-customer pricing, for example, means that any insurance-company-negotiated price or price schedule is immediately posted and available to everyone. No special profit advantage exists to an insurance company by such negotiation. With claims payment mandated for covered services rendered, utilization gatekeeping as a profit strategy also disappears.

It is also necessary that insurance policies be written in a form that allows comparison and competition.

C. Actuarially fair rating by age and sex

Application of Rule 8: Good Policy is in the Core.

It is a principle of fair insurance that no group identifiable-in-advance should be able to withdraw from the insured pool and do better for itself. This principle is violated in health care unless policies are rated by age and sex of the insured. Rating by age and sex is a minimal requirement. Further rating to pool like with like is within the proper insurance function. As a start, pro-competitive government policy should therefore mandate rating by age and sex of the insured.

Rating by age and sex of the insured also facilitates a second principle of good insurance, which is that health insurance policies cover all medical services unless the service is specifically listed in the list of exclusions. For example, services not generally used should be excluded, but available in additional options. Examples might be fertility services for women or hair transplants for men. Excluded services can be sold separately as policy riders.

D. Application of rules about insurance, deductibles, and co-insurance

The need to follow rules about insurance design, especially regarding deductibles, co-insurance, and co-payments have long been understood and urged by healthcare economists. For example:

- | **Application of Rules 2 and 3: Pay fully for what you take from society. Be fully paid for what you provide. Not paying one's debt is stealing.** | "Each person should pay a premium equal to the expected healthcare costs he or she adds" to the risk pool they are entering. If someone cannot pay, "they will either be left out of the pool, or others must make a charitable contribution on their behalf."[6]

- "Renewal is guaranteed, and if premiums are increased, they must be increased proportionately for everyone." Everyone's premiums are raised or lowered "at renewal time, based on whether the whole group's costs have been more or less than expected."[7]

- Plus, detailed insurance design advice is readily available the details of which we need not treat here.

E. Guaranteed renewability

In a given year each of us faces risks from two kinds of medical events. One, like breaking your arm, is treated during the year and you are returned to your previous health status. The other, like being diagnosed with a permanent condition requiring care and treatment for the rest of your life, changes your insurance classification (your "health status"). Both need to be insured against. Guaranteed renewability (the right to renew insurance at the same premium as others of one's age and sex) is equivalent to saying that everyone carries "reclassification risk insurance" (health status insurance) in addition to "short-term health event" insurance. National re-insurance mechanisms support this feature (described in *Health Care for Us All*).[8] Different means of supporting guaranteed renewability for individuals in good standing are included in the discussion above under "Guaranteed Issue and Portability."

---

[6]Goodman, 2012, p. 170-71.

[7]Ibid.

[8]Grinols and Henderson (2009). See pp. 143-145.

F. Equalized tax treatment

It is well known by health care economists that the differential tax treatment of health insurance offered though place of employment and insurance purchased in the individual market has led to great distortions and harm.[9] Tax treatment must be equalized to remove this distortion. Since health care insurance is a private good, the preferred way to do this is to remove deductibility for insurance offered through place of employment to match the lack of deductibility for individual purchase of insurance. When it comes to rules and regulations, less is better.

G. Freedom of Choice Provision

> **Application of Rule 10: It is government's job to enforce appropriate property rights.**

Free markets allow citizens to choose where and when to purchase. Equalization of tax treatment for insurance purchase can be coupled with a freedom of choice provision. Such a provision would stipulate in law that insureds could use whatever health care dollars are available to them— whether through employer contribution, private charity, or government subsidies—to buy insurance from their preferred seller. If an individual saves money by buying from a nationally competitive company, he or she keeps the difference.

Various ways to phase in and phase out such provisions are possible. For example, the freedom of choice provision could initially be applied just to the young and later extended to all ages.[10] Proportion of savings retained by the insured could be varied in time, and so on.

10.3   Market Incentives for Individuals to Buy Insurance

As much as possible, health care arrangements should honor natural market incentives. In a market the buyer pays for what he or she

---

[9]Grinols, (2015).
[10]Ibid.

gets. If the buyer does not pay now, then the buyer pays later. If another pays on the recipient's behalf, it is the charitable choice of the giver. Loans are tracked in a market and payment enforced. One can imagine various implications.

> **Application of Rules 2 and 3: Pay fully for what you take from society. Be fully paid for what you provide. Not paying one's debt is stealing.**

Plan A: To re-establish incentives for individuals to want to buy their own health insurance, The Emergency Medical Treatment and Active Labor Act must be reformed so that the amount of free and subsidized health care that they receive is recorded, tracked into the future, and paid back by the recipient. Recipients of unpaid care might be required to file annual statements, for example, that reveal their current ability to pay and required payments enforced.

Emergency care can be administered at the time of need (this is current law) regardless of ability to pay, but provision for tracking into the future must be added so that those who can pay back in the future are required to do so. There are various ways that government can be helpful to the tracking process. This might include federal tools such as a required annual income and asset filing with contact information. A never-fail biometric identifier might be required of EMTALA care recipients such as an eye scan or fingerprints.

> **Application of Rule 5: Competition is the only reliable way to keep prices as low as possible.**

Prices charged for EMTALA-based care may not exceed the best prices charged by the supplier to the most favored of its customers.

> **Application of Rule 10: It is government's job to enforce appropriate property rights.**

Rationale: It is appropriate for government to create the necessary property rights for a market to exist. In this case, EMTALA reform creates the property right for EMTALA care recipients to be traced, paying their debts in the future when able to, and so aiding the health insurance market.

Application of Rule 12: Government should not engage in theft. Forced charity is theft. Charitable Fund:
Many individuals may want patients to be given financial help in paying for their EMTALA-based care. A charitable fund established with government oversight allows private contributions to be given to it for that purpose. Charity is not a proper government activity because it does not promote the general welfare but only the personal welfare of some to the harm of others. Forced charity is theft. Government encourages and strongly affirms those who want to give so that others may receive help, however, by sanctioning and enabling the charitable function.

Plan B: If the above arrangements are not strong enough, a second incentive is possible that rewards health insurance purchase by lowering the price of all other consumer purchases. The plan involves imposing a broad-based tax such as a value added tax (VAT) that is rebated at point of purchase only to those who provide proof of having health insurance at time of purchase.

- Knowing that I will pay 10 percent less for all my purchases if I have health insurance is a strong inducement. (The actual amount can be set as needed.)

- Through this device, economic theory, in effect, creates a mechanism similar to posting a deposit on a bottle or can. Only those who do not properly dispose of their bottles and cans by returning them pay the "deposit tax." An incentive is created that affects only non-buyers of insurance (automatically singling them out).

- This price benefit for insurance purchase is accomplished at no budget cost. For example, imposing a uniform tax that raises all prices (such as a value added tax[11]) but rebates the tax back for (or does not collect it from) those who have purchased health insurance costs nothing to government, but does create an incentive.[12] Further, such an arrangement impacts only

---

[11] A VAT is recommended by this author only if it replaces the income tax and the 16th Amendment is repealed. The size of federal unfunded obligations may enable such a compromise in the immediate coming years.

[12] There are, of course, inconvenience costs that appear at the place and time of a sale.

those without insurance and has no impact on those who do. This arrangement is favored by *Health Care for Us All* because it is implied by economic theory. (See pp. 131-136, 27-29)

- If politics prevents the theory-implied mechanism, then some other means of motivation can be substituted.

Plan C: If Plans A and B are rejected, then other alternatives that cause the uninsured to want to buy health insurance can be substituted, though they will be less efficient.

One example is an income subsidy paid through an augmented Earned Income Tax Credit (EITC). An EITC to those who qualify, coupled with a tax penalty, would provide a once-per-year reminder and reach those uninsured who file taxes. Those who don't file, would need to be motivated in some other way. Another possibility might be whatever state by state plans that might be devised that respect the need to require personal accountability by aid recipients.

10.4 Targeted Intervention for the Small Group of Truly Needy.

Because they want to buy insurance, those needing financial aid have the incentive to self-identify and seek it. Those found qualified might be granted income aid through an augmented, incentive-compatible Earned Income Tax Credit. This is targeted aid, not a blanket expenditure for all people. Alternatively, those who want insurance but need financial help can receive income aid through a charitable fund for that purpose. Government could be involved in facilitating and overseeing the charity, with the source of funds being private charity.

As extensively discussed, income aid should be paid back in the future by those who are able in the future to pay it back. Those who cannot pay back in the future can become the beneficiary of charity. See "Charitable Fund" in C. above. RIP Medical Debt is discussed in the box below.

RIP Medical Debt.

Do you think it is wrong for households to have to pay medical costs that they cannot afford, especially when their need for care may have been outside their control? Here is a way you can help.

RIP Medical Debt is a not-for-profit 501(c)3 voluntary private organization that uses donors' money to buy bundles of medical debt instruments at prices that are as little as 10 cents on the dollar and even lower. Once acquired, those whose debts are in the bundle are told that their medical debt is forgiven. The following explanation is from the RIP website:

> RIP uses donors' funds to wipe out medical debt from the neediest cases up.
>
> Once we've pinpointed the portfolios for those in or near the poverty level, we buy up their debt and forgive it. Then we send forgiveness notices to the benefiting families, and subsequently help the recipients repair their credit reports—renewing their access to opportunities and resources that will allow them to rebuild and recover.

Several comments:

1. As we saw in the example on page 59 where the heart operation could be provided at **6%** of the hospital's stated price, medical charges are often based on fictions that do not reflect the true cost of care. *RIP Medical Debt* cancels that debt at low costs that come closer to reflecting the true costs incurred.

2. The Intervention Principle says that the best policy is targeted narrowly to the objective, which in this case is terminating medical debt for those who cannot pay it. There is no need to set up a massive system of national health care involving everyone in the nation. *RIP Medical Debt* is available, effective, and targeted.

3. Many profess to favor that those near poverty not be saddled with large, unfair, medical debt. They have a perfect vehicle to provide the help they want to give.

4. Disclaimer: I think *RIP Medical Debt* has a wonderful and clever business model. I have contributed to it myself.

5. If you were in medical debt that you could not pay, you would want someone to help you. By the Golden Rule, you therefore have an obligation to help others end their medical debt.

"Therefore whatever you desire for men to do to you, you shall also do to them; for this is the law and the prophets." Matt 7:12

10.5 Transition Details

Transition is a 6-18 month period in which everyone is transferred to insurance offered in free competitive markets. Everyone pays his or her own actuarially fair premium rated for his or her age and sex. Those who cannot pay receive targeted intervention as described above. Recipients of aid are tracked and those able to pay later pay back in the future. This "recycles" the help they get.

One way to think about transition arrangements is by insured type. Insureds consist of a healthy group and pre-existing-conditions group. Allow the healthy group plus adults without dependents on Medicaid to buy policies on ehealthinsurance.com using their current subsidies that are not Patient Protection Act compliant.

— Place those in the pre-existing conditions group into a temporary high risk pool charging them appropriate premiums as they are able to pay and until charity and other permanent arrangements can be established.
— An individual who is uninsured and remains healthy (no pre-existing conditions) who now wants insurance must pay a penalty (penalties of some size are necessary to support proper incentives for individuals continuously to carry insurance), but may buy insurance on the exchanges.
— Extend for a transition period the "slacker mandate:" those under 26 may be on their parents' policy up to age 26 if they are a dependent of the parents.

10.6   Sequencing of Changes

If only one could be made, what system-transforming change would accomplish the most good? If two? If three? The following list orders changes by their importance.

1.   **T**ransparency and competition: require posting of prices, most favored customer pricing, and insurance sold to any willing buyer at actuarially fair prices and ratings by age and sex. This legislation could be written on one page.

2.   **R**enewability and Portability: Require re-insurance mechanisms, allowed to vary state-by-state, to support guaranteed renewability and portability. Define role of good standing, how to maintain and restore good standing. This mitigates against companies avoiding obligations to sell.

3.   **A**ccountability: Change EMTALA and establish accountability accounts. This mitigates against citizens abusing and gaming the system.

4.   **I**nsurance Design: This leads to low fair prices and restores freedom to buyers of insurance.

5.   **N**eed-based Charity Only: Charity narrowly targeted to those currently unable to buy insurance means lower cost since aid goes only to those who need it. Everyone will have insurance and access to care. Federal mechanisms endorse, support, and encourage giving to provide premium support and support for paying back balances.

The preceding list forms the acronym TRAIN.

10.7   "Social Insurance"

The title of this section is in quotation marks because based on what we have learned in this book "Social Insurance" is in some sense an oxymoron. "Social" in the name "Social Insurance" suggests that it is insurance that should be (or is) offered by a government body for a social purpose. As noted earlier in this chapter, an insurance company is nothing but a paperwork processing office, collecting premiums and processing claims, neither of which requires government. The insured pays premiums and afterward receives in return contingent payment of private goods, or the money to buy private goods. Since insurance is a private good it should be produced and distributed in competitive private markets. The previous sections on heath care and health care insurance involve government only because they take as given that a list of non-market features be present. We explained the way that these additional objectives could be met consistent with efficiency and morality.

Nevertheless there are programs of "social insurance" such as Social Security that need to be squared with what we have learned. The two principles that apply are (1) that the premiums someone pays for his or her policy should cover the expected cost of the claims that he or she will have plus administrative costs and normal return to investment of the insurance the provider, and (2) those who buy insurance should get the benefits of their policy and those who don't shouldn't. Participation in insurance should be the choice of the insured.

We show how this works by dealing with some hard "hole in the bucket" type questions.[13]

Question 1: A news story reported that firefighters in a rural area let a home burn to the ground because the homeowner hadn't paid the $75 insurance premium! What do you say?

Answer: When the fire department received the emergency call, the homeowner should have been told the true cost of putting out the fire, been allowed to commit to pay that cost (including the option to pay the debt over time), perhaps with a reasonable penalty added, and the units sent out to put out the fire. Presuming the value of the lost home exceeded the true cost of putting out the fire and the fire is put out, the homeowner is better off, the fire department is better off. Presuming further that the penalty is large enough to induce the homeowner to keep current on his or her fire policy, he or she will not make the same mistake of being uninsured twice.

Question 2: What about a crack baby? Who should pay its

---

[13] In the folk song, the problem begins with a hole in the bucket, the response to which is "fix it." This is followed by the assertion of further problems such as the question "With What?" which when solved, evince yet the assertion of another complication. Hole to straw to cutting the straw to using an ax to sharpening the ax to using a whetstone to needing it wet to using water to needing to carry the water to using a bucket to "there's a hole in the bucket" is the sequence of the song. If a problem is made impossible, of course, there is no solution.

medical costs?

Answer: A baby cannot be expected pay his or her medical costs, they are the responsibility of the baby's parents. Crack babies are babies born to mothers who used crack cocaine during their pregnancy. People who know they will never have a crack baby (e.g. an 85 year old widow, a couple who do not abuse drugs, an unmarried male) do not want to buy an insurance rider that pays for crack baby costs. Thus, the costs of an insurance policy to cover the costs of a crack baby are likely to be very high, and purchased solely by those who know with near certainty they will have high claims. Such a policy is likely to be prohibitively expensive. Realistically then, medical costs for a crack baby (true costs, **not** fictitiously inflated prices invented by the hospital) become the debt responsibility of the parents, and the object of charity. See the grayed box on RIP Medical Debt.

Question 3: What if the baby has severe autism that is not the fault of the parents that results in higher costs throughout the child's life? Who should pay the medical costs?

Answer: A child's medical and other costs remain the responsibility of the child's parents. In this case, however, let us presume that every couple intending to bear children has the same probability of encountering the autism in their child. Now an insurance policy rider that covers autism-related claims would be attractive to a large number of buyers, all of whom will have reason to want the added coverage. Those who know going forward that they never will have children with autism (because they will not be having children is the most likely cause) will not buy such policies. As before, if medical costs cannot be paid now, they can become debts that are paid in the future (once more, we are talking about the competitively low true costs of care), and can be the object of charity.

REFERENCES:

Centers for Medicare & Medicaid Services. Medicare & Medicaid Research Review/ 2013 Statistical Supplement, Tables 13.5-13.11. https://www. cms.gov/ Research-Statistics-Data-and-Systems/ Statistics-Trends-and-Reports/ MedicareMedicaidStat-

Supp/2013.html

Centers for Medicare & Medicaid Services. Medicare-Medicaid Enrollee Information, National, 2011.

Goodman, John, "Designing Ideal Health Insurance", Priceless: Curing the Healthcare Crisis, Chapter 11. Oakland, CA: The Independent Institute, 2012.

Goodman, John, "Why I Don't Like Deductibles," *Health Alerts,* December 18, 2013, http:// healthblog.ncpa.org/ why-i-dont-like-deductibles/ ?utm_source=newsletter &utm_medium =email&utm_campaign=HA #mo re-35149.

Grinols, Earl L. and James W. Henderson, *Health Care for Us All: Getting More for our Investment.* New York: Cambridge University Press, 2009.

Grinols, Earl L., "Reforming Obamacare: Start with the Young," *Real Clear Policy,* http: //www.realclearpolicy.com /blog/2015/ 01/20/reforming_obamacare_start_with _the_young _1176.html20 January 2015.

Part 2: Chapter 11

Government Failure

The search for a scapegoat is the easiest of all hunting expeditions.

Dwight D. Eisenhower

Part 1, Chapter 11 suggested that government failure is probably an intrinsic feature, to some extent can be explained by human nature, and is likely influenced by identifiable incentives. Harming one group to help your own, or scapegoating one group to help your own is politics at less than best.

In this book we have rejected the organismic conception of government that says government has interests that go beyond justice, morality, and fairness, to include the crafting and adoption of policies that intervene to harm one group to help another. Creating a program that helps just one group but is paid for by all is an example. We should not be surprised that some businesses, affinity groups, and individuals try to turn government to selfish purposes, and not all politicians resist implicit bribery and blackmail if they anticipate not being caught.[1]

Section 11.1 in this chapter augments Chapter 11 of Part 1 by briefly considering the political source, Democrat or Republican, of selected US government failures of the past two centuries. We argue that two explanations seem to be at work. Section 11.2 follows

---

[1]Judges, for example, are supposed to rule "without favor, without fear." Nothing should deter them from rendering justice.

this by summarizing the economic costs of one particular form of government failure, Directly Unproductive Profit-seeking.

Before proceeding, we acknowledge that it is always dangerous to criticize one group or another. Team players identify with "their" team.   Historian Edward Gibbon in his monumental *The History of the Decline and Fall of the Roman Empire* reports that Roman sporting factions adopted certain colors, and so strong became the factional devotion that riots, fights and even deaths resulted between caerulean blues, whites, light greens, and reds.[2]

Nevertheless, we proceed. What a group did in one generation, all of whose members are now dead, is fair game for examination.

11.1   Democrat versus Republican Policy Failures

Historians prefer discriminating assessments of history. In hind sight, it is easy to see that the National Socialists in pre-World-War-II Germany were the primary source of that era's misguided government. Nazis were German, but not all Germans were Nazis.   The non-socialists' failure was inaction and failing to prevent Nazi policies.

A similar situation exists with respect to major policy failings of the United States over its history.   Table 11.1 lists a number of failings that relate to one group mistreating another, sometimes under government auspices, the relevant time frame, the political party responsible, and a short commentary.

---

[2]Chapter 40, *Fall in the East*, "The Factions of the Circus": "The race, in its first institution, was a simple contest of two chariots, whose drivers were distinguished by white and red liveries: two additional colors, a light green, and a caerulean blue, were afterwards introduced;" Gibbons describes as absurd,

> the blind ardor of the Roman people, who devoted their lives and fortunes to the color which they had espoused. Such folly was disdained and indulged by the wisest princes; but the names of Caligula, Nero, Vitellius, Verus, Commodus, Caracalla, and Elagabalus, were enrolled in the blue or green factions of the circus; they frequented their stables, applauded their favorites, chastised their antagonists, and deserved the esteem of the populace, by the natural or affected imitation of their manners. The bloody and tumultuous contest continued to disturb the public festivity, till the last age of the spectacles of Rome.

Table 11.1: **Sources of Government Failure**

Time Frame	Event	Party	Comment
1830s	Trail of Tears	Democrat	Andrew Jackson, Martin Van Buren. See page 124.
1788-1863	Slavery	Democrat	The Republican Party was founded in 1854 as the anti-slavery party. Republicans did not own slaves.
1856	Dred Scott Decision	Democrat	The seven members of the Supreme Court who voted against Dred Scott were Democrats. The two who voted in favor of Scott were a Republican and a Whig.
1865-1944	Ku Klux Klan (1865-71, 1915-1944)	Democrat	Nathan Bedford Forest, founder, was a Democrat. KKK operated in two distinct eras in the South as an anti-occupation group and anti-Black group.
1877-1954	Jim Crow Laws	Democrat	Laws that enforced racial segregation were passed in southern states between the end of Reconstruction in 1877 and beginning of the civil rights movement in the 1950s.
1866-1913	Government Pension Corruption	Republican	The story of Republican pension corruption and Democrat Grover Cleveland's opposition to it is told on p. 147.
1913	Re-Segregating Federal Government	Democrat	Theodore Roosevelt had desegregated the federal government. Woodrow Wilson reversed.

1930s-Present	Agricultural Support Programs	Republican	See page 146. Why are the risks of farmers underwritten by the government, but not the risks of stock market investors? Republicans tend to be more associated with this form of crony capitalism that artificially intervenes in markets to help one group at the expense of others.
1942-1945	Incarcerating American citizens of Japanese descent	Democrat	Franklin Roosevelt was responsible for Executive Order 9066 that placed Japanese-Americans in concentration camps and affected 117,000 people, most of whom were citizens of the United States.
1960s-Present	Abortion	Democrat	Abraham Lincoln said no one has a right to do wrong. Since it involves human life, abortion remains the pre-eminent moral issue of the nation.

What can account for the assignments in the table? We offer two. First, there is Lord Acton's previously-cited dictum in regards to government pensions and Grover Cleveland that "absolute power corrupts absolutely." The Republicans after the Civil War were masters of the political scene. Union Civil War veterans wanted pensions. The party in power found it convenient to provide them. It was especially easy to drift into pension corruption because the ready excuse was that the "worthy recipients" were war veterans, deserving of pity, thanks, and ... public money.

The explanation for the acts of Democrats listed in Table 11.1 is different. As already explained, the organismic view of government holds that it is permissible to weigh the well-being of one group against another when deciding social policy. At the outset it is deemed acceptable for policy to help one group even if it harms another, if the measure of social welfare is increased thereby. There is no universal or universally accepted way to decide which group will be favored and which group will be dis-favored.

The issue is whether such choices should be made at all. In

one generation, "rich" Indians are separated from their land to help poor whites. In another, one racial group is disadvantaged to advantage another racial group. In wartime the rights of one group, Japanese-Americans, are limited to reduce wartime risks to non-Japanese groups. Some think it acceptable to recognize no rights for unborn children in order to advantage the pursuit of happiness by already-born women. Disadvantaging one group to advantage another is acceptable in the social utility context of organismic government, it is not acceptable in the individualistic context of this book.

Organismic v. Individualistic Government Again
It is not difficult analysis. Once the organismic principle is adopted that it is acceptable to go beyond enforcing justice, fairness and morality, to balance the favorable impact on one group against the unfavorable impact on another, it is only a matter of time until policies that help one group at the planned expense of another are, in fact, adopted. If one political group learns that it can keep itself in power, thereby, it will fight ferociously to do so.[3]

---

[3] The reader may wish to revisit the statement by Bastiat on page 159.

Pareto Optimality, the Golden Rule, and the individualistic approach to government all lead to an entirely different calculus that honors the principles that you own yourself, that you create your own property, that taxes are legitimate only in proportion to the benefits provided to the payer by government from their use, that there should be unanimity about the quantity of what government provides, and so on.

Pareto Optimality and morality are inconsistent with the organismic approach. Moreover, the organismic approach activates incentives for political abuse and government failure.

11.2 Directly Unproductive Profitseeking

A continuing theme in this book has been that incentives must always be kept in mind and set correctly to allow human flourishing to occur. Pareto Optimality and the Golden Rule were our start-ing point for identifying what *essential economics* and morality im-ply. Frederic Bastiat's comment that the bad economist takes ac-count only of what is immediate and that "it almost always happens that when the immediate consequence is favorable, the later conse-quences are disastrous (p. 163)" is a statement about incentives.

Just how powerful incentives can be when they are properly aligned is illustrated in the following story.

Desert travelers A & B are both approaching the same oasis. As they converge, each complains to the other of having the slowest, worst camel ever. A disagreement ensues and they make a bet. Traveler C arrives some time later to find A & B on their camels standing foolishly and motionless in the desert sun hundreds of yards outside the oasis. He learns of the bet. They cannot stand in the desert forever. Amazed over what has happened, he whispers to them. The scene changes. Now the camels are racing at top speed to the oasis.

How did he solve the problem? The hint is that the original incentives were not set correctly. He whispered: "Switch Camels." Motionless camels now raced. Fixing the incentives fixed the prob-lem.

In the commercial realm, competition and markets harness in-centives for the people's good. Outside of competition and markets *there is no reliable, lasting, consistent force for social good.* Govern-ment, being naturally non-market, naturally works in the opposite direction. Social structures must understand this and actively work in the opposite direction and prevent environments that engender social harm. One of those harms is what economists call Directly Unproductive Profit-Seeking (DUP).

11.2.1   Description of DUP

Directly Unproductive Profit-Seeking, DUP, is defined as

> Ways of making a profit (i.e. income) by undertaking
> activities which are directly (i.e. immediately, in their
> primary impact) unproductive.[4]

---

[4]Bhagwati (1982), p. 989.

Stealing is an obvious example of DUP. By stealing your goods I produce nothing, but nevertheless enrich myself (unless prevented by the law, of course!). Whereas stealing is illegal, other examples of DUP are not. The favors from government that crony capitalists seek are often DUP. In Elizabethan England, Queen Elizabeth granted crown monopolies to selected and favored courtiers. This enriched her supporters by granting them the exclusive right to trade, but because monopolies are not competitive, was harmful to the public.

State licensed casinos are a modern example. Many states such as my former state of residence, Illinois, grant casino licenses to only a privileged few who are then able to provide gambling in designated parts of the state.[5] Such grants can be extremely lucrative. If casinos are truly good for the economy and society, then why is not everyone given the same privilege? In the first years after issue (1990-December 1993) the return was as high as 1244%! Where do you and I sign up for a similar return?

Revenue-seeking lobbying that diverts government money toward one's firm and oneself is another example of DUP. Tax evasion and smuggling, which may use a great deal of extra resources to accomplish, eliminate paying tax and implicitly generate returns. Professional gamblers might be able to make a living at it, but if their activity does not produce anything of value or generate utility (e.g two professional gamblers playing one another who don't gamble for enjoyment, but just to extract money from the other), it is wasteful of productive resources. Both could be usefully engaged in directly productive activity.[6]

11.2.2 Welfare Effects of DUP

DUP is wasteful in its primary impact and therefore tends to be harmful overall. International trade theorists, however, have been able to place DUP analysis into a general equilibrium context where primary and secondary effects matter. They show that in distorted equilibria, DUP can be welfare enhancing, as for example when tariff-

---

[5]See Grinols (2004).

[6]Of course, other possibilities exist. Just as professional golfers and football players are in the entertainment business, if the gamblers provide entertainment value to others who watch them and pay them for the privilege, their activity is no different than other forms of entertainment.

destroying lobbying occurs in a country for which free trade is optimal. The existence of paradoxical cases means one must balance wasted resources against the effect of DUP on correcting other distortions that may already be present in the system. If the initial situation is distorted the "shadow cost" (or hidden true cost to the system) of a factor of production might be negative. By drawing away resources, the original distortion might be attenuated and the net effect positive. While paradox is possible, that does not mean it is likely. Figure 11.1 provides a fourfold analysis. We start with

Figure 11.1: **Economic Effects of Directly Unproductive Profitseeking**

		HARM	PARADOX POSSIBLE
	Distortion	(Destroys resources + destroys efficiency)	(Destroys resources, may lessen distortion by "starving" the distortion.)
		(Monopoly Example)	(Paradox example.)
Final Situation			
	Distortion Free	HARM	PYRRHIC VICTORY
		(Destroys resources)	(Distortion-destroying lobbying may lower welfare.)
		(Tariff Example)	
		Distortion Free	Distorted

Initial Situation

the paradox case in the upper right hand corner. If the initial economy is distorted and the final situation remains distorted, DUP uses resources and by drawing them away might "starve" the distortion. The net effect could paradoxically be positive. Note, however, that a better policy would be to directly attack the initial distortion and remove it without wasting the resources devoted to DUP.

The bottom right corner labeled "Pyrrhic Victory" involves the reverse situation where DUP eliminates the distortion but wastes so much resources that the net effect on the economy is harmful. Again, directly attacking the initial distortion and removing it without wasting resources is superior policy. The two cells on the left

Figure 11.2: **Distortion Free to Distortion: Monopoly Example**

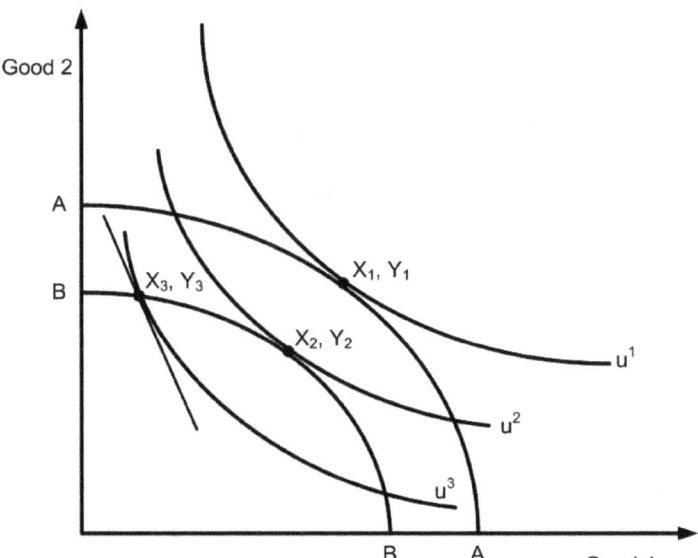

side of the diagram show that if the initial situation is distortion free, then the effect of DUP can only be harmful. If the final situation is distortion free, DUP has wasted resources. If the final situation is distorted, DUP has not only introduced a distortion, but wasted resources in doing so.

Figure 11.2 provides the example of a country where initial production Y_1 is on the production frontier AA and equals consumption X_1. Crony capitalist lobbying for a monopoly uses resources that shrinks the frontier to BB. Instead of producing at the lobbying point Y_2, however, a monopoly has been created that causes the economy to produce at point Y_3, which is even worse. Two sources of loss are introduced: DUP and monopoly. As the lower left corner of Figure 11.1 indicates, the only possible consequence is negative.

Now consider Figure 11.2, from which we can demonstrate two results. Production frontier AA applies to a small trading country. If

Figure 11.3: **Distortion Free to Distortion Free: Tariff Example**

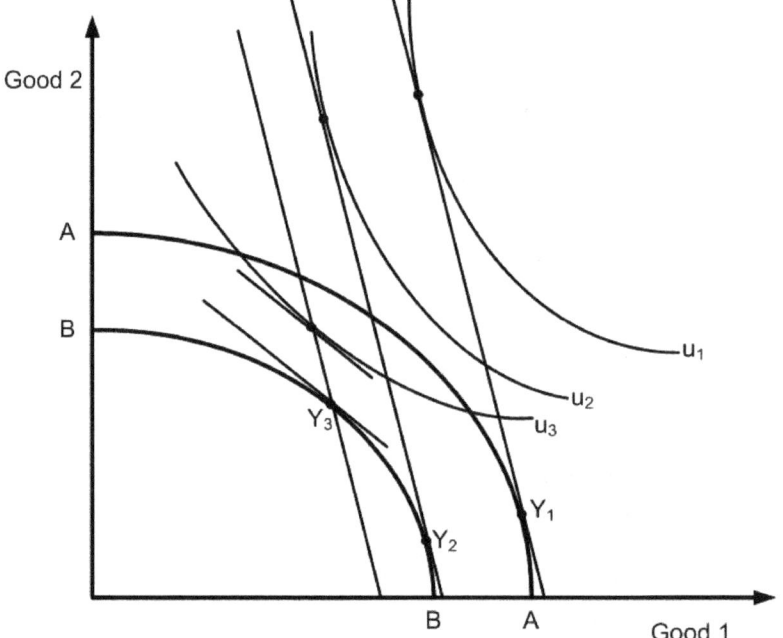

no distortions are present production takes place at point Y_1. Utility is u_1. Our first result is that if no distortions are present in the final situation (this corresponds to the lower left hand corner of Figure 11.1) then the sole consequence of DUP activity is to move the economy to point Y_2 on the post-lobbying frontier. Utility falls to u_2. Since that frontier is diminished by the loss of resources, welfare must fall.

For the second result, assume that the lobbying results in the imposition of a tariff on Good 2 (perhaps the DUP lobbyist competes with Good 2 imports and wants a tax on those imported goods). This corresponds to the upper left square in Figure 11.1. DUP resource use shifts the economy frontier to BB. Instead of producing at Y_2, however, which free trade would do, the tariff resulting from the lobbying shifts production to point Y_3, which lowers welfare further to u_3. The budget line tangent at production point Y_3 exhibits a higher relative price of Good 2 than the four other budget lines shown. This is due to the internal post-tariff price of Good 2 being higher.

The last result in Figure 11.4 shows the paradoxical possibility that Distortion + DUP need not *always* give less welfare than the distortion alone. Assume that the country in question begins with a tariff in place. Production is at point Y_1. Utility is u_1. Now introduce DUP lobbying, keeping the tariff in place. The loss of resources shrinks the frontier from AA to BB. It could happen that production shifts to a point like Y_2, which is on a better budget line for the country and shifts consumption to the northeast on the labeled income expansion path. Utility rises to u_2. Distortion + DUP has "paradoxically" given greater welfare than Distortion alone.

Our final comment is a simple one. The more government ventures outside its Table 10.1 (p. 120) assignments, the greater the inducement for crony capitalists and individuals to seek special favors. Government action generally invites, and may incite, DUP activity.

Figure 11.4: **Distortion to Distortion DUP Paradox: Tariff Example**

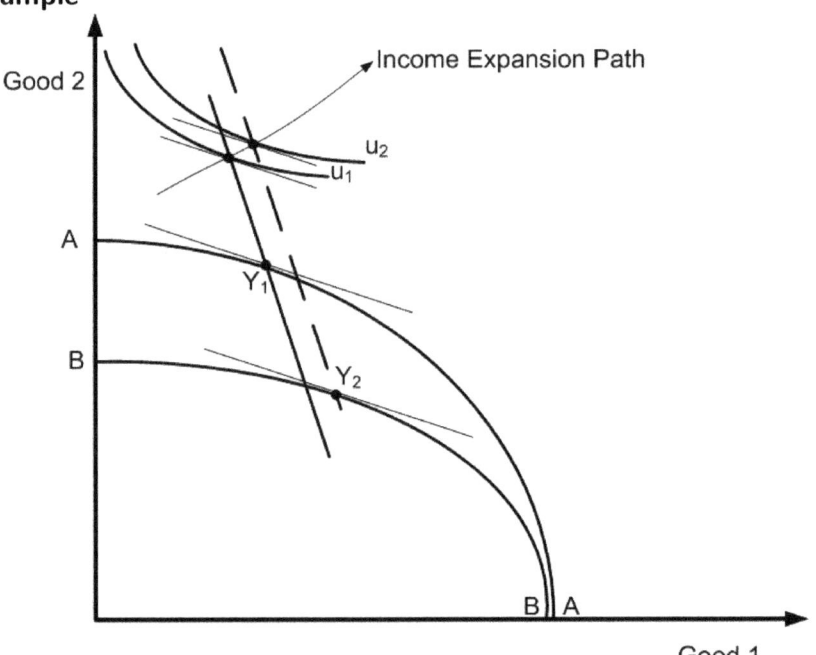

11.3 Conclusion

Government failure can be analyzed both for its economic consequences and for its origins. If a nation consists of individuals, it is not surprising that it might contain factions and parties to which government failures may be unequally assigned. No faction, party, or government is perfect, but the organismic approach to government appears prone to certain kinds of failures to which the individualistic approach is philosophically less prone.

References

Bhagwati, Jagdish (1982). "Directly Unproductive, Profit-Seeking (DUP) Activities," *Journal of Political Economy*, 90, 5, October, 988-1002.

Grinols, Earl L. (2004). *Gambling in America: Costs and Benefits*. New York: Cambridge University Press.

Shaded Boxes

Glossary

- **Actuarially fair** A term used to describe insurance that charges to each insured premiums that equal the expected payout to that individual in covered future claims.

- **Allocation** An allocation lists the consumption and production of every good and service for producers, consumers, and any other decision making unit.

- **Charity** Aid voluntarily given from one's own money or resources to benefit another individual in need.

- **Citizen** See **Household.**

- **Competitive market** In a competitive market, producers maximize their profit given the set of prices that apply.

- **Consumer** See **Household.**

- **Cost** $C[q]$ ("cost," "firm cost," or "total cost") is the cost incurred by the firm in production of q units of the good under consideration.

- **Cost-benefit analysis** A process for measuring the increase or decrease in households' utility attendant upon a change in economic circumstances. Cost-benefit analysis identifies and separates the components of utility change so that they are exhaustive and mutually exclusive.

- **Distributive Efficiency** The impossibility of re-arranging goods in the bundles of consumers to improve the well-being of one without harming the well-being of any other.

- **Economic development** The increase in the well-being of households from given resources. The creation of greater value by society from its available resources. Economic development is often associated with and connnotes the ability to better manage existing resources in response to conditions.

- **Economic growth** The increase in the well-being of households due to technological change—including the introduction of new industry—or increase in the availability and use of productive inputs.

- **Economy** A group of participants (e.g. consumers, households, individuals), endowments, and the production technology (techniques, production recipes) that allows the economy to function.

- **Edgeworth Box** A box whose dimensions equal the total quantity of two goods held between two economic agents. Placing a point in the box divides the two goods between the two agents.

- **Efficient** Accomplishing something in the best possible way. An economy is efficient if it is Pareto Optimal.

- **Endowment** Goods inherited from nature or the past that are not produced in the current production period. We use ω to be the list of endowment quantities.

- **Expenditure, Household** See also Lump sum income.

- **Externality** Direct effects that one economic participant's choices have on another economic participant that do not operate through market prices. A helpful effect is referred to as a positive externality; a harmful effect is referred to as a negative externality. A firm whose production process pollutes the air, for example, creates a negative externality. Since the positive or negative effect impacts others, it is the nature of externalities that the decision-making participant does not take into account the effect its actions have on others when making its choice.

- **Fixed cost** Fixed cost $= C[0]$. See definition of Cost.

- **Gross Domestic Product** The value of all goods and services produced by an economy.

- **Gross profit** Profit before a full accounting of costs, depreciation, and taxes; i.e. revenues after subtracting a subset of costs, depreciation, and taxes.

- **Household** The consumer decision making unit. A household may consist of a single individual, a family, or a group of individuals that makes decisions as a unit. Citizens are households that are the proper object of a political jurisdiction's attention. Residents are households living within a specified region.

- **Indifference curve** A curve whose points represent consumption bundles between which the consumer is indifferent.

- **Individualistic** A conception of government whose interest is establishing individual rights through rules of interaction that enforce justice between economic agents, all of whom are treated equally by the arrangements.

- **Inner product** The number produced from two equally long lists of numbers by multiplying the first component of one list by the first component of the other, the second by the second, and so on, and adding all such products.

- **Iso-quant** From "Iso" meaning same, and "Quant" meaning quantity. A curve whose points are all input bundles that produce the same quantity of an output.

- **First and Second Fundamental Theorems of Welfare Economics** Theorems that taken together imply that Pareto Optimality is equivalent to Competitive Equilibrium (Competitive Market Equilibrium).

- **Laissez faire** A policy of "hands off" or noninterference by government in the affairs of markets.

- **Lump sum income** Income whose amount is not changed by any current decision of the consumer. Wage income is not lump sum, for example, because it varies with the consumer's decsion about how many hours to work.

- **Marginal Cost** The additional cost per unit incurred to produce an additional unit of output.

- **Marginal Rate of Substitution** Written as $MRS^i_{X,Y}$, the marginal rate of substitution of consumer i of good X for good Y should be thought of as the consumer's personal valuation of good X just as the marginal rate of transformation, $MRT_{X,Y}$ should be thought of as the cost of good X. Technically, $MRS^i_{X,Y}$ is the number of units of good Y the consumer would be willing to give up to acquire an additional unit of X. $MRT_{X,Y}$ is the rate at which Y must be given up in the economy's production in order to get more X.

- **Marginal Rate of Transformation** See Marginal Rate of Substitution.

- **Non-economic** An objective that is arbitrary, not normal to or that arises from outside natural economic dealings and the economy would be non-economic.

- **Organismic** A conception of government that says the economy can be treated as an organic whole and managed by a central authority. The central authority seeks to maximize a numerical function of the utilities of the individuals in the economy and is willing to intervene in ways that harm one group to help another.

- **Pareto Optimality** The inability to re-arrange an economy to raise the utility of any consumer without harming another in the process. Economic Optimality, Economic Efficiency, Efficiency, Competitive Equilibrium (see First and Second Theorems of Welfare Economics) are synonymous terms.

- **Pareto Superior** Allocation A is Pareto Superior to allocation B if at least one consumer is better off in A and none worse off, when compared to B.

- **Pareto Inferior** Allocation A is Pareto Inferior to allocation B if at least one consumer is better off in B and none worse off, when compared to B.

- **Pareto Suboptimal** Allocation A is Pareto Suboptimal if a Pareto Superior allocation to it exists.

- **Pareto Non-comparable** Allocations A and B are Pareto Non-comparable if neither is Pareto Superio to the other.

- **Perfect competition** Competition between firms characterized by a standardized product, costless entry and exit, perfect information, and nonstrategic pricetaking behavior. Perfect competition is often associated with many competitors.

- **Private good** Goods exhibiting rivalness (One's consumption of the good prevents another from consuming the same good.) and excludability (the ability to prevent consumption of the good by someone who has not paid for it). Food is a private good.

- **Profit** Profit is calculated by valuing the output of a production process and substracting from it the cost of inputs used.

- **Public good** A good having the property of non-rivalness and non-excludability. Consumption of the public good (such as the safety provided by national defense) by one individual does not diminish the ability of others to consume the same units, and individuals can consume the good even if they have not paid for it.

- **Rational** Preferences of a consumer are rational if they are stable, the consumer can rank any two consumption bundles, any bundle is preferred or indifferent to itself, and if bundle A is preferred to bundle B, and bundle B is preferred to bundle C, then bundle A is preferred to bundle C.

- **Side payment** Any transfer in the economy that is imposed outside the rules of normal buying and selling at market prices. For example, were a system of bribes present where a person had to pay a bribe to some official or other individual before being allowed to engage in trade at market prices, the bribe would be considered a side payment.

- **Social Utility** The number representing the well-being of society as a whole. Social utility is produced by aggregating in some functional way the utilities of all members of the economy. Social utility rises if the utility of any member rises, all else constant.

- **Society** A group of individuals living together as members of a community.

- **Tax deadweight loss** The amount by which lost consumer surplus and firm profits due to a tax exceeds the amount of tax collected; the extra loss incurred by the private sector, beyond the amount of tax collected.

- **Transactions constraint** An impediment that limits the ability of a firm or household to make choices in their own best interest. For example, an individual who wants to work at the going wage and is otherwise qualified for the work, but who remains unemployed, is encumbered in choosing how much labor to supply and therefore experiences a transactions constraint.

- **Utility** The numerical measure of a consumer's level of well-being. A measure of the consumer's satisfaction or level of welfare. Well-being, welfare, utility are synonyms.

- **Value added** The value of a good or service minus the cost of the material inputs used to produce it.

- **Welfare** See **Utility.**

- **Wealth** Something of value. The claim to something of value.

- **Well-being** The state of satisfaction experienced by a consumer. Well-being is synonymous with utility.

REFERENCES

Adam Rose and Associates (1998). "The regional economic impacts of casino gambling: Assessment of the literature and establishment of a reasearch agenda." Report prepared for the National Gambling Impact Study Commission (August).

Adams, John (1787). "A Defense of the Constitutions of Government of the United States of America."

Alexander, Sophie, Tom Maloney, Tom Metcalf, and Bloomberg. "The Global Economy is crumbling—and Jeff Bezos is $24 billion richer." *Fortune* , 14 April 2020. https://fortune.com/2020/04/14/jeff-bezos-net-worth-2020-billionaires-amzn-amazon-stock/

Arrow, Kenneth J. and F. H. Hahn, *General Competitive Analysis*, San Francisco: Holden-Day, Inc., 1971.

Bartiromo, Maria (2020). "Candace Owens: Democrats Want Black Americans Dependent on Government Policies," *Sunday Morning Futures with Maria Bartiromo*, 'The Candace Owens Show' host reacts to the president's Black economic empowerment plan on 'Sunday Morning Futures', Fox News Channel, September 27, 2020. Online at https://video.fox news.com/v/6195035834001#sp=show-clips.

Bartiromo, Maria (2021). "Interview of Speaker Newt Gingrich," Mornings with Maria Bartiromo, Fox News, 6 May 2021.

Bastiat, Frederic. *The Government*. The title of this piece is usually translated from the French as *The Law*, but more accurately describes what modern usage would call the government.

_____. "What is Seen and What is Not Seen," reprinted in *Selected Essays on Political Economy I*, George B. de Huszar, ed., 1995.

Becker, Gary S. "Are We Hurting or Helping the Disabled?" Business Week, 2 August 1999, 21.

Bergstrom, T. "On the Existence and Optimality of Competitive Equilibrium for a Slave Economy," *The Review of Economic Studies*, 38, 1, 1971, 23-36.

Bhagwati, Jagdish. "Directly Unproductive, Profit-Seeking (DUP) Activities," *The Journal of Political Economy*, 90, 5, October 1982, 988-1002.

Binion, B. (2020) "Michigan Supreme Court Strikes Down Gov. Gretchen Whitmer's COVID-19 Executive Orders," *Reason* news, 5 October. Online at: https://reason.com/2020/10/05/michigan-supreme-court-strikes-down-gov-gretchen-whitmers-covid-19-executive-orders/ Accessed 21JAN2021.

Bradford, William (1651). *Of Plymouth Plantation.* Boston: Commonwealth of Massachusetts, 1998. (Many modern editions have been published.)

Brooks, Arthur (2006). *Who Really Cares?* New York: Perseus Books.

Brueck, Hilary. (2019). "Switzerland Has a Stunningly High Rate of Gun Ownership," *Business Insider*, 5 August. Online at: https://www. businessinsider.com/ switzerland-gun-laws-rates-of-gun-deaths-2018-2?op=1, accessed 23 January 2021.

Bryan, William Jennings (1896). Quoted in *Wall Street Journal*, "The Cross of NAIRU." Editorial, 20 June 1996, A18. [Non-Accelerating Inflation Rate of Unemployment, NAIRU, refers to a theoretical level of unemployment below which inflation would be expected to rise.]

Buchanan, James M. "The Pure Theory of Government Finance," *The Journal of Political Economy*, 57, 6, December 1949, 496-505.

Cavendish, Richard, "The Republican Party Founded," *History Today*, 54, 7, 7 July 2004 (available online at https://www.historytoday.com/archive/republican-party-founded).

Centers for Medicare & Medicaid Services. Medicare & Medicaid Research Review/2013 Statistical Supplement, Tables 13.5-13.11. https:// www.cms.gov/ Research-Statistics-Data-and-Systems/ Statistics-Trends-and-Reports/Medi careMedicaidStatSupp/2013.html

Centers for Medicare & Medicaid Services. Medicare-Medicaid Enrollee Information, National, 2011.

Chalmers, Thomas (1850). "On The Great Christian Law of Reciprocity Between Man and Man," Discourse V, in *Sermons and Discourses*, Vol. II, New York: Robert Carter & Brothers, 1850, 147-153. Available online.

Chapman, Michael W. "Democrats Introduce Bill to Prevent Trump From Being Buried at Arlington," *CNS News*, 18 February 2021. https://cnsnews.com/article/washington/ michael-w-chapman/democrats-introduce-bill-prevent-trump-being-buried-arlington

Chesney-Lind, Meda and Ian Y. Lind (1986). "Visitors Against Victims: Crimes Against Tourists in Hawaii," *Annalys of Tourism Research*, 13, 167-91.

CIA World Factbook, "North Korea," "South Korea," "Venezuela."

Cleveland, Grover (1887). *Congressional Record*, 49 Cong., 2d Sess., Vol. XVIII, Pt. II, p. 1875.

Coase, Ronald H. "The Nature of the Firm," *Economica*, 4, 16, November 1937.

_____. "The Problem of Social Cost," *Journal of Law and Economics*, 3, October 1960, 1-44.

_____. "The Nature of the Firm; Origin," *Journal of Law, Economics, & Organization*, 4, 1, Spring 1988.

_____. *The Firm, the Market, and the Law*, Chicago: University of Chicago Press, 1990.

Cole, Harold L. and Lee E. Ohanian. "New Deal Policies and the Persistance of the Great Depression: A General Equilibrium Analysis," *Journal of Political Economy*, 112, 41, 2004, 779-816.

_____. "How Government Prolonged the Depression," *Wall Street Journal*, 2 February 2009, online at https:// www.wsj.com /articles/SB123353276749137485.

Commager, Henry Steele (1963). "Jackson's Veto of Maysville Road Bill," *Documents of American History*, 7th ed., New York: Meredith Publishing Company.

Committee for Economic Development. *Crony Capitalism: Unhealthy Relations Between Business and Government*, A White Paper by the Committee for Economic Development of The Conference Board, Arlington, VA: CED, October 2015, pp. 1-44.

Confessore, Nicholas (2009). "Homeless Organization is Called a Fraud," *The New York Times*, City Room, 24 November 2009. https://cityroom.blogs.nytimes.com/2009/11/24/homeless-organization-called-fraud/

Coolidge, Calvin. (1890)–(1929) *Coolidge Speech Full Archive*, Calvin Coolidge Presidential Foundation. Available online at https:// www.coolidgefoundation.org/coolidge-speech-full-archive/

Coren, Courtney. "Dick Morris: Obama Wants to Turn US Into Japan, Mexico." *Newsmax*, 24 September 2014.

Debreu, Gerard. *Theory of Value: An Axiomatic Analysis of Economic Equilibrium*, Cowles Foundation for Research in Economics at Yale University, New Haven, CT: Yale University Press, 1959.

DeJesus, Juan (2010). "Judge Orders Homeless Organization to Disband," *NBC News*, New York, 24 June 2010.
https://www.nbcnewyork. com/news/local/judge-orders-
uho-to-disband/1914728/

de Tocqueville, Alexis, "Government of the Democracy in America," Chapter 13 in *Democracy in America*, 1835, 1840.

_____. *Democracy in America*, Harvey
Mansfield and Delba Winthrop, trans. Chicago: University
of Chicago Press, 2000, p. 663.

"East Germany," *DW*, https://www.dw.com/en/east-germany-
its-not-just-the-economy-stupid/a-45454241, online, accessed
2 October 2018.

Ehrlich, Eva and Andreas Boros-Kazai. "The Competition among
Countries, 1937-1986," *Eastern European Economics*, 29,
2 (Winter, 1990-1991), p. 90.

Eidsmoe, John A. (2009). "The Militia: In History and Today,"
The New American 5 March. https://thenewamerican.com/
the-militia-in-history-and-today/. This story is reported by
several sources. The earliest appearance seems to be in the
Lutheran journal: *Christian News*, New Haven, Missouri,
Feb. 4, 2002.

Ellis, Edward S. "A Sensible and Timely View of a Certain Constitutional Question." Chapter XIII in *The Life of Colonel
David Crockett*. Philadelphia: Porter and Coates, 1884.

Encyclopedia Britannica (2002). Chicago: Encyclopedia Britannica.

Encyclopedia Britannica (2018) "Golden Rule: Ethical Precept,"
https://
www.britannica.com/topic/Golden-Rule. Online, Accessed
13 November 2018.

Fagge, Nick (2019). "The Rich Kids of Venezuela—including
Socialist revolution leader Hugo Chavez' daughter—flaunt
their wealth with fist-fulls of cash and lavish holidays while
the nation starves," *Daily Mail*, UK, 4 February 2019, https://

www.dailymail.co.uk/news/article-6667889/Rich-Kids-
Venezuela-including-Socialist-leader-Hugo-Chavezs-daughter-
flaunt-wealth.html.; *Fox News*, "Hugo Chavez daughter is
the richest individual in Venezuela, report claims," 10 Au-
gust 2015, https://www.foxnews.com/world/hugo-chavez-
daughter-is-the-richest-individual-in-venezuela-report-claims.;
"Maria Gabriela Chavez podria ser la mujer mas rica de
Venezuela" (Maria Gabriela Chavez Could Be the Richest
Woman in Venezuela). *Diario Las Americas* (in Spanish).
Caracas. 7 August 2015.

Ferrell, Robert H. (1998). *The Presidency of Calvin Coolidge.*
University Press of Kansas. ISBN 978-0-7006-0892-8.

Foley, Duncan. (1970). "Lindahl's Solution and the Core of an
Economy with Public Goods," *Econometrica*, 38, 1, January, 66-72.

Fox, Jack V. (1959). "Khrushchev Visits Iowa Cornfields," UPI,
September 23, 1959. Online at https://www.upi.com/Archives/
1959/09/23/Khrushchev-visits-Iowa-cornfields/1112442791026/

Franklin, Benjamin (1766). "On the Price of Corn and the
Management of the Poor," *The London Chronicle, 1766,*
reprinted in *The Works of Benjamin Franklin*, Vol. II, Jared
Sparks, ed. Chicago: Townsend Mac Coun., 1882, 355-360.

Friedman, Milton. (1962). *Capitalism and Freedom.* Chicago:
University of Chicago Press.

Friedman, Milton. (1970). "The Social Responsibility of Business is to Increase its Profits," *The New York Times Magazine*, September 13.

Goodman, John, "Designing Ideal Health Insurance", Priceless:
Curing the Healthcare Crisis, Chapter 11. Oakland, CA:
The Independent Institute, 2012.

Goodman, John, "Why I Don't Like Deductibles," *Health Alerts,*
December 18, 2013, http:// healthblog.ncpa.org/ why-i-
dont-like- deductibles/?utm_source= newsletter&utm_medium
=email&utm_ campaign= HA#mo re-35149.

Graff, Henry F. (2002). *Grover Cleveland*, New York: Times Books, p. 19.

Grinols, Earl L. (1994). "Time for a National Policy," Congressional Testimony, Committee on Small Business, House of Representatives, One Hundred Third Congress, Hearing on the National Impact of Casino Gambling Proliferation, Washington, D.C.: U.S. Government Printing Office, Serial 103-104, 8-11, 1995, 76.

_____. (2004). *Gambling in America: Costs and Benefits*. New York: Cambridge University Press.

_____ (2007). Review of Arthur Brooks, *Who Really Cares?: The Surprising Truth About Compassionate Conservatism–*
America's Charity Divide, Who Gives, Who Doesn't, and Why It Matters in *Faith and Economics*, 49, Spring, pp. 50-55.

Grinols, Earl L. and James W. Henderson (2009). *Health Care for Us All: Getting More for Our Investment.* New York: Cambridge University Press.

Grinols, Earl L. (2015). "Reforming Obamacare: Start with the Young," *RealClearPolicy,* http://www.realclearpolicy.com/blog/2015/01/20/reforming_obamacare_start_with_the_young_1176.html, 20 January.

Hansmann, Henry. *The Ownership of Enterprise*, Cambridge, MA: Harvard University Press, 1996.

Hanson, Victor Davis (2019). *The Case for Trump*, New York: Basic Books.

Hawley, Josh (2021). *The Tyranny of Big Tech*, Washington, D.C.: Regnery Publishing.

Hayek, Friedrich (1994). "Preface," *The Road to Serfdom*, Fiftieth Anniversary Edition, Chicago: University of Chicago Press.

Henderson, David (2010). "Krugman Misstates Dickens's Point," 24 December, http://econlog. econlib.org/archives/2010/12/krugman_misstat_1.html

Henriksson L. E. (1996). "Hardly a quick fix: Casino gambling in Canada." *Canadian Public Policy.* XXII, 2, 1996, 116-128.

Higgs, Robert (2003). "Why Grover Cleveland Vetoed the Texas Seed Bill," *Independent Institute*, Research Article, 1 July. https://www.independent.org/publications/article.asp?id=1329

Hopper, Mike. "Pennies are Useless, Here's Why the Government Keeps Making Them," *Economy*, Generation Opportunity, 21 February 2016, https://generationopportunity.org/articles/ 2016/02/21/pennies-are-useless-heres-why-the-government-keeps-making-them/.

Hudson, Jerome (2016). "Eleven Great Thomas Sowell Quotes," *Breitbart News*, 28 December. Online at: https://www.breitbart.com/politics/2016/12/28/11-great-thomas-sowell-quotes/.

Hundley, Kris and Kendall Taggart (2017). "America's 50 Worst Charities Rake in Nearly $1 Billion for Corporate Fundraisers," *Tampa Bay Times*, 2 October 2017, https://www.tampabay.com/news/ nation/americas-50-worst-charities-rake-in-nearly-1-billion-for-corporate/2339540/

Jefferson, Thomas (1801). First Inaugural Address, 4 March.

Jefferson, Thomas (1802). Letter to Danbury Baptists Association in the state of Connecticut, 1 January.

Jefferson, Thomas (1816). Letter to Joseph Milligan, 6 April.

Jefferson, Thomas (1817). letter to Albert Gallatin, second Treasury Secretary, 16 June.

Leonard, Thomas C., Robert S. Goldfarb, Steven M. Suranovic. "[Wm.] New on Paternalism and Public Policy," *Economics and Philosophy*, 16, 2000, pp. 323-331.

Lindahl, Erik (1919). "Die Gerechtigkeit der Besteurung" (translated from the German in 1958). Erik Lindahl, "Just Taxation—A Positive Solution," in: Musgrave, R.A. and Peacock, A.T. (eds.) *Classics in the Theory of Public Finance.*

King, Martin L., Jr. "The Negro and the Constitution," *The Martin Luther King, Jr. Papers Project* 11 June, 1944, http://okra.stanford.edu/transcription/document_images/Vol01Scans/109_May1944_The 20Negro20and20the20 Constitution.pdf (Source of the quote in the chapter on morality.)

_____. (1963). "Letter from a Birmingham Jail," 16 April.

Kroll, Emily. "My Take: Hypocricy is the Word of the Day," *Sentinel*, Holland City, 27 May 2020. https://www. hollandsentinel.com/opinion/20200527/ my-take-hypocrisy-is-word-of-day

Krueger, Anne. (1974). "The Political Economy of the Rent-Seeking Society," *American Economic Review*, 64, April/May, 291-303.

Linder, Douglas O. (2021). "The Trial of John Peter Zenger: An Account," *Famous Trials,* Online: https://famous-trials. com/zenger/87-home.

Locke, John. *Two Treatises on Government*, London: Printed for R. Butler, etc., 1821 (originally published 1689).

McClanahan, B. *9 Presidents who Screwed Up America and Four Who Tried to Save Her*, Washington: Regnery History, 2018, pp.242-42.

McDonald, Heather. "Four Months of Unprecedented Government Malfeasance," *Imprimis*, 49, 5/6, May/June 2020.

McCullough, David. *The Pioneers*. New York: Simon & Schuster, 2019.

Madison, James (1792). Letter to Edmund Pendleton, 21 January, in *The Papers of James Madison*, vol. 14, Robert

A Rutland et. al., eds. Charlottesvile: University Press of Virginia,1984.

_____. (1794a). Speech to the US House of Representatives, January.

_____. (1798b). *(Annals of Congress 179.*

_____. (1831). Letter to James Robertson, 20 April

Makary, Marty, MD. *The Price We Pay: What Broke American Health Care—And How to Fix It.* New York: Bloomsbury Publishing, 2019.

Malinvaud, E., *Lectures on Microeconomic Theory,* New York: American Elsevier Publishing Co., Inc., 1972.

Mankiw, N. Gregory, Matthew Weinzierl, and Danny Yagan, "Optimal Taxation in Theory and Practice," *Journal of Economic Perspectives,* 23, 4, Fall 2009, 147-174.

Mas-Colell, Andreu, Michael d. Whinston, and Jerry R. Green, *Microeconomic Theory,* New York: Oxford University Press, 1995.

Meredith, James. "A Challenge to Change," *Newsweek,* 6 October 1997, p. 18.

Mintz, Steven, ed. *Andrew Jackson, Messages and Papers of the Presidents, Vol. 2, in Native American Voices: A History and Anthology,* St. James, New York: Brandywine Press, 1995, 115-116.

Moon, Ruth. "Founder of World's Largest Megachurch Convicted of Embezzling $12 Million." *Christianity Today,* 24 February 2014. https://www.christianitytoday.com/news/2014/february/founder-of-worlds-largest-megachurch-convicted-cho-yoido.html.

Nozick, Robert. *Anarchy, State, Utopia,* New York: Basic Books, 1974.

Olcott, Charles S., *The Life of William McKinley,* 2 vols. Boston: Houghton Mifflin, 1916. pp. 281-282.

Olohan, Mary M. "Whitmer Does Not Deny That Her Husband Sought Special Treatment Over Boating On Memorial Day Weekend," *Daily Caller*, 26 May 2020. https://dailycaller.com/2020/05/26/ gretchen-whitmer-husband-special-treatment-boat-memorial-day-coronavirus/

Pierce, Franklin (1854). Veto of measure to help the mentally ill.

Polk, James K. Polk (1846), Veto of "An act making appropriations for the improvement of certain harbors and rivers," 3 August.

Pollock v. Farmers' Loan & Trust Co. No. 893. Supreme Court of the United States, 157 U.S. 429 (1895); Argued March 7, 8, 11, 12, 13, 1895. Decided April 8, 1895.

Quirk, James and Rubin Saposnik, *Introduction to General Equilibrium Theory and Welfare Economics*, New York: McGraw-Hill Book Company, 1968.

Raut, Lakshmi (2004). "Two-sided Altruism, Lindahl Equilibrium, and Pareto Optimality in Overlapping Generations Models," *Economic Theory*, 27, pp. 729-736.

Roche, John P. (1984). *The History and Impact of Marxist-Leninist Organizational Theory: "Useful Idiots," "Innocents' Clubs," and "Transmission Belts,"* Cambridge, MA: Institute for Foreign Policy Analysis, January.

Rotman, Michael (2020). "Cuyahoga River Fire," *Cleveland Historical*, https://clevelandhistorical.org/items/show/63, accessed June 2020.

Sachs, Jeffrey. *The Next Money Crash*, Bloomington, IN: iUniverse, 2014.

Schlaes, Amity. "The Rules of the Game and Economic Recovery," *Imprimis*, 39, 9, September 2010.

Shlaes, Amity (2013). "Calvin Coolidge's faith was the secret to his success," Fox News, March 10, 2013, updated May 11, 2015, https://www.foxnews.com/opinion/calvin-coolidges-faith- was-the-secret-to-his-success

Sheehy, Kate. "Embattled Michigan Governor in Hot Water Over Hubby's Boat Request," *New York Post* 25 May 2020. https:// nypost.com/2020/05/25/ michigan-gov-gretchen-whitmer - in-hot-water-over-husbands- boat-request/

Starr, Ross M., *General Equilibrium Theory: An Introduction*, New York: Cambridge University Press, 1997.

Stepman, Jarrett. "This Case Against Western Ranchers Shows Why Americans Are Right to Fear Government," *The Daily Signal*, 8 January 2018, https:// www.dailysignal.com/2018/ 01/08/unprofessional-case-western-ranchers-shows-americans- right-fear-government/

Stiglitz, Joseph E. "Pareto Efficient and Optimal Taxation and the New New Welfare Economics," Ch. 15 in *Handbook of Public Economics*, Vol. 2, New York: Elsevier, 1987, 991-1042.

_____. *The Price of Inequality*, New York: W. W. Norton and Company, 2012.

Tampa Bay Times. "America's Worst Charities," Tampa Bay Times, https://www.tampabay.com/resources/topics/ specials/worst-charities/worst-charities.pdf.

Traverse City Eagle. "There Can't Be Two Standards," Editorial: Traverse City Eagle. 2 August 2020. https://www.record-eagle.com/ opinion/ editorial-there-cant-be-two-standards/ article_74eb3450-d414-11ea-8693- 9798eb7932b2.html

Tullock, Gordon. "Efficient Rent-Seeking," in *Toward a Theory of the Rent-seeking Society,* edited by James M. Buchanan, Robert D. Tollison, and Gordon Tullock. College Station: Texas A & M University Press, 1980.

Unruh, Bob. "State Fines Couple $4.1 million for Gate on Own Property," *World Net Daily,* https://www.wnd.com/2019/02/ state-fines-couple-4-1-million-for-gate-on-own-property/, 17 February 2019.

U.S. House. (1995). Committee on the Judiciary. National Gambling Impact and Policy Commission Act: Hearing on H.R. 497 Before the House Committee on the Jucidiary. 104th Congress, 1st Session.

Warren, Caroline M. (1828). *The Gamesters; or ruins of innocence. An original novel, founded in Truth.* Boston: J. Shaw.

Weather Channel (2020). "Russian City So Polluted Skies Turn Black, Residents Urged to Leave," 15 June 2020. https://weather.com/en-CA/international/videos/video/russian-city-so-polluted-skies-turn-black-residents-urged-to-leave.

Wesley, John Wesley (1872). Sermon "The Use of Money," http://www.umcmission. org/Find-Resources/John-Wesley-Sermons/Sermon-50-The-Use-of-Money

West, E. G. "The Political Economy of American Public School Legislation," *The Journal of Law and Economics*, 101-128.

Wimble, Lorie. "Gretchen Whitmer's lockdown hypocricy is the modern Democratic Party in a nutshel," TextitNOQ Report, 5 June 2020. https://noqreport.com/2020/06/05/gretchen-whitmers-lockdown-hypocrisy-is-the-modern-democratic-party-in-a- nutshell/

Zabilka, Ivan L. (1994). Editorial. *Gambling Economics*, 2, (November), 3.

Index

CPSIA information can be obtained
at www.ICGtesting.com
Printed in the USA
LVHW081749130922
728185LV00010B/364